Mental Health
in the
Workplace

MENTAL HEALTH
IN THE
WORKPLACE

An Employer's and Manager's Guide

Donna R. Kemp

Quorum Books
Westport, Connecticut • London

Library of Congress Cataloging-in-Publication Data

Kemp, Donna R.
  Mental health in the workplace : an employer's and manager's guide
/ Donna R. Kemp.
      p.   cm.
  Includes bibliographical references and index.
  ISBN 0–89930–703–5 (acid-free paper)
  1. Industrial psychiatry. I. Title.
  RC967.5.K45   1994
  616.89—dc20   93–27708

British Library Cataloguing in Publication Data is available.

Library of Congress Catalog Card Number: 93–27708
ISBN 0–89930–703–5

First published in 1994

Quorum Books, 88 Post Road West, Westport, CT 06881
An imprint of Greenwood Publishing Group, Inc.

Printed in the United States of America

The paper used in this book complies with the
Permanent Paper Standard issued by the National
Information Standards Organization (Z39.48–1984).
10 9 8 7 6 5 4 3 2 1

To my parents

Maybel A. Smith Kemp and Glen E. Kemp

Contents

Preface

Mental Health in the Workplace: An Employer's and Manager's Guide examines the way in which mental health issues impact the workplace and explores ways to create mentally healthy work environments. This book has been written for employers, managers, and students of management, organizational sociology, and employee assistance program administration. The goal of this book is to increase the understanding of how a mentally healthy workplace can enhance productivity, satisfaction, attendance, and longevity in employment.

Subjects covered include mental health problems in the United States; mental health policy, organization, and services; mental illness and disability; the physical/mental health connection; treatment of mental health problems; definitions of common mental disorders; employee selection and mental health issues; demographic and sociological changes; employment law; placement of the workers with a disability; psychological testing; graphology; drug screening; genetic testing; mental health issues and management; supervising employees with mental disabilities; supported employment; managing the substance abusing employee; personality and the workplace; grievances and termination; violence in the workplace; change in the workplace, including career change, organizational change, relocation, layoffs, outplacement and transition services, retirement, and the mental health issues of illness and death; the impaired manager; psychological needs of employees; creating a mentally healthy work environment; changing the corporate culture; quality of worklife; organizational policies; family oriented policies; substance abuse policies; diversity and discrimination policies; designing a healthy environment; management development; organizational development and design; workplace stress; wellness programs; employee assistance programs; critical incident stress debriefing; conflict resolution and reduction; and financing mental health care.

I extend my thanks to Kathie Pendo and the word processing staff for word processing of the manuscript and to Irv Schiffman, Chair of the Department of Political Science, and James D. Haehn, Dean of the College of Behavioral and Social Sciences, California State University, Chico, for word processing funding.

Mental Health
in the
Workplace

1

Mental Health and the Workplace

All organizations include a human resource component. For many organizations, human resources account for the greatest number of dollars expended in the organization, sometimes as much as 80–90 percent. Selecting people who are mentally healthy and maintaining the mental health of people within the organization, in sheer economic terms, means a savings of dollars within the organization. Having an emotionally healthy work environment means getting the best in terms of productivity, retention of good employees, and quality of life for managers and employees alike.

Mental health in the workplace also means dealing with the special mental health issues that arise in the workplace, such as employment of people with mental disabilities including mental illness and mental retardation. Federal law requires employers to accommodate people with mental as well as physical disabilities. Also, employers have come to understand that the emotional problems that employees experience are never left at the door to the workplace but impact the ability of the employee to function at work. In addition, researchers, health professionals, and employers are increasingly recognizing the extent to which mental health plays a role in physical health problems (Simonton, Matthews-Simonton, and Creighton, 1978; Siegel, 1986), and there are those who believe that separating mental health and physical health creates an artificial distinction because there is only one health (Sagan, 1987). At least 25 percent of general medical visits are because of mental health problems, and those problems are not always recognized by the patient or the physician. This means people may be inappropriately treated for physical problems without getting to the root of the mental health issue that lies behind the physical health problem. This is costly to the patient, insurer, and employer. Approximately 25 percent of all hospital inpatient days in the United States are still for diagnosed mental disorders, and at one time, 50 percent of all hospital inpatient days were for such problems (Kiesler and Sibulkin, 1987). This raises issues about the appropriate level of treatment and whether mental health insurance that emphasizes inpatient care encourages inappropriate treatment levels.

MENTAL HEALTH PROBLEMS

Mental health problems may involve psychiatric illnesses, substance abuse, emotional disorders, and developmental disorders. Estimates of mental illness are based on definitions that have been developed by the American Psychiatric Association's *Diagnostic and Statistical Manual of Mental Disorders — IIIR* (1987) (DSM III-R), which is currently being revised as the DSM IV, and the federally funded Epidemiological Catchment Area (ECA) surveys conducted during the 1980s (Regier et al., 1984). These federally funded studies indicated that 18.5 percent of all Americans suffered at least one mental health disorder during an average six-month period (National Institute of Mental Health [NIMH], 1986). An estimated 29–38 percent of people have been mentally ill at some time during their life (Robins et al., 1984). Many cases of mental illness never come to the attention of the mental health system, and mental health symptoms are often overlooked by non-psychiatric physicians, who tend to recognize only the most serious mental disorders (Kiesler and Sibulkin, 1987). At any time, 3 percent of the population is suffering from a long-term disabling mental illness. Because there have been no consistently applied measures of mental illness, there is uncertainty as to whether mental illness is increasing or not.

The most prevalent conditions in the United States are anxiety and somatoform disorders (phobias, panic disorders, and obsessive-compulsive disorders), affective disorders (depression, bipolar disorders, and manic episodes), substance abuse, and schizophrenia. The most prevalent problems in men are alcohol abuse and dependence, phobias, and drug abuse. In 1986, 3 percent of persons admitted to mental hospitals had drug-related disorders as a primary diagnosis, and 6.2 percent of all patients had a principal diagnosis of alcohol-related disorders (NIMH, 1990). The most common problems for women are phobias, major depression, and dysthymia (a form of depression). The second most common problem for women 18–24 is drug abuse, and for men and women over 65, severe cognitive impairment is the first and second, respectively, most common problem (NIMH, 1986). People in urban areas are at higher risk for mental illness, with a lifetime prevalence of 32 percent as compared with 27.5 percent for people living in small towns and rural areas (Robins et al., 1984).

Suicide is the third leading cause of death among teenagers and young adults, and 20 percent of suicides are committed by persons under 25. Approximately 30,000 Americans commit suicide each year (National Center for Health Statistics, 1990). A study of teenagers in South Carolina found 11 percent reported serious suicidal thoughts, 6.4 percent reported specific suicidal plans, 5.9 percent reported attempts that did not require medical care, and 1.6 percent reported attempts requiring medical care (Garrison et al., 1993).

Research has indicated links among alcohol abuse, depression, anxiety disorder, and aggressive behavior (Rich, Young, and Fowler, 1986; Robins et al., 1959; Shaffer, Gould, and Fisher, 1992). Considerable linkages have been made between alcohol abuse and suicide. There may also be a link between suicide and unemployment and population pressures on educational and occupational resources. There may be some connection to socioenvironmental factors in the explanation for the marked increase in the suicide rate over the past 30 years, particularly among males under 30 (Shaffer, 1993). Suicide rates for males also rise with age, and suicide is a problem for males approaching or having reached retirement. Suicide rates are rising in the United States, and the actual suicide rate may be three times the reported rate (Sagan, 1987). The suicide rate among native Americans is 2.5 times the rate for the general population, and this contributes to the fact that Indians have a shorter life span than any other population group in the United States.

The NIMH estimates that there are between 4 million and 5 million people (2.1–2.6 percent) with serious mental illness (SMI) in the adult U.S. population. This includes persons both in the institutions and in the community (NIMH, 1992). The National Health Interview Survey (NHIS) in 1989 found 3.3 million adults (18.2 adults per 1,000) 18 years of age or older with a serious mental illness in the past 12 months in the noninstitutionalized U.S. population. Approximately 78.8 percent (2.6 million) had one or more specific limitations in work, social functioning, school, or personal care. The rate of SMI was generally higher in the oldest age group. More females than males were represented (20.6 per 1,000). Prevalence rate were similar for blacks and whites, with other races reporting prevalences about half that for black and white persons. Prevalence was clearly related to poverty, with SMI being more than 2.5 times more likely for adults in poverty. Also, the rate was almost twice as high for people with less than 12 years of education (Barker et al., 1992).

Employees bring these mental health disorders into the workplace. Of any employee population, 11.5 percent will have personal problems serious enough to affect job performance. Of that group, 45 percent will have a primary problem with alcohol, 25 percent will have emotional problems, 13 percent, family problems, and 7 percent, a drug problem (Weaver, 1984). Certainly, employees are well aware when fellow employees are having problems. One study of 2,000 employees reported that approximately 26 percent of employees knew an employee whose work was hindered because of personal problems (Holoviak and Holoviak, 1984). In 1986 a study by the NIMH estimated that mental illnesses cost the United States $185 billion a year. Absenteeism from work and reduced productivity due to living problems cost more than $100 billion a year. Problems related to substance abuse, marriage, family, and other mental health problems contribute to 60 percent of absenteeism, 80–90 percent of industrial accidents, and 65 percent of terminations. Troubled employees as a group have the worst absenteeism and turnover rates, have higher grievance rates, have four times the average number of accidents, and use three times the usual sick benefits (Holoviak and Holoviak, 1984). Untreated problems result in a productivity loss of approximately 25 percent of an employee's salary through absenteeism, accidents, tardiness, use of medical benefits, and workers' compensation claims (Hurley, 1986).

Surveys by the NIMH in Baltimore, New Haven, and St. Louis found alcoholism to be the most common single disorder within a six-month prevalence (5 percent). The lifetime prevalence was 12–16 percent. This means that more than one of every ten Americans is affected by alcoholism (NIMH, 1990). One study of 500 executives reported 9.3 percent were admitted problem drinkers (Greenberger, 1983). If one assumes that between one-quarter and one-third of each problem drinker's salary is wasted due to alcohol-related absenteeism, inefficiency, and errors, there is anywhere from 2.25 to 3 percent of the average organization's payroll being lost to alcohol-related unproductiveness (Shore, 1984). A 1983 study by the Alcohol, Drug Abuse, and Mental Health Administration (ADAMHA) estimated the social costs of alcohol abuse at $117 billion, including $65 billion in lost productivity.

In 1983, alcohol resulted in 10 million injuries, 2 million of which were disabling, and there were 18,000 fatalities. The National Institute on Alcohol and Alcohol Abuse in 1981 estimated that problem drinkers use eight times more medical care and are absent 2.5 times more often than other workers, and it is estimated that they have 3.6 times more accidents on and off the job. In 1983, the social cost of drug use was estimated at $60 billion, including $33 billion in lost productivity. The loss in productivity from drug abuse was found to come from the heaviest drug abusers, those who used drugs daily for at least a 30-day period (ADAMHA, 1983). In 1987 the Research Triangle Institute estimated that the 1985 costs of drug abuse in U.S. industries in lost productivity, medical expenses, and theft and damage was $36.3 billion. Workers with substance abuse problems are absent 16 times more than the average employee; their accident rate is four times higher; they use one-third more sick time; and they have five times as many compensation claims (Wright, 1984). In 1986, the U.S. Chamber of Commerce estimated that substance abuse cost employers $60 to $100 billion annually in lost productivity (Abramowitz and Hamilton, 1986). Drug abuse in the United States is declining. From 1988 to 1991, the number of abusers dropped from an estimated 14.5 million to 12.6 million. However, the use of cocaine is still rising. In 1991, there were an estimated 1.9 million users, compared with 1.6 million in 1990. Since 1989, crack usage has fallen by probably 50 percent and has now leveled off. In Canada, the amounts of cocaine and heroin being seized have increased ("Drug Abuse Falls . . . ," 1993).

It costs an average $25,000 to replace problem employees who have to be terminated, and this does not include lost knowledge of the operation and experience (Wright, 1984). An organization usually spends 60 percent less to rehabilitate an employee than to replace a worker who is performing poorly because of personal problems (Topolnicki, 1983), and in some cases, the law requires the employer to attempt to rehabilitate the employee.

Employees' families may also suffer from mental disorders. More than 12 percent of U.S. children and adolescents (7.5 million) have mental disorders. Some of these disorders will last a lifetime. Treatment of children and adolescents costs $1.5 billion a year. Yet, less than one-fifth of children with mental disorders receive appropriate treatment. This increases the costs of lost lifetime productivity, because some of these children will never be able to enter the work force and will never live independently (National Advisory Mental Health Council [NAMHC], 1990). A study comparing the treatment costs of children's mental disorders and physical disorders, involving children who were dependents of employees of a large company, showed that from 1984 to 1986, $2.7 million (16 percent) of $16.7 million spent on hospital care was for mental disorders. About 23 percent, or nearly $2 million of $4.9 million, spent on outpatient care was for mental disorders. These costs involved only insurance reimbursement and did not cover unreimbursed inpatient or outpatient costs or costs for outpatient care by private practice psychologists, social workers, or counselors (NAMHC, 1990).

Many people with developmental disabilities are also in the work force. The American Association on Mental Deficiency defines mental retardation, and under their definition, approximately 3 percent of the U.S. population are persons with mental retardation (Stedman, 1971). Mental retardation is now included in the larger population of persons with developmental disabilities.

MENTAL HEALTH POLICY

Mental health policy in the United States has been marked by ambivalence. Policy cycles have fluctuated from control and containment to caretaking and custodial to prevention and cure. Depending on which focus is being taken, mental health policy has overlapped with criminal justice policy for social control, welfare policy for caretaking, and health policy for the medical model. Approaches have swung from medical and biological to humanistic and psychotherapeutic to social/cultural and back again. However, five themes have developed and remained largely consistent over time. First, mental health policy has most of the time been treated separately from physical health policy and has functioned in a separate policy arena. Second, mental health has been a stepchild and has not received the same level of recognition and support as physical health. Worsening this situation is the fact that, in recent years, fiscal problems at the national, state, and local levels have led to cutbacks in expenditure for public mental health programs. Soaring health care costs, which are climbing much faster than the rate of inflation, have also affected the availability of resources in both the public and private sectors. Third, mental health policy making has been marked by attempts to avoid responsibility and shift responsibility and costs to another source. Mental health policy in the United States is complicated by the federal system, in which there are many levels of government that may be involved in developing and implementing policy. In addition to the federal government and the 50 state governments, there are thousands of counties and municipalities, and, in addition, many services are provided through regional bodies and nonprofit and profit-making organizations. Fourth, mental health policy making has been dogged by stigma, denial that the problems exist, belief that many mental health problems are not really serious (just problems of living), and belief that those with mental illness are somehow responsible and would not have a problem if they "just pulled themselves up by their bootstraps." Fifth, the mental health policy arena has lacked cohesiveness. Various mental health problems over time have tended to develop their own interest group support and have redefined themselves to establish their own policy arenas. Examples of this are mental retardation and substance abuse. Each of these groups competes for limited dollars at each level of government. The consumer rights movement has led to powerful advocacy movements that attempt to target services for the seriously chronically mentally ill, substance abuse, mental retardation, and so on. Now, mental retardation is included under the federal government's definition of developmental disabilities which also includes epilepsy, cerebral palsy, and autism. The focus has shifted to functional limitations, away from intellectual criteria and particular diagnosis (Summers, 1981). Arguments have been made for expanding the definition to include learning disabilities. Under the definition of developmental disabilities, mental retardation and substance abuse also continue to be defined in the DSM III-R. Alcohol and drug programs have also moved away from the traditional mental health services. By 1983, half of the state alcohol and drug agencies were no longer a part of the state mental health authorities (Council of State Governments, 1983). This separation has resulted in more effectiveness in competition for funding by developmental disabilities and substance abuse but has also resulted in less effective coordination among systems (Hudson, 1993), and there are those who believe this fragmentation has been to the detriment of mental health (Finch, 1985). This has resulted in problems for people who are dually diagnosed. They may have problems finding suitable treatment, or they may be shuttled back and forth among service providers who do not want to treat them. These problems can involve substantial populations, because, for example, as many as 60–80 percent of seriously mentally ill persons may also have substance abuse problems. The proliferation of consumer and advocacy organizations has contributed to a growing politicization of mental health decision making (Hudson, 1993).

In recent times, mental health policy and services have followed largely a medical model, with psychiatrists as the dominant profession in the field. This model is disease oriented and emphasizes illness. The focus is placed on finding and treating causes of mental dysfunctions, and the emphasis is placed on diagnosis, treatment, and cure. Traditionally, the focus involved treatment in inpatient settings, usually large state hospitals. More recently, inpatient treatment has become increasingly shorter term but involving more frequent admissions to psychiatric and general medical units of general hospitals. In addition, there has been growth of community treatment and services. The emphasis has been on medication, with a limited focus on psychosocial and environmental issues. In the 1980s, attempts were made to broaden the base of service for the chronically mentally ill, provide more integrated services, and focus more on their environmental needs (such as housing), social needs, employment, and recreation.

There has been a growing number of professionals involved in mental health and a growing interest in team treatment approaches involving professionals, the client, and the client's family. Now, many psychologists, social workers, counselors, occupational therapists, recreational therapists, supported employment counselors, and others are involved in mental health. For people with less serious emotional disorders, there has been a rapid growth in outpatient treatment involving employee assistance programs, family treatment clinics, counseling services in heath maintenance organizations, individual practice therapists, and support groups. The growing numbers of professionals, approaches, and modalities involved in mental health for the seriously and chronically mentally ill and for less serious emotional disorders are leading away from the medical model and involving psychosocial, interpersonal, psychoeducational, developmental, and environmental approaches as well as the biological and medical. This is following the direction that developmental disabilities and substance abuse services have taken, in that they have shifted to community, developmental, and social models and focused on normalization and a continuum of care.

MENTAL HEALTH ORGANIZATION

At the national level the largest department involved in mental health is the Department of Health and Human Services (DHHS). Until 1992, the ADAMHA, with a budget in fiscal year 1991 of $2.6 billion, was the agency within DHHS most responsible for mental health policy. In 1992, legislation was passed to reorganize the mental health programs in DHHS; this resulted in the elimination of ADAMHA. Service programs that were formerly a part of the NIMH, the National Institute of Drug Abuse (NIDA), and the National Institute on Alcohol Abuse and Alcoholism (NIAAA) were placed under a new agency, the Substance Abuse and Mental Health Services Administration (SAMHSA), which is part of the Public Health Service (PHS). The SAMHSA consists of three centers: the Center for Mental Health Services, the Center for Treatment Improvement, and the Center for Substance Abuse Prevention. The three institutes with their research functions (NIMH, NIDA, and NIAAA) were moved to the National Institutes of Health, which is also under the umbrella organization DHHS. Mental retardation and developmental disabilities programs are managed by the Office of Human Development Services (OHDS) of DHHS. The President's Committee on Mental Retardation is part of OHDS.

At the federal level, the NIMH is the main research agency. The NIMH was originally mandated to fund research, conduct mental health planning, train mental health professionals, and conduct demonstration programs. Increasingly, however, the focus moved away from direct service and toward research. Now, with the new reorganization the Institute's mandate is research. Over time, the research focus has shifted from psychosocial orientations to biological theories of the causation of mental illness. In the late 1980s, research on schizophrenia and prevention were the main priorities but the Director of NIMH in 1990, Lewis Judd, referred to the 1990s as the "Decade of the Brain," in which research in biological psychiatry would be the NIMH priority.

The NIAAA provides a national focus for the federal effort to increase knowledge and promote effective approaches to deal with health problems and issues associated with alcohol abuse and alcoholism. The NIDA provides a focus for federal efforts regarding drug abuse. Research includes biological, psychological, and psychosocial aspects; epidemiology; treatment; and prevention of drug abuse and addiction.

Recently, the National Center for Injury Prevention and Control was established at the Centers for Disease Control. One of the principal goals of the center is to identify effective suicide prevention methods.

Direct service provision is made by the federal government to veterans through the Department of Veterans Administration, which administers 139 psychiatric programs through the veterans hospital system. Most of these programs include outpatient and inpatient programs for mentally ill and for substance abuse (NIMH, 1990). Native Americans are provided with services through the Bureau of Indian Affairs in the Department of Interior.

Funding for some mental health services is provided by Medicare for the aged, blind, and disabled and by Medicaid for the poor. Guidelines and standards for that funding come from the Health Care Financing Administration (HCFA), a part of DHHS. Funding is also provided to individuals through Social Security Disability Insurance (SSDI) and Supplemental Security Income (SSI). To qualify for SSI under Medicaid, an individual must be determined to be disabled under the guidelines of the program and must meet state income and resource standards.

About 703,000 (23.2 percent) of adults with SMI in households receive disability payments from a government program because of their mental problem. Most respondents receive SSDI (46 percent) or SSI (43.5 percent). The average payment for an adult in 1993 was $324 per month. The maximum SSI payment for an individual was $434 per month. An additional 12.3 percent of adults with serious mental illnesses receive veterans benefits, and 7.5 percent receive funds from some other program. Black males in poverty who are 35–64 years of age are disproportionately likely to receive disability payments. Of black adults with SMI, 44 percent receive disability compared with 21 percent of whites with SMI (Barker et al., 1992). In 1990, the U.S. government expended $24.8 billion for disability insurance benefits (U.S. Department of Commerce, 1992).

Requirements for protecting the rights of persons with mental disabilities are also established by federal law. In 1978 the federal Developmental Disabilities Assistance and Bill of Rights Act (P.L. 95-602) established rights and protections for persons with developmental disabilities, and similar legislation, the Protection and Advocacy for Mentally Ill Individuals Act of 1986 (P.L. 99-319), was passed for persons with mental illnesses. There are also laws at the state level, and many protection mechanisms have been put into place including advocates (Kemp, 1984b), peer review committees (Risley and Sheldon-Wildgen, 1980a), and human rights committees (Kemp, 1983; Risley and Sheldon-Wildgen, 1980b).

The 50 states, the District of Columbia, and some U.S. territories have mental health authorities, often housed in Departments of Health or Health and Welfare, Departments of Mental Health, or Departments of Human Resources. These departments are responsible for the state mental hospitals and mental health planning and provide funding and regulation for some community mental health programs. Among the state agencies involved with persons with mental disabilities are state Departments of Vocational Rehabilitation, Departments of Mental Health, and Departments of Developmental Disabilities.

MENTAL HEALTH SERVICES

In a year, 6 percent of the population receives specialty mental health and addictive services, and 5 percent of the population receives such services from primary care providers. Professionals estimate that between 10 and 20 percent of employees will use mental health and other counseling services in a year. About 70 percent of use will be related to behavior and social adjustment, and the remaining 30 percent will involve legal, housing, financial, and other related issues. Of the behavioral and social problems, half the cases will be directly related to problems reflected in the work environment (Holoviak and Holoviak, 1984). Most of the services received will be in the community on an outpatient basis, but some services will be inpatient. In 1989, about 7 percent of the serious mentally ill in households (2.4 million) had seen a mental health professional for their disorder. Among the 700,000 persons with SMI who had never seen a mental health professional, approximately 64 percent had seen a doctor who was not a psychiatrist or another non-mental health professional for the disorder. The oldest age group was most likely to have seen some type of professional other than a mental health professional, and persons 35–64 were more likely than other age groups to have seen a mental health professional (Barker et al., 1992).

Services are found chiefly in four sectors: (1) specialty mental health including public mental hospitals, veterans services, general hospitals with psychiatric units, private psychiatric hospitals, community mental health centers, private practices of mental health professionals, and residential treatment centers for children or adults; (2) human services including family service agencies, special education in schools, and forensic services in the criminal justice system; (3) the general medical sector including services in medical units of general hospitals, nursing homes, and practices of physicians without specialty training in psychiatry; and (4) a non-health sector including pastoral counseling and transportation services (NIMH, 1986).

In 1986 there were 3,039 organizations providing mental health inpatient services. Of these hospitalizations, 42 percent were in psychiatric units in general hospitals, 21 percent in public mental hospitals, 10 percent in private psychiatric hospitals, 4 percent in Veterans Administration hospitals, and 14 percent in residential treatment centers for children. There are also specialized facilities for mentally disordered offenders; of the 150 such institutions, most are operated by the states (NIMH, 1986). It is also estimated that at least 10 percent of the general prison population, which exceeds 1 million, have a severe mental illness and are largely untreated (Jemelka, Trupin, and Chiles, 1989).

The days of hospitalization in a state mental hospital are waning. By the beginning of the 1990s, there were 50,000–60,000 patients in mental hospitals (NIMH, 1992). An increasing number of people are being hospitalized in the community in psychiatric units in general hospitals or in medical units of general hospitals (Kiesler and Sibulkin, 1987). Inpatient treatment in the community occurs in freestanding mental health facilities, psychiatric units of general hospitals, and medical units of general hospitals. Some of these facilities specialize in offering only certain types of inpatient treatment, such as substance abuse, eating disorders, or depression.

Research by the NIMH (1990) found that 2.8 million clients (1.16 percent of the U.S. population) were receiving community mental health services from 2,946 organizations. Outpatient services include individual, family, and group counseling, information and referral, assessment and referral, crisis intervention, and medication monitoring. In addition, there are day programs aimed at maintenance and support of special populations, such as persons with chronic mental illness or patients with Alzheimer's; residential programs; and innumerable specialized support groups such as Alcoholics Anonymous, Narcotics Anonymous, and Overeaters Anonymous. Community mental health programs may be operated by state regional authorities, counties, or other public entities or may be controlled by private nonprofit or profit-making corporations. Thus service provision is fragmented and widely dispersed. At this level, there are organizations that provide treatment, residential care, maintenance and support, recreation, and employment.

Among the community organizations providing treatment are the child guidance clinics. Their predecessors were clinics established in the Department of Psychology of the University of Pennsylvania in 1896 and the William Healy Clinic founded in Chicago in 1909 as part of the first juvenile court in that city. The child guidance clinics began under the guidance of the Commonwealth Fund, with the first clinic opening in 1922. The clinics were originally meant to provide mental health professionals as consultants to workers in other community agencies who worked with children. The clinics were to include social workers, psychologists, and psychiatrists. However, the clinics almost immediately began working with individuals, and social workers became the dominant professionals. From the child guidance clinics have come many other types of psychiatric centers that serve children or families.

Community health centers were established under legislation in 1963. Since that time, these centers have developed in several ways. Some of them serve persons with severe and chronic mental illness and less emotionally disturbed outpatients, while others serve primarily outpatients with emotional problems such as marriage and family problems, substance abuse problems, and interpersonal and psychological adjustment problems. Some of these clinics have become entirely entrepreneurial, including becoming employee assistance programs. There are a growing number of specialized services, such as clinics for chronic pain, sexual problems, and substance abuse. In addition, there are counseling services provided by employers and employee assistance programs for assessment and referral for personal problems affecting the workplace. In addition, there are services in other organizations, such as educational psychologist services in the schools and mental health services in juvenile centers and adult detention facilities. Some of the fastest growth of services has been in private practice, where many states license such professionals as psychiatrists, psychologists, social workers, marriage and family counselors, and counselors to practice psychotherapy.

A growing number of people are requiring supervised living arrangements, and this has led to a wide array of private facilities that provide some form of supervised 24-hour care, including family care, family foster care, board and care, halfway houses, psychosocial rehabilitation facilities, satellite housing, and nursing homes (skilled nursing facilities). Family care, foster family care, or adult foster care involves placements with private families, usually someone other than an immediate family member. The caretaker is usually licensed and is supervised by a professional social worker, and the setting usually does not include more than four to six people. This type of care began in Belgium in the eleventh century. Homes there still provide this care to one or two people with disabilities who are perceived as an integral part of the community. Board and care homes developed during deinstitutionalization, and they lack any consistent format or direction. They developed individually under their owners and managers, with some being custodial, others being family focused, and some having a treatment orientation. Board and care homes range in size from a couple of residents to more than 200. Halfway houses and psychosocial rehabilitation facilities developed during the 1950s as temporary residences used to move people into living situations that are more fully integrated into the community.

Halfway houses may be small or may have as many as 20 or 30 residents while psychosocial rehabilitation facilities focus on specific training in social skills. Satellite housing, which began in the United States in 1963, focuses on independent living and does not have live-in staff but does have professional supervision. Apartments or houses are rented, leased, or purchased, and residents share in their own household work and expenses. Most apartments house one to four persons. Nursing homes also have housed many persons with mental illness. By 1976, nursing homes housed more persons with mental illnesses than state mental hospitals (Sirrocco and Koch, 1977). By the end of the 1980s, 1–1.1 million seriously mentally ill persons were residents of nursing homes (Strahm, 1990). The federal government through their funding mechanisms are making a concerted effort to prevent any more persons with mental illnesses from being placed in nursing homes and to stop funding of mentally ill persons in nursing homes. Many persons are also housed in boarding homes, which provide room and board but no care.

Problems involving residential housing have included community resistance to placement of the housing, ambiguity about what services are required, poor staffing, and the frequent lack of supplemental funding to enhance the limited SSI funding. Funding problems are increased in some cases by the high cost of housing in some areas and by situations like that in California where a two-tier system of funding allows for a higher payment for persons with developmental disabilities than for persons with mental illness, thus encouraging providers to not provide facilities for persons with mental illness (Segal and Kotler, 1989).

There are also services available for employment. Originally these were focused on institutional work, vocational rehabilitation, and sheltered workshops, but currently there is a trend to supported employment. In addition, there are many day activity and recreation services.

2

Mental Disabilities in the United States

Definitions of mental disabilities have changed over time. The basis of definition has moved from culturally deviant, to possession by the devil, to sickness, to disturbances in developmental, familial, genetic, and biochemical processes. By the late 1960s, an operational definition of mental illness was established. "An abnormality of behavior, emotions or relationships — which abnormalities are sufficiently marked and/or prolonged as to handicap the individual himself and/or distress his family or the community — which continue up to the time of assessment" (Chess, 1969). There have also been attempts to define the much broader term "mental health." The World Health Organization (WHO) (1946) defines health as "a state of complete physical, mental, and social well-being." Mental health is a part of that definition. In Canada, mental health is defined as

> The capacity of the individual, the group and the environment to interact with one another in ways that promote subjective well-being, the optimal development and use of mental abilities (cognitive, affective, and relational), the achievement of individual and collective goals consistent with justice and the attainment and preservation of conditions of fundamental equality. (Health and Welfare Canada, 1988)

There are two systems of diagnosis widely used in the United States: the Diagnostic and Statistical Manual of Mental Disorders, which is in a revised third edition (DSM III-R) (American Psychiatric Association, 1987), and the Manual of the International Statistical Classification of Disease, Injuries, and Causes of Death, Volume 1 (WHO, 1977), known as the ICD-9. Although some mental health providers dislike attaching labels to the people with whom they work, almost all of them do because insurance companies generally will not pay for counseling or psychotherapy services unless a diagnosis is provided. In addition, human services agencies may use classification as part of their demonstration of accountability to funding sources. Not all diagnostic categories are viewed as "mental illnesses." However, providers are forced into the illness viewpoint because most health insurers will not reimburse for categories not viewed as "illnesses." Depending on the insurance company, categories such as occupational problems or parent-child problems may not be reimbursed.

DIAGNOSTIC AND STATISTICAL MANUAL OF MENTAL DISORDERS

The DSM first appeared in 1952, and it is undergoing its fourth revision. It provides the most commonly used resource for U.S. mental health practitioners making diagnosis decisions. The third edition, which appeared in 1980 and was revised in 1987 (DSM III-R), is the current edition in use. It was developed by the American Psychiatric Association to provide a detailed description of all categories of mental illness and is based on a combination of research field trials and committee votes. The DSM III represented the most revolutionary change by being more descriptive and atheoretical. It no longer recommended the use of the term "neurosis" for diagnosis and changed the term "depressive neurosis" to "dysthymic disorder." Also, homosexuality was no longer classified as an emotional illness. DSM III and DSM III-R are based on three perspectives: biological, psychological, and social. This goes beyond the traditional medical model in which disease is defined by physical etiology and biological dysfunction and goes on to consider the psychological and social influences for a biopsychosocial model. Each disorder is given a description that usually contains a list of essential features plus a clinical sketch. There is also a summary of characteristics usually associated with the disorder, information on the usual onset and course of the disorder, including potential for impairment and complications, and information on the known predisposing factors and the frequency of occurrence. Diagnostic criteria are included, and information is provided on similar disorders that could be confused in diagnosis (American Psychiatric Association, 1987).

The DSM III-R makes minor improvements on DSM III and has been criticized for being too much like a cookbook. In fact, it is much like one and when applied properly, this is not considered a disadvantage (Amchin, 1991).

In DSM III-R each of the mental disorders is conceptualized as a clinically significant behavioral or psychological syndrome or pattern that occurs in a person and that is associated with present distress (a painful symptom) or disability (impairment in one or more important areas of functioning) or with a significantly increased risk of suffering death, pain, disability, or an important loss of freedom. (DSM III-R)

An attempt is made to distinguish mental disorders from the range of normal functioning and from psychological experiences and behaviors that are normal responses, such as bereavement (Amchin, 1991). The major categories in DSM III-R are disorders usually first evident in infancy, childhood, or adolescence; organic mental syndromes and disorders; psychoactive substance use disorders; schizophrenia; delusional (paranoid) disorder; other psychotic disorders; mood disorders; anxiety disorders; somatoform disorders; dissociative disorders; sexual disorders; sleep disorders; factitious disorders; other impulsive control disorders; adjustment disorder; psychological factors affecting physical condition; developmental disorders; and personality disorders.

MENTAL ILLNESS AND DISABILITY

There are a wide array of mental illnesses and disabilities that appear in people in the workplace. These conditions include severe mental illnesses such as psychotic disorders, affective disorders (mood disorders), and phobias (anxiety). Some people will experience an acute episode and will recover, never to suffer from that mental illness again. Other people will suffer from a chronic, severe mental disorder for the rest of their lives. Historically, the definition of serious mental illness (SMI) was based primarily on psychiatric diagnosis. The definition over time has evolved, and there is increased recognition that people with SMI are a heterogeneous group with different diagnoses, levels of disability, and durations of disability. However, definitions of mental disorder differ, and although alcohol abuse, drug abuse, and mental retardation are included in DSM III-R, they are not included in the National Institute of Mental Health (NIMH) definition. The NIMH was in 1992 developing a more precise definition for serious mental illness and disability. For a recent study of serious mental illness and disability in the adult household U.S. population, the National Center for Health Statistics defined SMI "as any psychiatric disorder present during the past year that seriously interfered with one or more aspects of a person's daily life" (Barker et al., 1992).

Most people who experience an acute episode and many people who have chronic, severe mental disorders are or will be employed in the workplace. There is insufficient information on the relationship between symptoms and impairment. Some people with multiple symptoms have minimal impairment, while others with few symptoms have significant impairment. It remains difficult to predict the length of a disorder or whether there will be a spontaneous remission. The 1978 Social Security Administration Survey of Disability and Work estimated that 1.1 million persons in households were seriously disabled mentally ill. Their definition included people 20–64 years of age who were limited in the amount or kind of work or housework they could do and who had been or were expected to be disabled for at least 12 months because of mental illness or nervous or emotional problems (Ashbaugh et al., 1983). In 1989 the NIMH collaborated with the National Center for Health Statistics (NCHS) on a supplement to the National Health Interview Survey (NHIS). That research found approximately 1.4 million (47.2 percent) of seriously mentally ill adults between the ages of 18 and 69 had difficulties in relationship to work. SMI limited the work of 529,000 people (18.4 percent) and left another 829,000 (28.9 percent) currently unable to work. Over 82 percent of those adults had had their work limitation for a year or longer. More black persons with SMI (43.3 percent) than white persons (26.8 percent) were unable to work because of their mental disorder. The majority of people with SMI are able to work, although 58 percent of those with no current work limitation reported other limitations, of which coping with day to day stress, reported by 52.6 percent, was the most common. In addition, 21–32 percent of respondents reported difficulty concentrating long enough to complete tasks and in making and keeping friendships (Barker et al., 1992). Because of the intense stigma attached to these disorders, many people will not want to disclose that they have had or do have one of these disorders, and hiring processes may not seek disclosure of this information (see Chapter 3).

Employers have workers with developmental disorders in the workplace, including mental retardation, and experience people with developmental behavioral problems, including young workers who have conduct disorders. One of the major problems employers face in the workplace is employees who are substance abusers or addicted to alcohol or other drugs. In addition, at some point, most employers will encounter employees with emotional disorders. These problems have sometimes been referred to in a derogatory manner with such terms as "the worried well." This is the least well-defined category and the area of mental health that has raised fears that if treated, there would be no end to needs and service provision. Yet, in this category of mental health problems are major personal and societal problems including marital problems; family problems; spouse, child, and elder abuse; relationship problems; stress; and lifestyle problems, including smoking. Some of these emotional disorders may, if unaddressed, lead to more severe mental disorders or physical problems or may even lead to suicide. Also, employers will find that employees who have physical problems may also have to address mental health problems that are a component of or are brought on by the physical disorder.

THE PHYSICAL/MENTAL HEALTH CONNECTION

Psychiatry has been influenced from the beginning by concerns regarding the mind and body as attempts have been made to define and differentiate the psychological, environmental, biological, and physiological factors. Increasingly, research shows that there is no clear delineation between mental and physical problems. Many mental disabilities are the result of physiological damage to the brain, including mental retardation and dementias, and increasingly, mental illnesses such a schizophrenia, depression, and some phobias are being seen as caused by or as resulting in changes in brain chemistry or brain structure. Interdisciplinary research is being conducted on early brain growth and the emergence of cognitive functions. The brain's frontal lobe development is being studied, with exploration of the relationship between tissue growth and behavioral function. Brain imaging techniques (including BEAM, MRI, PET, and SPECT scans) allow researchers to examine brain structure, metabolism, and electrical activity. These techniques have shown specific patterns of pathology in autism and schizophrenia (National Advisory Mental Health Council [NAMHC], 1990). The 1970s and 1980s have seen major advances in mental health research that have constantly redefined mental disorders. This research includes biological and psychosocial approaches to prevention and treatment; increased knowledge about the interaction of biological, social, and psychological forces and their relationship to mental health or illness; and knowledge about human development. The DSM III-R attempts to bridge the gap between general medicine and psychiatry by including a diagnostic category called "psychological factors affecting physical condition." Critics argue that the category does not adequately reflect the biopsychosocial approach and the perspective that psychological factors affect almost all physical conditions (Amchin, 1991).

How a person relates to others concerning their illness may also play a significant role. Research shows that cancer's severity plays less of a role in a patient's mental health than does how openly the disease is discussed. With survival rates growing for diseases such as children's cancer, psychological adjustment is also of increasing importance. Direct communication, the way the patient talks with family, peers, and others, is the variable most predictive of psychological functioning in a survivor. One study of children and young adults, ages 7–21, found that for those who were able to have open and supportive relationships during treatment, clinical depression, at about 6 percent, was no greater than among other children. However, for those with negative mental health outcomes, there may be problems such as severe weight gain, isolation, and dropping out of school (Fritz, Williams, and Amylon, 1989).

There has been a rapid growth in environmental medicine, which integrates many disciplines and focuses on organ systems, interdependency; and genetic, familial, and environmental aspects. Environmental medicine looks at all factors that influence a person's life and health, both psychological and physical. This includes childhood experiences involving emotional, psychological, and physical events; environmental influences and exposures; and genetic history (Anderson and Berger, 1991). This is in sharp contrast to traditional medicine, which focuses on the organ about which there is a complaint and is conservative, symptomatic relief focused, and drug oriented.

Another growing new field is psychoneuroimmunoendocrinology. This field focuses research on the inner communication between vital bioregulatory systems, including the central nervous system, immune system, endocrine system, and the psyche. The research is based on the theory that these systems are interconnected and inseparable and consequently influence each other. This means psychoemotional problems may lead to imbalances in the body's systems. For example, physical, psychological, or sexual abuse in children can led to dysfunctions in the immune, endocrine, or neurological systems that may later appear as physical symptoms such as seizures, migraine headaches, and stomach problems. It is hypothesized that a traumatized person who is experiencing tremendous fear, conflict, or rage is affecting brain circuits by constantly overstimulating some and understimulating others and that this leads to an imbalance in electrochemical activity in the brain; this then leads to physical problems and disease. "Abnormal, bio-chemical products are produced in the body, such as allergic mediators like histamine, serotonin, and insulin; mediators of inflammation, like some prostaglandins, or certain peptides that are secreted by the gastrointestinal systems" (Anderson and Berger, 1991). This process may lead to psychological dysfunction and neurological disorders, which may include anxiety and panic attacks, eating disorders, dementia, obsessive-compulsive behavior, and rage. This could be an explanation for addictions such as drugs, alcohol, and food. People use these substances originally to numb emotional pain, but this may lead to overstimulation of the pleasure centers and limbic system of the brain, which may change neurochemistry, thus, leading to addiction.

Some researchers believe as many as 90 percent of physical problems have a psychological component (Padus, 1986). The psychoemotional component of illnesses are often ignored because of the fear of the costs involved in diagnosis and treatment. Symptomatic relief is a quicker fix. However, in the long run, if the psychoemotional component is not addressed, this may mean the same problem may return or there will be new problems. For example, there will be further damage to the heart or continued cirrhosis of the liver if the underlying psychological and alcohol abuse problems are not addressed, and this could lead to heart bypass surgery or a liver transplant or early death, which in the long run are even more costly.

TREATMENTS OF MENTAL HEALTH PROBLEMS

Mental disabilities may be treated by medication and psychotherapy. However, many people are not treated.

Psychopharmacology

The psychological and behavioral effects of drugs were noted even in primitive medicine, and psychopharmacology is tied to a search for chemically or physiologically caused states. Psychopharmacology focuses on the ability of drugs to alter mentation and behavior, and more and more mental disorders are being treated with drugs. There are some 5,000 substances loosely referred to as drugs. Most of these drugs have been developed in laboratories and are manufactured by chemical processes. Many of them are synthetic forms of naturally occurring substances, and a few come from animal or botanical sources.

All drugs have three names: a generic name, which is the official medical term for the basic active substance, a name chosen by the U.S. Adopted Name Council (USAN); a brand name, chosen by the manufacturer; and a chemical name, which is the technical description. There may be several brands manufactured by different companies with the same generic substance that have only slight changes relating to convenience, absorption rates, or digestibility. Drugs may be available by generic or brand name or both (Clayman, 1988). All new drugs must undergo testing by the drug companies, and those tests are reviewed by the U.S. Food and Drug Administration (FDA) before the drug is approved for marketing to the public. The FDA does not do its own testing, and testing by drug companies frequently takes several years. Recently, federal regulatory changes have been aimed at shortening the testing and review period, but drugs may be available in other countries for some time before they become available in the United States. Under federal law, drugs must be considered safe and medically effective and their risks must be weighed against their benefits. Federal and state law determine which drugs require a physician's prescription and which drugs can be sold over the counter. Controlled substances laws regulate drugs under five schedules.

Disorders of the brain and nervous system frequently are successfully treated with drugs that modify the disorder by treating the symptoms but do not eliminate it. Drug treatments may provide symptom relief and, in rare cases, can restore normal functioning. The modern era of psychopharmacology began in 1951 with the synthesis of chlorpromazine. This was followed by the introduction of Thorazine in 1954. Drug therapy is based on observation of symptom changes in behavior. Notations are made concerning the therapeutic effect of a drug, and the relationship between the drug dosage and the psychopathology is quantified. Clinical rating scales and psychological test methods have been developed to establish criteria to determine the results of therapy. Drug therapy requires constant monitoring, and reactions of drugs with other substances need to be considered. The field of pharmacokinetics researches what happens to drugs after they enter the body. Food can play a significant role in enhancing or delaying the absorption of drugs. Mixing certain drugs and food can also cause dangerous reactions. For example, certain foods high in tyramine (an amino acid), including some fish, cheese, and red wines, can result in a dangerous rise in blood pressure when combined with certain antidepressants (Graedon and Graedon, 1988). This is an area to which professionals and consumers do not always pay sufficient attention. Alcohol can also be dangerous, even lethal, when mixed with certain drugs. Alcohol can make drugs such as benzodiazepines function more potently.

One of the major problems with the use of drugs is that for most drugs it is unknown whether greater or lesser amounts are needed in the treatment of women. Traditionally the National Institutes of Health (NIH) have funded research on primarily male animal and human research subjects. Women have usually been treated based on knowledge about male subjects. Differences regarding females have remained largely unknown. In the early 1990s, the Congressional Women's Caucus focused on this issue and the fact that predominantly female diseases have also been poorly funded. The Bush administration appointed a woman to head the NIH and established an agenda that included seeing that women subjects are included in research and predominantly female diseases are researched. In mental health research recently there has been some focus on the fact that women may not be treatable in the same way as men; this has particularly been recognized in regard to treatment of women with alcohol problems.

Some drugs that have been used to treat certain conditions have been found to have possible serious mental health consequences for some people. Benzodiazepines are used commonly to treat sleep problems and are also used to treat anxiety. They have been considered to be comparatively free of adverse effects and to be relatively safe, even in overdose. However, their relationship to depression and suicide for some people has been questioned. There are a number of reports in the literature that note an association between benzodiazepine use and the emergence of depressive symptoms (Hall and Joffe, 1972; Lydiard et al., 1989). A 1991 review of the literature concluded that although there were no data to support the belief that depression was a frequent or regular side effect, benzodiazepine use could occasionally lead to significant depression and suicide (Smith and Salzman, 1991). In addition, Halcion, a sleeping drug marketed by Upjohn company, which brings in 8 percent of that company's sales, about $2.5 billion ("Health: Upjohn Defends . . . ," 1991), has been charged with causing short-term memory loss and depression in some people.

Psychoactive drugs may have serious side effects. Many side effects are reversible if the drug is stopped, and many can be controlled by taking additional medication (Bouricius, 1989). Tardive dyskinesia (TD) is a serious neurological disorder that can affect people using neuroleptics for schizophrenia or affective disorders. TD consists of involuntary irregular movements, which may be of the face and mouth, such as chewing and smacking movements. Sometimes the involuntary movements may involve the arms and legs. TD in many cases is irreversible. Prevalence is estimated to be between 20 and 30 percent among psychiatric outpatients, and it usually occurs in persons who have taken high doses for long periods. Fortunately, less than 5 percent of these persons have serious symptoms (Bouricius, 1989). However, the visibility of this disorder can result in stigmatization of the person with it. The risks of the use of psychotropic and other drugs with mental health effects have to be weighed against the benefits for each individual. Although drug therapy, particularly with antipsychotic drugs, has been under heavy attack by some of the patients' rights movements, drugs may be helpful to many patients if carefully prescribed and monitored.

Non-Drug Treatments

Some psychiatric symptoms have an underlying organic cause, including cerebral tumors, that may be treated by surgery. However, surgery has also been tried to treat mental illness. From the 1930s through the 1950s a form of surgery called psychosurgery was popular, particularly in state institutions, to treat mental illnesses, usually schizophrenia and depression.

Psychosurgery

Psychosurgery involves removing, destroying, or severing some brain tissue. Prefrontal lobotomy was developed using various techniques. By 1949, 5,000 surgeries per year were performed, more than half in state institutions (Valenstein, 1986). Opposition to conducting the procedure became very strong in the United States and other countries in the 1950s. The introduction of psychoactive drugs during that decade sped the decline in psychosurgery. By 1970, only around 300 surgeries were being performed in the United States (Chorover, 1974). Oregon outlawed the procedure in 1982, and it is highly regulated in other states.

Modern psychosurgery techniques now include using exact stereotactic procedures for directing electrodes that place very small lesions in key areas of the brain, using radiofrequency waves or radioactive elements with a short half-life, or freezing using cyroprobes. On-line video monitors and x-rays are used in carrying out very precise procedures. Although these procedures are seldom used, they still are occasionally used to treat severe chronic anxiety, agitated depression with high risk of suicide, incapacitating obsessive-compulsive disorders, and intractable pain.

Electroconvulsive Therapy

Electroconvulsive therapy (ECT) is used primarily as a treatment for some forms of depression, particularly typical, endogenous, psychotic, and melancholic types of depression (Kiloh, 1982). It involves applying an electrical voltage to the brain through electrodes attached to the surface of the head. It is performed with the patient under a muscle relaxant or anesthesia to prevent problems with convulsions. There is considerable criticism of ECT, and it is now highly regulated by state laws.

Psychotherapy

The most commonly used non-drug treatment for mental health problems is psychotherapy. Psychotherapy has been described as the type of social influence exerted by a socially sanctioned and trained healer with a person who is suffering and seeking relief through a defined series of contacts (Frank, 1973). Psychotherapy has developed in many different directions, providing for widely divergent approaches based on different psychological theories. Some therapists use only one approach, while others are eclectic and combine various approaches. Strict Freudian psychoanalysis has rapidly declined in the United States in favor of shorter, more direct forms of psychotherapy. Researchers have also concluded that there is no evidence that psychoanalytic therapies result in better outcomes than less time-consuming approaches (Fisher and Greenberg, 1985). Researchers have concluded that roughly four-fifths of clients improve regardless of which type of therapy is used, because the elements that cause the change are a helping relationship with a therapist, suggestion, and abreaction (release of repressed emotions through retelling the experience). These are elements of all psychotherapies. The same researchers found that with major mental illness, success rates improved when psychotherapy and drugs were both used (Luborsky, Singer, and Luborsky, 1975). Psychotherapy is shown to be an effective treatment for many people (Malan, 1973), but 3–6 percent of clients do not improve but become worse (Strupp, 1978). It is estimated that one-third to one-half of people with less serious mental health problems who have no systematic psychotherapy improve symptomatically, but only an estimated one-fourth show constructive personality changes (Crowne, 1987). Without the constructive personality changes, problems are more likely to rearise.

Therapy may be provided to individuals, families, or groups. Some of the therapies commonly used are psychoanalytic, Adlerian, cognitive, rational emotive, Reality Therapy, humanistic existential, Rogerian, gestalt, family systems, and behavioral/social learning. Hypnosis and biofeedback may be used as adjuncts to other therapies. Hypnosis uses various relaxation techniques to lead to a trance state, and psychotherapy is conducted while the client is in trance. Hypnosis is also used for age regression, involving encouraging the client to experience an earlier age. Biofeedback became prominent in the late 1960s. Various techniques have been developed to enable people to develop some voluntary control over physiological functions, including blood pressure and heart rate. There are numerous electronic devices that provide the client with visual or auditory feedback on which modifications are made. The client is expected to learn from the feedback how to control a physiological function.

FAILURE TO TREAT

There is a cost to not treating someone with a mental illness that results in loss of productive lives in the workplace and in the community. In addition, occasionally there is also a cost resulting from violent behavior. Most people with mental illness are not dangerous; however, some people with untreated mental illness can be dangerous. Most people with psychosis who commit serious violence have been psychiatric patients, but only a few of them have received treatment within the six-month period before committing an offense, and research shows that 43 percent of those with psychosis who committed a violent act were driven by a delusion (Taylor, 1986). Research also indicates that 71 percent of all offenses committed by schizophrenic patients were motivated by delusions or hallucinations (Hafner, 1986). It is important for persons with serious mental illness to be encouraged and assisted in seeking, receiving, and staying in treatment.

Lack of treatment may lead to lifelong problems. Research indicates that untreated childhood and teenage depression may led to chronic problems, which later include adult depression, particularly by females. Anxiety disorders also often persist into adulthood, and almost half of the children and adolescents diagnosed with conduct disorder become antisocial adults (NIMH, 1990).

Failure to treat often results in the greatest effects on the families of the person with mental illness. When there is no or inadequate treatment and support systems, the families usually become the total caregivers. There may be severe consequences for children of parents with mental health problems. The prevalence of severe behavior problems among children of mentally ill parents is substantially higher than among children in the general population. One study found 53 percent of these children have already become "victims" (Feldman, Stiffman, and Jung, 1987). An affective (mood) disorder of the mother may be particularly detrimental for at-risk children, because it can impede the mother's ability to establish a good relationship with the child. However, the bond between mother and child is less susceptible to disruption by mental illness than is the bond between father and child. The risk to the child rises with the number of people with mental disorders in the home. Assistance for families with mental disorders may be difficult to find. More than 25 percent of families in one study failed to receive assistance from any organization or agency, and 42 percent of them had no help from relatives, friends, or neighbors. Of the variance in the behavior problems in children in these families, 40 percent was explained by the proportion of mentally ill persons in the family, the frequency of discord in the mother-child relationship, personal coping skills in activities and schools, and interaction between the proportion of mentally ill persons in the home and activity competence. Children with family members with mental illness exhibited more severe behavior disorders and much weaker coping skills, with especially low scores on interpersonal, school, and activity competence, and they suffered a higher incidence of stressful events each year. However, they did not differ from a comparison group in terms of academic achievement (Feldman, Stiffman, and Jung, 1987). The type of mental disorder influences the problems experienced by the child. For example, depression appears to be one of the major symptoms in children of alcoholics (Goodwin et al., 1977) (see Chapter 4).

Failure to treat emotional and mental health problems may lead to increased physical health problems, to increasingly severe mental health problems, and to costs to the workplace in the form of loss of productivity, accidents, absenteeism, increased sick leave, interpersonal relationship problems with other employees, and other problems that result from employees with mental health problems or employees who are relatives of persons with mental health problems.

MENTAL DISORDERS

The DSM III-R can be used to provide a summary of some of the many common mental health disorders found in the work force. These include psychotic disorders, dementias, mood disorders, anxiety disorders, somatoform disorder, sleep disorders, substance abuse, developmental disorders, and personality disorders.

Psychotic Disorders

DSM III-R defines several psychotic disorders, but the most well-known is schizophrenia.

Schizophrenia

Schizophrenia is a major mental disorder involving psychosis. Schizophrenia's typical onset is at adolescence or in early adulthood, around the time young workers are entering the work force, and it has a lifetime prevalence of approximately 2 percent. There are several different types of schizophrenia: catatonic, disorganized, paranoid, undifferentiated, and residual. Schizophrenia may have a gradual onset or a sudden one. In its acute phase it is characterized by distortions in thinking, disturbances in feelings and behavior, delusions, and hallucinations. After the acute phase, the person may enter a chronic phase, which may cause social withdrawal, inhibited behaviors, motor behavior problems, difficulties in affect (expressiveness), and loss of ego boundaries. People with schizophrenia may fail to make appropriate judgments about the behavior of others, may follow rigid rules that may or may not be appropriate under the circumstances, may be incompetent at making appropriate social judgments, and may follow the first cue they receive with little attention to the overall context. Research indicates that this is an intrinsic feature of the disorder and is caused by biological factors of the disease itself (Cutting and Murphy, 1990). Acute phases may reactivate from time to time, but the course of the disease is different with different people. With treatment, approximately one-third of patients improve, one-third stay the same, and one-third become worse.

The etiology or cause of schizophrenia is still under research, but most researchers now believe that there is a genetic component, which is not the total cause of the condition. Irregularities in brain chemistry may be the cause. Research on dopamine and other brain chemistry research are of major importance. Schizophrenia is actually believed to be a group of diseases with similar symptoms but different causes. Schizophrenia is still largely treated as one disease, although this is slowly beginning to change. Schizophrenia is now seen as having two major syndromes involving negative symptoms, such as lack of drive, loss of expression, loss of interest, and social withdrawal, and positive symptoms (psychosis).

Psychoactive drugs are used in the treatment of schizophrenia, and over the years, three classes of drugs have been developed: phenothiazines, butyrophenones, and thioxanthenes. Neuroleptics are the most commonly used drugs for schizophrenia, and there are now more than 30 of them, many with several names. Some drugs such as trifluoperazine (Stelazine) are given in pill form, and others such as haloperidol decanoate (Haldol) are given in a long-acting (depot) injection. There are many supporters of the benefits of psychopharmacology who believe that the benefits have been demonstrated for all forms of schizophrenia (Hollister, 1978). However, one of the problems with the use of psychoactive drugs is that they are a "shotgun" approach, going to every part of the brain. This causes unwanted drug side effects. As researchers have found receptors for brain chemicals such as dopamine, the chances of designing drugs that will affect only receptors linked to the disease are increased. This would avoid many problems with side effects. Researchers are also trying to develop drugs that will separately affect the negative and positive symptoms of the disease. Clozapine (Clozaril), a drug discovered in the late 1960s but not appearing significantly in the United States until the 1980s, has shown an ability to affect the negative symptoms as well as the positive. It appears to be able to stimulate and blockade at the same time (Stahl, 1990). The hope is that eventually psychosis will be controlled by a drug and the negative symptoms can be treated separately (Jones et al., 1990). Currently there are an estimated 10 to 20 percent of patients who do not respond to drug treatment (Issac and Armant, 1990).

Schizophrenia is also treated with sedatives, including barbiturates, and benzodiazapines, which have a calming and sleep-inducing effect. Unfortunately, these drugs are habit forming. Minor tranquilizers (anxiolytics) are also used, including chlordiazepoxide (Librium), diazepam (Valium), and alprazolam (Xanax) for relief of anxiety and side effects of antipsychotic drugs. Antiparkinsonian drugs are used to treat side effects and are probably the second most frequently prescribed medication for schizophrenia (Thorton, et al., 1985).

Delusional (Paranoid) Disorder

Delusional (paranoid) disorder involves persistent nonbizarre delusions. Hallucinations, if present, are not prominent. Apart from the delusions or the consequences of the delusions, the person's behavior does not seem obviously odd or bizarre. There are five types in DSM III-R: erotomanic, in which the delusion is that a person, usually of higher status, is in love with the patient; grandiose, in which there is an inflated sense of worth, power, knowledge, identity, or a special relationship to a famous person or deity; jealousy, in which the delusion is that the sexual partner is unfaithful; persecutory, in which the delusion is that the person or someone close to them is being badly treated in some way; and somatic, in which the person believes that they have some physical defect, disorder, or disease. If untreated, in some cases, delusional (paranoid) disorder can lead to violence in the workplace.

Dementia/Alzheimer's

The rate of organic and functional psychoses among people over 60 is estimated to be approximately 7–9 percent. The rate of dementia among persons over 65 is estimated to be 1.3–6.2 percent for severe dementia and 2.6–15.4 percent for milder dementia (Neugebauer, 1980). Epidemiological Catchment Area (ECA) research found 4–5.1 percent rates of severe cognitive impairment in people 65 and over (Robins et al., 1984). Dementia is included in DSM III-R under organic mental syndromes, along with several other disorders. Alzheimer's disease is the leading cause of dementia and the fourth leading cause of death among older persons in the United States. In the United States, 2 million to 4 million people suffer from Alzheimer's. Alzheimer's and other dementias are of increasing concern for employers because of the aging of the U.S. population, which increases the segment of the population that is vulnerable. Also, the removal of legally mandated retirement ages allows employees to continue work without consideration of age.

Alzheimer's disease is of particular concern to employers because it is the most common type of dementia and because early-onset Alzheimer's may affect employees as early as their forties and fifties, during the prime time of their careers. Alzheimer's is a progressive degenerative illness that impairs behavior, memory, and thinking. The primary site of the disease is the brain, therefore, it affects the mental and physical health of all those who have the disease. The disease has existed for a long time, but it remains difficult to diagnose. Dementia and major depressive disorders may have similar symptoms, including apathy, difficulty concentrating, memory loss, and disorientation. Because about 10 percent of noninstitutionalized older persons have clinically diagnosable depression (Harper, 1986), it may be difficult to correctly diagnose whether a condition is dementia or a major depressive disorder. Dementia is sometimes not revealed by MRI, CAT scan, or other neurological exams that have the ability to analyze the brain's active and inactive areas and increase the possibility of detection of brain defects (Buckingham and VanGorp, 1988).

Only in recent years has Alzheimer's received widespread recognition, and only slowly is biological medical research shedding light on this disease. There may be several ways in which Alzheimer's is developed. Although some cases have an inherited component, most appear sporadically. Researchers in Indiana in October 1991 published a paper concerning the finding of a mutation in the same gene on chromosome 21 in three generations of an Indiana family. The gene affected production of amyloid beta protein, which forms plaques, brain deposits, that are a mark of Alzheimer's. Recent research has also demonstrated for the first time in live animals that an accumulation of beta-amyloid causes the nerve damage which is characteristic of Alzheimer's and has shown that a protein, substance P, inhibits the destructive effects of beta-amyloid. There is a correlation between the loss of ability to transmit messages between nerve cells and the decline in ability to reason and think (National Institute on Aging, 1992).

Alzheimer's is a primary degenerative dementia. It results in a deteriorating course over a period of several years in which the person's mental and physical functioning are affected. Dr. Martin Farlow of Indiana University and a California company, Salk Institute Biotechnology-Industrial Associates, are working on a test to detect the disease. They published research in *Lancet* in August 1992 documenting how their genetic test showed the onset of Alzheimer's in a 39-year-old Indiana person who appeared symptom free. The patient is a member of the intergenerational family with a history of inherited Alzheimer's that has been followed by researchers since the 1960s. An abnormally low level of amyloid beta protein was found in another family member who was 44 years old. Family members who developed the disease usually had symptoms in their early forties and died within a few years. If a test can be developed, it would allow identification of patients in the early stages of the disease before clinical symptoms appear ("Scientists Home in . . . ," 1992). This approach is still experimental and will require further research and regulatory review before general use. At present there is no way to detect Alzheimer's until clinical symptoms appear.

There is currently no effective treatment for Alzheimer's. A controversial drug, tacrine, raised hopes when a California doctor reported dramatic results with it in the late 1980s, but in October 1992, doctors reported in the *New England Journal of Medicine* that a major study showed disappointing results. Researchers found no across-the-board improvement in 215 patients who received the drug at 16 hospitals. When results of the study were reported to the FDA in 1991, an advisory panel of the FDA declined to recommend approval. The drug did improve some abilities on tests such as naming common objects and following simple commands, but there were no significant changes. The manufacturer, Warner-Lambert Co., was continuing with trials, hoping for better results. Preliminary results of a study on 468 patients indicated that doctors of the two-thirds of the patients who were on tacrine judged those patients improved compared with the one-third of patients who were on a placebo. The drug boosts the brain's levels of acetylcholine, a chemical that diminishes in Alzheimer's patients. A third study is under way to determine if higher doses of the drug produce better results. Currently around 5,000 patients are being treated through various studies. Because the drug is not available for general use, some relatives of Alzheimer's patients have sued to have the drug released (Haney, 1992).

Mood/Affective Disorders

The 1970s were called the decade of affective disorders (Dunner, 1988). By the end of that decade, diagnostic criteria were standardized by the DSM III-R (1987) under the term "mood disorders," and the term "manic depressive illness" was replaced in DSM III by the term "bipolar disorder." The DSM III established the following categories of mood disorders: major depression (single episode or recurrent), dysthymia (depressive neurosis), biopolar disorders (mixed, manic, or depressed), and cyclothymia. The NIMH (1990) has found that serious depression has two major onset ages: 15–19 years and 25–29 years. Depression in adolescence may double the risk of later drug abuse or dependence (NAMHC, 1990). Serious depression, thus, first appears in many young people as they are entering the work force or in the early years of developing careers.

Mood disorders involve physical and behavioral components and subjective feelings, thoughts, wishes, and fantasies. Only one of five people with a significant depression is treated, and half of those receive only short-term treatment. Some of the common symptoms of depression are a sad or irritable mood, decreased ability to concentrate, difficulty in making decisions, diminished or absent pleasure, loss of interest in normal activities, social withdrawal, guilt or sense of worthlessness, lack of appetite or excessive appetite, physical agitation or slowed motion, irritability, blunted affect, decreased energy and fatigue, insomnia or sleeping all day, and suicidal thoughts or actions. Bipolar disorders involve alternating depression and manic episodes. Manic episodes are characterized by elevated or irritable mood of one week or longer, including distractibility, impulsivity, increased activity, overtalkativeness, racing thoughts, and decreased need for sleep. Depression has been described under two categories: endogenous and exogenous. Endogenous depression includes bipolar disorder and is believed to result from biochemical or hormonal imbalances and is not related to external factors. Exogenous depression is believed to be precipitated by external stress, including work stress and loss of a loved one (Atwood and Chester, 1987).

Antidepressants are the most commonly used drugs for treating affective disorders. Antidepressants usually reverse a depression in two weeks to a month, but their use is often combined with psychotherapy for the most effective treatment (Esajian, 1991). Endogenous depression is treated with tricyclics, a group of one of four major groupings of antidepressants. They were introduced in 1959 and now include amitriptyline (Elavil) and clomipramine (Anafranil). Monoamine oxidase inhibitors (MAOs), which were introduced in 1954, are also used, particularly for people who are also anxious or have phobias as well as depression. They include phenelzine (Nardil). Mood stabilizers such as lithium and carbamazepine are also used to treat affective disorders, particularly bipolar disorder. Lithium treatment of biopolar illness has saved the United States an estimated $39 billion in lost productivity over the past 20 years (NIMH, 1990). Minor tranquilizers are more often used to treat exogenous depression. They became very popular during the 1950s and have become subject to abuse.

DSM III-R recognizes seasonal patterns to mood disorders. Seasonal affective disorder (SAD) is a disturbance of behavior and mood connected to seasonal change. It is cyclical, with depressions occurring in fall and winter alternating with normal mood or mild elation in spring and summer. Research has shown that SAD resembles seasonal behavioral rhythms of lower animals. Approximately 20 percent of people complain of moderate to marked changes in mood and energy across the seasons. Symptoms increase with increasing latitude. Although some children are affected, onset is usually in the twenties and thirties (Rosenthal et al., 1986), which are also the early years of career development. Women are four times more likely than men to experience it, and there may be a genetic link to some forms of the illness (Weissman et al., 1985).

Phototherapy has been developed to treat SAD. High-intensity, full-spectrum fluorescent lights are usually used, and special lights are available for use at home and at work. Light manipulation is used to try to regulate the hypothalamus of the brain. Although the cause is still unknown, there are currently three major theories as to causation.

Anxiety Disorders

Anxiety involves apprehension or fear not caused by real danger. Brain activity can be increased by certain brain chemicals, and this increased brain activity can result in stimulation of the sympathetic nervous system, resulting in physical symptoms such as breathlessness, digestive disorders, headaches, muscle aches, tension, frequent urination, palpitations, sweating, and shaking, as well as feelings of fear. There may be difficulty concentrating and difficulty sleeping, including nightmares. Anxiety disorders in adolescence may double the risk of substance abuse (NAMHC, 1990). Under anxiety disorders, DSM III-R includes panic disorder with or without agoraphobia (the fear of being in places/situations from which it could be difficult to escape); agoraphobia without history of panic disorder; social phobia; simple phobia; obsessive-compulsive disorder; posttraumatic stress disorder; and generalized anxiety disorder.

Agoraphobia can result in people avoiding travel, being unable to leave home, or requiring a companion to be with them when leaving home. Even if they are able to leave home or travel, they experience a high level of anxiety. Social phobias leave people fearing scrutiny by others and fearing that they will be embarrassed or humiliated; this may cause avoidant behavior that interferes with their occupational or social life. Simple phobias involve fear or avoidant behavior regarding a specific object or situation, for example, specific animals, such as snakes; substances, such as blood; closed spaces (claustrophobia); heights (acrophobia); or air travel. Obsessions involve recurrent and persistent ideas, thoughts, impulses, or images that a person originally tries to ignore or suppress but that, over time, impose more and more upon the ability of the person to function. Obsessions may involve food, contamination, violence, or the need to perform a certain act. Compulsions are the repetitive and intentional behaviors that are performed in response to the obsession. Some examples of compulsions are hand washing and counting. Obsessive-compulsive disorder often begins as early as 15–19 years of age ("Peak Ages . . . ," 1990). Employees may be able to hide anxieties or obsessions for a while, but if they become severe enough, they will affect the employee's productivity and may eventually lead to the inability to work.

Antianxiety drugs such as anxiolytics or minor tranquilizers are used to alleviate the symptoms of anxiety but do not address the underlying causes. Benzodiazepines are the most commonly used drugs and are usually given for a short time to create relaxation. Unfortunately, they are among the most abused of legal drugs, and long-term use can lead to addiction. Beta blockers are used primarily to reduce physical symptoms of anxiety. Psychotherapy, including cognitive behavior therapy, may be used to address underlying causes, but research shows that some anxiety may be the result of chemical brain imbalances. Further drug research may lead to new drugs to address those forms of anxiety.

Posttraumatic stress disorder involves experiencing a traumatic event outside the range of normal human experience, which would be very stressful to most people. There also is persistent reexperiencing of the traumatic event, persistent avoidance of stimuli associated with the event or a numbing of response to it, and persistent symptoms of increased arousal. Reexperiencing the event may involve dreams or flashbacks in which the event is relived; avoidance or numbing may include avoidance of activities or situations associated with the trauma, amnesia or failing to remember the event, a restricted emotional range, feelings of detachment or estrangement and a sense of a foreshortened future; increased arousal may include difficulty sleeping, irritability or outbursts of anger, difficulty concentrating, and hypervigilance. There may also be an avoidance of responsibility, depression, and substance abuse. Employees who have been Vietnam veterans or who were abused as children may be suffering from posttraumatic stress disorder. If untreated, in some rare instances, posttraumatic stress disorder may lead to workplace violence.

Somatoform Disorders

Somatoform disorders are characterized by physical symptoms that indicate physical disorders, but no organic cause can be found. In this category, DSM III-R includes body dysmorphic disorder, which involves a preoccupation with an imagined defect or a slight physical imperfection; conversion disorder, which involves a loss or change in physical functioning that would seem to be from a physical disorder but for which psychological factors are the cause, for example, false pregnancy or the loss of the use of an arm when there is no physical cause; hypochondriasis, in which there is a preoccupation with having a serious disease that has not been diagnosed; somatization disorder, which involves a history of recurrent and multiple physical complaints or the belief that one is sickly over a period of several years; and somatoform pain disorder, which involves a preoccupation with pain in the absence of any physical finding.

Sleep Disorders

Sleep disorders were a new official category for DSM III-R. There are several defined sleep disorders, but all must exist for more than one month, and it must be the predominant complaint. Dyssomnias involve disturbances in the amount, quality, and timing of sleep. They include insomnia disorders, which involve difficulty in initiating or maintaining sleep or having nonrestorative sleep. Sleep wake schedule disorder involves a mismatch between the sleep wake schedule demanded by the person's environment, often their work setting, and the person's normal circadian sleep wake pattern, resulting in insomnia or hypersomnia (excessive daytime sleepiness with a tendency to fall asleep easily and quickly or sleep attacks of irresistible sleep, or sleep drunkenness, a prolonged transition to a fully awake state). Sleep wake schedule disorder is a problem that occurs with shift workers and can lead to difficulties on the job, such as increased accidents. New approaches being taken to adjusting sleeping patterns for shift workers include special lighting treatments and a new experimental drug in pill form. There are also parasomnias that involve an abnormal event during sleep or at the threshold between sleep and wakefulness; these include dream anxiety disorder, nightmare disorder, and sleepwalking disorder. Sleep research labs or sleep recording data may be used in determining the diagnosis. Employees with sleep disorders may have difficulties at work, including lost productivity and increased accidents.

Substance Abuse

People have self-medicated themselves for centuries in their search for relief of psychological pain. Alcohol, opiates, and marijuana were widely used for self-tranquilization. Abuse of some drugs has led to their control. The peak age for onset of alcohol or drug abuse or dependence is 15–19 years (NIMH, 1990). Substance abuse takes a major toll in the workplace of workers of all ages. Most researchers believe that it is a combination of psychological, social, and biological factors that lead to a user becoming an addict (Franklin, 1991).

In DSM III-R, substance abuse is included under psychoactive substance-induced organic mental disorders, which are various organic mental syndromes caused by the direct effects of psychoactive substances on the nervous system, and under psychoactive substance use disorders, which relate to symptoms and maladaptive behavior associated with regular use of psychoactive substances that affect the central nervous system. Eleven classes of substances are included in the DSM III-R: opiates; hallucinogens; PCP and similar drugs; cocaine; amphetamines or similar sympathomimetics; sedatives, hypnotics, and anxiolytics; cannabis; inhalants; alcohol; nicotine; and caffeine.

Substance abuse may be difficult to diagnose, because substance abusers are often in denial, provide unreliable histories, withhold information, and alienate mental health workers (Amchin, 1991). Psychoactive substance use disorders involve substance dependence or abuse, and the person requires the continued use of the substance despite occupational, social, psychological, and physical problems. Psychoactive substance dependence involves cognitive, behavioral, and physiological symptoms that impair control over the use of a psychoactive substance. Severity is designated as mild, moderate, severe, in partial remission, or in full remission. Possible symptoms include marked tolerance requiring increasing amounts of the substance to achieve the desired effect and possible physiological tolerance and/or withdrawal. If several substances are involved, the person may be diagnosed as a polysubstance abuser. Signs of a substance abuse problem include an abrupt change in mood or attitudes, decline in attendance or performance at work, resistance to correction or discipline, impaired relationships with other employees, unusual flares of temper, stealing, secrecy, associating with a new group of people, and increased money problems (Alcohol, Drug Abuse, and Mental Health Administration [ADAMHA], 1991).

Heroin

In 1977, 3.2 percent of young adults surveyed by the National Institute on Drug Abuse (NIDA) admitted to having used heroin at some time (NIDA, 1981). The number of regular heroin users by the late 1980s was estimated to be 500,000–750,000. In 1991, NIDA surveys indicated that 0.8 percent of 18–25 year olds and 1.7 percent of 26 year olds and over had ever used heroin, and 0.1 percent of 18–25 year olds were current users. Death and emergency room visits linked to heroin stabilized in the 1970s but grew 25 percent in the 1980s (NIDA, 1991).

Scarcity and impurity were believed to have limited heroin use in the 1970s, but from 1986 to 1990 opium production doubled, purity rose from 10 percent to 35–50 percent, and prices stabilized, making it economical to smoke the drug rather than use a needle. Speed ball (heroin/cocaine mix) use tripled from 1985 to 1989. Because every stimulant epidemic has been followed by increased use of sedatives, some experts believe that if there is a decline in cocaine use, there will be an increase in heroin use ("Heroin Use," 1990).

Heroin addicts may suffer irreversible metabolic changes. Methadone treatment is a common form of treatment for heroin addicts. It is based on the model of insulin treatment for diabetes and is used to relieve the metabolic deficiency created by heroin use, which may be irreversible (Moccia, 1983). Methadone is an opiate, like heroin, and allows the addict to cope without heroin. It prevents withdrawal symptoms, provides an effect without the highs and lows of heroin, and does not result in euphoria.

Methadone was developed during World War II in Germany as a synthetic pain killer and began to be used in the 1960s in New York to treat heroin addicts. By 1968 a New York study showed 59 percent of those under treatment were working and only 12 percent of patients failed the program (Chambers and Brills, 1973). By 1977 another New York study reported that 50 percent of patients were working and only 2.7 percent of those in treatment were arrested (Newman, 1977). Thus, people receiving methadone maintenance may be successfully employed. The success of methadone maintenance programs has led to their spread around the country. To receive treatment, addicts usually have to show proof of at least two years of addiction; however, some clinics are not careful about these procedures, and it is possible for a substance abuser to get methadone from more than one clinic at the same time. Methadone is administered at clinics and drug levels are monitored regularly by urinalysis. If there is inadequate monitoring, drug overdose and death may occur. Counseling programs sometimes also are provided to deal with the psychological aspects of addiction. The courts have upheld the right to confidentiality in methadone treatment. Treatment may cost $40–50 a week, because it is largely provided through profit-making clinics. There is considerable controversy about the ability of addicts to get off methadone. There is a family movement aimed at getting addicts off methadone. The NIDA is also trying to develop alternative drugs ("Lukewarm Turkey," 1989).

Lysergic Acid Diethylamide

Lysergic acid diethylamide (LSD) was synthesized in Switzerland in 1938, and its hallucinogenic properties were discovered in 1943. Originally it was thought that LSD could be used to create artificial model psychoses for research. Research showed that although altered behavior was induced in all subjects who received an adequate dose, some subjects did not produce a model psychosis but showed altered thinking processes without psychotic behavior. The individual's personality was found to be a variable, along with mood, setting, cultural factors, and psychological expectations. Timothy Leary, a faculty researcher at Harvard, became an advocate of LSD and other mind-altering drugs in the 1960s. After dismissal from Harvard, he became a crusader for altering human consciousness by psychedelic drugs. The rapid spread of the drug through the countercultue of the 1960s led to its being made illegal in 1966.

Hallucinogens like LSD can result in panic reactions, high anxiety, loss of contact with reality, paranoia, confusion, flashbacks, psychosis, and hallucinations. LSD and other hallucinogens are also known for sometimes leading to self-destructive behavior or violent acts. They may reduce response to pain and create the appearance of super strength. In 1991 NIDA estimated that 1.2 percent of 18–25 year olds were current users of hallucinogens and 1.7 percent of 26 year olds and over had at some time used them.

Cocaine

Cocaine was isolated in 1859–60. It was first used for its anesthetic properties in local anesthesia and ophthalmology. It was also seen as possibly therapeutic for mental illness. In the 1800s it was viewed as a "wonder drug." As an unregulated drug, it was readily available to the public and was dispensed in coca tonics. The widespread use of cocaine products led to many cases of psychosis and addiction. Abuse of cocaine declined with the passage of the Pure Food and Drug Act of 1906, the Harrison Narcotic Act of 1914, and regulations on production and sale in Europe after World War I. It was not until the 1970s that widespread illegal use of the drug appeared. In 1991 NIDA found 2.5 percent of 18–25 year olds were current users of cocaine and 0.8 percent of 26 year olds and over were current users.

Cocaine affects the brain and can result in a range of reactions from mild agitation to seizures, convulsions, and death. Research indicates that cocaine abuse can lead to significant alterations in the pleasure centers of the brain and that these disturbances may lead to craving states and withdrawal. Alterations in the reward centers and intense euphoria of intoxication result in this drug being classified as physically addictive. Euphoria and craving alternate, leading to a cycle of addiction. Recreational use can progress gradually to compulsive addiction, dominating the addict's life. Researchers are proposing using medications to treat the craving and withdrawal states in cocaine addiction (Gawin and Ellinwood, 1988; O'Brien, Childness, and Arndt, 1988). Drugs might also be used to treat cocaine-induced depression and to reverse cocaine overdose (Dackis and Gold, 1990). Cocaine in the 1980s was a popular drug, with some middle- and upper-income employees seeing it as a recreational drug. As its addictive qualities and its ability to cause sudden death in some individuals received increased media attention, there was increasing recognition of its dangerousness by that population. At the same time, cheap and dangerous crack cocaine became popular with lower socioeconomic groups.

Amphetamines

Amphetamines were first marketed in the United States in 1932 in nasal inhalers (Benzedrine inhalers). As the drug began to be abused, abusers broke open the inhaler containers and swallowed the drug, but the Benzedrine inhalers were not removed from the market until 1949. All amphetamine inhalers were banned by the FDA in 1959. Methamphetamine remained uncontrolled, and inhalers were available until 1970. In 1936 amphetamine tablets became available, and their addictive quality was noted in 1937 and amphetamine psychosis was reported in 1938. Benzedrine tablets appeared on college campuses in the 1930s, and the drug was sold without prescription until 1939. Amphetamines were used by U.S. soldiers during World War II, and after the war, amphetamine production was measured in tons. By 1966 enough amphetamines were manufactured to supply every person in the United States with 35 doses (Sadusk, 1966). Amphetamine abuse was widespread in the 1960s and 1970s, and increasingly, there were cases of psychosis reported with its use. Amphetamine use was referred to as an epidemic (Angrist, 1990). Although production in illegal laboratories and illegal importation have remained a problem, some control has been gained through legislation controlling overproduction of legally prescribed drugs, increased physician awareness, and limitation of legal prescribing. In 1991 NIDA found 1.5 percent of 18–25 year olds and 0.3 percent of 26 year olds and over were current users of inhalants and 0.8 percent of 18–25 year olds and 0.2 percent of 26 year olds and over were current users of stimulants.

Cannabis/Marijuana and Hashish

Minor drugs, like marijuana, can also have serious impacts on the workplace. More than one-third of the injured patients treated at the Shock Trauma Center of the Maryland Institute for Emergency Medical Services Systems in Baltimore had used marijuana several hours before being seriously hurt. Marijuana alone or in combination with alcohol was the reason for a substantial percentage of injuries (18 percent marijuana, 16 percent alcohol, and 17 percent both) in a study of 1,023 patients over a nine-month period. About two-thirds were in car accidents, and others were involved in falls and other accidents and were injured in assaults. Of those injured, 73 percent were men and almost 60 percent were 30 or younger (Soderstrom, Birschbach, and Dischinger, 1990). Research shows 7–13.4 percent of drivers in fatal car crashes test positive for marijuana (Simpson, 1986). Employees who use marijuana and drive company vehicles and equipment are a substantial risk management problem.

The first scientific study of hashish was made in 1845, when the drug was determined to produce a state similar to insanity, and resulted in the development of the first model psychosis in psychiatric literature. This work is considered to be the beginning of psychopharmacology. It is now recognized that marijuana usually results in changing levels of consciousness rather than hallucinations and that it can create both physical symptoms similar to depression, involving relaxation and drowsiness, and the effects of stimulants, such as increased respiration and heart rate. NIDA in 1991 found 13 percent of 18–25 year olds were marijuana users and 3.3 percent of 25 year olds and over.

Chronic long-term use of marijuana can result in behavioral and learning difficulties, memory impairment, reproductive problems, increased rate of chromosomal breakage, respiratory problems, decreased strength of heart contractions, and worsening of prior psychotic states and also may negatively affect growth-hormone production and the immune system. Episodic users may suffer from impaired judgment and experience panic attacks and flashbacks. A study reported in 1990 concluded that teenagers who often use marijuana may suffer short-term memory problems for at least six weeks after they stop smoking and that heavy users have much lower scores for their ability to remember than non-users (Schwartz, 1992). These memory impairments can affect productivity in the workplace.

In 1990 scientists at the NIMH cloned a "button" that marijuana presses in the brain. They found the chemical makeup of a protein structure on the surface of brain cells to which marijuana's main ingredient binds. Although large parts of the public view marijuana as relatively harmless, some of the effects of marijuana clearly are negative for the workplace. The debate whether to legalize marijuana continues, with public support still being insufficient for legalization. The drug is allowed on a limited basis by prescription for some medical conditions, but there is continuing controversy over wider use of the drug for medical purposes.

Alcohol

Until recently, the peak risk age for males for alcohol abuse was believed to be mid-to-late twenties and for women it was believed to be approximately 40 years of age (Russell, Henderson, and Blume, 1985). However, in 1990 the NIMH reported the peak age for the onset of alcohol abuse or dependence to be 15–19 years ("Peak Ages ...," 1990). It is believed that there is a genetic factor in the development of alcohol abuse, and some studies have indicated that this is more prevalent in males. In 1991 NIDA found 63.6 percent of 18–25 year olds were current users of alcohol and 52.5 percent of 26 year olds and over. On a lifetime basis, 3.4 percent of respondents to surveys reported they had gone to professionals, programs, or agencies for a drinking-related problem (Room, 1991).

As many as one-third to one-half of alcoholics display depressive symptoms at some time during their illness (Lord, 1983). Antisocial personality disorder is also found more often than can be accounted for by chance in alcoholics (Solomon and Hanson, 1982). There is also a high degree of association between drinking and the use of cannabis and other drugs (Gibbs, 1982).

Misuse of Prescription Drugs

Prescription drugs may be abused by consumers and also by providers who are caretakers. In 1987 the American Psychiatric Association started a program to train physicians in appropriate prescribing of psychotropic drugs, and in 1989 Medicare regulation revisions added stronger controls to the use of antipsychotic drugs in nursing homes. Of prescribed sedatives and hypnotics, 35–40 percent are for the elderly, even though they make up only about 12 percent of the U.S. population (Clifton, 1989).

Minor tranquilizers are overused and widely abused. They may be prescribed by physicians rather than confronting the cause of a problem and referring to an appropriate source. Many cases of anxiety, compulsive disorders, and other problems are inappropriately handled. This unnecessarily increases health care costs, because people may continue to receive costly prescription drugs for long periods without resolving the underlying problems. Valium topped the federal government's Drug Alert Warning Network (DAWN) List in 1977 as the drug most often mentioned as prompting emergency room visits. The use of tranquilizers, legally or illegally obtained, continues to contribute to car and other accidents, including those on the job, as well as suicide attempts. NIDA in 1991 found 0.6 percent of 18–25 year olds used tranquilizers for nonmedical use and 0.4 percent of 26 year olds and over.

Inappropriate use of tranquilizers can be a hazard in the workplace. Tranquilizers may impair psychomotor skills and cognitive performance. One study of benzodiazepine tranquilizers, which were introduced in the United States in 1962, showed that the risk of accidental injury increased with prescribed benzodiazepine use. The probability of an accident-related medical encounter was higher during months in which a prescription for benzodiazepine had recently been filled. Persons who had filled three or more prescriptions in the six months following the beginning of therapy had a significantly higher risk of accident than those who had filled only one prescription. After controlling for age, sex, and prior utilization, there was an approximately two-fold risk of accident-related care (Oster et al., 1990).

Treatment

Employees may be sent to inpatient/residential or outpatient substance abuse treatment centers. With substance abuse treatment and prevention expenditures at $2.4 billion (Butynski, Canova, and Rada, 1990) and $925 million for treatment intervention for fiscal year 1990 under the National Drug Control Strategy (White House, 1989), there is a high level of investment in prevention and treatment.

Drug abuse treatment is successful in lowering drug use for some clients (Anglin and Hser, 1990; Hubbard, et al., 1989). Over 60 years ago Dr. Bob and Bill Wilson founded Alcoholics Anonymous (AA), a self-help group that recognized the medical aspects of alcoholism and established a 12- step recovery program. Other self-help groups such as Narcotics Anonymous (NA) have been patterned after it. In the mid-1960s, group health insurance began reimbursing for alcoholism treatment, and this stimulated the growth of a wide array of inpatient and outpatient facilities, many of which also require the use of support groups such as AA. Treatment costs vary greatly, with high cost treatment running $13,000 and up and low cost treatment running $8,000 or lower (Burger, 1992). More than 85 percent of substance abuse treatment is by outpatient providers (Office of Technology Assessment [OTA], 1990). The most common treatment is drug-free therapy, which involves a combination of individual and group counseling and supervision to eliminate drug use. Another common treatment modality is the use of methadone as a substitute for the abuse of opiate drugs. Although the public sector has traditionally assumed the major responsibility for the operation of treatment programs, the role of the private sector has been increasing. Programs that receive most of their revenue from private insurance or out-of-pocket payments are likely to treat more affluent clients. Public and nonprofit treatment centers accept a higher percentage of nonpaying and reduced-fee clients.

An example of how an outpatient chemical dependency treatment program operates is the program at Community Psychiatric Centers (CPC) Vista Del Mar Hospital in Ventura, California. That program is a highly structured one-year evening outpatient program. Clients must undergo psychiatric and medical evaluations. If detoxing is required, a period of inpatient hospitalization can be required before the outpatient program is joined. Clients are required the first month to participate for three hours five times a week. Many of the center's staff are themselves in recovery. A typical three-hour group session begins with an hour of process group therapy, in which the counselor helps the group members to identify current issues, resolve conflicts, and learn to communicate feelings. Then, for another hour, clients are encouraged to share their experiences with community 12-step groups, which they are required to join as part of the outpatient program. The last hour is devoted to topics such as relapse prevention, self-esteem, leisure awareness, family therapy, and spirituality. Although attendance requirements decline after the first month, clients are monitored through individual conferences and urine screening. The number of meetings clients are required to attend then varies by individual. The support of family members and, in the case of employee assistance program referrals, of employers is enlisted. Outpatient treatment minimizes costs to the employer in terms of treatment charges and lost work hours, because people attend evening sessions ("Outpatient Treatment . . . ," 1992).

Developmental Disorders

Developmental disability is defined as "A severe chronic disability which is attributable to mental or physical impairment or a combination of mental and physical impairments, is manifested by age 22, is likely to continue indefinitely, and results in substantial limitations in three or more areas of major life activity" (Grossman, 1983). Developmental disorders are characterized by major disturbance in the acquisition of cognitive, language, motor, or social skills. Developmental disorders under DSM III-R include mental retardation, autism (classified by DSM III-R under pervasive developmental disorders), disruptive behavior disorders/conduct disorders, anxiety disorders of childhood or adolescence, eating disorders, gender identity disorders, tic disorders, elimination disorders, speech disorders, and other disorders of infancy, childhood, and adolescence.

Mental Retardation

Biomedically, mental retardation involves a distortion or pathology in the central nervous system, usually in the higher centers of the brain, which causes intellectual and behavioral dysfunctions (Plog and Santamous, 1980). The American Association for Mental Deficiency classifies mental retardation as mild (IQ 50–55 to approximately 70), moderate (IQ 35–40 to 50–55), severe (IQ 25–35 to 35–40), and profound (IQ below 20–25). Approximately 85 percent of people with mental retardation have mild retardation, 10 percent are moderately retarded, 3–4 percent are severely retarded, and 1–2 percent are profoundly retarded. Thus, most people with mental retardation have mild retardation and are capable of working in general employment. Mental retardation is also described in terms of functional levels by focusing on the level at which a person performs below that expected for the person's age. Three criteria are used to define mental retardation: onset during the developmental period, significantly subaverage intellectual function, and concurrent deficits in adaptive behavior. It is believed that a high percentage of cases of mental retardation exist prior to birth, and many cases of mental retardation are now linked to alcohol abuse by the mother. Some of the causes of mental retardation are infections and intoxications, including use of alcohol during pregnancy (fetal alcohol syndrome [FAS] may include substantial mental retardation), trauma, inborn errors of metabolism, nutritional deficiencies, gross brain disease, chromosomal abnormality, gestational disorders including prematurity, environmental influences, malformations of the brain, and childhood schizophrenia.

"Mental retardation" is a term that should be used with caution and only after a careful diagnosis. In response to negative connotations being attached to defining words, the words used to describe this mental condition have changed over time. Terms like "idiot" or "imbecile" are no longer acceptable. The more commonly used terms now are a person with "mental retardation," "intellectual handicap," or "developmental disability." However, employers and coworkers should be sensitive about applying any labeling terminology.

There are a variety of reports on the extent of mental illness and/or emotional disturbances in persons with mental retardation. It appears that individuals with mental retardation are nearly twice as likely as the general population to develop mental illness (Menolascino, 1989). The most consistent reports for the incidence of psychoses are 4–6 percent. Estimates for serious psychiatric disorders, including psychoses and personality disorders, are 8–15 percent (Parsons, May, and Menolascino, 1984). Studies indicate a 20–35 percent frequency rate of emotional disturbances in persons with mental retardation (Menolascino, 1983). When serious mental illness and major and minor emotional problems are included, estimates reach as high as more than 50 percent (Parsons, May, and Menolascino, 1984). One clinical study (Eaton and Menolascino, 1982) found personality disorders comprised 38 percent of the sample, with almost half of these individuals classified as passive dependent. Organic brain syndrome with behavioral or psychotic reactions was the diagnosis for 34 percent (21 percent with behavioral reaction and 13 percent with psychotic reaction). Pollock (1944) identified four reasons for the high incidence of mental illness in persons with mental retardation: reduced capacity to withstand stress, poor ability to resolve emotional and mental conflicts, lack of social competence and the ability to deal with difficult situations, and emotional instability that may lead to loss of self-control. There is a lack of knowledge regarding the incidence of suicide or suicidal behavior among persons with mental retardation, but what little research there is indicates an incidence close to the general population rate of 1 percent (10 per 1,000). Although suicide and suicide attempts are not common among this population, it is recognized that suicide attempts occur, and suicide threats should be taken seriously (Parsons, May, and Menolascino, 1984). What little evidence there is indicates that alcoholism and drug addiction appear to be rarely reported for people with mental retardation (Parsons, May, and Menolascino, 1984).

Mental illness may go unrecognized due to the effects of mental retardation (Sovner, 1986). However, it is important to identify mental illness or emotional disorders. Persons with mild mental retardation (IQ greater than 50) seldom fail on the job because of low intelligence; the most common cause of failure is "temperamental instability, neuroses, or psychoses" (Kirman, 1973). Persons with mental retardation usually come to the attention of society and employers because of a failure in social adaptation (Phillips, 1971). There are a number of approaches that work successfully with persons with mental retardation, including behavior modification, psychodynamic psychotherapy, group psychotherapy, social learning, and parental counseling. Also, psychotropic drugs can be used to treat behavioral and emotional problems in persons with developmental disabilities, but the use of such drugs for that population is a distinct clinical discipline (Sovner, 1987). Appropriate mental health services for the person with mental retardation may be difficult to obtain. Four obstacles have been identified to the provision of mental health services to individuals with mental retardation: failure of mental health professionals to respond to treating this population for reasons that include ignorance and bias; failure of mental health professional organizations to effectively promote treatment of this population; interdisciplinary disagreements between various professions and professionals involved in the treatment of mental retardation and mental illness; and negative attitudes toward mental health professionals on the part of persons with mental retardation, their families, and society in general (Cushna, Szymanski, and Tanguay, 1980).

Autism

Autism is a disorder that begins early in life and causes distortions in development. Three-fourths of persons with autism also have mental retardation, and two-thirds of persons with autism require 24-hour structured care even as adults. Only a small number of persons with autism at this time are or will become capable of employment, but clearly there are people with autism who can work.

People with autism do not establish normal affectionate relationships but respond in unusual or bizarre ways to the environment, resist change, have impaired speech development, have ritualistic behaviors, and have too much or too little response to stimuli. Genetic research and brain imaging studies indicate that autism is primarily biological in origin. Genetic research also shows that in families in which there is autism, 2–3 percent of family members will have autism and another 25–30 percent will have less severe variants such as social deficits and language disorders. A mutant gene may be responsible for social and language deficits, with additional factors leading to full clinical autism. Parents with one autistic child have a 4.5 percent chance of having a second. The chance of an average couple having an autistic child is only 1 in 2,500 ("Autism Seems to Cluster . . . ," 1990). Brain imaging studies show that some autistic persons have an underdeveloped cerebellar vermis. Various approaches are being taken to treat this disorder, but only a few people with the disorder have recovered sufficiently to function independently or semi-independently as adults.

Disruptive Behavior Disorders

Under DSM III-R, conduct disorder, attention-deficit hyperactivity disorder, and oppositional defiant disorder are listed as disruptive behavior disorders. Conduct disorder is a disorder that may begin in the preschool years but becomes fully apparent in late childhood or adolescence. It is characterized by a persistent pattern of behavior involving violating the basic rights of others or social rules, physical aggression, truancy, and running away. The risk of substance abuse is also increased. Conduct disorder leads to the vast majority of serious antisocial behaviors in adulthood. Almost half the adolescents who have conduct disorder become antisocial adults (NAMHC, 1990).

Research shows that environmental influences, including the family, may influence the adaptability to the biological inheritance. In times of economic problems, parents and children may experience high anxiety, stress, or depression, which may lead to behavioral problems or disorders. Economic dislocations of the 1980s and early 1990s contribute to these conditions. The 1970s and 1980s have seen considerable progress in developing techniques to measure environmental influences (NAMHC, 1990).

Eating Disorders

Eating disorders are characterized by gross disturbances in eating behavior. The group of disorders covers four specific eating disorders under DSM III-R: anorexia nervosa, which involves a refusal to maintain a minimal normal body weight, intense fear of gaining weight and being fat, a disturbance in body image, and amenorrhea in females; bulimia nervosa, involving recurrent episodes of binge eating, feelings of lack of control over eating behavior during binges, and a regularly practiced behavior such as self-induced vomiting, use of diuretics, and laxatives, strict dieting or fasting, or vigorous exercise; pica, consisting of repeated eating of nonnutritive substances; and rumination disorder of infancy, involving repeated regurgitation of food without gastrointestinal illness, associated with weight loss or failure to achieve an expected weight gain. Employees may have children with these disorders, and anorexia nervosa and bulimia nervosa may be found in adult employees, usually females. Because these disorders may go on for years, if untreated, employees of all ages may suffer from them, and they may result in physical health problems and even death. There are clinics that specialize in treating eating disorders.

Personality Disorders

"Personality" refers to long-standing, deeply ingrained patterns of behavior which include ways of perceiving, thinking about, and relating to the environment. "Personality traits" are relatively stable patterns of behavior. "Personality disorders" relate to rigid, maladaptive personality traits that result in significant functional impairment or distress. DSM III-R lists several personality disorders, including paranoid, schizoid, schizotypal, antisocial, borderline, histrionic, narcissistic, avoidant, dependent, obsessive-compulsive, and passive-aggressive.

Paranoid personality disorder involves a tendency to interpret actions of people as threatening or demeaning; schizoid personality disorder involves a pattern of indifference to social relationships and limited emotional experience and expression; schizotypal refers to a personality disorder that involves a pattern of deficits in interpersonal relations and peculiar ideas, appearance, and behavior; antisocial personality disorder involves a pattern of irresponsible and antisocial behavior; borderline personality disorder involves a pattern of unstable mood, unstable relationships, and unstable self-image; histrionic personality disorder relates to a pattern of being excessively emotional and attention seeking; narcissistic personality disorder involves a pattern of gradiosity, hypersensitivity to the evaluation of others, and lack of empathy for others; avoidant personality disorder involves a pattern of social discomfort, timidity, and fear of negative evaluation of oneself; dependent personality disorder involves a pattern of submissive and dependent behavior; obsessive-compulsive relates to a personality disorder with a pattern of perfectionism and inflexibility; and passive-aggressive personality disorder involves a pattern of passive resistance to demands for occupational or social performance, which may include procrastination, irritability, or argumentativeness when asked to do something or deliberately working slowly or poorly, protesting unjustifiably about others, avoiding obligations by forgetting them, believing one is doing a good job when one is not, resenting suggestions, obstructing the efforts of others, and criticizing or scorning others in positions of authority. Many of these personality problems may cause disruptive behavior in the workplace. They are difficult to treat and often require long-term treatment.

Other Mental Health Problems

DSM III-R recognizes other mental health problems that are not attributable to a mental disorder. These problems may be seen in some employees and include adult antisocial behavior, borderline intellectual functioning (IQ 71–84), malingering, marital problems, noncompliance with medical treatment, occupational problems, other interpersonal problems, other specified family circumstances, phase of life problems or other life circumstance problems, and uncomplicated bereavement. Employees who have children may also be involved with issues such as academic problems, childhood or adolescent antisocial behavior, and parent-child problems.

PHYSICAL DISEASES WITH MENTAL HEALTH COMPONENTS

Some chronic medical disorders may increase the risk of specific mental disorders. For example, people with cancer have increased prevalence of depression and anxiety disorders. Also, in families where there is congenital heart disease, there is an increased risk in children of adjustment disorders and substance abuse. Acquired immune deficiency syndrome (AIDS) is a major illness that combines physical and mental health components, and premenstrual syndrome (PMS) is a disorder that was originally thought to be all in the mind but is now known to be physically caused but to have mental health components.

Acquired Immune Deficiency Syndrome

In January 1991 the U.S. Centers for Disease Control (CDC) reported 164,129 cases of AIDS in the United States. In 1989, the CDC reported that intravenous drug abusers remained the second highest transmission category, with 16,805 cases (20 percent).

AIDS is an example of a physical disease with a mental health component that includes an organic brain syndrome with psychological symptomology. Other mental health factors involved in AIDS are the mental health responses common to persons who suffer from major life-threatening diseases; the unusually high levels of psychological fear and stress response expressed by coworkers and the general population; and the fact that drug use involving the use of contaminated needles is a major transmitter of the disease.

Because AIDS is an extremely complex disease that affects every aspect of the infected person's life and because the long-term outlook for those diagnosed with AIDS is poor, with the recognition that few, if any, will survive, diagnosis is an especially stressful event. The age at onset may increase the trauma, because people between the ages of 25 and 49 do not expect to develop a potentially fatal disease (Christ, Weiner, and Moynihan, 1986).

In 1981, soon after the recognition of AIDS, reports began to appear regarding a neurological syndrome. Research involving patients who demonstrated significant confusion, disorientation, and memory loss prior to death revealed the presence of human immunodeficiency virus (HIV) in the brain. Because HIV has been found in the cerebrospinal fluid, the macrophage (white blood cell) found in the central nervous system is believed to be a kind of Trojan horse that the HIV uses in crossing the blood-brain barrier (Dilley and Boccellari, 1988). Based on research findings, the CDC changed the definition of AIDS to include the AIDS dementia complex (ADC), which involves the deterioration of mental capacities caused by direct infection of the brain by HIV. ADC is defined as "persistent impairment of intellectual function with compromise in at least three of the following spheres of mental activity: language, memory, visuospatial skills, emotions or personality, and cognition abstraction, calculation, judgment, etc." (Buckingham and VanGorp, 1988). The diagnostic criteria of the CDC include a positive antibody test for HIV, a negative lumbar puncture, and a negative Computerized

Tomography (CT) or Magnetic Resonance Imaging (MRI) scan or findings consistent with atrophy. Clinical tests can be administered that include an assessment of attention, judgment, language abilities, memory, and orientation. An important part of assessment includes interviews with family and friends regarding their observation of the patient. Neuropsychological assessment includes a neurological exam, neuroradiological procedures, and neuropsychological testing. Psychiatric symptoms and mood state can also be measured (Dilley and Boccellari, 1988). ADC remains difficult to detect, particularly when the patient shows no physical signs but shows mental disturbance symptoms of social withdrawal, apathy, and emotional blunting. Failure to correctly diagnose may result in a person with ADC being inappropriately referred to a mental health facility for treatment or a person with a major affective disorder such as depression being left untreated because he/she is believed to have ADC. Dementia is viewed as a brain pathology, which is largely untreatable, but affective disorders such as depression can be treated (Buckingham and VanGorp, 1988). Dementia and depression can exist simultaneously, and if that is suspected, the person can be placed on a trial of antidepressants to see if there is improvement (Dilley and Boccellari, 1988).

Researchers estimate that early during the course of AIDS, approximately one-third of patients will develop moderate to severe ADC and an additional one-fourth will have mild dementia that could be documented only by careful neuropsychological assessment. This population would include employees who are probably still well enough to be in the workplace. As the infection progresses, as many as two-thirds of patients may develop some signs of dementia. AIDS dementia can be treated with azidothymidine (AZT), a widely used AIDS treatment. It can return people to approximately 90 percent of their previous mental functioning while the drug is effective for them (NIMH, 1990).

Persons diagnosed with AIDS, even if they do not have ADC, may suffer from stress and depression. Multiple doctor visits, painful tests, and isolation procedures in hospitals may contribute to the individual's stress level (Christ, Weiner, and Moynihan, 1986). Persons diagnosed with AIDS may feel socially isolated, guilty, and unsure how to deal with a terminal illness. The most common mental disorders in people diagnosed with AIDS, in order of prevalence, are adjustment disorder, major depression, dementia, delirium, and panic disorder (Faulstich, 1987). At any point during the disease, the person may become depressed. A study at San Francisco General Hospital found depression was the reason for 13 of 40 inpatient referrals to psychiatric consultation-liaison of AIDS patients (Faulstich, 1987). Depression may lead to possible suicide. Reports regarding suicide vary. Some feel that suicidal ideation is common but that actual suicide attempts are not common. More self-destructive behavior is found in patients who also have personality disorders (Faulstich, 1987). Others believe that not only are suicidal thoughts high but also attempts are increasingly common. Depressed patients may see taking their own life as a rational act in light of the social stigma and ultimate fatal progression of the disease (Perry and Markowitz, 1986).

Premenstrual Syndrome

PMS was originally thought to be all in the mind and was often considered to be a pseudodisease of the "weaker sex." However, research has now shown that PMS is a bona fide, physically based disease with a mental health component. The disease is biologically based, with a linkage having been made between PMS and the hormones estrogen and progesterone. The diagnosis is based on a set of criteria that include symptoms in a cycle, which must appear in a consistent pattern over at least two or three months; being symptom-free at least two or three weeks per month; and the presence of some of the identified physical and emotional/psychological symptoms. At least 180 symptoms have been identified and are categorized into four categories: emotional/psychological, pain, water retention, and miscellaneous, including food cravings, fatigue, nausea, vomiting, and poor concentration. Among the emotional/psychological symptoms are anxiety, tension, depression, low self-esteem, withdrawal, and irritability (Sperling, 1988). In extreme cases, PMS may lead to violence. Researchers at the Premenstrual Syndrome Clinic at University College Hospital, London, believe that although PMS will cause only a small minority of women to be violent, it may be responsible for many violent acts. Their research found that of 156 female prison inmates, 49 percent were sentenced for crimes committed during their eight-day paramenstrum. In a study of women in psychiatric hospitals, they found that 46 percent were admitted during their paramenstrum. They also found that 53 percent of women attempting suicide were suffering from premenstrual tension (Restak, 1988).

It is estimated that 20–30 percent of women have PMS, but less than 5 percent have it severely enough to interfere with functioning (Sperling, 1988). Late luteal phase dysphoric disorder (PMS) is currently listed in DSM III-R under proposed diagnostic categories needing further study.

3

Employee Selection and Mental Health Issues

There are many issues concerning mental health that are raised in the selection process. Employee selection is influenced by demographic and sociological changes, including an increasingly diverse work force. The law also impacts the selection process in regard to workers with mental disabilities, and there are a growing number of programs focused on placement of people with disabilities into the workplace. The selection process itself is increasingly involved in mental health issues such as psychological testing, drug testing, and genetic testing.

DEMOGRAPHIC AND SOCIOLOGICAL CHANGES

As employers and managers are increasingly aware, the work force in the United States is changing as a result of demographic trends and sociological changes. The largely white male work force of the past is rapidly disappearing in all work sectors. Increasingly, the labor market from which employers select their employees is made up of women, minorities and ethnic group members, mentally and physically disabled people, and older workers, and research shows this is likely to be the labor force of the future to an even greater extent. Demographic trends have a major bearing on the selection and retention of the employees of the future.

The Changing Work Force

According to demographic projections, after 1995 the population may grow more slowly than ever before, more slowly than even during the Great Depression of the 1930s. The U.S. Census Bureau made a series of 30 projections of possible U.S. population growth from the 1988 population base of 245 million. The lowest projection is 264.5 million in 2020, followed by decline, and the highest projection is 501 million in 2080 (U.S. Census Bureau, 1989). By 1992 the most likely projected population for 2020 was 320 million. The work force of the 1990s is expected to grow by only 1.2 percent annually compared with the 2 percent growth from 1976 to 1988.

An Older Work Force

As the 77 million people of the baby boom generation (born between 1946 and 1964) grow older, they will continue to dominate the work force until they start to retire, beginning around 2000, as the first baby boomers turn 55. As the smaller cohorts of the baby bust generation, 41 million people born from 1965 to 1976, and the following younger generations enter the workplace, the average age of the work force will rise while the pool of young workers entering the job market will shrink to its lowest level since the 1930s. The share of the population under age 35 may never again be as large as it was in the late 1980s (55 percent), as it drops to 48 percent in 2000, 46 percent in 2010, and 41 percent in 2030. The median age of the U.S. population will be 36 by the year 2000. The age of the work force will change from 50 percent 16–34, 38 percent 35–54, and 13 percent 55 and older in 1985 to 38 percent 16–34, 51 percent 35–54, and 11 percent 55 or older in 2000 (U.S. Census Bureau, 1989).

People are living longer. In 1985, there were 28.5 million people 65 years of age or over (12 percent of the population). The elderly population will grow more slowly after the mid-1990s, during the years the Depression and World War II cohorts are in that age group, and will reach 14 percent of the population by 2010. After 2010, there will be an acceleration again as the baby boom generation moves into that age group and the population 65 or older rises to 17 percent. By 2030, that age group will account for 21 percent of the population (U.S. Census Bureau, 1989). With changes in mandatory retirement laws, more older workers can be expected to be in the work force. Under current law the retirement age gradually will be raised to 67 for full Social Security retirement and 65 for early retirement by 2027. Under proposed 1993 legislation, this change would be phased in by 1999 at the latest. By 2020, the retirement age could be 70 or higher to reflect increased life expectancy (Fosler et al., 1990).

Women and Minorities in the Work Force

Women, minorities, and immigrants will account for most of the new work force. Almost two-thirds of the new entrants by the year 2000 will be women. White males are now a minority in the work force, and only 15 percent of new entrants to the work force will be white men. In 1985 the labor force consisted of 47 percent nonminority males, 36 percent nonminority females, 5 percent minority males, 5 percent minority females, 4 percent immigrant males, and 3 percent immigrant females. The new workers in the labor force from 1985 to 2000 will be 15 percent nonminority males, 42 percent nonminority females, 7 percent minority males, 13 percent minority females, 13 percent immigrant males, and 9 percent immigrant females (U.S. Census Bureau, 1989).

For the past 30 years, women's average earnings have been approximately 60 percent of those for men for full-time, year-round workers (Reskin and Hartman, 1986). There has been much discussion concerning a glass ceiling that bars women from high-level positions (Milwid, 1987). In 1992, Catalyst, a New York research and advisory service, reported the results of a survey of senior and middle management employees and human resource personnel in Fortune 500 and Service 500 industries. They found evidence of glass walls, barriers preventing women from gaining the needed experience for top management positions early in their careers. Women were not getting the lateral mobility they needed to achieve experience in core areas of the organizations, a prerequisite for advancement to senior levels. Senior managers most often cited stereotypes as still being barriers to women's promotion (Dominguez, 1991).

Most studies show that employment appears to improve the mental and physical health of unmarried women and of married women who have positive attitudes toward employment and that the increased social support associated with employment has beneficial health effects for women (Repetti, Mathews, and Waldron, 1989). Researchers at Ohio State University and Hobart and William Smith Colleges in New York found in a study of 164 new mothers that among the mothers who wanted to return to work and did, there were good feelings about their choice and they did well as both mothers and workers. They did not experience conflicts about their dual roles, because they received personal validation from their ability to contribute financially to the family and to contribute as mothers. The women who wanted to work but stayed home had the worst results, with more stress and depression, probably as a result of role conflict and confusion ("Moms Reap Benefits . . . ," 1990). Other social trends are also affecting women in the work force: an increase in one-parent families, most of which are headed by a woman; delays in marriage; delays in childbearing; and growing numbers of women with children, including women with preschool children, working.

There are unclear data available on the effects of sex discrimination on mental health. Most research has been focused on sexual harassment. Some surveys have reported symptoms of anger, fright, helplessness, and guilt along with some somatic symptoms and difficulty in concentrating among women who have experienced discrimination (Hamilton et al., 1987). Discrimination can also have a detrimental effect on the physical and mental health of minorities.

In 1984, blacks and Hispanics accounted for 19 percent of the U.S. population. In 1984 the black population was estimated to be 28.6 million (12.1 percent) and was projected to be 44 million by 2020 (U.S.

Census Bureau, 1984). The number of blacks in the 18–24 age group has declined along with the general population decline in that age bracket. This raised hopes that their problem in finding employment would be eased, but this has not held true, because of the poor economic performance and employee reductions of the 1980s. In 1987 the number of Hispanics was estimated to be 18.7 million (7.8 percent). The Hispanic population is growing twice as fast as the black population and four times as fast as the non-Hispanic white population. Hispanics are projected to reach 47 million in 2020 and to surpass the black population. The number of Hispanics in the 18–24 age group is also increasing. By 2020, blacks and Hispanics are expected to account for 35 percent of the population. The white population is expected to decline in 2030, while the black population and other races are expected to continue to increase. At some point in the twenty-first century, non-Hispanic whites will become minorities, along with blacks, Hispanics, and Asians. This is already occurring in many local jurisdictions and is projected to occur statewide in California and Texas by 2010. Asian Americans are now the fastest-growing minority group. They grew in number by 95 percent from 1980 to 1990. In 1990 there were 7.3 million Asians, 3 percent of the U.S. population. By 2020 they are expected to grow to 20 million, or 6 percent of the population (U.S. Census Bureau, 1993). Native Americans are another fast-growing population group.

In recent years the number of people officially admitted as economic migrants has been small and concentrated in skilled jobs. Most immigrants have come as relatives of U.S. residents or as refugees. Illegal immigration, however, has been predominantly economic, and only recently has the Immigration Reform and Control Act of 1986 attempted to regularize that immigration and threatened sanctions against employers who hire illegal immigrants. By 2030, there could be as many as 32 million immigrants who entered the country after 1986, and they and their descendants could make up 12 percent of the population (U.S. Census Bureau, 1989). As immigration now overwhelmingly consists of people from Asia and Latin America, this means an increasingly diverse racial, ethnic, and cultural work force.

An increasing number of jobs will require college degrees; however, the number of people with the qualifications to fill those positions is expected to decline (Johnston and Packer, 1987). For many employers, their work is becoming more technical and knowledge-intensive while the labor market for recruitment is becoming more competitive. Alternative labor sources are becoming increasingly important for economic reasons. Employers need to be aware of discrimination and stereotyping, which have traditionally kept women, minorities, and people with disabilities out of the workplace, have not allowed them to enhance their careers by job change or promotion, and have created work environments that have been detrimental to their mental health and ability to be productive. Also, managers need to be aware that work environments that are not receptive to a diverse work force may take a toll on recruiting and retaining the best workers. Among the potential workers who are capable and productive but have not been provided a full opportunity for selection and advancement are people with disabilities.

People with Disabilities

Of the 43 million people with disabilities in the United States, 8.5 million are classified by the U.S. Department of Labor as unemployed but employable (DeLuca, 1991). According to a Louis Harris poll, only one-third of all Americans with a disability work, and two-thirds of unemployed people with disabilities report that they want to work (Waldrop, 1991). Excluding 10 million people with disabilities from the work force costs U.S. society $300 billion annually (Pati and Stubblefield, 1990). Societal costs include loss of income and tax revenues and the costs of public assistance for nonworking disabled persons. In 1990 the U.S. government spent more than $6.2 billion annually on programs for people with disabilities. Changing hiring opportunities could drastically reduce taxpayer costs. Although there are several factors that have inhibited the employment of people with mental disabilities, discrimination is a major factor. Legislation has been passed in the United States to try to prevent this discrimination. Department of Labor surveys have found that "impaired persons" have fewer disabling injuries than the average worker exposed to the same work hazards. Studies have shown that the mentally disabled overall are more loyal employees and have lower absenteeism and turnover rates than workers in the general population (Bellamy et al., 1989).

Persons disabled by mental illness make up a disproportionate number of the unemployed in the United States. Employment rates among persons discharged from psychiatric hospitals range between 10 and 30 percent, and only 10–15 percent of those who find work are still employed one to five years later (Anthony and Liberman, 1986; Jacobs, 1988). It is estimated that as many as 70 percent of all persons with chronic mental disabilities remain unemployed (Goldstrom and Manderscheid, 1972). However, many of even the most severely mentally disabled may be able to engage in work. A long-term follow-up study of persons severely incapacitated with schizophrenia found that half of them were able to engage in some form of work in a later phase of their illness (Harding et al., 1987).

Other countries are far more successful than the United States in placing people with disabilities into the workplace. Denmark uses the principles of normalization, integration, and decentralization through a case advocate system that, combined with flexible upper secondary vocational options, results in 75 percent of high school graduates with disabilities attaining competitive employment. In Italy the Genoa Approach places 90 percent of high school graduates with severe and moderate disabilities in competitive employment. Sweden's policy of "Employment for All" has resulted in the creation of 80,000 subsidized jobs for people with disabilities. Japan's Quota-Levy Program requires employers to hire persons with disabilities in proportion to their representation in the overall labor market, and organizations that fail to achieve their employment quota must pay a levy; originally, the program covered only persons with physical disabilities, but it now includes people with mental retardation (Brodsky, 1990).

The Washington Business Group on Health, a nonprofit coalition of more than 150 of the largest U.S. employers, has founded an Institute for Rehabilitation and Disability Management to help U.S. employers improve their disability policies to facilitate the hiring and retention of people with disabilities. The Institute has received a three-year grant from the National Institute on Disability and Rehabilitation Research to create curriculum materials on disability issues for professional schools of public policy, law, and social work, with the objective of making graduate students aware of the magnitude of the constituency made up of people with disabilities, the power of the disability rights movement, and the importance of consumer empowerment. The hoped-for result is to impact these career professionals, who will be in policy positions, so as to increase their recognition of people with disabilities as good job candidates and their awareness of the importance of consumer involvement in making policy and laws and delivering services.

Integration and Development

The economic development of modern nations is highly associated with three aspects of rationality: science and its applications, economic processes involving central planning or market discipline, and integration. Integration involves "the capacity for productive inter-action among the elements of a national or international system." It includes "the facilitation of exchanges across time and space" involving improved communication and transportation and developments in finance, markets, currency systems, measurement, and laws. "Integration also implies reducing the inefficiencies caused by making distinctions without a difference: if a person can do a job, it is inefficient to deny it because of sex or color [age or disability], just as it would be inefficient to treat identical sacks of wheat differently according to who grew them" (Fosler et al., 1990).

EMPLOYMENT LAW

Not only the personnel manager but also all managers in an organization should know what their legal responsibilities are in regard to nondiscrimination. The legal basis for equal employment opportunity can be found in the U.S. Constitution, presidential executive orders, federal laws, state constitutions, state laws, and judicial decisions. The fifth amendment of the Constitution in its due process clause provides through court interpretation for "equal protection" from federal government action. The equal protection clause of the fourteenth amendment provides for protection from state and local government action. All state constitutions also have equal protection clauses that provide protections in regard to actions of that state and its local governments. For example California's Constitution Article I, Section 7 provides due process and equal protection clauses. There are also many laws at the national and state level that forbid discrimination in employment, including the 1964 Civil Rights Act.

Protected groups in 1989 were restricted in their ability to file and prove discrimination cases by the federal court decision, *Ward's Cove Packing Co.* v. *Antonio* (U.S., 109, 2115, 1989), which shifted the burden of proof to the individual. The 1991 Civil Rights Act remedied the 1989 court decision. The act allows women and the physically handicapped to sue private employers for emotional trauma caused by job discrimination, broadens the grounds for racial harassment suits, and removes obstacles to challenges of employers' practices that have discriminatory effects. In 1993 the Ninth Circuit Court of Appeals ruled that the 1991 law was retroactive. That action was viewed as particularly important to victims of sexual abuse.

Federal agencies, state and local governments, and private employers who receive federal grants or contracts over specified amounts may be required to develop and implement affirmative action programs to eliminate historic underrepresentation of designated groups. Affirmative action is considered a means for reaching equal employment opportunity. The goal for affirmative action is for employers to recruit, hire, and promote protected classes who meet the minimum requirements for the job. Employers may be required to have numerical goals and timetables for employment of protected classes and to make a "good faith" effort in meeting those goals and timetables. Quotas for hiring of protected group class members who meet the minimum job qualifications may be required by court order. The Supreme Court has consistently upheld affirmative action, although various court decisions have defined its appropriate use.

Two types of discrimination claims can be made, disparate treatment and disparate impact. Disparate treatment cases involve treatment of an individual (or group) in a less favorable way because of their protected group status, for example, disability, sex, race. This type of case requires proof of discriminatory motivation or intent. Disparate impact cases deal with cases that on their face seem neutral in the way in which they treat individuals but that impact more severely on protected groups and cannot be justified by business necessity (Modjeska, 1988).

Enforcement of equal opportunity may be by filing a case with the Equal Opportunity Commission, a federal agency established by the 1964 Civil Rights Act; filing a case with a state civil rights agency, such as the Department of Fair Employment and Housing in California; or filing a civil case in a state or federal court.

The Law and Mental Disabilities

The Rehabilitation Act of 1973

Section 503 of the Rehabilitation Act of 1973 requires affirmative action in the hiring and promotion of qualified mentally and physically handicapped persons. This act applies to employers who receive grants and/or contracts from the federal government in excess of $2,500 per year. The legislation affects primarily public employers and large private corporate employers, because these tend to be the employers receiving federal funding. These employers must regard persons with disabilities as a protected class, which involves the same affirmative action procedures as for other protected classes. Both this law and the 1990 Americans with Disabilities Act (ADA) are aimed at decreasing discrimination and enhancing opportunities for the person with disabilities, but neither law requires an employer to hire an unqualified applicant.

Between 1985 and 1990, over 500 complaints were filed under Section 503 of the Rehabilitation Act by people who were under the designation "mentally disabled." Only 10 percent of the complaints filed were successful. Although there were variations by region, the 1973 Act was rarely implemented to assist people with mental disabilities. Therefore, even if case law is used from the Rehabilitation Act in interpreting the ADA, it may not be particularly helpful for those with mental disabilities. However, one useful case is *Allen v. Hecker* (780 F. 2d 64, 66, D.C. Cir, 1985). The U.S. Court of Appeals held in that case that former psychiatric hospital patients were covered by the Rehabilitation Act, although no longer institutionalized, because of the continuing stigma and the fact that the disability does not disappear upon discharge. A report published by the Mental Health Policy Resource Center suggests that federal agencies need to find more effective ways to monitor and enforce implementation of the Rehabilitation Act of 1973 and the ADA for people with mental disabilities (Moss, 1992).

The 1990 Americans with Disabilities Act

The ADA (P.L. 101-336) was passed in May 1990. The ADA is a comprehensive antidiscrimination law aimed at integrating the disabled into society and the work force. The law is expected to cover some 43–45 million Americans (almost 20 percent). Of an approximate 200 million people in the workplace, the law is expected to apply to 25 percent (Schneid, 1992). The law applies to employers of 25 or more employees effective 1992 and applies to employers of 15 or more employees as of 1994. The law covers public accommodation access; removal of physical barriers or provision of alternative services; access to public transit systems, including comparable paratransit such as vans, for those who cannot use a fixed-route bus; accessibility of all new buses and rail vehicles; and employment.

The law defines disability as a mental or physical impairment that "substantially limits one or more of the major life activities of such individual; a record of such an impairment; or is regarded as having such an impairment" (ADA, 1990, Subtitle A, Section 3[2]). The definition is comparable to that in Sections 501 and 504 of the Rehabilitation Act of 1973 but uses the word "disability" rather than "handicap." A mental impairment is defined by ADA as a "mental or psychological disorder, such as mental retardation, organic brain syndrome, emotional or mental illness and specific learning disabilities" (Equal Employment Opportunity Commission [EEOC], 1991). Awareness of the law originally was low. A national poll found that 90 percent of respondents were unaware of the law (Rice, 1992). Many government agencies, nonprofit organizations, and community organizations are working to increase awareness.

On July 26, 1992, Title I went into effect for employers of 25 or more employees. It contains employment provisions that apply to people with disabilities regardless of their national origin or immigration status. That section intends to remove barriers that prevent qualified persons with disabilities from employment opportunities. Title II prohibits discrimination by public entities including state or local governments, instrumentalities of state or local governments, and Amtrak and commuter authorities. The law forbids discrimination by an employer if the applicant or employee can perform the "essential" functions of the job with "reasonable proficiency." Thus, there is an obligation on the part of the employer to eliminate nonessential duties from a position when considering the hiring of a disabled worker. If a disabled worker can perform the essential duties of the job but is unable to perform some of the peripheral, nonessential duties of the job, the expectation is that the worker should be considered for employment. Thus, the employer must decide whether the person will be able to perform the job if the nonessential duties are eliminated. Under ADA, like under the 1973 Rehabilitation Act, there is a requirement for "reasonable accommodation," which may mean modifying examinations, training materials, or policies; acquiring new equipment or devices to assist the person in the work; restructuring the job; modifying work schedules by staggered or flexible work hours; providing for part-time work or job sharing; providing qualified readers/interpreters or personal assistants; keeping positions open when the person requires leave; reassigning a worker to a different position when necessary; and removing physical barriers. ADA is a nondiscrimination law, but it is not an affirmative action law. It does not require active recruitment of persons with disabilities. However, employers must be sure their recruitment activities do not screen out potential applicants with disabilities.

ADA puts limitations on what questions are allowable on application forms and in the job interview. Employers should review applications, testing processes, and interview guidelines to remove discriminatory matter. The law does not allow employers to ask applicants about disabilities, including their past mental illness or alcohol and drug use. Even if a disability is visible, inquiry concerning the nature or severity is not acceptable. Preemployment questions must stay focused on the applicant's ability to perform the job duties.

Under ADA, medical examinations can be given only after a job offer has been made contingent on satisfactory results of the exam. Exams must be specifically job related and necessary to the business. Medical exams may occur before the applicant begins work, with the job offer conditional on the results. If a medical exam screens out an individual with a disability, the exam must be shown to be job related. After the conditional offer of employment, the employer may inquire into the individual's workers' compensation history in a medical inquiry, but only if medical exams are required for all applicants in that position. Information can be used to screen out applicants with a history of fraudulent workers' compensation claims or who are a "direct threat" to the health or safety of themselves or others and where an acceptable level of behavior or reasonable accommodation could not be made. Decisions cannot be based on speculation about the future costs of workers' compensation claims. Most employees with some percentage of disability rating will probably qualify for ADA protection (Schneid, 1992).

The American Psychological Association (APA) is working with the EEOC on drafting policy guidelines for the ADA and medical tests. As of 1993, it was not yet known whether psychological tests would be treated as medical exams, with the same restrictions. The issue of psychological exams and ADA is discussed in more detail later in this chapter. Testing job applicants for alcohol and controlled substances is allowed; such testing is not considered a medical exam (Section 104d).

In addition to new requirements that employers must meet when hiring employees, there is an incentive to employ mentally or physically disabled workers. A demand-side subsidy provides targeted job tax credits for employers who hire people with disabilities. These tax credits are aimed at helping employers cover the costs of making adaptations for disabled workers. Programs such as the Small Business Tax Credit and Targeted Job Tax Credit may also apply. Employers who do not comply are subject to having complaints or civil suits filed against them. The same enforcement and remedies as Title VII of the Civil Rights Act of 1964 and the Civil Rights Act of 1991 are provided under the ADA. Compensatory and punitive damages are remedies for intentional discrimination, and there is a right to a jury trial. Complaints must be brought to the EEOC within 180 days from the alleged discrimination or within 300 days in states with approved enforcement agencies such as Human Rights Commissions. EEOC has 180 days to investigate and sue or issue a right-to-sue notice. The complainant has 90 days to then file a civil action. Arbitration may also be used. Remedies include those of the Civil Rights Acts of 1991: hiring, reinstatement, promotion, back pay, reasonable accommodation, or other actions that will make the individual "whole." Payment of attorneys' and expert witness fees and court costs are allowed. It is estimated that between 12,000 and 20,000 ADA-related claims will be filed with the EEOC against employers and others who do not comply (Schneid, 1992).

The Fair Labor Standards Act

The Fair Labor Standards Act (FLSA) was enacted in 1938 and has been amended many times (29 USC Sections 201 et seq. 1949). It covers employees of firms engaged in interstate and foreign commerce and sets standards for minimum wage, overtime pay, and record keeping. The act exempts executive, administrative and professional employees from the minimum wage and overtime provisions. The Supreme Court upheld the provisions of the act in 1941. The original FLSA excluded state and local governments and their employees from coverage. Beginning in 1961, Congress extended provisions of FLSA to public employees employed in enterprises engaged in commerce or in the production of goods for commerce, and in 1966 the exemption of states and their political subdivisions was removed regarding employees of state hospitals, institutions and schools. In 1974, Congress extended the minimum wage and overtime pay provisions to virtually all state and local government employees. In 1976, the Supreme Court ruled in *National League of Cities* v. *Usery* (426 U.S. 833) that the 1974 amendments were unconstitutional and the minimum wage and overtime pay provisions were not applicable to integral and traditional governmental functions of state and local governments. In 1985 the Supreme Court overturned the *Usery* decision and ruled in *Garcia* v. *San Antonio Metropolitan Transit Authority* (469 U.S. 528) that Congress does have the authority to apply the FLSA requirements to state and local governments' employees engaged in traditional governmental activities. The impact of the decision was estimated by the Department of Labor to bring 7.7 million state and local employees in approximately 83,000 government units under the Act and to increase wages by an estimated $612 million annually (U.S. General Accounting Office [GAO], 1988).

When the 1966 amendments to the FLSA extended minimum wage and overtime provisions to all nonprofessional and nonsupervisory employees of institutions and hospitals, this included facilities for people with mental illness or mental retardation. Patient and resident workers were not explicitly exempted, but the Department of Labor, which was responsible for the administration and enforcement of FLSA, never enforced the provisions for those workers (U.S. Department of Health, Education, and Welfare, 1975). Many patients and residents of the large state institutions were paid substandard wages to work for the institutions, a form of peonage.

In 1973 a suit, *Souder et al.* v. *Brennan et al.* (367 F. Supp. 80 D.C., 1973) was filed in U.S. District Court, District of Columbia by the American Association on Mental Deficiency, the National Association for Mental Health, and three patients/residents with mental illness/mental retardation in state institutions in Ohio and Pennsylvania. The suit sought to require the Secretary of the Department of Labor to enforce the 1966 amendments to the FLSA for hospital patient-workers.

The Court addressed the defense argument that it was difficult to distinguish between work and work-therapy or vocational training:

> Economic reality is the test of employment and the reality is that many of the patient-workers perform work for which they are in no way handicapped and from which the institution derives full economic benefit. So long as the institution derives any consequential benefit the economic reality test would indicate an employment relationship rather than mere therapeutic exercise (*Souder* v. *Brennan*, 1973).

The Court ordered the Secretary of Labor to enforce the FLSA standards, and, on December 7, the Court issued a declaratory judgment and injunction order granting relief. The defendants were required within 120 days to notify the superintendents of all nonfederal facilities for residential care of persons with mental illness or mental retardation that resident/patient workers were covered under the FLSA and that the Secretary of Labor would enforce the act on their behalf. Superintendents were also to be required to keep records and inform resident workers at their facilities of their rights.

The *Souder* case affected some 200,000 institutional patient/ resident workers who performed institutional work frequently in excess of 40 hours per week and seldom for more than $10 a month ("Court Rules . . . ," 1974). The final regulations concerning employment of patient-workers in hospitals and institutions at subminimum wage were published in February 1975 (20 CFR Sec. 529.1-.17, 1975). They covered employment of patients whose earning or productive capacity was impaired and allowed employers to pay them a prorated share of the full minimum wage adjusted to the actual productivity of the handicapped worker relative to that of a "regular" employee (Friedman, 1974). This effectively resulted in the end of what was referred to as "institutional peonage" and brought the last group of persons with mental disabilities under established procedures for vocational training and employment under federal law.

A 1977 survey of large state institutions for mentally retarded persons based on a response by 44 institutions (30 percent of state institutions) in 28 states (56 percent of states) found that although a few institutions increased their number of resident workers, a considerable number of institutions decreased their resident workers (39 percent), and at least 20 percent of the reduction was associated by administrators with the *Souder* case (Kemp, 1981).

Under the FLSA, the Wage and Hour Office of the Department of Labor establishes requirements for payment of workers with disabilities in noncompetitive employment such as sheltered workshops or vocational training sites. Traditionally, output norms for training are established by a nonhandicapped person performing the task for a specified time. The output norm becomes the basis for determining the wages for workers with disabilities (Evans, 1983). Thus, if workers with disabilities perform at 25 percent of the norm, they are paid 25 percent of the normal wage, which is often minimum wage.

PLACEMENT OF THE WORKER WITH A DISABILITY

Self-esteem suffers when socialization does not facilitate competency in skills needed to master the environment (Disabatino, 1976). People who are socialized into a "secondary" role with limited expectations and who do not have sufficient opportunity to dwell in fantasy about various jobs and fields of work may have difficulty with adequate goal setting (Super, 1963). Aspirations affect choice, with present aspirations molding future behavior (Hahn, 1974). In the past, women, minorities and people with disabilities were socialized into "secondary" roles, were limited as to what futures were open to them, and were not encouraged to have high aspirations. Slowly, society is changing in regard to how these populations are viewed, but some of these individuals may have experienced a scaling down of their vocational aspirations as a result of the realities they faced and may require assistance in obtaining employment and promotions that in the past were closed to them.

Society as a whole values meaningful employment. Given the opportunity to work, people with disabilities are able to attain dignity and feelings of self-worth (Pati and Stubblefield, 1990). However, for the general population there is also satisfaction and well-being in leisure and free time. Surveys of the general population show that higher levels of involvement in free time and leisure activities are associated with higher ratings of overall life satisfaction and well-being (Andrews and Withey, 1976; London, Crandall, and Seals, 1977). In chronically mentally ill persons, deficits in living skills and social leisure involvement can lead to an absence of meaning in life (Barris, Dickie, and Baron, 1988). These individuals need to be involved in meaningful activity (Anthony, 1980). They need environments that do not understimulate them, but they also need environments that do not overwhelm them (Cournos, 1987).

One study of life satisfaction of 83 adults with severe mental disabilities found that at the beginning of the project, 91.7 percent of the individuals were neither in competitive employment nor in sheltered employment Almost one-third described themselves as "sitting around with nothing to do" most or all of the time. They described themselves as "not busy; having a hard time getting out of bed; with no spending money or transportation and no opportunities for jobs, school, or social activities; unhappy with personal accomplishments; bored; and lonely" (Champney and Dzurec, 1992). The study concluded that involvement in activities and receipt of a housing subsidy were significantly associated with satisfaction over a ten-month period. Clients who originally had little or nothing to do showed the greatest increase in satisfaction over time. Changes in functioning or symptomatology had very little to do with changes in satisfaction when activity level was controlled for. Involvement in self-determination in activities and involvement in meaningful activities are necessary for a good quality life for persons with severe mental illness.

Applicants with mental disabilities may pursue employment through regular employment application procedures or may be assisted in seeking employment by community-based agencies that provide rehabilitation/habilitation, training, or other employment assistance. A person with a disability may require special assistance, because their vocational, psychological, social, and physical development can be hindered by the type and severity of their disablement. A congenital disablement may result in a child spending a significant amount of time in special medical or treatment facilities, which can result in loss of socialization experiences. Children with chronic and severe disabilities may sometimes be overprotected and, again, may have experienced more social isolation. Isolation experiences may have a negative effect on vocational and psychosocial development (Hollingsworth and Mastroberti, 1983). Onset of a disability in later life affects a person's established roles. The impact of a mental disability or a serious emotional problem disrupts one's lifestyle, particularly the work role. The disruption of the vocational self-image is in addition to the psychological devastation of the mental disability, such as a major depression or a substance abuse problem. Disability affects all aspects of life. A number of difficulties may contribute to problems in returning to work, including problems with sustaining a job search, work tolerance, endurance, problem solving, judgment, concentration, and cooperating with others.

Occupational Therapy

Occupational therapy can be used to help people with severe mental illness integrate into the community. Occupational therapy may be provided through public, nonprofit, or private profit-making agencies. Clients may be referred from a variety of state agencies, community programs, and independent facilities. Such programs work with individuals with a primary diagnosis of severe mental illness. Some individuals may be dually diagnosed with mental illness and substance abuse. There are also programs for people with development disabilities.

Occupational therapy programs involve planning with the client, family, and caregivers to identify the client's goals and resources for achieving them. Long-term goals such as holding a job may be identified. An example of this type of planning is given by a program in the state of Maine. The Maine program worked with a seriously mentally ill woman who, although she was under state guardianship in a long-term care facility, had the goal of returning to a job similar to one she had held several years before. In that job she had sorted and hung items in a clothing store. An individualized plan was made for the woman, coordinating with the Maine Department of Mental Health, the mental health facility, the Bureau of Vocational Rehabilitation, a Goodwill agency, and a local grocery store. The woman was helped to overcome a problem with control of screaming by providing her with an organized and structured setting that decreased her sensory stimulation. With this program, she was able to work four hours per day at a thrift store while awaiting a community placement (Learnard and Devereaux, 1992).

Occupational therapy can be used to develop an environmental structure to provide necessary support to facilitate learning and improve functioning, and skill building can be used to develop on a day-to-day basis the functional skills of a person with mental disabilities. The Maine program also provides an example of skill building with a 35-year-old man with continual crisis. Because the man did well on prevocational testing and expressed a desire to work in the community, the occupational therapists began to build on the knowledge of the assessment that showed he responded best to clear limit setting, positive reinforcement of success, and visual cues. They found his memory and attention also could be improved with continuous cues. A daily schedule was developed, including yard work at his boarding home, and he visited several work sites as a means of giving him visual cues of work options. A multidisciplinary team was developed consisting of his state guardian, his parole officer, his boarding home operator, and someone from a Goodwill agency. Various approaches were worked out to help the man enter and maintain a volunteer job at a soup kitchen. This led to the vocational rehabilitation agency being willing to place him in a sheltered workshop (Learnard and Devereaux, 1992). These types of individualized occupational therapy plans and interventions can lead to helping persons with severe mental disabilities eventually enter a competitive job environment.

Vocational Rehabilitation

Vocational rehabilitation focuses on getting the person back into the workplace, and vocational habilitation focuses on preparing for the workplace a disabled person who has not yet been employed. Work is considered a critical factor in the rehabilitation of persons with mental illness. It provides therapeutic effects as well as provides financial independence. Work enhances self-esteem and self-concept and provides meaningful structuring of the day's activities. It provides valuable learning experiences, a measure of status, and an opportunity to develop social skills a well as vocational skills. Time on the job has been shown to result in more substantial salary increases for older workers than increments of education or training (Ferber and Birnbaum, 1981).

Various methods have been found to improve success rates when employing people with mental disabilities (Rusch and Hughes, 1989; Wacker et al., 1989). Important factors include job/position analysis, job match and placement, job training, follow-up services, client advocacy, and interagency coordination.

Job/Position Analysis

Job/position analysis is used widely by large public and private employers. Under ADA it may become necessary for smaller employers to also adopt job analysis, because they must determine the essential functions of the job. Job analysis involves breaking the job into elements. The job description describes the specific tasks and duties required to perform the job, and to meet ADA, it is necessary to focus on only the essential elements of the job. The job specification describes the required skills and knowledge to perform the job. Artificially high levels of skills or knowledge must be eliminated to meet ADA. Job requirements are determined by a job/position analysis, which may involve several techniques to collect the task- and person-oriented data. These include observation, interviewing, supervisory conferences, critical incidents, work sampling, questionnaires, and checklists.

Job Match and Placement

Job match and placement involve matching the right applicant to the right job. Attention must be paid to the occupational grouping the disabled person is entering. Job design means more than just workplace engineering. Disabled workers may need to be matched with job groupings that maximize their specific assets and minimize their specific deficits. Trait-and-factor job matching and placement are important. Certain types of jobs may be better suited for certain symptom behaviors; for example, withdrawn persons might work more successfully on a night shift alone, while someone who is more easily agitated might do well working outside in a position involving a lot of physical movement. Placement in a familiar work field also may encourage appropriate work behavior. To attract and retain workers, more flexible benefits and work environments may also be needed (see Chapter 6).

Mentally disabled persons may work in a number of work settings, including sheltered employment involving employment in a controlled environment; transitional or training employment, which is time limited and aimed at developing skills for moving into competitive employment at a job site; supported employment, which involves long-term intensive ongoing support; and competitive employment, which is unsubsidized and unsupported employment in the regular job market. Job clubs have become a successful approach to help persons with mental disabilities obtain competitive employment, while supported employment and buddy systems are helping people with greater disabilities gain employment and, in some cases, move on to competitive employment.

Job Training

The employment specialist, job coach, or employer will need to use specific systematic training techniques to prepare the worker for the job. Depending on the disability, a supervisor may need to develop more detailed and extensive training to help the individual successfully learn the position. The supervisor, new employee, and the job coach may need to discuss what will be needed in the training process. At that time, any necessary modification to adapt the job will be put in place, and a plan will be made for maintenance of the work behaviors learned during training. Training in social survival skills may also enhance the placement and retention of the worker. Follow-up services should be planned that fit the job performance standards and that can be used to maintain the appropriate level of productivity and provide ongoing support.

Client advocates may be available to assist the worker with a disability. They can serve as a liaison between the employee and employer or between the disabled person and community services. Advocates may sometimes perform activities helpful to the employee and employer, such as making sure the employee gets to work on time and giving the employee positive feedback on work performance (Wacker et al., 1989). Persons with mental disabilities may receive services from many organizations, and the advocate may also assist in interagency coordination. Coordination of all services provided to the employee is important in assisting job placement and retention.

Job Clubs

Job clubs are an innovative approach to vocational rehabilitation that have had successful outcomes (Mitchell, Jacobs, and Yen, 1987). An example of this approach is the Brentwood Job Finding Club, founded in 1981 in the Los Angeles area to help persons with psychiatric impairments find competitive employment in the community. Early program results led to 55 percent of participants obtaining competitive employment and 10 percent entering vocational training programs (Jacobs et al., 1984). Early results were based on individuals recruited from a Veterans Administration (VA) hospital, which provided a predominantly male population with generally stronger work histories than the overall psychiatrically impaired population.

A new and wider recruitment was made from late 1985 through early 1987 to study the effects of the job clubs with a more diverse participant population. Persons between the ages of 18 and 65 with DSM III criteria diagnosis were recruited from the Brentwood Veterans Administration Medical Center the Neuropsychiatric Institute at the University of California, Los Angeles, and various day treatment programs, board and care facilities, self-help programs, and community mental health centers in urban Los Angeles. An effort was made to include persons who received Social Security Disability Insurance (SSDI) and Supplemental Security Income (SSI). The job-finding club included a training in job-seeking skills phase and a job search phase. The training phase consisted of 20 hours of assessment and training over a three-day period in small group sessions of three to eight persons. After training, participants began job searches on a full-time basis with the guidance of vocational counselors. The club provided job leads, a place to work from, daily goal setting and problem solving workshops, frequent contact with vocational counselors, and an incentive system.

Eighty-nine individuals participated. The most common diagnoses were depressive disorders (32 percent), bipolar disorder (25 percent), schizophrenia (23 percent), substance abuse (15 percent), and anxiety disorders (5 percent). Eighteen percent received SSDI, and 30 percent received SSI. Of the 89 participants, 16 percent dropped out during skills training, 40 percent dropped out during the job search, and 8 percent were discharged by program staff because of symptom exacerbations or lack of progress. Of the participants, 36 percent had positive outcomes, with 29 percent obtaining a job and 7 percent entering vocational training.

Three factors were found to be strongly related to outcome: psychiatric diagnosis, vocational history and job seeking skills, and SSDI support. Persons with psychotic disorders such as schizophrenia or with bipolar disorder were less likely to obtain jobs. Persons with nonpsychotic diagnoses were more likely to find employment, with 50 percent of those with a diagnosis of depression and 36 percent of those with a substance abuse diagnosis finding employment. Persons who found jobs were also those who had worked most recently. This held true regardless of diagnosis. The average duration of unemployment for those finding employment was ten months; for those entering training programs, 24 months; for those who dropped out during the program, 28 months; and for those discharged from the program, 50 months. Those with good job histories in competitive employment in the past five years and those who scored higher on job interview skills during training did better. Excellent job interview skills were found to help override other negative factors, but persistence in the job search was found to be not enough. Combining the interview skills and persistence could make the difference between success and failure. No significant difference was found between those receiving only SSDI and those receiving no support, but persons receiving SSI benefits had significantly poorer outcomes. A comprehensive training module for job-seeking skills was developed and made available to mental health and rehabilitation organizations, based on the study's findings (Jacobs et al., 1992).

Supported Employment

There are four supported employment placement models for obtaining competitive employment for persons with disabilities: the individual placement model, the clustered placement model, the mobile crew model, and the entrepreneurial model (Rusch and Hughes, 1989). The individual placement model uses the skills of an employment specialist to locate jobs in an organization in the community and to help the individual with a disability obtain employment and learn the job in that organization. A job coach provides continuous on-site training until the supported worker performs the job at an acceptable standard. The type and level of assistance is gradually decreased over time. Usually the job coach maintains a minimum of two monthly contacts, and, if necessary, the job coach will return more frequently. For example, if job duties are added, the coach will return to help with the learning of those duties. The cloistering, mobile crew, and entrepreneurial models all involve placing mentally disabled persons in groups and are primarily used with individuals with more severe disabilities who require more intensive support (Rusch and Hughes, 1989). Chapter 4 discusses supported employment in more detail.

Buddy Systems

Unions have played an important part in providing job placement and supported employment for their members. The buddy system was patterned after European models as a way to provide on-site, long-term support services to coworkers. Union members with disabilities are paired with employees who provide them with role modeling and assistance. As union membership shrinks, workers with disabilities, like women workers, will be of increasing interest to unions as new members. Accordingly, unions can be expected to be more interested in addressing issues of workers with disabilities. The International Association of Machinists (IAM) has already developed a program to serve people with disabilities that has become so large that it has become a nonprofit organization, IAM CARES. They have placed more than 5,300 disabled workers, while the AFL-CIO's Human Resources Development Institute placed 4,165 people with disabilities. between 1977 and 1989 (Traiforos, 1990).

Employers who hire disabled workers not only are complying with the law and may be eligible to receive tax credits but also are enhancing their public image. Successful public relations has the direct benefit of making it easier to recruit qualified applicants. Providing a welcome for persons with disabilities will attract the best employees both with and without major disabilities. A secondary benefit gained is that a positive public image contributes to the organization's overall well-being (Bellamy et al., 1989), which enhances creating a mentally healthy and productive work environment. The organization is also demonstrating its social responsibility, an important part of many organizations' stated mission.

SELECTION PROCESS

Mental health issues are raised in several selection processes, including psychological testing, polygraphs, and graphology.

Psychological Testing

Psychological testing is used to determine the psychological well-being of the individual. Psychological testing was widely developed and used by the military during World War I and World War II to determine individuals unfit to serve. Government psychologists also developed standardized tests that were used for determining military assignments. As tests expanded to measure intelligence, aptitude, vocational skills, and personality, testing became popular with employers during the 1950s and 1960s. In the 1980s, psychological assessment techniques for selection purposes became much more sophisticated.

Psychological testing can be used to measure mental thought processes, emotional traits, stability, attitudes, personality characteristics, and behaviors. The information gained from tests is then used to predict future job performance and to make hiring decisions. The tests can be used to screen out or select in individuals. Although psychological tests based on self-reporting and interviews are good predictors of psychosis, they predict only probabilities of job performance success or failure (Inwald, 1988). Long-term predictions of job performance for selecting in are not very accurate, because a person's behavior may change over time. As the employee matures and ages, the person's outlook, attitudes, and expectations may change. Screening out seeks to use the test to eliminate individuals whose present behavior is a potential liability (Taylor and Zimmerer, 1988).

Employers are interested in using personality tests as predictors of job performance, as a way to go beyond the usual screening process and reliance on past history, and as a way to gain some insight into the personality of the applicant. Employers are interested in personality factors because it is recognized that job failures are more frequently caused by personality factors and conflicts than by insufficient job skills (Rotman, 1983). Job analyses indicate that personality traits, attitude, motivation, and interest are generally more important determinants of job success than basic intellectual abilities (Davey, 1984). However, personality tests are not very good predictors of future job performance, and even if an organization is successful in determining certain preselected traits, identifying them, and hiring people with them, developing a "personality pool" of similar individuals who have similar reactions may stifle creativity (Taylor and Zimmerer, 1988). As Janus warns in *Group Think* (1982), selection of individuals who are too much alike may lead to a sameness in thinking and a lack of challenging of ideas, which may be detrimental to organizations. Some employers are also interested in the ability to predict violence or dangerousness. However, testing has not been successful in determining violent behavior and dangerousness. This has clearly been shown in attempts of mental health professionals to predict dangerousness in mentally ill patients. Also, most individuals are aware enough not to self-report violent tendencies on tests that are non anonymous (Inwald, 1988).

Psychological testing has been used by a variety of employers to determine a number of different factors regarding prospective employees. Because in the late 1980s employee theft was estimated at $40 billion annually, ten times the cost of street crimes (U.S. Department of Commerce, 1988), organizations involved in sales have used honesty testing, psychological tests to determine if an individual possesses the personality traits and characteristics linked to employee theft, to determine the likelihood of an applicant's stealing from the company. Personality testing has been used to determine traits of employees, such as assertiveness, that are sought for particular positions. Health care facilities have used psychological testing to evaluate the mental healthiness of people they hire and to predict their ability to function in that environment. Psychological testing is used widely in placement of police officers to determine suitability for the job. However, most employers still do not use psychological testing. The American Management Association conducted a survey in 1985 of 7,000 human resource managers nationwide and found that most managers did not use psychological tests (Inwald, 1988).

Testing guidelines are provided by the APA, the International Association of Chiefs of Police Psychological Services Section and the EEOC. Testing requires the skills of a professional psychologist, and the psychologist and employer determine the appropriate tests to be used, based on the organization's needs. The psychologist who conducts the testing should be very familiar with the organization. Tests should not be used mainly to screen out undesirable candidates but should be considered more appropriate as tools for matching an individual to a job, for the best job fit. This approach involves determining personality traits that distinguish individuals who perform well in particular jobs from individuals who perform poorly in those jobs. This requires administering the test to employees who perform that job and who have a range of performance levels in that work. Tests must also be administered to enough employees to validate the test by having statistically significant findings. Once a test is standardized on a pool of employees who hold a specific position and is shown to be valid for that position, the test(s) can be administered to applicants and a report written up based on the results. Tests administered to applicants should continue to be followed up to see how well people perform on various measures of success or failure on the job over time. The test should continue to be evaluated as to its ability to predict. Because of the limitations of psychological testing, many employers use a combination of various psychological tests, intensive interviews, and background checks. Employers typically receive an interpretative report summing up the written test(s) and interview and a recommendation to hire or not to hire.

If a test is questioned, the vendor's and the assessor's qualifications will be called into question. Credentials of vendors and of assessors should be carefully screened. The test must have been developed and validated by a credible source, and the test must have been administered using proper procedures, including a credible assessor. Most states require a Ph.D. degree and licensure for psychologists. Psychologists may receive diplomate status through the APA's American Board of Professional Psychology.

Frequently Used Tests

Tests have changed over time to meet greater demands for accuracy and to meet legal requirements. The most common types of psychological testing have been testing for honesty, personality inventories, and integrated assessment tests (Kovach, 1986). The Minnesota Multiphasic Personality Inventory (MMPI) is the most widely used psychological assessment test. It has been widely used as a screening instrument in law enforcement. Relationships have been found between the MMPI scales and academy performance and attrition, supervisor's ratings, automobile accidents, promotions, job problems, and job tenure (Hargrave and Hiatt, 1987). The test was updated in 1989 to remove sexist language. Because it has been widely used in the workplace, a number of items that might offend an employee's sense of privacy have been omitted, including references to sexual preference.

The California Personality Inventory addresses personality characteristics related to social living and interaction. It is also widely used for law enforcement screening and has relationships between the scale scores and academy performance and supervisor's ratings (Hargrave and Hiatt, 1987). It is also used to select child care workers and has significant relationships between scale scores and employee job failure (Mufson, 1986). Another widely used test is the

Inwald Personality Inventory (IPI), which addresses a wide range of topics related to law enforcement. A five-year study of 219 public safety officers who were hired over a one-year period for a large urban public safety organization found that the most successful predictor for officers who were subsequently terminated was use of both MMPI and IPI scores. This method accurately identified 21 (70 percent) of terminated officers (Inwald, 1988).

Confidentiality Issues

The employer who uses psychological testing has a responsibility for maintaining the confidentiality of that testing. Some feel that only those most vitally concerned with selection or growth and development should see the report and that the individuals tested should not see the reports or have material read or quoted to them from the reports (Rotman, 1983). Others feel that from an ethical standpoint, the employer should offer to share the assessment data with the people from whom it is collected, regardless of the purpose for the collection. Making assessment feedback available also enhances people's attitudes toward assessment. Not everyone, however, will wish to receive feedback. One executive assessment program had over 90 percent of internal candidates but only 60 percent of external candidates take advantage of a feedback option (Fletcher, 1986). One psychologist recommends giving the feedback only verbally so that a balanced approach may be taken and clear explanations given (Fletcher, 1986). This should help alleviate some of the problems with feedback, such as defensiveness on the part of the candidate. In some cases, such as with some public safety personnel, psychological test results are sealed and made available only upon a court order.

Legal Issues of Psychological Testing

Psychological testing is losing favor because it is increasingly under legal scrutiny. Poorly constructed or inadequately researched test instruments lead to lawsuits, and lawsuits or legislation may eventually outlaw the use of all such tests (Inwald, 1988). As noted earlier, the use of psychological testing under the ADA is under investigation. An employer risks court challenges and possible damages for the incorrect use of testing and employers should be extremely careful about the examiners, the tests, and the reasons for which they use the tests.

The widespread use of psychological exams led to allegations that they had racial and sexual bias and concerns that they were dehumanizing. Adverse impacts on protected groups must be considered in any selection process. Tests that have an adverse impact on a protected group are subject to challenge even if it is possible to prove that they accurately reflect the group's expected performance (Davey, 1984). One example of adverse impact is if an organization chose its management trainees on the basis of such traits as assertiveness, independence, and self-confidence. There is an increased chance that the trainees would be predominantly male, because those are traits encouraged in male children. If a charge were made of adverse impact and sexual discrimination, the organization would have great difficulty proving those traits were job related (Taylor and Zimmerer, 1988).

The 1971 U.S. Supreme Court case *Griggs* v. *Duke Power Co.* (401 U.S. 424) required that a link be made between a selection process and the specific job. Any organization using a psychological test must be able to demonstrate the validity and job-specific necessity of the test. Tests should measure only personality traits related to job performance, and a linkage should be shown between test scores of applicants and their future job performance. That decision had a chilling effect on the use of psychological testing by corporations (Kovach, 1986). The main reason most employers do not use psychological testing is their concern that the test will not meet validity standards for a particular job and will be open to a complaint for enforcement by the EEOC (Aberth, 1987).

In the public sector, where there is a constitutional protection of the right to privacy in regard to governmental action, federal, state, and local employees may challenge psychological testing as an invasion of their right to privacy. Because the right to privacy is a core or fundamental right, the burden of proof is on the government using the test to show they have a compelling governmental reason to do so. In the case *McKenna* v. *Fargo* (451 F. Supp. 1355, 1377 DNJ, 1978), the right to administer a battery of psychological tests to firefighter candidates was allowed because the court viewed that it had a job related purpose. However, as will be seen later in regard to drug testing in the public sector, a crucial part of that decision making was the view of the court that the firefighting occupation was a life-endangering public safety occupation in which there were unique psychological factors. The court held that there would be very few other occupations in which there would be such a need for psychological and emotional assessment.

The federal government's Office of Personnel Management's (OPM) regulations do not permit psychological testing, but Representative Barbara Boxer of California has maintained that the practice persists. She introduced a bill in 1990 to amend the 1989 Whistleblowers Protection Act to prohibit psychological testing (Bureau of National Affairs [BNA], 1990).

ADA and Psychological Testing

Experts at the APA's 1992 convention warned employers to be careful about giving psychological exams to job applicants. The APA is working with the EEOC on policy guidelines for the ADA and medical tests, and the EEOC may decide that psychological tests are equivalent to medical exams and will be subject to the same restrictions. The psychologists did not expect EEOC to exempt personality tests from the ADA. Catherine Flanagan of Psychological Consultants for Management advised against using the tests but provided some guidelines for employers who wished to continue using psychological exams. She advised the elimination of test questions that would be considered offensive, such as "I often have dizzy spells," and recommended that after the test results were considered, a written diagnosis not be placed in personnel files because it could be considered a medical test ("ADA Could Restrict . . . ," 1992).

There are some major problems with using psychological tests, including problems with acceptability, because many people view such tests as an invasion of privacy, which may result in public relations problems; problems with finding a test that has true validity, because many times there may be subjective elements to the test and personality tests are generally poor predictors of future job performance (Taylor and Zimmerer, 1988); possible legal challenges and costs, including the likelihood that they will have to meet the restrictions on medical exams under ADA; the hidden costs of testing, including the fact that assessment data are not usable beyond five years at most (Fletcher, 1986); and the costs incurred from incorrect predictions of the applicant's future performance and an unnecessary loss of job applicants because there are individuals who do not want to take the exams (Taylor and Zimmerer, 1988).

Graphology

Graphology, which involves analysis of a handwriting sample, is another method that is used to try to determine personality traits. Handwriting is a product of human behavior and may be considered a psychological instrument. The characteristics in writing reflect the nature of the activity in the brain that is producing the writing (Wallner, 1975). Graphology is not widely used in the United States and is subject to the same ethical and legal concerns as psychological testing, as well a serious concerns about proven validity. Even though it is not well established in the United States, it is estimated that 5,000 firms have employed graphologists as consultants, including Firestone, Ford, H & R Block, General Electric, and Mutual of Omaha (Kurtz et al., 1989). Fortune 500 companies use it primarily to analyze top executives, while middle-sized firms tend to use it more widely. Graphology has been used in hiring and promotion of employees, to identify dishonest employees, to handle other problem employees, in negotiations, and as a career counseling tool. It is usually used as only one method to determine who to hire, not as the sole determinant.

Traits commonly analyzed include decisiveness, empathy, enthusiasm, organizational skills, persuasiveness, problem-solving ability, and being a self-starter. It also helps to determine what motivates applicants and employees, including approval, ego drive, money, or the opportunity to grow in management or responsibility. Findings from the most successful personnel in an organization are sometimes compared with the handwriting of applicants. Traits are not labeled good or bad but are determined to be more or less suitable for a particular job.

Graphology is practiced extensively in Europe, where U.S. multinational corporations are very likely to experience its use. Some estimates place the use of graphology for personnel selection, particularly at the management level, as high as 85 percent in Europe (Fowler, 1991). Only the British, like the Americans, seem strongly opposed to its use, based on their belief that research does not support its validity and may even show that it is invalid as a technique to select personnel (Fowler, 1991). Training is more extensive in Europe. Graphology may be studied at universities in Europe and Israel at the master and doctorate levels, and many European universities require it in applied psychology and for education majors who are going to teach. In the United States, virtually anyone can call themselves a graphologist; therefore, if a consultant is to be hired, an employer must look carefully at credentials and track record. The International Graphanalysis Society and the American Association of Handwriting Analysts require strong qualifying exams.

Graphology is subject to being used without the knowledge or consent of an applicant. An ethical and legal approach requires knowledge and consent of applicants before this procedure is used. Reputable graphologists request employers to notify job applicants that their handwriting is being analyzed and to share the results with them. Graphologists view handwriting samples anonymously, with no information as to gender or age. Because of legal requirements in the United States (addressed earlier), employers should be careful about using handwriting analysis in their selection processes.

DRUG SCREENING

One approach employers have taken to deal with substance abuse is drug screening of job applicants and drug testing of employees. In 1988, survey research found that 25 percent of the respondents for Fortune 500 companies reported conducting drug testing, and another 20 percent stated that they planned to implement a drug testing policy within the next two years (Davidson, 1988). By 1991, 50 percent of the Fortune 500 respondents reported using drug testing, and 10–15 percent of all organizations employing 50 or more people reported they were planning to start drug testing programs (Konovsky and Cropenzano, 1991). More than 90 percent of Fortune 100 companies had instituted preemployment testing, which is the most prevalent form of screening (Kupfer, 1988).

Many employers perceive drug abuse as a problem. A survey of 224 top U.S. company chief executives found that 79 percent felt drug abuse was a serious problem in their corporations, and 18 state governors and 23 city mayors felt drugs were a serious problem in their organizations (Konovsky and Cropenzano, 1991). In 1990, according to an American Management Association survey of employers, job applicants in California were reported as more than twice as likely as applicants in other states to fail preemployment drug testing. Of 13,146 job applicants tested in California, 17.8 percent tested positive for illicit drugs, compared with 8.1 percent in other states. However, the study had a high margin of error, 7.8 percent, meaning that the true figure could be between 10 and 25.6 percent ("Californians Flunk . . . ," 1990).

Drug testing is a response to the substance abuse problem in society and its effect on the work force. Employers justify drug testing on the grounds of integrity on the job, employee safety, and safety of others (Reuter, 1988). Under the ADA, employers may continue to test job applicants for alcohol and controlled substances prior to an offer of employment (Section 104D). As noted earlier, this testing is not considered a medical examination under the ADA definition. This chapter will focus on screening applicants, and the following chapter will look at testing current employees.

Of all drug tests administered in organizations, 85 percent are for preemployment screening (Kupfer, 1988). Such screening is viewed as a way to prevent hiring an employee who will be a problem in the workplace. Either preemployment drug testing occurs prior to the employee being offered the job or successful passage of the test is made a condition of the employment offer. Employees are willing to see certain occupations as more acceptable in terms of drug testing. These include airline pilots, air traffic controllers, and police officers (Murphy, Thorton, and Prue, 1991). However, job applicants have more positive attitudes toward agencies that have not instituted drug testing programs (Crant and Bateman, 1990). There are many issues of concern regarding testing. Some of these issues such as organizational substance abuse policies, administration of tests, and test accuracy will be discussed in a later chapter.

The Drug-Free Workplace Act of 1988 requires all private sector employers with contracts of $25,000 or more to take steps to maintain a drug-free workplace. Although the act does not require testing of applicants or employees, many employers see testing as one way to ensure a drug-free environment. The ADA requires all employers to conform to Drug Free Workplace Act requirements, and most existing preemployment and postemployment alcohol and controlled-substance programs that are not specifically part of the preemployment medical examination or ongoing medical screening program will be permitted to continue (Section 102C). Individuals who currently engage in the illegal use of alcohol or illegal drugs are excluded from the protection of ADA.

Applicants in the private sector generally have no constitutional protections regarding the use of drug testing. Protections rest largely on whether union contracts address the issue. However, in some states, for example, California, the state constitution, Section 1, provides a privacy protection in regard to private as well as public employers. A California court case involving a private employer and drug testing held that the California constitutional right of privacy was not absolute and that individuals who sought employment also necessarily chose to disclose certain information. The court allowed the testing in spite of the constitutional protection because the applicants had a choice of consenting to the limited invasion of their privacy by accepting the testing or declining a conditional job offer and the test. The court held that they were not prevented from seeking employment elsewhere (*Wilkinson et al.* v. *Times Mirror Corporation et al.*, 215 Cal. App. 3d 1034, 1989). In the public sector there is U.S. constitutional protection against government action (fifth amendment for federal action; fourteenth amendment for state and local action). These constitutional protections are in regard to due process and equal protection. There are also constitutional protections in regard to search and seizure (fourth amendment) and privacy (U.S. Supreme Court decision, *Griswald* v. *Connecticut*, 381 U.S. 479, 1965). Although blanket testing of all applicants is restricted in the public sector, applicants to many positions may be tested based on the ability of the government employer to sustain a court challenge that there is a compelling reason, for example, "safety," that supersedes the right of the applicant. However, basically, drug testing of applicants is more limited in the public sector.

According to a 1987 survey by the Clearinghouse on Drugs and AIDS Testing of the American Society for Public Administration's Section on Personnel Administration and Labor Relations, which surveyed personnel directors of the 50 states, 100 largest cities, all counties over 500,000 population, and 114 federal cabinet-level departments and independent agencies regarding public agency drug testing policies, only 10.9 percent of respondents tested all applicants and 66.4 percent tested only public safety applicants. Almost two-thirds of respondents informed applicants that they would be tested prior to employment, and another one-fourth informed them during the preemployment physical. Over two-thirds of the respondents required the applicant's written consent prior to testing; over one-half informed the applicant in writing of positive test results, over one-third informed them verbally, and another 13 percent did both. Of the respondents, 80 percent informed the applicant that positive test results were the basis for refusing employment. More than three-fourths of respondents conducted a second test for verification of positive results (Klingner, O'Neil, and Sabet, 1987).

GENETIC TESTING IN THE WORKPLACE

Genetic testing also raises mental health concerns in the workplace. Genetic screening and monitoring have the potential to significantly change the workplace by detecting occupational and nonoccupational diseases by identifying genetic abnormalities that may be associated with inherited traits, susceptibilities, and diseases in an otherwise healthy-appearing person.

Every gene is a unique fragment of deoxyribonucleic acid (DNA). Scientists are now in the process of attempting to determine the exact location of specific genes on the 23 pairs of chromosomes by analyzing the structure of human DNA. This involves determining the sequence of approximately 3 billion chemical components, the base pairs of human DNA (U.S. Congress, Office of Technology Assessment [OTA], 1988). The task involves finding the genetic chemical components for diseases, their location, and how to sequence them to allow testing for predisposition to diseases or disorders. Some specific genes have been found that carry the predisposition for certain diseases/disorders. For the most part, however, genetic markers have been found, rather than direct identification of disease- and disorder-carrying genes. There are some 4,000 known inherited diseases that are caused by single-gene defects (U.S. Senate, November 9, 1989).

The Human Genome Project

In 1989 within the National Institutes of Health (NIH), a center was created to conduct research on the human genome. This division is the Human Genome Project, which evolved out of the Office of Genome Research, in response to the high priority given by NIH to the mapping and sequencing of human genomes. Successfully mapping the human genome is expected to take between 20 and 25 years. The new technologies developed through the Human Genome Project's research will be used to assess public health needs. The project will also accelerate diagnostic applications. Because the ability to diagnose a genetic abnormality usually precedes the ability to treat or prevent the abnormality, how these diagnostic applications should be used and who should have the information obtained from them is a matter of concern. In January 1989, the Program Advisory Committee on the Human Genome was established as a working group on ethics to address these types of issues, and some of the federal genome budget was designated to study the ethical issues of the genome research.

Genetic Testing of Applicants and Employees

In the 1970s a few companies started to use genetic testing. In 1990, it was estimated that occupational illness cost the U.S. economy over 1 million work days (U.S. Department of Commerce). Individuals who have a greater risk for certain illnesses or disorders may spend fewer years in the work force and may cause greater health costs for employers. Excluding those at risk may lower employers' costs for recruitment and training (Council on Ethical and Judicial Affairs, American Medical Association, 1991). Thus, there is a strong incentive to want to use new technology to address this problem.

At present, with the exception of a few specific diseases, testing for genetic predisposition is done by probability methods and linkage markers. Unless the testing is for a known trait that appears in a high-risk population or for a gene that has been directly located, the process is lengthy and not yet proven to be scientifically valid. Thus, widespread use of the procedure is relatively unrealistic for the workplace. Although a few large U.S. corporations do some sort of genetic testing, it has not been employed as a mass-screening mechanism for prevention.

In the workplace, genetic testing involves two activities: genetic screening and genetic monitoring. Several techniques are used to examine workers for particular inherited genetic traits or disorders (screening) or environmentally induced changes in their genetic material (monitoring). The testing carries the assumption that these traits or changes may predispose them to illness. There are four general purposes for genetic testing in the workplace: research, information, diagnosis, and exclusion. In every purpose of genetic screening or monitoring, ethical questions are unavoidable, because the tests focus on a person's genetic makeup, which is an unchangeable, unchosen, and fixed component of human life (Murray, 1983). Research is primarily done by companies to establish links between genetic predispositions and reactions to workplace hazards. Information learned from tests can be provided to managers and workers for decision making regarding the workplace. Diagnosis involves the actual clinical diagnosis of an individual worker in regard to his/her condition. Also, genetic testing can be used for exclusionary purposes; this would involve excluding from work an applicant or a worker who tested positive for a genetic condition believed to result in a heightened susceptibility to the everyday work environment or who showed genetic damage linked to the work environment.

Genetic Screening

Genetic screening is a one-time testing procedure to determine if a person has particular genetic traits. The traits are identified through laboratory tests on body fluids, usually blood. The assumption behind this testing is that genetic traits may make an individual more susceptible to certain environmental or emotional stressors in the workplace. Screening has the potential of determining individual susceptibility but it is less well-developed than genetic monitoring, because only a few specific disease-carrying genes have been located. Genetic screening can be used to screen a job applicant or employee to identify a genetic predisposition to an occupationally related disease or to detect general heritable conditions, not just those that are occupational specific. Screening could be used to improve productivity and lower workers' compensation claims; promote and encourage general health awareness; and improve employers' health care cost containment, particularly for health insurance. This could be done by not hiring those with genes that potentially could lead to health insurance claims. Screening for nonoccupationally related diseases may be of particular interest to companies that have adopted self-insurance plans, which are not subject to state insurance regulations. Because these companies assume the risks for the health care expenses of their employees directly instead of purchasing health insurance, they may feel the most pressure to use any method available to help control costs (U.S. Congress, OTA, October 1990).

Information gained from screening can also be used to help target company wellness programs to identified problem areas or even to specific employees. If specific gene connections are unknown, genetic screening involves looking for linkages by blood testing of the individual; blood testing of parents, siblings, and grandparents; establishing a file of familial medical records; and using the test results as well as probability methods to determine a person's genetic makeup, damage, and predisposition to disease. Obviously this is not practical in the work setting in most situations because of the involvement of people other than the worker and the risk of unreliability. In addition, many diseases and disorders will never be pinpointed to a single genetic factor but will be found to be carried by multiple genes. Therefore, it will require much more research to understand the complex linkages between genetics and the environment, and it will remain a matter of probabilities to try to define how much influence the genetic factors have in determining the likelihood of any particular individual having any particular disease or disorder.

Genetic Monitoring

Genetic monitoring involves examining individuals periodically for environmentally induced changes in the genetic material of their cells, such as chromosomal damage or evidence of increased occurrence of molecular mutations. This procedure may indicate exposure to a hazardous substance or may indicate the possibility that the exposed tested group will be at an increased risk of developing an illness. Monitoring can be used to assess an exposed population to determine if that population is at risk because of exposure to certain hazardous substances and to assess the extent to which an individual is currently at risk. Because genetic monitoring is more preventive than exclusionary, it is a more viable option for employers to use. However, current techniques are not exposure specific, so detected changes could come from ambient exposures, personal habits, and life-style decisions, such as use of tobacco, as well as from the workplace. Changes may also be caused by age. The Council on Ethical and Judicial Affairs (1991) of the AMA believes that there may be a very limited role for genetic testing for exclusion of workers who are genetically susceptible to occupational illness and that several conditions would have to be met: the disease would have to develop so rapidly that serious, irreversible illness would occur before monitoring of exposure to the substance or the worker's health status could be effective in preventing harm; the genetic test is highly accurate; empirical data exist that the abnormality results in an unusual susceptibility to the occupational illness; measures have been taken to protect susceptible employees and the costs of lowering the level of the substance are extraordinary, relative to the costs of the genetic testing; and testing is performed only with informed consent. The council believes that future unemployability is not an adequate basis for performing genetic tests, because they are poor predictors of disease and even poorer predictors of disabling disease. When a gene manifests itself it is characterized by variable expression, which varies widely from person to person; for example, Huntington's disease manifests between the ages of 30 and 50, and in many cases, modification of behavior can limit expression of a gene.

Psychological Effects on Workers

For workers, genetic screening may single out individual workers because of a perceived genetic inadequacy. There are those who argue that selecting out employees based upon their genetic makeup is in effect labeling them as different, stereotyping them. For a job applicant or employee who is told that he/she cannot obtain a position or can no longer work for an organization because of the results of a genetic test, this could be psychologically traumatizing (Lappe, 1987; Murray, 1983; U.S. Congress, OTA, 1982). This could force the worker into states of depression or anxiety and even suicidal tendencies (Annas, 1989; Murray, 1983).

Because genetic traits may be linked to racial/ethnic lines, this could lead to increased stigmatizing of groups and exclusion of large numbers of individuals who are members of certain races/ethnicities (Lappe, 1987; Murray, 1983; U.S. Congress, OTA, 1988). Such stigmatizing has negative emotional and psychological consequences for the individuals involved.

Mental Disabilities and Genetic Screening

Gradually, linkages between mental disabilities and genetics are being found. Scientists have mapped the location of a gene involving risk of Alzheimer's disease at the twenty-first chromosome, the same chromosome associated with Down syndrome. Research has shown that schizophrenia, bipolar depression (manic depression), and Alzheimer's disease are probably carried by multiple genes. These findings may eventually help to prevent certain mental disorders. However, they also increase concerns regarding protecting the rights of persons with mental disabilities. There are concerns that genetic testing could lead to eugenics. "Eugenics" refers to past movements at the turn of the century and again during World War II to racially improve the human race. Such movements have been aimed against persons with mental illness, mental retardation, the poor, criminals, and various racial/ethnic groups, the most well-known of which are the Jewish people.

Legislation and Law

Existing legislation may not adequately cover a worker who feels that he/she has been discriminated against. Title VII of the Civil Rights Act of 1964 (42 U.S.C. 2000e) prohibits discrimination based on race, color, national origin, religion, or sex, but racism may be difficult to prove in relationship to genetic testing (Annas, 1989; U.S. Congress, OTA, 1988). This act may apply not only to intentionally discriminatory actions but also to neutral employment practices that have a disparate impact on a protected group. Some genetic screening procedures have a disparate impact that could fall under Title VII.

The 1973 Rehabilitation Act (29 U.S.C. 791 et seq.) and the ADA (Public Law 101-336) provide protection for people with disabilities. The Rehabilitation Act of 1973 bans discrimination against individuals with mental or physical disabilities by employers who are federal contractors or recipients of federal grants. An otherwise-qualified employee must prove his/her genetic trait is or is regarded as an impairment. An individual with a genetic predisposition for a disease may not be denied employment or promotion just because of the predisposition (U.S. Congress, OTA, October 1990). The employer is required to make reasonable accommodation for the person. The ADA extends a prohibition of discrimination on the basis of disability to the private sector. Whether genetic traits will be an impairment under this legislation is unclear. Preemployment medical examinations or inquiries are to be limited to determining the applicant's ability to do the job; thus, genetic screening for nonoccupationally related conditions would seem to be prohibited (U.S. Congress, OTA, October 1990). However, the legislation does not specifically address genetic testing, so in the future, court cases will probably clarify this. The Council on Ethical and Judicial Affairs (1991) of the AMA believes the ADA will have a significant impact on the ability to use genetic testing. They believe the act will probably allow some consideration of future employability but that it will probably be tied to whether the individual can continue employment for more than a very short time, and such people could be identified by medical testing rather than genetic testing.

The National Labor Relations Act (29 U.S.C. 151 et seq.) covers relationships of employees, unions, and employers Included in mandatory subjects of bargaining are safety and health matters such as fitness for duty, physical examinations, and medical testing. Genetic testing may be considered a mandatory subject of collective bargaining. The Occupational Safety and Health Act (OSHA) (Public Law 91-596) has been used to regulate some employer practices that could also impact genetic testing; these include access to medical records and communications about hazards by employers to employees. OTA (U.S. Congress, October 1990) believes that OSHA is likely to have the most immediate impact on the use of genetic screening and monitoring because it has dealt extensively with related practices of biological monitoring and because its rules on access to medical records and hazard communication are among the most applicable. "Thus, OSHA is the most appropriate candidate for regulating in the area of genetic monitoring and screening in the workplace" (U.S. Congress, OTA, October 1990).

Few Supreme Court cases have dealt with genetic issues. However, the trend of the court has been to expand the protection of handicapped and disability laws to diseases such as tuberculosis and acquired immune deficiency syndrome (AIDS) (Annas, 1989). The courts have consistently rejected employers' arguments that they should be able to deny employment based on the fact that future work might be compromised by health problems (Gostin, 1991).

The U.S. Congress has been concerned about genetic testing since the 1970s. Reports of genetic monitoring and screening in the workplace attracted the attention of Congress in the late 1970s and early 1980s. Concern about scientific and social issues of such testing led to the House Committee on Science and Technology holding hearings and requesting an OTA assessment. OTA surveyed U.S. industry and unions in 1982 and again in 1989 (U.S. Congress, OTA, 1982; October 1990) regarding their involvement in genetic screening and monitoring. Congress has also recognized that current legislation is disjointed and that it is probable that new laws will be required.

In some states, such as California, there is legislation that specifically prohibits discrimination based on disease. Assemblyman Lloyd Connelly (D-Sacramento) intended to introduce an amendment to California's legislation that would add genetic characteristics to the list of protected classes ("Who's Been Peeking . . . ," 1991). In 1983 there were four states that had statutes limiting the use of genetic information in employment decisions (U.S. Congress, OTA, 1982). In Florida, Louisiana, and North Carolina, the laws are specific to testing for sickle cell trait. In New Jersey, however, the law bans employment discrimination based on genetic traits. States are also involved because of their role in workers' compensation programs (see Chapter 7). The role of genetic data as evidence, the admissibility of the data, and the coverage of a susceptible employee, as well as many other issues involving genetic testing, are unresolved.

Changes in common law relating to work place genetic testing have been incremental. The more advanced case law regarding employer screening for drug use and AIDS may also be used to project a trend. There are growing exceptions to the employment-at-will doctrine. That rule forms the basis for most employment relations without an explicit contract between the parties and gives the employer virtually unlimited authority to terminate the employment relationship at any time. It is the most common employment situation in the private sector. Public sector employment comes under many more restrictions and much more scrutiny. Traditionally, at-will doctrine has included the right to terminate employment because of a belief that the employee is no longer able to perform adequately and would have allowed an employer to terminate for genetic test results regardless of their accuracy. In recent years, the courts have been eroding the scope of the at-will doctrine, and employers must be very careful about applying it.

Privacy

Another concern is the issue of privacy and protecting the confidentiality of the information obtained. One of the dangers involving genetic information is that health insurance carriers might be able to obtain this information as part of the person's medical history and determine that such a person is either high risk or uninsurable. Eventually, genetic screening may become part of routine medical examinations, which would increase this danger.

Dr. Paul Billings, Chief of the Division of Genetic Medicine at Pacific Presbyterian Medical Center in San Francisco, has reported that he has collected approximately 60 cases of employment and insurance discrimination resulting from genetic tests ("Who's Been Peeking . . . ," 1991). With a new 1992 Supreme Court decision that supports insurance companies' rights to terminate insured individuals' policies for current conditions, this danger may be enhanced. In 1988 the Human Genome Privacy Act was introduced to provide confidentiality for genetic information maintained by the federal government. As of 1993, that legislative initiative remained unresolved.

However, there is a expectation that there will be a revolution in advances in genetic medicine in the decades to come. Early in the 2000s, when the database from the Human Genome Project is in place, it is anticipated that the science of molecular genetics will significantly enhance longevity and that the baby boom generation will reap the benefits (Rosenfeld, 1992). This has enormous implications for retaining workers in the work force. In addition, researchers expect to conquer disorders caused by defects in single genes, including cystic fibrosis, muscular dystrophy, and sickle-cell disease. Later, they expect to have effective therapies for major diseases such as heart disease, cancer, arthritis, emphysema, and schizophrenia.

4

Mental Health Issues and Management

There are many mental health issues that affect the management of employees once they have been hired. These issues arise in relationship to supervising employees and retaining them in the workplace and also occur in relationship to discipline and termination. Some of the mental health issues that arise are supervising employees who have mental disabilities in regular employment or supported employment; managing the substance abusing employee; supervising employees with specific personality types that may impact the workplace, including children of alcoholics, members of abusive families, and Type A and Type B personalities; mental health issues and discipline and termination; dealing with potentially dangerous people in the workplace; mental health issues of career change, layoffs, and retirement; mental health issues of illness and death, including acquired immune deficiency syndrome (AIDS); and the impact of the impaired manager.

SUPERVISING EMPLOYEES WITH MENTAL DISABILITIES

In supervising an employee with a mental disability, there are several important considerations. An employee with a mental disability is a person first. Persons with a mental disability, like persons with a physical disability, should not be defined by their disability. The mental disability is not who the person is but simply one aspect of them that may or may not have to be addressed in the workplace.

Supervisors should be sensitive about any language that they use regarding disabilities. Individuals should be referred to as a person with a disability, not as "crippled," "handicapped," "mentally ill," "mentally retarded," or even "a disabled person." It is better to say "person with a mental or emotional illness" rather than "the mentally ill" or "a mentally ill person." This is using what is referred to as "people first" language, putting the emphasis on the person, not the disability. Whenever possible, it is preferable not to refer to the disability at all. People should not be labeled with their disabilities. Causal references to people's disabilities, such as "she is the person with depression" or "he is the person with a developmental disability," should not be made. Such references are tactless and demeaning. Would you refer someone to "see the man in the wheelchair" when "see the person at the second desk to the right" would get the person to the proper personnel just as readily but without labeling based on a disability? It is the responsibility of the supervisor to see that all employees also have proper training in appropriate language. This will reassure persons with disabilities that there is no prejudice against them and will create a positive work environment. The supervisor should make the person feel comfortable in the work setting and should also be sure that coworkers do the same. This may require some in-service training. Employees may need to be educated about different types of disabilities, the productiveness of persons with disabilities, the correct way to talk about disabilities, and how to work with someone with disabilities. The supervisor should not assume that all the employees are sensitive and knowledgeable about people with disabilities. It is important to help workers with disabilities integrate into the work force and be treated like all other workers. The McDonald's Corporation has trained more than 8,000 persons with disabilities over nine years (DeLuca, 1991). As part of their McJobs program, before a McJobs trainee enters the workplace, managers and staff undergo sensitivity training designed to make them more empathetic to the new worker. Employers who work successfully with persons with disabilities are more than repaid for their effort. Studies show that persons with mental disabilities in general are more loyal employees and have less incidence of turnover and absenteeism as a group than the work population as a whole (Bellamy et al., 1989).

The disability should be referred to only when it is necessary to do so for a job-related reason or if the person with the disability wishes to bring up the subject. As previously discussed, under the 1973 Rehabilitation Act and the 1990 Americans with Disabilities Act (ADA), employers are expected to make reasonable accommodations for their employees with a disability but do not have to make accommodations that cause undue hardship on the employer. The ADA applies to all terms, conditions, and privileges of employment, including training, compensation, advancement, and discharge (P.L. 101-336).

Someone in the organization should be designated to be the expert on ADA and to help to see that there is full compliance. Supervisors who have questions can then turn to this person for advice. An employer not in compliance can have a case filed against them with the Equal Employment Opportunity Commission (EEOC), and the remedies are the same as under Title VII of the Civil Rights Act of 1964. Through consent agreement with the EEOC or a court order, an employer can be required to hire or promote a qualified person, provide reasonable accommodation, or pay back wages and attorney fees. With increasing proportions of the population aging and living with disabilities and with older workers likely staying longer in the work force, disabilities will become increasingly common in the workplace.

If a supervisor believes a person has a disability that is affecting job performance, the supervisor should not be hesitant to bring up the subject and offer ways to alleviate the problem. Supervisors should be aware, however, that many employees with disabilities are hesitant to bring up the subject even if they are aware they need help, either because they feel this will put them in a bad light and make employers reject them or because they believe they must pull their own weight, no matter what. This view may be enhanced for people with disabilities who are the only person with that disability in that organization or the only one who has reached a higher level of the organization. The factor of tokenism, being the only one, can add additional pressure, making the person more conscious of their actions. Managers should also be aware that many people with disabilities in effect are part of a different culture because they have a different perspective on life as a result of their life experiences. People have probably become most aware of this in regard to people with severe hearing impairments, but it is equally true of people with mental retardation or mental illness and people who have experienced abuse.

It is the supervisor's responsibility to stay job focused and, when necessary for the job, to bring up disability issues. The ADA does not prohibit employers from making inquiries or requiring fitness for duty or medical examinations when it is necessary to determine if the employee is still able to perform the essential functions of the job. Also, if periodic physical exams are required by medical standards under such laws as the federal Occupational Safety and Health Act (OSHA) or state or local law, they are allowed under the ADA (EEOC Interpretive Guidelines, 56 Fed. Reg. 35,751, July 26, 1991). Supervisors should also not hesitate to take corrective or disciplinary action with employees with disabilities. People with disabilities are competent and incompetent the same way people are who do not have disabilities. In turn, supervisors should consider them as readily for training and promotion as any other employee. Managers should make themselves aware of any prejudices that prevent them from seeing these employees as good sources for advancement.

Any discussions involving a disability should be made only with people who need to know based on job related reasons. When information is being transmitted to the appropriate people, it is important to be wary of the means of transmission. Using a fax machine or a cellular car, mobile, or cordless phone should be avoided. Fax messages are subject to misdialing and going astray. If a fax machine is to be used, it would be wise to have a clause giving permission to use a fax on the signed release of confidentiality authorization. Also, fax cover sheets should include a warning describing the confidential nature of the transmission and providing instructions on what to do if there is a misdial. As for the phone transmissions, all such phones involve broadcasts that can be intercepted if the channel is not secured ("New Technologies . . . ," 1992).

Disabilities should be treated as confidential matters the same as medical issues. For example, when an employee has signed a written waiver of confidentiality with an employee assistance program (EAP) and it is necessary to make an appropriate accommodation for a substance abuse problem, such as leave for inpatient treatment, it is appropriate for the supervisor, personnel, and the employee to discuss the substance abuse specifically for that purpose, or if a supervisor believes an employee may have an alcohol problem that is affecting his/her work, it is acceptable and necessary for the supervisor to discuss the work-related issue with personnel; what is not appropriate is discussing the possible alcohol problem with coworkers or customers. In cases that involve leaves, it is not necessary to discuss with coworkers more than the fact that the employee is on leave. However, it is better if permission is given by the employee to discuss the matter frankly. For example, in the case of substance abuse, it is helpful, if confidentiality has been waived, for an EAP professional to discuss the role of codependents and how supervisor's fellow workers should avoid that type of behavior upon the employee's return from rehabilitation.

Deciding what is appropriate and what is not is largely a matter of common sense, sensitivity, and considering if you were the employee how you would feel if this were said or done. However, the bottom line remains that in supervising an employee with a mental disability, supervision should be the same as for all employees; it should remain work behavior focused, the law should be followed, and the ultimate question to be answered is, what does this have to do with getting the job done?

Employee Support Services

Special programs can be made available to help persons with disabilities in the workplace. Support services are programs developed to integrate physically or mentally disabled or injured employees into the work force. The organization may provide an internal service that directs the process from identification through work reentry and that can be coordinated with other support services, such as vocational training and job modification, EAPs and wellness programs, disability management, vocational rehabilitation, and supported employment.

Supervision and Supported Employment

Employers can take advantage of various rehabilitation services, including supported employment, to bring persons with mental disabilities into their work force. Supervisors need to be made familiar with supported employment and the fact that their supervision in that case involves a job coach as well as the employee. It is the responsibility of the supervisor to train the job coach and employee. The supervisor or another staff person may provide the basic instruction, but the job coach will continue the training in aspects of the work that it takes the employee longer to learn or for which the job coach may need to use special training techniques for teaching the person.

Supported employment is a new approach toward people with serious mental disabilities. In 1984, Public Law 99-506 called for professionals to reevaluate services to persons with handicaps, to design service delivery systems to provide meaningful employment in community integrated work settings, and to include these people in service delivery systems. In 1986, the federal supported employment initiative was expanded in the reauthorization of the Vocational Rehabilitation Act. A new formula-based funding was established to enable state agencies to provide supported employment services and to allow funds to be used from the Basic State Grant Program under Title I. This led to supported employment programs becoming available in all 50 states. Under P.L. 99-508, supported employment must be provided by vocational rehabilitation services and mental health and mental retardation agencies. Over 25,000 persons with disabilities are believed to have entered the job market as a result of supported employment legislation (Wilson, O'Reilly, and Rusch, 1991).

Because individuals in supported employment may have severe disabilities, they are not suited for many jobs, but there are many other jobs that they can perform, and they are working in growing numbers in many organizations. One study found that proportionally more larger urban employers hired supported employees, but in real numbers, more supported employees were found working in smaller organizations. Public organizations hired more persons with disabilities by percentage, but service organizations hired more by raw numbers (Craig and Boyd, 1990). Some employer associations are encouraging employment of people with disabilities, including the National Restaurant Association.

A recent study of supported employment found that 30 percent of individuals with mental retardation were still employed in their original employment placement, 20 percent were employed in a subsequent employment situation, and 31 percent had lost their jobs and were awaiting new employment. Eighty-four percent were employed in food service and custodial work, and most of the positions required simple training (Shafer, Banks, and Kregel, 1991). Another study indicated that the majority of supported employees had a primary diagnosis of mild mental retardation (not the severely disabled at whom the program was aimed) and received wages equivalent to other employees hired under a minority status (Wilson, O'Reilly, and Rusch, 1991). Research has also shown supported employment to be cost effective. The wage earning capability of supported employees reduced the need for government expenditures for Supplemental Security Income (SSI), Social Security Disability Insurance (SSDI), public aid, Medicaid, and Aid to Dependent Children. Savings amounted to $26,138 per supported employee (Tines et al., 1990). Costs to employers to accommodate employees with disabilities is relatively low, with many accommodations being less than $50.

Supervisors need to have a clear understanding with the job coach regarding the responsibilities of the job coach, the length of time they will be available to assist the employee to do the job and train them, and their availability to return and provide support if the employee later becomes destabilized. The job coach is specially trained to work with people with mental disabilities. The job coach is there not only to help the employee learn the tasks of the job but also to help them learn the necessary social skills for the workplace. For example, many of these individuals lack the social skills necessary for good interpersonal relations and to be competitive and successful. Social skills elicit positive, neutral, or negative responses from others. The job coach can help the trainee learn appropriate social skills in the workplace.

Social skills are learned and governed by rules and include nonverbal as well as verbal behavior. In fact, nonverbal skills are sometimes the more difficult to learn, and this is true for people who have sustained brain damage through injury or disease as well as for individuals with mental retardation and some forms of mental illness such as schizophrenia. Nonverbal communication includes such things as the appropriate distance to stand from people, appropriate eye contact, and appropriate times and places for touching other people, as well as what parts of the body are acceptable to touch. This nonverbal communication is made more complicated because it also varies by culture. Verbal communication skills include appropriate communication skills such as when it is appropriate to speak, when not, what to talk about with whom, and in what manner. It is very important for supported employees to learn what communications are and are not appropriate in the work setting. Supervisors can learn from the job coach how to facilitate this process, and if they have several supported employees, they can provide language and social skills workshops. If the organization requires considerable interpersonal communication, the organization may include communication or nonverbal communication workshops for all employees.

Social skills are goal directed and determined by the individual. For example, they can be used to attract attention. If the method chosen by an employee to attract attention is inappropriate, the supervisor can work with the job coach to extinguish that behavior and to provide appropriate attention for desired behaviors. Enhancing these kinds of skills can be useful to the supervisor in working with all employees. Social skills are specific to specific situations; therefore, if a situation changes, a supported employee may need to be shown new appropriate responses. It should not be expected that a person can be taught one set of social skills that will be applicable to all situations. The supervisor should be prepared to assist in modifying behaviors as new situations arise. In some cases, it may be found that an employee does not develop adequate interpersonal skills, and in that case, an attempt should be made to place the employee in a situation where minimal interpersonal skills are required.

Another of the responsibilities of the job coach is promoting social acceptance of supported employees by encouraging interactions with coworkers. This assists the supported employee from becoming isolated in the workplace. Supervisors also need to make sure coworkers understand supported employment and the role of the job coach. They need to understand that the job coach is there to help the supported employee do the job and to train that employee and is not an extra employee available for other work.

Coworkers may adapt readily to having a supported employee coworker. One study found that a large percentage of coworkers advocated for supported employees at the workplace and that supported employees associated extensively with their coworkers at work, although there was little interaction outside the workplace. Over half of supported employees received training from coworkers. Employers were receptive to having coworkers assist supported employees. Two-thirds of employers would always allow a coworker to repeat an instruction, 71 percent would always allow a coworker to show the supported worker what to do, and 57 percent would always allow the coworker to physically assist the supported employee (Rusch et al., 1991).

MANAGING THE SUBSTANCE ABUSING EMPLOYEE

The employer and manager must also address the problem of the substance abusing employee, because they are a risk to the workplace and a potential liability. There are also legal requirements regarding addressing substance abuse.

A Drug-Free Workplace

There is a growing focus on establishing drug-free workplaces. Executive Order 12564 (September 15, 1986) established the Federal Drug-Free Workplace Program. That Executive Order required each executive branch agency of the U.S. government to establish drug testing programs for employees in sensitive positions and to determine its own random testing frequency. Testing coverage among agencies ranged from 4 percent to 100 percent (U.S General Accounting Office [GAO], 1992). In 1986 a president's commission issued a report saying that every employer should have clearly stated policies prohibiting drug use, possession of drugs, or being under the influence of drugs on the premises. The Drug-Free Workplace Act of 1988 established guidelines for employers to ensure a drug-free workplace. The law required employers receiving federal contracts or grants of $25,000 or more to develop a formal antidrug policy. The guidelines included drug awareness education, counseling, information about penalties for drug use violations, and the use of EAPs. Employees must notify the employer of any criminal drug conviction for a violation occurring in the workplace not later than five days after the conviction takes place. Notification must be made by the employer to their federal contracting agency within 10 days after receiving notice from the employee. The act requires that if an employee is convicted of any violations of the act, the employer must impose a sanction on or require satisfactory participation in a drug assistance or rehabilitation program. Failure to comply can result in termination of the grant or contract. The act does not require testing, but many employers do use urinalysis as a means to ensure a drug-free work environment. The Rehabilitation Act of 1973, which also covers employers taking federal funds, categorizes substance abuse as a disability. If an employee is identified as a substance abuser, the employer must make available assistance such as counseling to rehabilitate the employee before termination.

Drug Testing

The original ADA was amended to address concerns that drug abusers might use the protections of the ADA. The legislation now expressly excludes job applicants or employees who are currently using drugs and who are not otherwise disabled from the definition of a "qualified individual with a disability." The employer may prohibit the use of alcohol and illegal drugs by all employees and may require that all employees not be under the influence of those substances at work. Employers are not prohibited from using drug tests with applicants or current employees (P.L. 101-336, Section 105d, 1990). Information obtained during a medical exam and/or drug test must be confidential. Supervisors may be informed only of those aspects of the exam, including drug testing, that it is necessary for them to know about in order to make alterations to the new employee's work duties (P.L. 101-336, Section 102, 1990). Employees who have successfully completed a supervised rehabilitation program and are no longer addicted to or using the substance are covered by the ADA as a "qualified individual with a disability" (Section 511b).

The highest group of drug users are in the age group of 25 and younger, the age group over 40 seldom uses drugs, and the large bulk of drugs that are consumed are used by a small number of abusers (Reuter, 1988). Survey data indicate that professional/managerial workers, clerks, women, and those over 34 are significantly less likely to show evidence of current use of cocaine or marijuana. As of 1985, current cocaine use for those groups amounted to no more than 1 percent and marijuana use, 7 percent. Marijuana use was markedly higher among laborers, skilled trade, semiskilled trade, and service workers (Cook 1989).

A survey by the Department of Labor found that 3.2 percent of businesses had drug testing programs, but because more large firms tend to drug test, 20 percent of all private employees were in firms with drug testing. Nine percent of current employees and 12 percent of job applicants tested positive (U.S. Department of Labor, 1989). Employers test all of their employees; test employees based on the type of positions they hold, usually related to the need for public safety or security; or test employees based on whether the employee is suspected of drug use on the job or has been in a work-related accident. Organizational policy should clearly spell out the organization's substance abuse policy, and employees should be educated concerning those policies in orientation and training.

There have been many court challenges to drug testing. Federal and state employees are protected by the federal and state constitutions, and private employees are covered by some state constitutions or laws. The courts have established that drug testing in the workplace is constitutional for those employees who hold jobs that are sensitive to public safety and/or may jeopardize national security (Ban and Riccucci, 1991). In 1989 the U.S. Supreme Court upheld a federal regulation requiring railroads to administer drug and alcohol tests to workers involved in major train accidents or who violate certain safety rules (*Skinner* v. *Railway Labor Executives Association*, 489 U.S. 602) and upheld a drug testing program by the U.S. Customs Service requiring a urinalysis for employees seeking transfers or promotion to jobs having a direct involvement with or requirement of carrying firearms (*National Treasury Employees Union* v. *William Von Raab, Commissioner, United States Customs Service*, 109 U.S. 1384). In 1990, the Ninth Circuit Court of Appeals approved the random drug testing program of the Federal Aviation Administration and declared that it did not violate constitutional prohibitions against unreasonable searches (*Bluestein* v. *Department of Transportation*, 90 Ninth Circuit Court of Appeals 5183, July 10, 1990). The unannounced testing does not require any individualized suspicion of drug use and is not triggered by either a promotion or transfer, as in the Treasury case, or a specific event like a train accident, as in the Skinner case. Where there is a privacy right, typically employers must have reasonable suspicion in order to require an employee to participate in drug testing, or where there is random testing, the employee must be engaged in work related to public safety or national security.

Legal protections may be found in right to privacy, protection from unreasonable search and seizure, due process, negligence law, and contract law. Laws vary state by state in regard to drug testing of employees of private companies. The California Constitution has been found by the California Supreme Court to apply to private employers as well as government agencies. Employers can also be held liable for slander due to wrongful accusations of drug use. There also have been challenges to drug tests by employees who have been incorrectly tested as positive. An employer should seek legal advice before instituting a drug policy. If employees are represented by a union, the union also should be consulted.

If an employer decides to use drug testing, a written policy is needed. The policy clarifies rights, establishes authority and mutual responsibility, establishes procedures and consequences, and provides a means for communication regarding the problem. The policy should define the problem in workplace terms and avoid legal, moral, and medical definitions; safeguard privacy, due process, and confidentiality; avoid conflict with federal, state, and local laws; and should be applied equally through the organization (Smits and Pace, 1988).

Urinalysis is the most widely used method of drug testing and is one of the country's fastest-growing businesses (Schachner, 1990). The National Drug Institute on Drug Abuse in 1989 published a list of certified drug testing laboratories in the *Federal Register* on November 1, 1989. Breathalyzers are the most widely used alcohol testing device. Urinalysis screening consists of testing for a variety of chemicals and substances and may include alcohol but typically will identify only recent and heavy use. Confirmation testing identifies the existence of specific chemicals present in the body. Costs of drug testing vary. Use of drugs may also be determined by blood testing during a physical examination, and enzyme testing of the liver may provide information about alcohol use. Between October 1990 and March 1991, the federal government's agencies spent an average direct cost of $73.46 per test. Direct costs included review of test results by a medical doctor, purchase and submission of blind testing specimens for quality control, providing for employee urine collection, and obtaining laboratory testing services (GAO, 1992).

An employer must not only decide which employees to test and under what circumstances (mass random testing or fitness for duty testing, for example, at the time of an accident) but also determine what testing laboratory to use and what procedures will meet the requirements of that laboratory and the needs of the employer. In order to ensure that a specimen comes from the subject and not another person, observation of the act or other procedures are necessary. People have been known to obtain or buy urine samples of others and to secrete a sample on their body to substitute for their own. Direct observation is very offensive to many people and in most cases would be a violation of privacy rights and illegal. Instead, other procedures can be used, such as requiring presentation of a photo ID at the time of the test, not allowing purses or other large objects into the bathroom at the time of the test, restricting access to faucets to prevent dilution of the sample, use of a tamper-proof container, and testing for body temperature of the specimen. The sample should be carefully labeled and sealed by the person supervising the taking of the sample. The donor and collector should initial the container. Complete records regarding who took the sample, the donor of the sample, who had access to the sample for transportation, who tested the sample, and by which method it was tested must be carefully maintained. Confidentiality is essential. Until tested, the sample should be secured at all times.

The most common approach to drug testing is to screen with one test method and then to run a second test on any positive results from the first screening. Guidelines set up by the Department of Health and Human Services (DHHS) require the initial screening method to be immunoassay and the confirmation method to be gas chromatography/mass spectrometry. Testing has to be done very carefully, because there are legal substances that can be mistaken for illegal drugs. Of the people who test positive for drug use, 95 percent have families and have no criminal convictions (Finegan, 1990). Drug testing is a tool and not a complete substance abuse program, so it is important to also establish a prevention program.

Identifying the Substance Abusing Employee

The manager has a responsibility to identify substance abusing employees. This is important from a risk management standpoint, because supervisors and employers may be held accountable for the actions of their employees, and from the standpoint of maintaining a productive and rewarding work environment.

Substance abusing employees are not easy to identify, and women are more adept at hiding their substance use than men (Pape, 1992). Certain behaviors may indicate to a manager that an employee is having a substance abuse problem. These behavioral cues include absenteeism; accidents; excessive use of sick days; excessive compensation claims; difficulty with authority figures; isolation and withdrawal; apathy; chronic fatigue; persistent depression; frequent crying; major changes in eating or sleeping patterns; loss of interest in previously liked activities; anxiety; frustration; wild mood swings, hostility, or abusive behavior; wholesale changes in with whom the person associates; lying, especially about whereabouts; stealing; and sloppy appearance and carelessness about grooming. Some other possible signs of substance abuse include chronic eye redness, sore throat, or dry cough. A report of the results of investigations of employees who were involved in the use or transaction of drugs in the workplace revealed that drug users have some common characteristics. All employees who were involved in the selling of drugs were workers who had access to all areas of the business. Drug using employees tended to meet in remote areas of the facility and had at least one on-the-job injury but still maintained steady work habits. Over time, the productivity of the drug users always went down (Lousig, 1990).

If the supervisor believes an individual is under the influence in the workplace, the supervisor must take action. An employee under the influence is a liability, and if action is not taken, the supervisor and employer could be held liable for the action of the employee. This is especially critical if the employee is operating equipment or has contact with the public. Although it is essential to remove the employee from the workplace, the supervisor also needs to be aware that this type of confrontation may get an angry or abusive response. The supervisor should try to avoid confronting an employee under the influence of alcohol or other drugs alone. If possible, the supervisor should get the assistance of the personnel office, EAP professional, union representative, or security personnel. The first goal is to safely remove the employee from the workplace without injury to the supervisor or anyone else. This also means that the employee is not allowed to drive home. If the employee is cooperative, arrange for someone to drive them home or call and pay for a taxi to take them home. If they drive home and are in an accident on the way, that is a potential liability. The second goal is to provide due process and handle the procedure correctly so that the supervisor can collect evidence of the incident with proper documentation that can be used in a disciplinary proceeding. If the organization personnel policy requires drug testing for someone reasonably suspected of being under the influence, the policy should be invoked, the personnel office notified immediately, and the policy's procedures followed precisely.

Intervention

If a manager suspects that an employee is a substance abuser, the manager should seek to provide for an intervention. The manager should contact the personnel office and/or EAP and follow their advice. There are two goals to be accomplished. First, getting an appropriate professional intervention, for example, by an employee assistance professional, and second, documenting any work-related behavior to use in disciplinary proceedings. Providing assessment, referral, and counseling for substance abuse is a major function of EAPs. Managers need to be aware that they are on the front lines for identifying substance abuse and work problem behaviors and need to take action but that they are not professional counselors and should not try to diagnose or counsel the employee regarding substance abuse or other mental health problems. The EAP is the most important resource for dealing with these problems, and the supervisor can advise the employee on how to get help through that organization. If there is no EAP or other organizational program for counseling employees the manager must rely upon the personnel office to arrange an appropriate referral to a mental health professional. Under no circumstances should managers take it upon themselves to make an outside mental health referral (see Chapter 6 for more detailed information on EAPs).

Managers should be aware that when they are making a referral to the EAP or to the personnel office, they may meet with resistance. It is important not to prejudge how the employee will act — cooperative or rebellious. If employees rebel, they may try to engage the supervisor in a power struggle to prove their worth to the supervisor and themselves and to increase their self-esteem. The supervisor should be aware that rebellion usually results from underlying feelings of vulnerability and fear, shame, or hurt and that the employee may have trouble identifying these feelings and will display anger and rebellion instead (Cosgrove and McLellan, 1992). The supervisor should avoid entering into the power struggle and stick to discussing the problem job behavior, what change is being asked for and what help, such as the EAP referral, is being offered. The manager should stay focused on the specifics. Most organizations use voluntary referrals but if the organization uses a mandatory referral, the supervisor should be clear with the employee that the employee must go to the EAP. Also, the supervisor needs to make it clear to the employee that any disciplinary action is a separate process from the EAP and will continue regardless of the referral. The confidentiality of the EAP and any exceptions to that confidentiality also need to be pointed out. Because rebellion is about power, the supervisor can reduce the chance of rebellion by not providing power cues, for example by having a balanced seating arrangement, by sitting near the employee in an identical chair (not behind a desk), and by holding the conversation in a private closed door location where the employee cannot play to an audience. Supervisors should not take rebellion personally. Rebellious employees are able to "push buttons and pull strings only when you have lost perspective" (Cosgrove and McLellan, 1992). If supervisors have problems with getting hooked into power struggles, they might want to observe or take the advice of a supervisor who does not have this problem or they might want to have some personal counseling to resolve their own power issues.

If an organization has an EAP, they will be able to make referrals for substance abuse treatment. If there is no EAP, the personnel department needs to develop resources for handling employees with substance abuse problems. This may involve using the local public mental health services for referral or having a list of other mental health services available. Obviously, this will not be as helpful or professional as having EAP services for assessment and referral. The Rehabilitation Act of 1973 requires employers to make a reasonable accommodation to help an employee with an addiction problem. Although the employer is not required to accommodate an addicted employee if it would cause an undue hardship on the organization, it is expected that the employer will give the employee some assistance.

Preventing Relapse

Even after the substance abusing employee is identified and treated, the role of the employer is not over. The employer also has a responsibility in preventing relapse. Relapse is not an event but an ongoing process that can be interrupted at any time (Muchowski, Gorski, and Miller, 1982). The relapse process is progressive and gets worse until it is interrupted or changed. Relapse brings a return of the previous symptoms or the formation of other related symptoms. The person is in either the process of recovery or the process of relapse.

Although relapse is an internal process and is not the result of the environment, the manager can assist the process of recovery and intervene in the case of relapse. Society tends to blame women more for substance abuse problems, and their support systems are less likely to be retained than men's. The woman is more likely to be expected to return from treatment and immediately fulfill her role as employee. Managers need to be aware of this double standard and guard against it in themselves and the coworkers. The manager also needs to be aware of the signs of relapse so that a new intervention can be made promptly. The symptoms of Post Acute Withdrawal Syndrome (PAWS) are believed to be the leading causes of relapse. The most common symptoms are anguish; difficulty in conceptualizing; impaired thought process, including periodic confusion; long-term memory loss; low stress tolerance; memory impairment, including distractibility and impaired ability to concentrate, with limited attention span; mood swings, including emotional overreaction or numbness; overreaction to stress; physical coordination problems; preoccupation with negative emotions; and sleep disturbances. Employment is a predictor of a successful treatment outcome, but vocational counseling and financial and budget problems may also need to be addressed. For women, another predictor of success is the ability to relate with other women (Pape, 1992). Other women in the workplace may be helpful to recovering women.

Changing the Corporate Culture

For some organizations there has been a long history of substance abuse, particularly alcohol use, being accepted as part of the culture surrounding the work. The U.S. military has been one of those organizations, and they, like some other organizations, began in the 1980s to make a concerted effort to change their corporate culture. Heavy alcohol use and cigarette smoking have been characteristics of being a soldier (Bray, Marsden, and Peterson, 1991). This is also true for other occupations, such as police officers, and many blue collar workers. In the 1980s the military introduced new policies and programs to try to change this image. In 1984 the army discontinued "happy hours" at officer and enlisted clubs. Since 1986, the army has placed official letters of reprimand in the personnel files of any soldier convicted of driving while intoxicated and has given mandatory referrals to alcohol and drug abuse prevention programs. Base military police now conduct random stops of drivers and administer Breathalyzer tests. In 1987, the army established regulations to protect occupants of army buildings from passive smoke and prohibited smoking in many buildings. Many employers, like the military, have now created smoke-free work environments. The recreational drug use policies of the military are viewed as highly successful (Gardner, 1991).

PERSONALITY AND THE WORKPLACE

Personality factors and life experiences can have a major impact on the workplace. Disciplinary problems and terminations are often related to personality conflicts and emotional reactions. Many of these personality factors and ways of reacting were learned in the employees' families of origin.

Learning from the Family

Childhood dynamics play an important role in the workplace. It is important for managers to understand the role played by what one has learned from one's original family or one's family of origin. The way one learned to relate in the family carries over into adult relationships, including those in the workplace. The family and the work group share common group dynamics; these include norms regarding authority and leadership, cohesion, role stereotyping, and stages of development. People may take on a role in the workplace like the one they had in their families, such as gatekeeper for information, supportive member, negotiator, or maintenance leader (O'Sullivan, 1992). These roles may or may not be helpful. Language styles and patterns of communication may also come from the family. Families and work groups are held together by having a common identity. For some people, the work group may be even more important than their family. Supervisors need to be able to identify how their own family learning experiences affect how they function in the workplace and how their employees' childhood experiences affect how they function in the workplace. This will help the manager better understand why people are doing the things that they do and will help the manager separate what are really work-related issues that should be addressed through supervision and the disciplinary process, what are personality issues, and what are mental health issues that should be referred to the EAP (see Chapter 5).

Children of Alcoholics

Approximately 28 million children under the age of 18 live with at least one alcoholic parent, and at least 50 million adult children of alcoholics are in the work force. Children of alcoholics and other substance abusers often develop behaviors that enable them to survive their childhood years in the family but that, if carried into adulthood and the workplace, can be destructive. Children who grow up in families in which one or both parents are substance abusers may carry emotional scars into adulthood that can affect their relationships at work as well as their personal relationships. Employers may find making available support groups such as Adult Children of Alcoholics (ACA) is a helpful approach. The coping behaviors the child learned helped the child survive, but they may get in the way of the adult. These employees are often unaware of their dysfunctional behaviors, or if they are aware of the behaviors, they are unaware of where these behaviors have come from and joining a self-help support group may help them identify these behaviors and make changes.

People who have grown up with codependent behavior may use this behavior in the workplace, including being attracted to supervisors or coworkers with substance abuse problems. In an alcoholic family, rather than communication being clear and straightforward, it is often oblique, mystifying, and conducted through a third party (Black, 1981). Family crises are usually denied, minimized, or handled in a negative way, including violence (O'Sullivan, 1988). Characteristics of ACAs include judging themselves without mercy, overreacting to changes over which they have no control, being overly responsible or irresponsible, guessing at what is normal, giving loyalty where none is deserved (Woititz, 1983), seeking acceptance, and operating from a defensive posture (O'Sullivan, 1992). They and other employees who have suffered traumatic childhoods may suffer spontaneous age regressions. As John Bradshaw writes about himself:

> I began to have vivid memories of my childhood. I remembered one Christmas Eve when I was about 11 years old, lying in my darkened room with the covers pulled up over my head and refusing to speak to my father. He had come home late, mildly drunk. I wanted to punish him for ruining our Christmas. I could not verbally express anger, since I had been taught that to do so was one of the deadly sins, and especially deadly in regard to a parent. Over the years my anger festered in the mildew of my soul. Like a hungry dog in the basement, it became ravenous and turned into rage. Most of the time I guarded it vigilantly. I was a nice guy . . . until I couldn't take it anymore. Then I became Ivan the Terrible. . . . What I came to understand was that these . . . behaviors were spontaneous age regressions. When I was raging and punishing . . . with withdrawal, I was regressing to my childhood, where I had swallowed my anger and expressed it the only way a child could — in punishing withdrawal. . . . What I now understand is that when a child's development is arrested, when feelings are repressed, especially the feelings of anger and hurt, a person grows up to be an adult with an angry, hurt child inside of him. The child will spontaneously contaminate the person's adult behavior. (Bradshaw, 1990)

Codependence

Children and spouses of substance abusers often learn to be codependents, and children carry this behavior with them into adulthood. The codependents have a loss of identity. They are out of touch with their own feelings and needs. They feel someone else's feelings rather than their own. They worry over someone else's problems. The nonalcoholic spouse of an alcoholic tends toward anxiety, depression, phobic anxiety, obsessive-compulsiveness, interpersonal sensitivity, hostility, and psychosis (Steinglass, 1987).

Codependence is fostered in unhealthy families where there is alcohol or drug abuse or violence. Because the situation is life threatening, family members adapt by becoming chronically hypervigilant. Stress becomes a daily event, not a temporary state. Under this chronic stress, persons living with the alcoholic or abuser lose touch with their own desires, feelings, and needs. Children have trouble separating their thoughts from their feelings. The children focus on the outside and over time have trouble identifying their own feelings and difficulty generating self-esteem from inside. Fulfillment is looked for outside, in other people or work. This is codependence and indicates that as a child the person's needs were not met and as an adult the person has a wounded inner child (Bradshaw, 1990).

Managers can function as codependents, enabling substance abusing employees to continue their substance abuse by covering for them and by refusing to address job performance issues (Blair, 1987). However, organizations can also provide the structure and support necessary to transform addictive behaviors and other dysfunctional family behaviors such as sabotage into productive ones (Riley, 1990). EAPs and wellness programs and other approaches to establishing and maintaining healthy work environments can be provided to help employees develop their positive personality characteristics (see Chapter 6). These programs may also be of assistance with Type A personalities.

Type A and Type B Personalities

One way people's personalities have been characterized is by examining their behavior patterns and classifying them as Type A or Type B (Friedman and Roseman, 1974) or some type in between. This classification was developed by cardiologists, not psychologists. Type A people are characterized as quick tempered, with a low tolerance of incompetence and inefficiency. They attempt to accomplish or achieve more and more. Underlying the personality is insecurity and a driving need for approval. Type B people are characterized by being even tempered and slow to speak and act. They see themselves as worthwhile regardless of their achievements (Friedman and Ulmer, 1984). Most people fall someplace in between. Robert and Marilyn Kriegal (1990) have defined a Type C behavior pattern, involving transcendence, effortlessness, positiveness, spontaneousness, focus, and vitality.

Numerous national studies have demonstrated that high-strung Type A behavior pattern people are more prone to heart disease. In 1981 an authoritative panel, after examining the available evidence, judged Type A behavior pattern to be a risk factor for coronary heart disease, comparable in impact to smoking, elevated blood pressure, and elevated cholesterol. Subsequent research indicates that underlying hostility is the aspect of Type A behavior that is most strongly predictive of coronary heart disease (Dembronski and Costa, 1988). Researchers are trying to determine which Type A people are most at risk. A recent nine-year cohert study found that Type A behavior appeared to be associated with more rapid increases in two well-accepted coronary risk factors in young adults: the Type A pattern may reinforce the smoking habit and motivate people to use more cigarettes, and it may stimulate more rapid escalation of blood pressure. A stronger association was found in women and blacks than in men and whites. One possible explanation the researchers gave was that women and blacks find themselves engaging in Type A coping responses as a response to the challenges of social discrimination. "Those who measure as Type A in their late 20s are more likely to have experienced a steeper increase in blood pressure and smoking during the preceding decade than their Type B counterparts" (Garrity et al., 1990). One recent study found that Type A people with at least one hypertensive parent seemed to be at greater risk for developing heart disease (Collar, 1992). Wellness programs, addressed in Chapter 6, can help employees cope with personality characteristics that may be detrimental to their health. However, regardless of organizational assistance, not all employees will continue to be satisfactory employees for the organization, so managers must also be able to deal with discipline and termination.

DISCIPLINE AND TERMINATION

One of the least-liked aspects of management deals with discipline and termination. Managers are concerned about conflict and how the employee will react. That reaction likely will come from how they learned to respond as children. Children learn about authority from their parents, and as adults, they often respond to discipline in the same way they did as children. The most common responses are "(1.) becoming overly apologetic, (2.) becoming angry, (3.) remaining untouched by the discipline, and (4.) feeling hurt but yet able to accept the criticism" (Stark, 1992). Children learn from what their parents do, not what they say. Parents who did not model self-discipline may have undisciplined children who later appear in the workplace with problems such as procrastination, refusing to delay gratification, rebelliousness, stubbornness, and acting impulsively without thinking. Children who have been overdisciplined may appear in the workplace as rigid, overly controlled or controlling, obedient, and people pleasing (Bradshaw, 1990). Employees whose parents promoted their self-esteem and who learned at home that it was all right to feel slightly hurt at being corrected but also learned to use correction for change and growth are able to hear feedback and criticism and make appropriate changes. However, employees who are overly apologetic are often more concerned with whether the manager likes them than they are with listening to what was done wrong and correcting the problem. It may be difficult for them to make appropriate changes. More difficult are employees who take the attitude that discipline does not matter or they don't care. They disregard accountability for what they do, and it is difficult to get them to accept feedback or follow rules. However, employees who respond with resentment or anger may present an even greater problem and can be dangerous in the workplace. They do not hear directions or respond appropriately to limits (Stark, 1992). They will sometimes do what they want regardless of limits and may engage in sabotage or other destructive acts around the workplace. In extreme cases, they may resort to violent behavior.

Discipline

Most managers dislike disciplinary action, and many try to avoid it, which usually results in even more serious problems. Managers dislike discipline because it usually involves conflict, and sometimes that conflict includes anger. Anger can be out of control and result in verbal and physical violence. If anger is properly expressed, it can be positive. If handled properly by all parties concerned, anger can be a spur to positive corrective action. A positive action can be to ask questions, to clarify the issue, and to find a compromise. Anger is often an expression of fear. By the manager being compassionate and hearing the person out in an objective way, the problem may be resolved. However, it is also important to recognize when there is genuine anger and when someone is very angry, volatile, and potentially dangerous. In this situation, it is important to try to diffuse the situation. It is better to get both persons to agree to come back later to discuss the matter when everyone is better able to deal with it than to risk escalating the situation into violence.

When dealing with employees with suspected problems, whether substance abuse or other problems, the supervisor should stay work focused and follow the progressive discipline or other process called for by the organization's disciplinary process. The Department of Labor makes some recommendations for dealing with employees with suspected problems: develop and communicate objective job performance standards, so deteriorating performance can be documented; talk with the worker about the need to improve performance and determine whether workplace factors such as inadequate training are contributing to the problem; prepare a written memorandum documenting incidents and examples of the performance or attendance problems; hold a private meeting to discuss problems addressed in the memo and discuss needed improvements; set a timetable for improvement; and inform the employee of the availability of assistance for personal problems and encourage use of those resources (U.S. Department of Labor, n.d.). The supervisor should follow up to see if behavioral changes have occurred. The supervisor should remain behavior and performance oriented and continue the disciplinary process. If the employee uses the EAP, this may help the employee to make changes that will then result in termination of the disciplinary process. Because of confidentiality, the supervisor usually will have no feedback on whether the employee has used the EAP. However, that is not important; what matters is that positive behavior changes are made.

Termination

Unfortunately, in some cases an employee cannot be salvaged, and termination must occur. This is the most disliked job requirement of managers. Termination again raises the issue of conflict, and it also means an organizational failure. Either the organization has failed in its selection process in finding the right person for the job, or something has later gone wrong in the employer/employee relationship, and the employer has not been able to correct it. It is important that management analyze what has gone wrong with this particular placement, so that, if possible, they can take corrective action.

Termination is the final step in the discipline process. Usually it comes after a lengthy process of attempts to correct behavior and disciplinary actions under systems such as positive employee performance or progressive discipline. Generally, by this point, there have been informal warnings, formal written reprimands, and actions such as suspension. Occasionally, in the case of a major infraction, dismissal will occur virtually immediately. There will also be terminations when employees' services can no longer be used, for example, when an organization is downsizing or doing cutback management because of reduced budgets.

Before termination, most public employees of state and local governments must be told of the charges against them and given an opportunity to respond. The U.S. Supreme Court in 1985 ruled that most public employees have a constitutional right to a hearing before they are fired (*Cleveland Board of Education* v. *Loudermill* [105 U.S. 1487, 763 F. 2d 202] and *Parma Board of Education* v. *Donnelly* [105 U.S. 1489]). Federal regulations provide similar protections for most federal employees. Some state civil service systems, including California, and most union contracts covering employees in the public and private sectors have even more protections. Most employees in the public sector have tenured employment (a permanent employee), which provides job protections and requires cause for termination. Most employees in the private sector are hired as at-will employees, which traditionally allowed termination without protections and without cause. However, if there is any implication by the employer of supplying tenure to the employee, such as a personnel manual or someone in authority saying the employee is permanent or that termination is only for just cause, an at-will termination will probably not withstand a court challenge. Increasingly, even for private sector at-will employers, there is risk in trying to terminate without proper procedures and cause. For example, employees in both the public and private sectors can claim termination was based on discrimination, and the employer must be able to document the real work-related reasons for termination in order to defend themselves against such a complaint. As of January 1, 1993, a new law in California took effect providing protection from discrimination based on sexual preference. Almost immediately, five homosexual men filed suits against their employers for wrongful termination. It makes sense for all employers to have a written discipline and termination policy, to have specific procedures to be followed, and to document all cases. Terminations should be based and documented on undesirable work behavior. Wrongful termination cases can be very expensive and may even include compensation for emotional damage. This also reduces the stress on supervisors, because they have specific procedures to follow and are not left in an unclearly defined situation in which justifying their actions may be difficult.

From the standpoint of the manager who must terminate a subordinate, there is again a risk of an unpleasant and, occasionally, even dangerous encounter that may be even more intensified than disciplinary encounters. Managers should be trained in how to handle a termination. Supervisors should avoid terminations at already stress-filled times, such as holidays. If the termination is based on a disciplinary action, it is best to carry it out as soon as possible and not continue the stress on the manager of waiting to carry it out or on the employee of waiting to find out the outcome. The termination should be carried out in a private location, and unless the supervisor is very sure there will be no negative reactions, it is a good idea to have someone else there, such as someone from personnel. If a union is involved, the union representative should be present. The meeting should be kept formal and specific. Information should be provided concerning what the employee should do about vacating work space, seeing personnel to finalize the employee's benefits and paycheck, and informing the employee of any assistance still available to him/her such as EAP services or outplacement services. In disciplinary situations, it is best to have the employee complete all necessary business and leave the organization as soon as possible.

If the termination is because the employer can no longer use the services of the employee, including widespread layoffs, it is helpful to provide outplacement services to help the employee locate a new position. It can even be useful to provide outplacement services for employees who are terminated for disciplinary reasons. The service may be able to help them correct their situation. An employee may be able to perform better somewhere else if redirected to a different type of work or working environment. The offer of such assistance also improves the atmosphere at the time of termination and reduces the chance of a complaint or lawsuit being filed or feelings of hostility that later could result in violence.

Grievance and Arbitration

It is not unusual for an employee to grieve a termination. There are various grievance processes available. Most public sector organizations are covered by a central personnel system that provides for a grievance process that generally ends with a hearing before the civil service or merit system protection board. Much of the public sector, as well as some of the private sector, is also covered by collective bargaining agreements, which require grievance processes involving union representation and usually end with an arbitration procedure established in the Memorandum of Understanding (MOU). Most other private profit and nonprofit organizations have an established organizational grievance process.

It is important to have developed a written grievance process that can be followed by employees. A good grievance or arbitration process will usually result in a resolution of the conflict without an employee resorting to the court system. Otherwise, if the employee has grounds, he/she may seek redress in the civil court system, which may prove a lengthy and costly process for the employer. Where a formal grievance process is in place, the court will, in almost all cases, require the grievance/arbitration processes to be followed before the court hears the case. This gives an opportunity to settle the dispute without court action.

In order to successfully withstand a challenge, the manager must be sure the case has been carefully documented, and in the case of addictions, the courts and arbitrators will be looking for a response by the employer that tries to salvage the employee. An example of a case in which this did not happen is a case study in which an employee was observed at a distance by a supervisor who saw smoke, a flicker of light, and something being thrown away by the employee. The supervisor believed that the smoke smelled like marijuana. The use or possession of intoxicating drugs was not permitted on company property, and company rules allowed for medical examinations of employees at any time, but the employee refused to submit to a urine drug screen. The employee, who had seven years of a clean work record with that company, was discharged for allegedly smoking marijuana. The arbitrator ordered reinstatement of the employee with full back pay minus earnings and unemployment compensation that he received while not working for the company. The company was also allowed to drug test that one employee only for unannounced periods over the next 18 months, and the employee was to be assessed by a competent counselor for drug dependence at the time he was reinstated. The supervisor and company lost this arbitration because the supervisor's observation of what he believed to be marijuana use was not sufficient, because he did not see the employee put anything up to his mouth and what was thrown away was not recovered — there was no physical evidence. However, more important to other organizations are the other findings:

> The medical exam policy mentions nothing about drug testing. The company had not negotiated drug testing procedures with the union, a mandatory subject for bargaining. The severity of punishment is not commensurate with the violation. It is too severe. . . . After the hearing, the arbitrator informally suggested that the company seriously consider implementing a formal EAP and negotiating a drug testing policy with the union. (Burger, 1992)

This points up the importance of three aspects of successful discipline, termination, and arbitration: clear written organizational policy on discipline, drug testing, and termination; if a union is involved, negotiation of procedures with the union and clear incorporation of them in the MOU; and access to an EAP for referral of substance abuse and other problems so that employees may be appropriately treated and salvaged without having to resort to termination unless absolutely necessary.

There are many court cases and arbitration awards concerning termination and substance abuse. In 1983 an employee's grievance for wrongful discharge was upheld when the arbitrator held that the employee's discharge was discriminatory because of the leniency it had awarded to other employees with alcohol problems (*Youngstown*

Hospital Association v. *Service Employees Union* [82 LA 31]). This case emphasizes that arbitrators expect that employees in similar situations will be treated the same. In 1985 a court upheld an employee's grievance of wrongful discharge because the employer did not give the employee an opportunity to rehabilitate herself (*Allegheny Ludlum Steel Corporation* v. *United Steelworkers of America* [84 LA 477]), and another case that year found that an employee had been improperly discharged for intoxication because the finding of intoxication had been made by nonmedical personnel and there was no documentation of the cause (*Darron Company* v. *United Steelworkers of America* [85 LA 1127]).

In another 1985 case, the Supreme Court of Iowa held that under the Iowa Civil Rights statute, similar to the federal statute 29 USC section 706(7)(A), which prohibits discrimination against handicapped persons, alcoholism is a disability, and the employee's condition did not prevent him from performing his job, a prerequisite in both the Iowa and federal statutes. The employer's insurance carrier paid for the employee's treatment, and the director of the treatment center concluded that the employee had successfully completed the program. However, in another case, the court denied the employee's grievance for reinstatement because the court believed the employer was not required to reinstate the employee. Although the employee had successfully completed the company's alcoholic rehabilitation program after his discharge from the company, the court found the employee had an ongoing history of absenteeism that had ultimately been caused by alcoholism, and the employee had been disciplined for his absenteeism on many occasions. Although the company had offered to let him enroll in their EAP to enhance his prospects for future alternative employment, they had not promised to reinstate him (*Bemis Co.* v. *Paperworkers Local 914* [1983, 81 LA 733]). Thus, clearly, employees must be given an opportunity for rehabilitation, but this doe not mean such opportunities are limitless.

There have also been cases regarding mental illness. In the 1970s a court ruled that a company's mandate that an employee seek psychiatric evaluation before returning to work was unfounded because the only basis for the mandate was an unsubstantiated rumor that the cause of the employee's hospitalization was three self-inflicted gunshot wounds. There was also no evidence that the employee was not physically able to work (In re *United States Steel Corporation Sheet and Tin Operations, Fairfield Works* v. *United Steelworkers of America* [1970, 54 LA 572]). In 1973 a court ruled that the employer's requirement that the employee submit to a psychiatric evaluation before returning to work was not justified when there was no substantial evidence that she could not perform her work or that she constituted a threat to her health and safety or to the health and safety of coworkers (In re *Jamestown Telephone Corp.*

v. *Jamestown Telephone Workers Union* [61 LA 121]). Although a court did not see that employee as dangerous, some employees may be a danger in the workplace.

VIOLENCE IN THE WORKPLACE

As mentioned above, an employee can react to discipline with anger and violence, or violence may occur during high-stress times of organizational change in the workplace, such as closures or layoffs. There is a potential for violence with substance abuse and some other mental health problems. Some occupations and work sites are particularly vulnerable to violence, such as police officers, mental health workers, and nursing home staff. For example, one study listed the following injuries reported by nursing home aides: black eye, eye injury, swollen arm, torn shoulder cuff, knee injury, injured jaw, and dislocated thumb; verbal abuse also occurred (Lusk, 1992a). The numbers of violent incidents to nursing staff are small, but the rate of injuries from assaults may exceed the rate of injuries to construction workers, the most hazardous U.S. industry (Lusk, 1992b). A study in Ohio identified police officers, gasoline service station employees, real estate employees, and hotel/motel employees as being at the greatest risk for occupational violent crime injury and death. Employees of convenience food stores and those in the real estate industry had the most reported rapes (Hales et al., 1988). The U.S. Post Office has had several incidents of employees or former employees entering the workplace with guns and shooting supervisors and fellow employees. In addition, domestic violence may be brought into the workplace when a spouse or lover attempts to injure or kill their loved one (16 percent of cases of violence in the workplace) (Davis, Honchar, and Suarez, 1987). Also, there is the risk of a client or customer who has developed a grudge returning to do violence.

The fastest growing type of homicide in the United States is murder in the workplace. Also, the number of workplace suicides appears to be on the rise (Thornburg, 1992). We increasingly see on the evening news incidents of violence in workplaces. There are an estimated 800–1,400 people murdered at work each year and an unknown number of nonfatal injuries due to workplace violence. Homicide is the third leading cause of death in the workplace (13 percent), following motor vehicle injuries and machine-related injuries. Although the majority of victims are male, it is the leading cause of occupational death for females, resulting in about 150 deaths per year. Victims are also more likely 65 or older and in sales, although laborers and transportation workers also have a high risk (Centers for Disease Control [CDC], 1987). Approximately 42 percent of fatal occupational injuries for women are due to murder. For men, the percentage is 11 percent (CDC, 1990). Causes of death include gunshot wounds, stab wounds, asphyxiation, and blunt trauma (Levin, Hewitt, and Misner, 1992).

Just one of many recent workplace incidents occurred in September 1991, when a gunman, angry because his wife couldn't have more children, entered a maternity ward of a hospital in Utah and threatened to start shooting babies unless the doctor who sterilized her was brought in. The obstetrician had performed a tubal ligation on the man's wife two years before, and the couple had eight living children. In addition to guns, the man had explosives and threatened to blow up the hospital. Over an 18-hour period, the gunman took nine hostages, and one nurse was killed when she tried to get the gun away from him. Another nurse, who delivered a baby in a booby-trapped office during the hostage taking, finally persuaded the man to surrender ("Hostages Recall . . . ," 1991). Cases such as this one show how difficult it is to determine when a violent incident may occur.

Incidents of violence also put the organization at risk for a civil action. Police and social service agencies have been held liable for inappropriate actions of their employees, including negligently retaining an unfit person as an employee (Meier, Farmer, and Maxwell, 1987), and lawsuits over negligent security may occur after an incident, as in the case of a woman and her supervisor who were shot by her husband (*Tepel* v. *Equitable Life Assurance Society of the U.S.* [Case No. 801363, San Francisco Superior Court, 1990]). As noted in the previous chapter, there is no reliable test to predict dangerous or violent tendencies or behaviors. It is the responsibility of the organization to catch problems early and handle them through the disciplinary process. Even so, risk of violence in the workplace remains. Every organization should have a basic plan of what to do when confronted in the workplace with someone who may be dangerous, and training should be given to managers and employees on what to do and not to do under such circumstances.

Offender behavior is usually the result of childhood violence, suffering, and unresolved grief. The once-powerless child takes on the role of the offender adult. Physical, sexual, and severe emotional abuse may be the precursors of adult violence. It is a form of identification with the offender. A psychiatrist, Bruno Bettelheim, developed this concept in work with survivors of German concentration camps and it has been carried on in work with prisoners of war and terrorism and adult survivors of severe child abuse. Children learn to survive severe violence by abandoning themselves and taking on the identity of the offender. Under stress, the adult may regress to the behavior learned as the child. In less frequent cases, the offender may have been overindulged and oversubmitted to by adults and left with feelings of superiority. These children learn to believe that they deserve special treatment from everyone and that they can do no wrong. As adults, they have no sense of responsibility and blame their problems on someone else. Also, in a few cases, the person has serious psychological problems resulting from mental illness or disorder that results in violent behavior (see Chapter 2). Regardless of the reasons for the violent behavior, however, the safety of others must be considered primary.

The physical setting should be addressed first. All organizations should make sure that there is an emergency number clearly visible on all phones. If the organization has its own police or security force, their number can be used; if not, the community emergency number can be used. The object is to use the number of the closest source of professional help. This assumes the organization's security or police force is trained in how to deal with this type of potential or actual violence. It should not be assumed that in an emergency, people will remember the number. A simple sticker can be made up and placed on all phones. The numbers should be large, so someone can read it even if they have lost their glasses. All employees should be trained in the location and use of all emergency exits, and those exits should be kept free and clear for emergencies at all times.

If employees work in situations where there is a lot of exposure to other people and do work in which conflicts with persons sometimes arise, they should be trained in how to set up their personal work space for escape. They should arrange their space so that the potentially dangerous person is not between them and escape. For example, the interview chair should not be set up between the only door and the employee doing the interview. Emergency hidden silent alarms should be installed. Doors should be left open, and coworkers should be trained to intercede or to phone for help when there is an indication of trouble, such as shouting, or when a silent alarm is triggered. A trained emergency response team should respond while other employees and clients/customers are quietly evacuated.

Some work environments will require controlled access to the building, increased exterior lighting, camera surveillance, bullet-proof cubicles, bulletproof vests, limitations on firearms on the premises, restricted hours of public contact, and provisions for money handling, such as drop safes and cash register visibility (Levin, Hewitt, and Misner, 1992). The physical environment should also be examined to reduce opportunities for suicide. For example, if the organization is located in multistory buildings, are the windows and open stairwells accessible for jumping? Closing off or screening high jumping points that may be an invitation for someone looking to commit suicide should be explored. (This should be done while keeping in mind fire safety.) Many universities, for example, have closed off public access to their bell towers because they were being used for suicide attempts.

Employees working with customers should be taught how to greet each customer and how to deter robbery (Levin, Hewitt, and Misner, 1992). For employees who have a lot of exposure to working with others and for all managers, there should be training in how to react to a conflict situation with conflict resolution techniques. They should be trained in how to contain a situation, how to negotiate, and how to respond or take action only when all else fails. This should cover how to defuse a situation, including the importance of body language. Eye contact and other body language must show neither fear and submission nor hostility and violence. Violence can be triggered by either acting like a victim or an aggressor; in the language of transactional analysis (TA), the person should stay in the adult.

TA has been used to improve communication in conflict situations. TA has been used for training police personnel to help them understand people better and to bring situations under control more easily. The New York City Police Academy has taught this approach. TA has also been used to work with potentially violent clients in high-risk settings, such as welfare eligibility offices. Kaplan and Wheeler (1983) show how to use TA as well as anxiety management training and assertive training to defuse violence. Staff are warned to stay with their adult when faced with anxiety, because a humorous response from the child is risky and a parental stance can spark rebellion. "Communication that implies equality is defusing and helps the client reclaim a sense of control and power. At any point in the assault cycle it is helpful if the client can be hooked into his adult" (Kaplan and Wheeler, 1983, p. 342) (see Chapter 5 on TA). There is even a computer software program that can be used in training for how to handle workplace conflicts peaceably. A threat to kill a coworker is among the ten scenarios offered. The program describes a situation and then asks a question, with five different courses of action. If the wrong answer is chosen, the program tells why it was wrong and reviews the facts of the case. After the case is resolved, the program offers additional information on the issue (Wisdom Simulators, Inc., 1992).

Employees should be trained to put their safety and that of other employees and clients/customers first and to not take risks in trying to disarm an armed perpetrator. However, employees must realize that every situation is different and the only overall advice that can be given is to stay calm, think through any action to be taken, and stay in the adult, acting rationally and avoiding escalating the situation. An example of using these behaviors in handling a dangerous situation occurs in the following case, which a professional recounted. An employee was determining the eligibility of a client for a program. She made the mistake of being in an isolated room with a closed door for the interview. During the interview, she realized the person was severely emotionally disturbed. When asked why he had quit his last job, he refused to respond, turned sideways in his chair, and folded his arms across his chest. The interviewer realized his nonverbal expression meant he was angry and potentially dangerous. She was afraid she could escalate the situation by calling for help (there was no hidden alarm) or going for help, so she asked if he could write down the reason. After writing the reason, very laboriously, she read his account of his being pursued by people from Oregon with guns. His nonverbal communication had remained very hostile, so by keeping her presence of mind, remaining rational, and calm, she told him that because he was being pursued by people with guns from Oregon, he had to quit his job, therefore, it was not a voluntary termination, and he was qualified for the program for which he was applying. His nonverbal expression immediately relaxed. She had accepted his view of the world, even though she knew it was paranoid; therefore, she decreased his hostility and was able to get him to leave without escalating the situation. She then informed her supervisor, and they contacted the proper authorities.

Security personnel or the police are frequently the first to respond to a crisis. They provide emergency assessment of the crisis, violence, substance abuse, unusual behavior, or altered mental status. When help is obtained from security or the police, the offending employee or client may be taken to jail or to a psychiatric facility. Some communities have emergency psychiatry mobile crisis programs that are coordinated with police services.

If criminal actions occurred, the employer should seriously explore options regarding pressing charges and should obtain the advice of the organization's attorney. If the person is charged by the police or a complaint is filed by the employer or others, the person may be released with or without bail pending a trial or, in a mental health case, a hearing. If the person appears to have a psychological problem, he/she probably will be taken to a mental health facility. Involuntary civil commitment may be difficult to obtain, because there are many legal protections for someone being involuntarily committed. If people refuse to voluntarily commit themselves and they do not appear dangerous to themselves or others at the time they are examined, they will probably be released immediately. If they are held, unless they are seriously disturbed, they will probably not be held for longer than a 72-hour examination period.

Because even in the case of serious violence, the offender may be back on the street in a very short period, the employer must immediately make a plan to secure the safety of the work site and employees. It may be possible to obtain a restraining order from the court. In cases of serious violence and a potential return of the offender, this should be pursued. It will not prevent the offender from returning, but it will make it easier for the police to remove the person if he/she returns. It may be necessary to hire a private security firm for a period of time. Although most offenders will not return to do violence, this should not be assumed, and precautions should be taken. If the offender is an employee, the safety of supervisors and other personnel who must work with this person in the disciplinary or termination process must be considered.

Every organization should have a policy regarding confidential reporting of any threatening statement to human resources or security. Such reporting should result in careful interviewing of the person reporting. Information needs to be gathered, documented, and then assessed by a specialist who deals in assessing potentially violent employees. If warranted, a crisis management team of legal counsel, human resources, and security should be formed to oversee other needed steps, such as background checks and interviews by a psychologist with the reporting source, other witnesses, and the person believed to have made the remarks. Various alternatives may be explored based upon a finding of dangerousness by the psychologist. These include referral to counseling, resignation, termination, restraining orders, and additional security depending on the type of organization and the state law (Cawood, 1991).

If, in spite of all precautions, a violent incident occurs, managers need to be aware that the emotions that result from the incident need to be addressed. If painful emotional memories are not dealt with, the defense mechanism of repression may take over, shifting them to the unconscious mind, where they may later cause many problems. This can result in posttraumatic stress disorder (PTSD) (see Chapter 2), and the failure to dissipate psychic energy may result in inhibition of the immune system and many physical problems or later mental health problems (see Chapters 2 and 3). Research shows incidences of PTSD are similar among hospital staff, police, and fire and rescue personnel who have been victims of violence or other traumatic experiences (U.S. Department of Health and Human Services, 1987; Carmel and Hunter, 1989; Williams, 1987). One of the most hazardous work settings is that of mental health facilities. In one study, 62 percent of 138 clinical staff respondents reported experiencing a critical incident involving a serious threat to life or physical harm or witnessing a serious injury or death, with 62 percent having had such experiences within the previous six months. Of that staff, 61 percent reported having symptoms of PTSD, and 10 percent of them would have been given the DSM III-R diagnosis of PTSD because of the number of symptoms reported. Of the nonclinical staff, 28 percent of the 76 respondents had experienced a traumatic critical incident, and 12 percent had had such an experience in the previous six months. Eighteen percent had PTSD symptoms, with 7 percent having enough symptoms to qualify for a diagnosis (Caldwell, 1992).

An event such as a shooting, being taken hostage, or being physically attacked or verbally threatened is referred to as a "critical incident" (CI). We now know that the stressfulness of traumatic situations can be assessed and appropriate action such as debriefing and therapy can be taken. Organizations that are subject to traumatic events, such as police and fire, may have special critical incident debriefing teams available at all times. Other organizations, if an incident occurs, may be able to use their EAP or mental health counselors in the community. Chapter 6 discusses in more detail programs to address critical incidents.

For employees who have been in a hostage situation, a special intervention model by trained professionals may be required. That model emphasizes the importance of creating a healing social environment immediately upon release, which encourages cohesiveness with other victims, isolates the victims from external groups, promotes abreaction (release of feelings), and restores a sense of power to the victims and reduces their feelings of isolation and helplessness (McDuff, 1992).

Violent behavior also may not be directed specifically at other persons but may appear in the form of damage to property through sabotage or fire setting or may be directed against the self as suicide. With many organizations dependent on information management systems, computer systems may be at risk. Viruses can be used to infect computers, and an employee seeking revenge or an ex-spouse wanting to strike back can cost hours of work and cause many dollars' worth of damage. Employees need to be made aware that when they are having domestic problems, they need to be especially careful about bringing disks from home to use in company computers. One woman who received a floppy disk from her ex-husband found that it erased everything on her computer, resulting in the loss of 800 hours of work, worth more than $9,000 ("Poetic Man . . . ," 1992). Many states have laws that make it a felony to introduce a virus into someone's computer without the person's knowledge or permission.

Some acts against property have the potential of endangering people as well, and a suicide at the workplace can be very damaging psychologically to other employees. Any threat of suicide, violence, or sabotage should be taken very seriously. Pathological fire setting is a not uncommon behavior among persons with serious mental illness, and pyromania is a disorder that involves a lack of ability to control the impulse to set fires. Fires may also be set in revenge or as a way to communicate. Communicative arson may be the most common form of pathological fire setting, and psychiatric facilities and prisons are particularly subject to that type of behavior. Fire is a medium of expression for people who avoid confrontations and verbal exchanges. Fire setting is relatively easy and has a high success rate, and this may encourage people who have had many failures in life (Geller, 1992). People with personality disorders, especially antisocial personality disorder, may be dangerous to people or property at the workplace (see Chapter 2). One way to reduce the chance of violence in the workplace is to deal effectively with change in the workplace.

CHANGE IN THE WORKPLACE

There are many changes that can occur in the workplace, including career change, organizational change, layoffs, changes from the external environment, and retirement which can cause emotional distress.

Career Change

There is a need for managers to be more aware of the impact of career change on mental health and the workplace. Career change has become a major area of interest. In 1978 it was estimated that 40 million Americans were in some form of career transition, and in 1980, Rochelle Jones referred to midcareer changers as a new social phenomenon, where midlife crisis brings on career crises 80 percent of the time and where 40 percent of working people over the age of 40 have seriously thought of changing their careers. Some of the reasons for that need for change are rebellion at others' expectations, a need to see the results of one's own work, and a desire to control one's own life (Jones, 1980).

A Dutch anthropologist, Arnold van Gennep, was one of the first to discuss life transitions at the beginning of the century and coined the term "rites of passage." Erik Erikson went on to define life cycles and establish an eight-stage model from infancy to old age. Daniel Levinson (1978) recast Erikson's work into a broader social context and established nine phases from ages 17 to 65. He viewed these periods as alternating between stable, structure-building times and changing transitional times. Timothy Lehmann (1978) separated out male- and female-specific tasks and events. He saw males in midlife as facing the realization of the gap between their dreams and the compromises they made and traditional women beginning to build dreams as their nests emptied. Gail Sheehy in *Passages* (1974) viewed traditional women as being rejuvenated as they moved out of parenting roles and saw men as seeing their lives much more in terms of their career advancement, with the family in a helping or hindering role.

Managers need to be aware that the work force is increasingly dynamic, with younger workers expected to make as many as five career changes over their working lives. Many employees will have a need for change over their careers. Sometimes this need can be met through training or career advancement in the organization. Some organizations have career development centers that help employees identify what they would really like to be doing and reach that goal. However, for some employees, the need for change will require a change in environment. The supervisor needs to respect their desires and provide them with assistance in making the transition. Trying to talk employees out of change and to hang onto them may prove counterproductive because if they remain dissatisfied, that dissatisfaction will eventually affect their productivity.

Organizational Change

The 1980s and early 1990s have been a time of organizational change. Many organizations have decided to flatten hierarchical organizations and eliminate large numbers of middle managers. Other organizations have decided to discontinue certain types of work and, in some cases, have shifted that work to contractors. This has been a time of downsizing for many organizations, and this is likely to continue for some time. Downsizing may involve the closure of whole facilities or reductions in numbers of employees at facilities that will continue to operate. Because organizational change in recent years has meant job losses, management should be aware that any organizational change they make, even if it will not include a loss of jobs, is likely to be met with concern. It is not surprising that in the atmosphere of the 1990s, employees associate change with loss. Even outside the current environment, organizational development specialists know that people tend to be insecure about change.

Organizational change should involve careful planning, open communication, and a designated change agent who oversees implementation of all changes and who can answer any questions or concerns about the change. Managers should be aware that change is stressful and that the stress can be reduced by open communication and allowing as much participation as possible by those whose positions will be involved. Participation means empowerment, and empowering people in the change process will enhance their psychological well-being. Employees who are more secure will adapt to change better, and a smooth change process will enhance the environment and productivity of the organization.

Relocation

Even relocations in which there will be no layoffs may be stressful. A study by Runzheimer International, an Illinois consulting firm, found that over 90 percent of employees resisting relocation did so because of concerns about uprooting their families. Among other concerns were that the new location was too far (47 percent); they did not like the new location (36 percent); they were the family's secondary wage earner (26 percent); they thought there were limited job opportunities for their spouse at the new location (26 percent); and the new location was high cost (22 percent). The consultant recommended being sure the right location had been selected to provide for a high quality of life with reasonable housing and living costs and good schools. Other ways to ease the transition were by offering all employees the same relocation package, involving the families in all communications about the move, and sponsoring orientation trips to the new location ("Study Addresses . . . ," 1992). Preparation and special assistance can aid employees and their families in making a successful transition (Anderson and Stark, 1986).

Relocations may be national or international. Alcoholism is cited as one of the major ways in which employees adjust to international relocation. Expatriate communities have been estimated to have alcoholism levels twice as high as home communities, and spouses are noted to be particularly at risk, not only for alcohol abuse but also for stress-related mental health problems (Fontaine, 1983). Overseas relocation programs should be involved with the assessment, recruitment, and evaluation of people suitable for the assignment, their orientation, on-site support, and reentry. Reentry programs are aimed at helping government and corporate employees who have been working overseas to return to the United States. Research shows that reentry into the original culture is a more difficult transition than moving to a foreign culture (Adler, 1981).

Layoffs

When employees begin to suspect that a closure or layoffs are going to occur, the grapevine becomes superactuated. Rumors are rife. It is important that management prepare careful and accurate formal communications for all employees. Having good up-to-date written communications on what is happening and what will happen is vital. Maintaining open communication with the employees is essential. If decisions have not yet been made, management should tell the employees that and explain to them the process that is occurring to make decisions. Channels should be provided via the union or supervisors for employees to make their concerns known.

When layoffs are being planned, there should be a committee to address that action. Members of the personnel department and EAP should be a part of that committee. The committee should plan programs that will help employees who are being laid off. Severance packages should be designed, including health benefits, that will continue the mental health as well as the physical health coverage of the employees. Also, plans should be made for outplacement services for helping laid-off employees find new employment and for transition services. If possible, an outplacement firm or transition services should be contracted. Included in these programs should be enhancement programs, such as an extension of EAP services for six months after the layoff. The committee should also make sure that there are procedures in place for handling possible violence and a critical incident response team. Any threat of violence should be taken seriously, because there is a potential for violence during times of high-stress change. These programs are aimed at keeping the employees working until the final layoff or closure, helping the employees adjust to the change, and providing proper benefits to help the employees and their families undergo transition and get through a period while seeking new employment.

Dislocated workers frequently have emotional problems that affect them and their families. The job loss adjustment process has been likened to the stages of death described by Kubler-Ross (1969), including denial, anger, bargaining, depression, and acceptance (Amundson and Borgen, 1982; Jones, 1979). The National Commission on Unemployment and Mental Health identifies five stages of the dislocation experience: first, there is a pre–job loss period, characterized by shock, anxiety, fear, and increasing stress as the layoff date nears; second, there is a stage of separation from the job, characterized by an initial decrease in stress and anxiety and new hope for the future; third, there is a denial stage, characterized by positive attitudes while financial resources like severance pay and unemployment insurance are available; fourth, a critical point is reached as financial deprivation increases, family relations are strained, and personal and financial risk increase, along with hopelessness; and fifth, is the period of extensive job search when financial resources are exhausted and personal relationships are very strained as the person feels lost, desperate, confused, and out of control. Serious problems like substance abuse and suicide may appear at this time. Problems may be intensified for older workers, who may find their age is a major barrier to reemployment.

Unemployment is related to a low level of self-esteem, often accompanied by self-blame. Laid-off employees blame themselves for being unemployed, for not finding work, and for having initially made their career choice. Divorce and separation rates are 3.5 times higher among the unemployed (Neece et al., 1991), and there is an increased risk of substance abuse and mental health problems (Institute of Science and Technology, 1986). Economic deprivation has been suggested to be the key variable in the correlation between economic change and mental health (Ferman and Gardner, 1979). A 1983 study indicated that displaced workers reported higher levels of agitation, depression, difficulty sleeping, and frustration when compared with other unemployed persons (Benson, 1990). It is estimated that for each 1 percent increase in the unemployment rate, suicide rates increase by 4.1 percent, state mental hospital admissions rise 3.5 percent, homicides increase 5.7 percent, state prison admissions increase 4 percent, cirrhosis mortality rises 1.9 percent, cardiovascular deaths increase 1.9 percent, and total mortality rises 1.9 percent. It is also estimated that 20–40 percent of the increase in outpatient mental health service utilization is attributable to unemployment rates (Benson, 1990).

Managers should be provided training to deal with the situation. They should be taught what and how to communicate to their employees; they should be given a resource person who can address questions or problems that they encounter; they should be told what their role is in regard to selecting employees to be laid off; and they should be encouraged to continue their supervisory activities, to not ignore problems, and to continue disciplinary actions and EAP referrals.

Outplacement and Transition Services

Outplacement and transition services are very important to easing the stress of layoffs. Outplacement counseling is provided by contract consultants. Typically, the contractor receives 15 percent of the person's total earnings for the 12 months prior to termination, with the terminating company paying the fee. The consultants work with the employees on improving their employment appearance and skills. They are not employment agencies, although some do provide sources for possible employment. Typically, the employee is kept on salary while the outplacement team administers assessment tests, helps write a resume, and puts the employee through a series of videotaped mock job interviews.

The Stroh Brewing Company provides an example of the use of transition services that go beyond outplacement. In 1985, Stroh decided to close their Detroit brewery, which employed 1,159 employees. They decided to set up two local transition centers: one for salaried employees and one for hourly employees. Program elements included outreach, orientation, job-search skills workshops, basic remedial education, job development, skills training, and ongoing counseling. The union was consulted and made a part of the process. Subcontractors with specialized skills were hired to deliver the services. Some employees were transferred to other Stroh facilities, but job developers contacted more than 4,000 employers to help find work for those laid off. Approximately 1,400 job orders were obtained through that job development. The transition centers were kept open 13 months, and during that time, continuous efforts were made to keep former employees coming in. At the end of 13 months, there was an overall placement rate of 98.3 percent, with over 80 percent finding comparable work. The company spent $1.5 million plus $600,000 in government funding, but the company believed that it had been worth it for the past employees and their current ones.

The program also had a positive effect on employees who were not affected by the plant closing. These employees, who were very much aware of how the affected employees were being treated, now perceive Stroh as more than just a good place to work. They see Stroh as a company with a genuine concern for its employees. (Franzem, 1987)

As already noted, loss of employment is like other major life losses; it involves the grief process, and employees experience stress and the major symptoms of loss, including shock, denial, anger, guilt, and fear. It is important to help employees overcome denial and develop a realistic sense of what is happening and to help them to plan how to deal with it. If the organization has an EAP, the EAP can provide workshops to help employees adjust and cope. If there is no EAP, a consultant with experience in doing this type of work can be hired. It is important to provide employees with this type of support. One experienced consultant suggests holding initial workshops to deal with fear, shock, and loss, followed by additional workshops two months later to deal with the practical issues such as basic financial planning, preparing for new employment, new career development, continuing education, entrepreneurship, and handling personal and family stress (Bibby, 1992).

When the closure or layoffs are complete, it does not mean everything is over. Managers need to realize that workers who remain may experience survivor guilt. Employees may remain frightened and wonder when this will happen again and will they be next. Bonds among employees may have been broken. Workshops and counseling should continue to address these problems as there is a return to normalcy (Bibby, 1992).

External Changes

The outside environment may also cause changes that need to be addressed. For example, Operation Desert Storm affected large numbers of employers. Many employees were traumatized by the events unfolding in the Middle East and could hardly tear themselves away from televisions and radios. For some of these employees, their loved ones were a part of the military forces, and many employees who were in the National Guard were themselves called up to either go to the Middle East or replace troops that had gone there. The context of Desert Storm also played a significant part in the reaction to it, as it helped to release emotions that had been suppressed about Vietnam.

There are several things for an employer to consider when a major event outside the organization causes change in the organization. In the case of Desert Storm, it was important for employers to realize that they were going to lose some productivity and that they should recognize the emotional significance of the event. Employee concerns could be eased by allowing televisions and radios in the workplace, even if that was not usually the accepted norm. Also, supervisors could show some leniency in allowing more than the normal social intercourse. In that type of event it is important to let people talk about it, process it, and reassure each other. Allowing people to deal with the shock and trauma by talking about it and supporting each other while it is happening is very important in preventing more serious problems later. It is also important for supervisors to take on a very supportive, reassuring, and comforting role at that time. Within a few days, people will begin to recover, and they will respond with renewed productivity. They will have positive feelings about having been well-treated at a time when they needed support.

An event like Desert Storm also calls for making sure professional resources are available through the EAP or other resources. Those who have loved ones in the military may need some group or individual counseling, and in the case of Desert Storm, because it awoke memories of Vietnam, Vietnam survivors and their loved ones needed assistance as well as others who at any time had suffered any type of war trauma. An event like Desert Storm can reawaken memories of other wars, and some people need to receive assistance for PTSD. Also, events such as war can exaggerate dysfunctions already in families or trigger dysfunction in previously functional families, therefore, counseling resources need to be available to families, particularly children, and readjustment services need to be available for employees and their families for when the employee returns to the home and workplace.

Fortunately, the rates of psychiatric evacuation from the Gulf War theater were the lowest in modern conflicts, only 2.7 per 1,000 evacuations per year or 6.6 percent of total medical evacuations from that area (Hale, 1992; Labbate and Snow, 1992). The Department of Veteran's Affairs committed funds and personnel for transition to civilian life upon return. One small study of U.S. troops who returned to Germany found that personal injury appeared to contribute to psychological trauma and the later development of PTSD. The results of that study also suggested that soldiers often turned to alcohol after their return to alleviate nightmares and other sleep disturbances. That study concluded that soldiers who directly experienced combat and who suffered physical injury might have increased risk for mental health problems (Labbate and Snow, 1992).

Retirement

It is easy to think that people look forward to retirement and that it is a positive change in their lives. This is true for some employees, but the supervisor needs to be aware that this is not true for all and that even for those looking forward most positively to retirement, there will be some moments of anxiety. Retirement is a major life change, and it can be very difficult for some people, who may experience stress and depression. Some of the reasons for this distress are role loss, loss of power, unattained goals, lowered self-esteem, financial difficulties, and change in relationships with family and friends (Bradford and Bradford, 1979). One of the reasons people avoid retirement is that they have not yet completed major goals, and many women are more reluctant than men to retire, because they are reaching career peaks and are not interested in giving up what they have acquired (Karp, 1989). For other people, the question of what to do after retirement frightens them.

Like that to layoff and unemployment, reaction to retirement may be similar to the grief process for those who find retirement difficult to accept. Depression may be made worse if the person suffers health or financial problems or has begun to experience the death of close family members and friends. Failure to adjust can have serious consequences, including suicide. Men are at greater risk for suicide than women, because their suicide rate rises with age. The national rate of suicide is 1.28 per 100,000. For those over 65 years of age it is 2.16. Most older people intend to die, so their attempts are more successful (Jones et al., 1990).

Retirement affects not only the person retiring but also the family. Someone who was previously gone many hours is now around the house and may try to make changes and take control, and this may create new power struggles in the family. Employers need to help people plan for their retirement early. Unfortunately, many organizations do not provide retirement planning, and if they do, it is only financial planning. However, some corporations have retirement programs, and the American Association for Retired Persons (AARP) offers a retirement preparation program. Among the advantages of offering retirement planning are keeping employees motivated, supporting early retirement, and facilitating the transfer of information from retiring people (Barry, 1989). With a work force that is growing older, this is a program that will be of benefit to increasing numbers of employees, and with people living longer, they need to have a better understanding of what is involved in retirement and what resources will be available. With a shrinking pool of new job applicants, employers may want to help their older employees consider the benefits of staying in the workplace longer, or with the removal of mandatory retirement ages, an employer of a largely older work force may want to help employees see the benefits of retiring, which will make room for new employees. Employees need a comprehensive retirement planning package that will let them look at the pluses and minuses of retirement for their particular situation and will help them to make adjustments early so that when they decide to retire, it will be a relatively smooth process.

Preretirement planning can start with employees before they are 55 by providing short workshops to get them thinking about retirement and making plans early. As retirement grows closer, more extensive workshops can cover retirement issues such as pensions; health benefits; family issues; retirement activities; physical and mental health issues including living wills and advanced directives; and survivor's issues including survivor's benefits, wills, and trusts. Personal retirement counseling sessions may also be made as employees approach retirement. Spouses should be invited to attend all retirement planning and counseling programs.

MENTAL HEALTH ISSUES OF ILLNESS AND DEATH

Illness and death will cause crisis for employees and will affect the workplace. A crisis is defined as "a turning point marked by sharp improvement or sharp deterioration . . . a decision or event of great psychological significance for the individual" (Chaplin, 1968). There are predictive life crises, such as the death of a parent, but most crises will be unpredictable.

In many cases the law provides protections for employees who are ill. In some states, like California, medical condition is included in the state's equal protection legislation (Article I, Section 7), and in five states, including California, and Puerto Rico, state law provides funding for temporary disability, and in 1993 Congress passed and President Clinton signed family leave legislation (see Chapter 6).

HIV/AIDS

Human immunodeficiency virus (HIV)/AIDS has become a concern in the workplace and is an example of the effects of a life-threatening illness in the workplace. The Rehabilitation Act of 1973 has been interpreted by the courts as protecting people with HIV/AIDS against discrimination. The courts have found that contagious diseases that are not transmitted at work cannot be the grounds for discrimination against workers with such diseases (*School Board of Nassau County* v. *Arline* [480 U.S. 273]).

Employers must attempt to provide alternatives for people with AIDS to help them continue employment. This includes job modification, flexible hours, job sharing, part-time work, or transfer (Elkiss, 1991). The 1990 ADA specifically states that people with contagious diseases are handicapped and are protected.

In the one-third of AIDS patients who experience the slowly progressive AIDS dementia complex that incapacitates the patient, there may be signs of confusion, disorientation, and memory lapses, or they may experience psychiatric symptoms, which may also be progressive. As the disease progresses, mental activity as well as physical movement becomes more difficult and usually leads to severe dementia. In the earlier phases, there may be a slowing of speech, an unsteadiness of movement, language disturbances, or an inability to learn or remember information (Buckingham and VanGorp, 1988). In some patients the physical problems may level off while the mental problems progress to manic or organic psychosis; in others, the mental degeneration slows but the physical problems grow worse, leading to complete paralysis (Price and Brew, 1988). These psychological changes may alienate coworkers and may eventually lead to the inability to continue work. The manager needs to help coworkers understand and adapt; also, the manager needs to be aware that people with HIV/AIDS may be depressed or suicidal (see Chapter 2).

Bereavement

Loss of a loved one is recognized as a major life crisis or stressor. The Social Readjustment Rating Scale developed by Holmes and Rahe of the University of Washington assigns points called "life change units" (LCUs) to life events and then ranks them in order of importance. People with a higher rating on the life change scale are more likely to contract illness after they have experienced the stressful events (Schwartz, 1982). The death of a spouse receives 100 LCUs, the highest number of points on the scale. Death of a close relative receives 53 LCUs, and death of a close friend receives 37 LCUs. Bereavement can be felt for anyone or anything that a person has loved.

Emotional involvement relates to how central someone has been to somebody else and the amount of time spent together. Many people who have loved their pets and for whom those pets have filled a major place in their lives will suffer just as much grief for the loss of the animal (Gustafson, 1992). It is important for managers not to allow their own beliefs to determine for others for whom they should grieve and how. The manager should respect each person's grief as personal and individual.

Grief may also be anticipatory, because those who recognize an impending loss may begin the grief process. People who are experiencing the prolonged fatal illness of a loved one may experience anticipatory grief, as do many individuals with elderly, failing parents. Grief may make worse or cause the return of problems such as alcoholism. Among people with mental illness, grief symptoms are like those among other grievers except that ideas of guilt or self-reproach may be more frequent. In addition, persons with mental health problems are likely to grieve for a longer period, even though there is a tendency for the reaction to bereavement to be delayed (Parkes, 1972).

Managers need to be trained in the legal aspects and organizational policies regarding the illness and death of employees. Many organizations now allow fellow employees to donate sick or personal leave time to an employee who has used up the benefit. Managers need to be trained in how to deal in an empathetic manner with employees who are ill and how to deal with employees who have family members who are ill. Managers also need to be trained in how to sensitively deal with the death of an employee. Managers should recognize that how the situation is handled when an employee dies provides a message to other employees regarding the value and worth of individuals to the organization. Although the organization must go on and replace the employee, this needs to be handled in a sympathetic manner. There should not be an unseemly rush to dispose of the personal effects of the former employee and to reassign the work space. In large organizations it may be necessary to send out a memo regarding the employee's death so that people in other parts of the organization who may have worked with the employee will be informed. This is also a way to inform people of the death of former employees who retired. Some organizations like to acknowledge the death of an employee or former employee with a public symbol, such as lowering the flag to half-mast for the day.

Consultation should be made with the family in respect to what might be helpful for the organization to do and what role the manager and coworkers might play, for example, in a memorial service or permanent memorial. Personal communication should be made by the supervisor with the family to express condolences and to find out if the organization can help them in some way. If an EAP is available, their services should be extended for a period of time to the family and the family should be informed of their availability. Not until some time after the funeral or memorial service should the organization request the family to come to the office and go through the employee's work area to collect the personal effects. The supervisor should provide someone to assist the family when they do this. In workplaces that require security, an employee may have to remove personal effects and bring them to the family. In such a case, care should be taken to make sure the family has received everything that they wish to have returned.

Grief is a state of psychological crisis. Such a crisis may lead to personal growth, development, and self-awareness or to lifelong suffering. Kubler-Ross (1969) described the grief process as stages involving denial, anger, bargaining, depression, and acceptance. The major characteristics of grief are yearning for the one who has died and anxiety provoked by loss. There is a sense of abandonment and loneliness. Initially, there may be a shock stage that may last a brief time or for several weeks. During that phase there is a strong sense of denial. The person either is unable to understand what has happened or does not want to. The person may appear stunned and unable to pay attention to what is being said. The person may have difficulty making decisions. Even though a person may appear outwardly calm, inwardly there may be chaos. The person may later find it hard to remember what he/she said or did. This is not the time for the manager to try to get the person to make decisions.

The reaction stage begins when the person realizes what has happened. At this point, people try to find some meaning for what has happened. The person may also experience the physical manifestations of grief, such as tiredness, sleeplessness, headaches, loss of appetite or compulsive eating, and loss or gain of weight. The person may have trouble concentrating and find it difficult to get involved in work. The person may withdraw from others or be quick to anger and easily irritated. Depression and apathy may alternate with anger. The anger will, in most cases, begin to dissipate by the end of the first month. Guilt feelings are also common, and employees may in some way blame themselves for the death or for the way they treated the person. The manager should not try to persuade the person that it is futile to mourn and that the person should focus on the future, because by doing this, the manager is denying the person's feelings and the employee may react with irritation or even aggressiveness.

The ability to handle grief is also influenced by what other crises are occurring. The more losses that occur simultaneously, the more difficult is the grief. It is important that the supervisor not apply more pressure to the employee at this time. The manager needs to recognize this is a time when the same productivity cannot be expected, and the supervisor should be alert to helping the employee find ways to lighten the burden. It might be possible to lighten the person's work load by redistributing some of the work. Coworkers are usually more than willing to help out and pull together under such circumstances, especially when they know they will be treated in the same way if they should have a problem. Some persons will hide their unhappiness, but this does not mean they are not feeling anything. Women and men generally express their grief differently and because of cultural factors, many men still try to inhibit their grief and not show it publicly. If the employee represses or denies too much, this may cause later physical or mental health problems. If an EAP or other mental health resource is available, the manager might encourage the employee to make an appointment.

The supervisor should not try to be a psychologist but should act as a compassionate person rather than a professional. Some key points to remember are do not try to console with words like "It could be worse"; listen actively and do not give advice, but, instead, accept and confirm feelings; if you feel like crying too, don't be afraid to; don't run away; help them find the words, and don't shut off the process because they have trouble talking; and accept that the person will repeat things, because that is part of the process and will gradually cease, so you shouldn't tell the person he/she has told you that before. Finally, assume responsibility for how things are, and check back with the employee periodically to see how he/she is doing (Koskinene, 1992). Each person will have his/her own way of working through grief. Some people will want time off, and the supervisor should work with them to arrange this; others will want to return to work immediately. The desires of the employee should be respected.

Grief is a major stressor and lowers the immune defense system. It is important for one's mental and physical health to recover from grief. After three to six months, grief for most people will have abated somewhat; if intense grief continues beyond this period the person may need help in dealing with some aspect of the grief. An EAP is a very important resource in this situation. Employees are not the only ones who may suffer from organizational change or loss; so may managers, and they may also be affected by mental health problems.

THE IMPAIRED MANAGER

When the manager in the workplace is impaired by a mental health problem, many of the same dynamics and adverse consequences occur as for employees. However, an impaired manager has consequences that go beyond those of the impaired employee, because the manager's impairment may result in failing to carry out management effectively. Also, in the case of problems such as alcoholism, the manager becomes a poor role model for the employees. In addition, a substance abusing manager may create a work environment that resembles an alcoholic family system.

An impaired manager can lead to communication problems in the work group. Communication tends to be unclear and indirect, often delivered through a third party. This sets up a situation in which informal communication or rumor can start to run rampant. During times of conflict, the alcoholic manager usually denies or minimizes the problem. The work group begins to take on the roles found in an alcoholic family, including the responsible one/enabler, who covers up for the manager and takes care of his/her work when necessary; and adjuster/avoider, who ignores the problem and stays clear of it; the placater/controller, who looks after the manager's interests in order to gain power for him/herself; the scapegoat/victim, who is the person held accountable and blamed for whatever is going wrong in the workplace, often assumes the blame, may be the first to appear in the health care system as a client, and suffers the most damage; the blind employee, who operates independently and is little affected; and the acting-out child, who responds to the pressures of the workplace by always getting in trouble (Black, 1981; Phillips and Milliken, 1980; Wegscheider, 1981). In this type of enmeshed system the drinking behavior has interrupted normal work tasks and caused conflict, shifts in role, and abnormal demands on the group members to adapt. The alcoholic manager uses passive-dependent behavior to try to control and yet avoid responsibility. The work group may break down into coalitions. The entire work group becomes increasingly dysfunctional and less productive until intervention occurs (O'Sullivan, 1992).

Some work groups appear to function even with an impaired manager. In this type of situation, the excessive drinking usually occurs outside the workplace, and the group isolates the alcoholic behavior. The greatest risk occurs from decisions that are made by the manager while under the influence of alcohol or drugs or while in withdrawal. This situation can become serious and may even reach the point where the manager does not remember agreements or work directives because of blackouts.

The organization is profoundly affected when a key person is addicted (Schaef and Fassel, 1988) or suffering from some other mental health problem. The workplace's objective moves from the work goals to the hidden objective of survival. It is essential that higher management intervene, and intervene early. By the time intervention occurs, there usually has been some damage done to the work group, and intervention then needs to occur not just with the impaired manager but also with that person's work group. The later the intervention, the more the work that will be necessary with the work group. Educating and treating the work group helps the group to become functional again and helps prevent relapse when the impaired member returns (Abrams, 1987; Sherman, 1985; Steinglass, 1987).

5

Psychological Needs of Employees

Managers, to work effectively with their employees, need to know why employees think, feel, and behave as they do. Organizational psychology has become firmly ensconced as a full-fledged discipline of applied psychology. This branch of psychology combines management science with behavioral science. Management science is an outgrowth of applied social psychology, and behavioral science is largely dependent on personality theories. Personality theory is grounded in Freudian and Adlerian concepts and modern theorists of motivation in organizational psychology.

No effective transformation in human behavior can occur without intervention in human psychodynamics: "examining all clinical therapeutic techniques . . . and the human motivation theories which encompass . . . applied psychology [one finds] that [by] ignoring psychodynamical characteristics of the groups and individuals no functional modification of human beings is possible" (Deb, 1982). Individuals cannot be understood or changed without an understanding of psychodynamics, and organizations cannot be changed without changing individuals.

Values are necessarily embedded in processes involving humans. There is some feeling that there exist some values that are held universally. Abraham Maslow declares, "Instead of cultural relativity, I am implying that there are basic underlying human standards that are cross cultural." (1970). Bergin (1985) defines 23 value statements under seven headings as a distillation of a consensus on values. Those identified value headings for enhancing the mental health of individuals are freedom, responsibility, and self-regulation; love and relationships; identity; truth; values; symptom management; and work.

The evolution of psychiatric diagnosis and organizational psychology has been affected by over 50 years of intensive research on collective influence and group impact on individual behavior. Mental health professionals have discovered a whole new area of psychodynamics "which can no longer be handled exclusively by separating one individual from the group and treating the isolated patient with traditional methods" (Brocher, 1976). Organizations created to serve and facilitate human needs "acquire a life of their own, a functional autonomy . . . by virtue of which they henceforth play a profoundly important role in shaping the personalities of human beings who grow up in their sphere of influence" (Marmor, 1974). A preliminary diagnostic question involves defining the relationship between the individual and the organization. What may at first be seen as economic or political problems may in fact be character problems.

The intraorganizational dynamics of interrelated functions are not abstractions, none of these functions can be performed by other than human beings. Whatever automated programs can achieve, they cannot work with human beings — human beings who are motivated by psychological needs such as well-being, the search for a stable environment, reduction of fear through predictability, recognition, satisfaction, communication, and trust. (Brocher, 1976).

Organizations may be pathological, and one must avoid always assuming that one individual or group is to blame for dysfunctional systems (Singer, 1980). This is the danger of basing an employee assistance program (EAP) on treatment of individuals whose problems are affecting the workplace. One must always consider that the reverse may be true, that is, a dysfunctional organization is impacting the individual. There is a need for effective methods of mental health maintenance to alleviate the symptoms of organizational dysfunction; "the growing alcoholism in industry and business, more frequent coronary attacks and psychosomatic illness . . . can no longer be ascribed exclusively to individual intrapsychic conflict. The impact of organizational conditions and structures might cause a high percentage of these allegedly individual symptoms" (Brocher, 1976).

Freud, Nietzsche, Niebuhr, and Fromm have all pointed to the pathologies of social organizations at a general level of society. Singer (1980) has explored pathological organizations using the metaphor "crazy system." Singer interviewed business, government, and media people in Canada and found that a majority of them had had disturbing experiences with, or played roles in, organizations they described as crazy systems. Using these interviews, public records, and reported incidents, Singer concluded that different kinds and levels of crazy systems do exist and some may justify the use of terms drawn from the literature of psychopathology. What they had in common was their effects which were ambiguity, confusion, and error. Such systems frequently breed what Singer calls "Kafka Circuits," "organizational or procedural traps for individuals, blind alleys, crazy situations that resemble the nightmarish mazes in Kafka's novels." The crazy system may include the entire organization or just a part of it. Hostility, grandiosity, secrecy, and suspicion are displayed at various times in the organization. Some are prone to paranoid symptomology. Manipulation and denial may be rampant. There may be a pathological clinging to unworkable rules and regulations. Kafka Circuits may emerge in three ways: consciously contrived by using organizational machinery, without specific intent through bureaucratic complexity and size, or facilitated by or embedded in technology. Objections to what is happening may be treated as abnormal. When the environment has been abnormal long enough, it becomes the norm. For years, applicants for some government jobs in Los Angeles did not question why they were being asked strange, unjustified questions about sexual behavior in the regular interview process, and some 50 clients of a Pennsylvania bank did not complain to legal authorities when a bank executive spanked them for being late in making loan payments. "Ordinariness masks the crazy and destroys perception of the truth" (p. 52). This same phenomenon has been seen recently, in a case where a well-known attorney spanked his clerical workers. That case, which went unreported for a long time, is now being handled as sexual harassment. People in these situations also often are intimidated into silence.

The most important aspect of organizational diagnosis is the exploration of relationships within organizations and the psychological agendas of individuals within the organization: the individual's motivations and defense mechanisms for implementing, procrastinating, avoiding, or delegating. It would be an oversimplification to suggest that individual symptoms are simply reflections of organizational conditions, but one must explore the adaptation of the individual and organization to each other. One must address the individual, the subsystems, and the organization as a whole and their interactions with each other (Peck, 1970).

Employees bring technical skills, experience, and intellect to the job, but they also bring personality. Their personality includes an orientation to work and helps determine their attitude toward a specific job in a specific organization. The ability to implement strategies to increase organizational effectiveness and efficiency is significantly affected by the individual's susceptibility to organizational management and control. Personality and motivational theories are well-known to management, but gradually we are also seeing the application of modern clinical psychotherapies for understanding and influencing organizational behavior (Hirschhorn and Gilmore, 1980). Modern psychotherapists can provide insights into the values, motivations, and behaviors of individuals and the interrelationships between individuals and organizations. Among those who have theories and applications of value to organizational theory and management are Eric Berne, William Glasser, Albert Ellis, and family systems psychotherapists.

PSYCHOLOGICAL CONTRACTS

When people accept job offers from organizations, they enter into unwritten, unverbalized agreements that consist of each person's expectations about the job and the organization as well as the organization's expectations of the individual. In addition to job performance expectations, the organization has other expectations, including that the employee will be receptive to the organization's value system and culture. Many employees expect that they will be appreciated by their organization and the clients or customers that they serve. They may also expect meaningful work, a supportive and friendly environment, fair treatment, recognition and approval, and career development and promotion. The greater the gap between the image portrayed by the organization during recruitment, the employee's expectations, and the actual reality of the job, the greater the jeopardy to the psychological contract. Discrepancies between reality and expectation cause the psychological contract to be renegotiated. In many cases, this results in continued socialization into the organization and a reformation of the contract until the next crisis. If the socialization process is successful, a bond forms between the employee and the organization, and the individual accepts a self-image and values compatible with the organization. However, if the disparity is too great or the employee is unable to overcome the organizational culture shock, the likelihood of a successfully renegotiated psychological contract is diminished. Then, employees may increasingly feel like outsiders who do not belong. They may leave the organization, or they may remain with the organization but be alienated and demotivated (Louis, 1980).

Alienation involves the effects of psychological deprivation in the workplace. Symptoms of worker alienation include apathy, boredom, resignation, frustration, nervousness, gastric disorders, aggressiveness and low self-esteem. Workers may or may not recognize the cause of their own symptoms, and managers may have difficulty identifying them. Job dissatisfaction may be expressed openly and cause a worker to look elsewhere for work, or it may be suppressed while the worker continues to unhappily accept the consequences, which may result later in physical or mental health problems.

Various theorists have tried to explain personality. There are over 50 definitions of the term (Heffron, 1989). Clearly, personality has an impact on how people will react in a work environment and how they can be motivated. The quest for productivity has led to research in worker psychology. This has spurred investigation of human nature and what it takes to make people happy and to work at their best. Prominent theories on personality in relation to the organization emerged in the 1950s and 1960s. In order to develop or renegotiate psychological contracts, the manager must know how the employees look at the world and what their wants and needs are. An exploration of some of the research in this area may be useful to that understanding.

PERSONALITY AND MOTIVATIONAL THEORIES

Many well-known theories have been developed in the nineteenth and twentieth centuries, and there are many theories regarding personality and motivation that may help a manager understand employee behavior.

Traditional Theories

Freud and Psychoanalytic Theory

Sigmund Freud developed psychoanalytic theory in which he developed the concepts of the id, ego, and superego. The psyche (personality) was seen as an expression of a conflict between the pleasure-seeking impulses of the id, the attempts of the ego to match the desires of the id with external realities, and the superego's attempt to censor thoughts and actions. The conscience is used to punish behaviors that do not comply with the standards internalized by the superego; this results in feelings of guilt. There are forces in conflict within the individual that appear in thought, emotion, and behavior, some of which are adaptive and others psychopathological. These forces exist at varying levels of awareness, and some are entirely unconscious; thus behavior often is seen as an expression of unconscious forces within the personality. Society and organizations constrain the individual's autonomy and self-expression. The individual attempts to find an acceptable way to accommodate. The psychoanalytic approach focuses on explaining psychological events after they have happened.

Taylor and Scientific Management

At the beginning of the twentieth century, Frederick Taylor (1911) based his theory on the economic man and inducing or motivating people to work by means of wage incentives. He preferred wage systems like piece rate, which made the closest tie between the actual work performed and the monetary reward. He spent most of his time seeking to find the best way to do a specific job. Although his work was later referred to as turning workers into machines and was sometimes used for exploitation of workers, that was not Taylor's intent, and there was nothing inherent in his work that preordained its abuse.

Skinner and Behavioral/Learning Theory

Behaviorists view personality as a collection of learned behavior. Behavior is seen as influenced by rewards and punishments through a learning process of cue, response, and reward. Skinnerian behaviorists deny that motivation has any effect at all. What they believe is important is positive and negative reinforcement. Thorndike's law of effect holds that an event or consequence is reinforcing if it increases or strengthens the probability of the occurrence of a given behavior in the future. Primary reinforcements are natural and unlearned and include food, water, sex, and most physiological satisfactions. Secondary reinforcements are learned through a process of association, or chaining, from primary reinforcements. Thus, most organizational reinforcers are secondary. Money is a secondary reinforcer associated with a primary reinforcer, for example money can buy food. Managers can use combinations of positive and negative reinforcement. Behavior is affected because people seek to minimize pain/unpleasantness and maximize pleasure/pleasantness. By controlling the administration of consequences, the conditioning takes on direction or shaping. When reinforcement is withheld, the behavior begins to decrease and can be extinguished (Skinner, 1961).

Social learning theorists have expanded traditional behavioralism with the concepts of psychological situation, expectancy, and reinforcement value. The psychological situation views the person as able to think, interpret, or define situations. Responses are affected by interpretations. "Expectancy" refers to knowing what a person expects to be the result. Expected reinforcement is viewed to be a more important predictor than actual past reinforcement. "Reinforcement value" is used to refer to the fact that people attach different values to different activities or rewards.

Organizational behavior modification theorists have used the concepts of learned behavior to determine how employee behavior can be controlled by conditioning. Some organizations have implemented programs of positive reinforcement for desired employee behaviors. This is based on the premise that employees will repeat behaviors for which they are rewarded. Positive reinforcers include praise and recognition, and negative reinforcers include criticism and discipline. Negative reinforcement may not ensure the desired behavior, because the employee may avoid the undesired behavior only when there is an immediate possibility of punishment.

An example of an organization using behavior modification principles of learning theory is Emery Air Freight where supervisors were trained in the use of nonmonetary rewards such as praise and recognition to reinforce desired behaviors. In the first three years of implementation of a continuous feedback program, the company attributed a $3 million savings to it. However, in subsequent years, the program's effectiveness declined because the effect was reduced with repetition. Behavior modification programs appear to work best when the desired behavior can be very clearly specified, as in a program of monetary rewards to reduce absenteeism (Heffron, 1989).

Expectancy Theory

Victor Vroom's (1964) expectancy theory dealt specifically with motivation in the workplace and held that workers who expect rewards for a certain type of behavior will modify their behavior to gain the reward. Expectancy is a major determinant of whether or not an incentive will motivate an individual. The strength of a tendency to take action in a certain way depends on the strength of an expectancy that the act will be followed by a given consequence or outcome and on the value or attractiveness of that outcome to the person taking the action. An outcome is positive if a person prefers attaining it to not attaining it, neutral if the person is indifferent to it, and negative if the person prefers not attaining it. "Valence" refers to an outcome's anticipated reward value rather than its actual reward value when obtained. Any action may be interpreted as leading to a number of outcomes. A person will be motivated to perform well only if performing well has the highest expectancy and valence force in that particular situation. Vroom also believed merit pay was a good means to motivate workers.

Humanistic Theory

Humanistic theories have received more emphasis in the study of organizational behavior than have other theories (Heffron, 1989). Humanists believe that people are motivated to survive and to strive for fulfillment of their potential, self-actualization. Human behavior is seen as the result of gratifying an unmet need. The Hawthorne Studies of the 1920s and 1930s by Elton Mayo (1933) at Western Electric Company became world famous and led to the development of the Human Relations School. Initially, the experiments were focused on environmental factors. The early studies sought to see if better illumination increased productivity. As the experiments went on, over time, the researchers found that regardless of how they varied the lighting, schedules, or rest periods, productivity did not decline. This led the researchers to conclude that increases in productivity were due to psychological factors. The recognition, attention, and prestige gained by participating in the experiments seemed to be the motivator for productivity and morale.

Barnard

Chester Barnard (1948) emphasized that an organization can operate efficiently and survive only when the organization's goals and the needs of the employees are in balance. The function of the executive is to maintain that balance. Barnard emphasized the importance of the informal organization. He stressed the need of the organization for persons to focus on organizational needs, not personal needs; however, to accomplish this, the wants and needs of employees must be met, whether rational or not. A goal of management is to get people to accomplish purposes beyond their own immediate needs. Problem employees are those whose personal ends have taken precedence over the goals of the organization. Barnard urges managers to recognize the contradictory nature of human cooperation.

Maslow and the Need Hierarchy Theory

Abraham Maslow's personality theory, the Need Hierarchy Theory, asserts that people share common needs arranged in an hierarchical order. His theory was introduced in an article "A Theory of Human Motivation" in 1943. Human motivation can be understood as a response to this hierarchy of needs. A need that remains largely unsatisfied causes a person to act to satisfy that need. These needs include survival or physiological needs such as hunger, thirst, shelter, and sex. As each level of need is met, the individual moves on to a higher level of need: safety (protection from danger and a secure environment), social (the need for friendship, affection, and love and the need to be kind, helpful, and a responsible community member), esteem (the need for approval and recognition, dominance, appreciation, status, respect, independence, achievement, adequacy, competence, and confidence), and self-actualization (self-fulfillment and recognition of one's own unique characteristics and potential). The highest level, self-actualization, is viewed as striving to become the person you ideally envision yourself to be, and it can never be totally satisfied. Maslow believed that very few people in their lifetimes reached self-actualization (Maslow, 1962, 1965, 1970).

Under Maslow's theory, in order to motivate and satisfy employees, organizations should offer outcomes that are consistent with the worker's current or emerging needs. In developed countries, the first level physiological needs have little effect on worker's attitudes and motivation (Dunham and Smith, 1979). Obviously, for some workers and at some times, like in the Great Depression, the survival needs become very important. This may be true sometimes for striking and laid off workers also. Safety and security needs have traditionally been met in large organizations, but during the 1980s, with downsizing, closures, and layoffs, many employees' safety and security needs were shaken. Also, when employers try to separate social needs from the workplace by desiring them to be met only outside the workplace, potential work-related motivation is lost (Dunham and Smith, 1979). If unsatisfied needs are the cause of behavior, the organization should look to the job to determine if it satisfies the needs of the employee. If the employee's needs are not met by the job, the employee would be dissatisfied and performance would be lowered. Each level of need can be used to motivate the worker, but once that level of need is satisfied, it can no longer be used as a motivator. The employer then would have to use the next level of need to motivate the employee (Maslow, 1954).

Attempts to confirm the validity of Maslow's theory have met with difficulty, and predicted causal relationships between variables have not been found (Shostrom, 1965; Heylighen, 1992). Wahba and Bridwell (1976) concluded that although the theory was widely accepted, there was little research evidence to prove or support it. They felt that there was difficulty with the concept of need. They were concerned whether need was psychologically or physiologically based and how needs could be identified, isolated, and measured. They felt there was considerable evidence that people sought objects and engaged in behavior that was not related to the satisfaction of needs. They also believed that although Maslow's theory would not be discarded, by testing it in modern work organizations, one could see that the needs of workers did not always follow Maslow's hierarchy. Schwartz (1983) contended that the theory as it was generally understood did not make any sense. He could find no organizational psychology literature that could explain why the stages of the hierarchy were in the order in which they were placed by Maslow. Mook (1987) criticized Maslow's subjectivity and his U.S. bias for his criteria for mental health. He argued that an individualistic, autonomous self-actualizer in Japan would not be considered well-adapted.

A five-year panel study of 40 AT&T executives involving interviewing the executives over time to determine changes in relative strength of needs hypothesized that the satisfaction of a given need level would correlate strongly with the strength of the next higher level. For example, high correlations were expected between safety needs and achievement and esteem needs. However, the study found no strong relationships to support the hierarchy of needs (Hall and Nougain, 1968). Makin, Cooper, and Cox (1989) concluded that the theory is weak in many respects but that some levels of the classification do appear to exist for some people. Also, they felt that rewards appear to fit into more than one classification. For example, money can be used to purchase essentials of life, but it can also be a status symbol. They also believed there are considerable individual differences in what constitutes sufficient satisfaction at any level. "Empirical research, therefore, has failed to support the theory, and most psychologists would rate its accuracy, on a scale of 1 to 10 somewhere about 2 or 3" (p. 35). They, however, viewed the model as useful because they believed people's needs probably were organized in a hierarchical manner, but they believed that the nature of the hierarchy varied from person to person.

Need-Satisfaction Models

Various need-satisfaction models have developed from Maslow's work. Basically, this view believes that people have basic stable, identifiable needs and attributes (personalities) and that jobs have stable, identifiable sets of characteristics that are relevant to the needs of individual workers. Individuals' attitudes toward their jobs are thought to result from the degree of correspondence between the needs of the individual and the characteristics of the job or job situation. For some theorists, this is also connected to motivation. When the characteristics of the job are compatible with the person's needs, the theory predicts that the person is satisfied. Some theorists believe also that the person will be more motivated (Salancik, and Pfeffer, 1977).

Alderfer

Clayton Alderfer (1972) in his Existence, Relations, and Growth (ERG) Theory identified three groups of core needs, existence, relatedness, and growth, as an alternative to Maslow's needs hierarchy. ERG Theory arranges needs in a hierarchy but does not strictly order them as does Maslow's theory. All people are seen as alike in that they possess some degree of each need, but they differ in the strength of their needs. Existence needs reflect a person's requirement for material and energy exchange and for the need to reach and maintain equilibrium. They include material and physiological desires, including hunger, thirst, physical working conditions, pay, and fringe benefits. They can be divided so that one person's gain is another person's loss. Frequently a person's satisfaction, beyond a bare minimum, is dependent upon a comparison of what he/she gets with what others get in the same situation.

Relatedness needs involve relationships with significant others. The satisfaction of these needs depends on a process of sharing or mutuality, including sharing thoughts and feelings. Relatedness involves acceptance, confirmation, understanding, and influence. Significant others can be groups as well as individuals. The opposite of relatedness is a sense of distance or lack of connection.

Growth needs impel persons to make creative or productive efforts in relationship to themselves or the environment. Satisfying growth needs comes from people engaging in problems that call upon them to utilize all capacities fully and, sometimes to develop additional capacities. A greater sense of wholeness comes from satisfying growth needs. Growth needs are dependent on persons finding opportunities to be themselves most fully and to become what they can be. Relatedness and growth needs can be motivating without the lower needs being met.

Empirical studies by Alderfer have directly compared predictions based on ERG Theory and Maslow's work (Alderfer, Kaplan, and Smith, 1974). Alderfer believed that ERG Theory was more useful for explaining the data than Maslow's theory but that better empirical proof was needed for such theories as Maslow's and even his own ERG (Alderfer, 1989).

Argyris

Chris Argyris concluded that there is a fundamental conflict between the individual and the organization that causes frustration and failure. This conflict between individual needs and organizational demands is seen by Argyris as a continuing problem that the leader has to face. Argyris utilizes the need-satisfaction model to propose that what people need in their work is the opportunity to develop their personalities. They will mature as they move from passive to active, from dependence to independence, from shallow interests to deep interests, from accepting subordination to desiring equality or superiority to peers, and from lack of control to self-control. Argyris views hierarchically arranged organizations as rigid and authoritarian. This places them in conflict with the needs of mature personalities and forces the mature personality back to a less-mature stage of development. The readiness of employees to self-actualize is stymied by organizational demands to behave in a passive, dependent manner. Employees grudgingly accept money in exchange for dissatisfaction at work in order to buy satisfaction outside work. Jobs and authority should be redesigned so that every position in the organization requires a mature person. Job enlargement and democratic participative leadership help ameliorate the situation (Argyris, 1957).

Herzberg and Two-Factor Theory

Frederick Herzberg elaborated on the need-satisfaction model in his two-factor theory, motivation-hygiene theory, in *Work and the Nature of Man* (1966). The basic theory suggested that employees have two sets of needs, one involving the avoidance of pain and the other involving the pursuit of psychological growth. This original work was based on a study of 203 accountants and engineers who were asked to describe satisfying and dissatisfying events or incidents at work (Herzberg, Mausner, and Snyderman, 1959). Herzberg (1966) then contended that there was no linear relationship between job satisfaction and dissatisfaction. He suggested that different sets of variables are related to separate dimensions of work satisfaction and dissatisfaction. Work satisfaction (motivators) is intrinsic and related to variables that comprise job content, including the task itself, achievement, autonomy, recognition, responsibility, and acquisition of new skills. Work dissatisfaction (maintenance, hygiene factors) is extrinsic and related to variables that comprise the job environment, such as security, salary, working conditions, organizational policy, and relationships with fellow workers and supervisors. The work itself influences workers' satisfaction, which in turn influences their level of effort on the job. Basic needs would not act as satisfiers to motivate employees but, if left unfilled, could be dissatisfiers. If basic needs were met, then satisfiers could be used to encourage optimal performance.

Herzberg used the term "motivation-hygiene theory" because it implied that there are certain personal needs that, unless met, detract from worker performance. When workers are given opportunities to increase the complexity and responsibility of their jobs, they derive greater satisfaction from work and have enhanced performance. It is possible for an individual to be both satisfied and dissatisfied with a job. To decrease dissatisfaction, one improves the hygiene factors, but this will not lead to satisfaction. To increase satisfaction, a manager must provide more motivators. Herzberg stressed education in the workplace to improve workers' attitudes about themselves and their jobs. He stressed job enrichment, positive reinforcement, increased worker responsibility, and new opportunities for growth.

Herzberg's work has been expanded by other researchers. Research indicates that both job content (satisfiers) and job context (hygiene factors) contribute to both satisfaction and dissatisfaction, although the satisfiers seem to have an overall greater influence on satisfaction or dissatisfaction. However, studies of worker performance involving job enlargement suggest that performance is not enhanced for all workers whose jobs are enlarged (Dubin, 1976). Maidani (1991), in exploring the two-factor theory in relationship to public and private sector employees' job satisfaction, found that employees' motives for work in both the private and public sectors tended to emphasize intrinsic factors. He also found that hygiene factors could be sources of satisfaction rather than dissatisfaction and were sources of satisfaction for both sectors, as were the motivators. Employees in the public sector put more emphasis on hygiene factors than employees in the private sector, and a larger majority of satisfied employees were found in the public sector.

Critics have also questioned Herzberg's work. Vroom (1964) argued that the critical incident method of testing the theory was at least partly responsible for the results and that human defense processes lead people to attribute causes of satisfaction to their achievements while attributing causes of dissatisfaction to the work environment over which they have little control. House and Wigdor (1967) also felt that the research design produced inaccurate results, and they produced research results that were contradictory to Herzberg's two-factor theory. They concluded that a given factor could cause job satisfaction for one person and dissatisfaction for another person; a given factor could cause both satisfaction and dissatisfaction; intrinsic factors were more important to both satisfying and dissatisfying; and Herzberg's theory was an oversimplification of the relationship between satisfaction and motivation. Marriner (1992) criticized Herzberg's study design for examining only two kinds of jobs and having only one measure of job attitude, accounts from interviews.

McGregor's Theory X and Theory Y

Douglas McGregor developed a topology of management styles that sought to recognize the conclusions of the need-satisfaction models. Theory X represented the conventional view of management and their view of subordinates' personalities. Subordinates are viewed as either passively or actively resistant to the organization's needs. The average man is seen as lacking ambition, disliking responsibility, and indolent. Management must intervene to modify and control employees' behavior to meet the needs of the organization. Interventions occur in the form of persuasion, rewards, and punishment. Under theory Y, the needs-satisfaction model developed by Maslow and his followers is recognized. Theory Y views people as motivated with a potential for development and a capacity for assuming responsibility. They are able to direct their behavior toward organizational goals. People are not by nature passive and resistant to the needs of the organization but have been brought to that by negative experiences with organizations. It is the responsibility of management to recognize human potentials and help them develop. The essential task of management is to arrange organizational conditions and methods of operation so that people can achieve their own goals through directing their efforts toward organizational objectives. Management's role is to create opportunities, remove obstacles, and encourage growth. McGregor suggested the use of decentralization, job enrichment, and participatory decision making (McGregor, 1960).

Rotter and External and Internal Personalities

The psychologist Julian Rotter (1990) explored the effect that expectation of rewards and punishments have on personality and concluded that people develop expectations about the source of control of outcomes. He divided people based on their perception of the locus of control into two personality classifications: internal and external. Internals are personalities who believe that their rewards and punishments are controlled by what they do. Their own actions are the determining factor. If they perform well or if they perform badly, appropriate consequences will occur. Externals are people who believe that forces outside themselves are responsible for their rewards and punishments. Factors such as chance, luck, and powerful other people control their consequences. Sometimes, outcomes are appropriate, but often they are not related to what the person does. Research indicates that internals are better adjusted, have more self-control, and are more achievement oriented and externals tend to be more flexible and more subject to social influence through conformity. Internals tend to be skill oriented, and externals are chance oriented. Internals have the confidence to develop, control circumstances within an organization, and manage. Externals often make dedicated, loyal employees who follow directives well. Internals demonstrate a higher degree of work motivation.

Managers tend to treat people as either internals or externals because of the manager's assumptions about people. The locus of control is the personality equivalent of McGregor's theory X and theory Y. Managers who have theory X assumptions about their people view them as externals, and those with theory Y assumptions view them as internals. Cross-mixing of personalities and assumptions will result in organizational friction. A theory X type manager will have difficulties dealing with internals, and externals will not perform well under a theory Y style manager (Sanzotta, 1977).

Ouchi and Theory Z

Between 1973 and 1980, William Ouchi conducted research in the United States and Japan. In his book *Theory Z: How American Business Can Meet the Japanese Challenge* (1981), he went beyond McGregor with his theory Z. He concentrated on the humanitarian side of employees and concluded that relationships and feelings were important factors. Material incentives were not enough. Trust, subtlety, and intimacy were important factors in relationship to performance. Ouchi combined aspects of U.S. and Japanese management approaches for what he believed was the best combination.

Kaplan and Ziegler (1985) criticized Ouchi's work. They felt there was no reason to believe clan-like methods of social control were necessary to higher productivity than hierarchical methods and that the degree to which a firm was involved in innovation might be an important factor in explaining whether an organization relied on clan or hierarchical methods.

Consistency Theory of Behavior

Leon Festinger (1973) developed a theory based on the assumption that when a person has contradictory thoughts or ideas that are inconsistent with their established behavior pattern, dissonance occurs. When this happens, individuals attempt to maintain consistency among various attitudes, beliefs, and self-perceptions within their cognitive structure. If dissonance occurs, disequilibrium produces tension and a state of psychological discomfort that motivates the individual to seek balance and consistency (Zunker, 1990).

Modern Psychotherapists and Organizations

Modern psychotherapists such as Berne, Glasser, and Ellis can significantly contribute to concepts impacting organizational theory and behavior. They offer personality theories that address people's needs and motivations, and they provide techniques that can be used in the application of management theory to improve individual, group, and organizational functioning.

Eric Berne and Transactional Analysis

Eric Berne (1910–70) was the founder of transactional analysis (TA). Educated as a psychiatrist in the eastern United States, he moved to Carmel, California, after World War II and published his first paper on psychoanalysis in 1958. The International Association of Transactional Analysis was founded in 1964. A prolific writer, Berne's main theoretical ideas were set out in *Transactional Analysis in Psychotherapy* (1961) and *Principles of Group Treatment* (1966). His most widely read books include *Games People Play* (1964), *What Do You Say After You Say Hello?* (1972), and *Beyond Games and Scripts* (1976).

TA is a complete theory of personality and a model for explaining interpersonal communication. It has been used extensively in organizational and leadership skills development. The personality theory defines three ego states, states of mind and their related patterns of behavior — parent, adult, and child — that operate in every individual. The parent ego state, extro-psyche, contains beliefs, values, and morals; attitudes; and behavior incorporated from external sources, primarily the parental figures. The parent is subdivided into a critical parent, who focuses on good, bad, and "shoulds," and a nurturing parent, who cares for and promotes growth in others. Inwardly, the old parental messages continue to influence the inner child, while outwardly, the parent is expressed in critical, prejudicial, or nurturing behavior. The adult ego state, neo-psyche, is oriented to current reality and the objective gathering of information. It is professional and rational. The adult figures things out by looking at the facts; it serves as the "computer," estimating probabilities and computing dispassionately. The mature adult ideally is the rational part that mediates wisely between the parent and the child, respecting and modifying both positions. Wise mediation of the adult reduces internal conflict and increases the ability to satisfy basic desires in both the short and long term. The child ego state, archaic-psych, contains feelings, impulses, and intuitions. The child is subdivided into a natural child of uninhibited feeling and behavior and an adapted child who has responded to the requirements of other people through compliance or rebellion. Berne sees ego states as denoting the state of mind, behavior, and feelings in the normal waking state. All people exhibit three ego states and shift easily from one state to another, although some people may have problems with being fixated primarily in one ego state. TA can be used to explain the values people hold based on their parent ego states and to explain their motivations and behaviors based on from which ego state they are operating.

TA has also been used as a development theory to explain patterns of the adult life cycle. Pam Levin-Landheer (1982) holds that human growth is a cycle of development composed of seven stages (the powers of being, doing, thinking, identity, being skillful, regeneration, and recycling) that begin in childhood and repeat throughout life. The significance of this developmental cycle is its application for individuals to understand issues of personal growth and for organizations to use as a framework for needs common to all members of the group. She describes the seven states in terms of ego states, common clues for recognizing when one is in that stage, the power developed through the associated tasks, and the fundamental transactions that nourish growth. For example, Stage One, the power of being, involves the natural child and the need to develop the power of being. People reenter that stage when they are under stress, during periods of rapid change or growth, or when they are beginning a new job. Stage One may involve difficulty in thinking, a lack of concentration, a questioning of self-adequacy, and a desire to eat frequently and sleep for longer periods.

Communication Patterns. TA also deals with communication patterns between the ego states of individuals. A transaction is an exchange between two people, either verbal or nonverbal. Transactions can be classified as complementary, crossed, or ulterior. A complementary transaction occurs when a message is sent from a specific ego state and gets the predicted response from the specific ego state it was sent to in the other person. Lines of communication are open, and people can continue to transact. However, even if communication lines are parallel, they may not always be helpful to the workplace. For example, a parallel conversation may occur between the child of two people; this child-to-child transaction may involve play and forgetting what they are suppose to be accomplishing or a fight to enliven a dull work setting. A parallel parent-to-parent can result in oversolving of problems, alarms, memos, and emergency meetings. The most frequently seen transaction in the workplace is the supervisor's parent to the employee's child. It can be either destructive or nurturing, depending on the way it is used. It is destructive if it is used to derogate the employee and get obedience through threats. Some nurturing can be productive, but it also can be counterproductive and abused if there is overprotection and the employee is encouraged to be helpless and dependent. The supervisor is seeking to appear competent and self-controlled at the expense of the employee (Bennett, 1980).

A crossed transaction occurs when an unexpected response is made to the stimulus. An inappropriate ego state is activated. This causes people to withdraw or switch the conversation in another direction. The person who sent the transaction is often left feeling discounted. Some 72 different variations of crossed transactions have been defined. An alert manager who picks up on a hurt child or parent state will continue to transact from the adult in order to hook the employee's adult to accomplish the job. At some point the manager may offer the employee a chance to discuss the problem or the behavior. For example, a clerical person who is complaining from their child state about always having to answer the phone can be answered from the supervisor's adult that if they feel they have too much responsibility then a time can be set to sit down and talk about it (Bennett, 1980).

Ulterior transactions involve more than two ego states. They are disguised under a socially acceptable transaction. An ulterior message is given when the secretary gives poorly typed work to the boss, inviting a parental put-down. An ulterior transaction also occurs when a recovered alcoholic comes to work with a hangover and boasts to coworkers about how he blew it; on the surface, he gives factual information from the adult, but on the ulterior level, he's looking for the parent in the coworker to condemn his drinking. If the coworker laughs from either his/her parent or child state, he/she reinforces the parental injunction "Get lost, you bum," which was usually learned nonverbally by the alcoholic as a child. Inappropriate laughs or smiles are called "gallows transactions." They tighten the noose and reinforce destructive behavior. The gallows transaction, like other ulterior transactions, is often used to promote psychological games (Jeppesen, 1974).

Games. People structure time by withdrawal, rituals, activities such as work, pastimes, intimacy, and games. Berne (1964) defines games as common ulterior transactions in which there is a psychological payoff and at least two basic roles. For example, the secretary noted above with the letter full of errors is playing Kick Me, a game in which one role is victim and the other is persecutor. Another game is See What You Made Me Do. The player accepts advice and assistance from anyone and then carries out the advice in a way in which the player will fail. The player then uses any mistake he/she makes to blame the helpers. The payoff is that the player confirms that not only is he/she not okay but neither are the helpers: he/she wins by losing. People play games as part of a lifelong script based on early decisions about the world and other people. Games are learned as children to get others to do something we want done. Sometimes meeting other people's needs is the response in order to maintain a stable home with a substance abusing parent. There are four basic life-positions: I'm OK, You're OK; I'm OK, You're Not OK; I'm Not Ok, You're OK; and I'm Not OK, You're Not OK. When employees feel or fear rejection, competition, or too many responsibilities, they may resort to games. Life scripts based on "I'll always be a failure" or "I am weak and helpless" are deeply entrenched (unconscious) life scripts that can undermine a conscious effort to live productively. Life scripts, as well as collections of bad feelings, are collected to justify the scripts and are used to form the basis of decisions. People may seek out situations that support anger, hurt, depression, or guilt in an effort to reinforce those familiar feelings. When people are aware of the games and scripts that are being used, they can make decisions to make changes. Sax and Hollander (1972) developed a set of reality games to help people develop their real selves and allow their real intimacy to emerge.

Strokes. Berne (1964) also believed people respond to strokes, any act implying recognition of the other's presence. The need to be stroked (need for attention) is one of the reasons people play games. In a study conducted by Firth and Shapiro (1986), they found that most of the distress that employees suffer is self-concept problems. One of the frustrations that employees expressed the most was that they had a need for constant feedback (strokes); they wanted to know if they did a good job. Strokes can be positive, making a person feel OK, or negative, telling a person they are not OK. Strokes can also be either conditional, given for what you do, or unconditional, given for who you are. Organizations can promote mental health by providing physical and psychological positive stroking in the form of benefits and recognition, rewarding productive behavior, providing counseling services where employees can explore self-sabotaging behavior, and encouraging honest self-disclosure concerning desires so that the organization and the employee can find a way to meet those desires without playing costly games (Zare, 1990).

Management Applications. When TA is applied to results other than reorganization of human personality, its application is called "special" and the targeted area is called a "field," an area of human behavior in which it is believed that application of TA theory can result in positive change. Management development has been used as a special field. It has been suggested that the basic requirements for that special field are "demonstrated knowledge of organization theory, organization behavior, management theory, small group theory and TA" (Underhill, 1982).

TA can be used to understand the behavior of individuals, groups, and organizations. Berne felt that internal processes were reflective of an organization or group's etiquette (parent), technical culture (adult), and character (child) (Berne, 1963). Roger Blakeney (1983) used general systems theory and TA to explain human behavior at the individual, group, and organizational levels. He felt from a TA perspective, there were two important keys to individual effectiveness: the use of ego states appropriate to the situation and the use of OK parts of ego states. With the adult in executive control, it could choose an appropriate ego state and assess the effectiveness of the behavior.

Roger Blakeney (1986) used TA to explore the role of trust in interpersonal communication in organizations. Lower levels of organizations filter information to avoid overloading higher levels (Ackoff, 1967). In conditions of low trust, subordinates filter favorable information upward, whether it is important or not. In conditions of high trust they filter information on the basis of importance (O'Reilly, 1978). Managerial decision making is facilitated when important, unfavorable information reaches upper levels and faulty group decision making processes may be avoided. Trust is related to safety, expertness, and dynamism (Giffin, 1967). Blakeney relates safety to the parent ego state, expertness to the adult ego state, and dynamism to the child ego state and concludes that trust develops when people express themselves effectively using all three ego states in both the sender and the receiver. "Thus, trust can be enhanced and interpersonal communication in the organization improved by using the OK parts of all the ego states as appropriate to the situation in an organizational context" (Blakeney, 1986).

TA has also been used to analyze power and leadership styles. With power defined as "the ability to influence the actions of others, individuals or groups" and leadership defined as "the way power is used in the process of influencing the actions of others" (Hersey, Blanchard, and Natemeyer, 1979). Rosa Krausz (1986) found that in an organizational setting, behaviors of superiors have some modeling influence on subordinates, especially if the behaviors are institutionalized as part of the organizational culture. A manager who uses ego states that are inappropriate to the management function will be modeling inadequate behavior that negatively influences the organizational culture. In a coercive leadership style, a symbiotic relationship will develop between the leader and the subordinates. The adult ego state will be excluded, so resistance to change will be high. The leader will be transacting from the critical parent to the subordinate's adapted child. Conditional or unconditional negative strokes are given. To maintain a more favorable stroke balance, subordinates will adopt passive behaviors, doing the minimum of work, and they will engage in one-down power plays, which may include organizational sabotage or violence (Wallgren, 1975). A controlling leadership style also results in symbiotic relationships, with overadaptation and agitation. The supervisor transacts from the critical or nurturing parent to the natural or adapted child of the subordinate. In a coaching leadership style, a semisymbolic relationship occurs. Each person uses the adult ego state and either child or parent, excluding the third ego state. Transactions tend to be adult to adult or critical nurturing parent to natural or adapted child. Some dependency is created, and the person's ability to solve problems tends to be discounted. A participative leadership style is free of symbiosis, and all ego states are used positively to solve problems and act with options. People relate as equals. Life positions for both supervisors and subordinates are "I'm OK, You're OK." Time structuring involves activities and intimacy; no games are played. The organizational climate is one of trust and openness. Although pure leadership types are rare, leaders have predominant styles. "Empowering people may be understood as the process of enhancing individuals' abilities to act with options. . . . And being powerful often brings with it the tendency to share organizational power more effectively, as well as to stimulate the use of personal power in the group" (Krausz, 1986). For a manager who has difficulty relinquishing control and who becomes enmeshed in office politics, TA can stress the need to explore the deep unconscious script that underlies the behavior in order to bring about long-term change that could enhance the manager's life and the work environment (Zare, 1990).

TA can also be used to understand and defuse certain types of behavior. For example, Molly Cole (1984) used TA to explain how the power struggle game can lead to passive-aggressive behavior. The power struggle game is played by a persecutor intent on making someone do what is supposedly good for them and a victim who will not or cannot refuse directly to do what is wanted. The victim signals the desire to play the game by doing nothing when something is expected of him/her or by doing what the persecutor does not want done. The gimmick is the persecutor's vulnerability of wanting some behavior from the victim. The response is when the persecutor tries to make the victim do what the persecutor wants. The switch is when the victim turns persecutor and behaves passive-aggressively by procrastinating, forgetting, saying he/she can't and believing he/she can't, or eventually doing the job intentionally inefficiently. The payoff is the persecutor feeling extreme frustration and feeling misunderstood, while the victim probably shows nothing but feels triumphant and vindicated. With a negative self-image, the victim may lose the job; however, at this point, the persecutor may rescue the victim to continue the game.

> The passive-aggressive person's target door is feeling. Although he may act tough, ... he usually feels bad. ... Kindness and empathy are the keys to connecting with his feelings. ... Winning his trust may be difficult; ... many other people have seen him as not OK. The persecutor has to give up the game and not take responsibility for him. He will then be free to act responsibly. (Cole, 1984)

Positive encouragement and stroking are needed.

TA has been used extensively to train managers to promote organizational development. TA has been taught to middle managers as a method for analyzing not only people but also organizational scripts and as a tool to help people and organizations work together (Jeppesen, 1974). It has been used to help business organizations improve their integration and productivity by helping managers operate more effectively, improve their interpersonal skills, and stimulate their personal growth. It has been applied to management problems by explaining games that business people play and the role of stroking and job satisfaction (Bennett, 1976).

In organizational development, TA has been used to open communication and facilitate productive and honest relationships. Consultants have used TA for training and development activities to improve interpersonal communications and understanding of organizational communication. Identification and analysis of trans-actions has been used to determine what managerial or team efforts facilitate or block task accomplishment (Christen and Nykodym, 1986). Consultants have also used TA as a self-assessment process when one-on-one working relationships are dysfunctional (Kurpius, 1985). It has also been used in workshop settings as a model to help individuals look at their own interpersonal style and has been applied to specific tasks such as team building (Bennett, 1980).

Research on TA in organizational development (OD) has been positive. In research on the impact of TA as a strategy in team skill training with an OD project, TA has been found to improve organizational climate through employee perception of increased listening, supervisory approachability, teamwork, information level, decision making, and job-related data. That research also indicated that TA could be used as an effective substitute for team skills training in preparing organizational participants for more in depth OD interventions (Nykodym, Nielsen, and Christen, 1985). Research has found TA to be useful in improving the effectiveness of quality circles and shows that TA has increased worker perception of how the work group contributes to a sense of personal worth and importance. It also has improved goal emphasis through "the extent to which the group behavior encourages and maintains high standards of performance, perceived increase in peer group facilitations," and perceived problem solving (Nykodym, Ruud, and Liverpool, 1986).

William Glasser and Reality Therapy

William Glasser is a psychiatrist living in Los Angeles. He published *Reality Therapy: A New Approach to Psychiatry* in 1965 and founded the Institute for Reality Therapy in Los Angeles. His many books include *Schools Without Failure* (1969), *The Identity Society* (1972), *Positive Addiction* (1976), and *Stations of the Mind* (1981). He also coauthored *Both-Win Management* (1980) with Chester Karrass.

Reality Therapy is a method of psychotherapy that emphasizes the need for people to face reality and fulfill their basic needs. Glasser suggests all human beings have certain needs: belonging/love (cooperation), gaining power and recognition (competition), having fun, and being free. People feel pleasure when they satisfy these needs and pain when they do not. If the emotional pain is severe enough, undesirable symptoms such as depression will threaten the ability to function productively. People develop their identity on a continuum. The power need is often the most difficult to meet. It can create tension and conflict, and in the workplace, the need for power is often a motivation. People are competitive as they strive for attention, achievement, and recognition, but they also need the security of belonging and being cared about. People need fun and to feel free. The ways in which they find the ability to satisfy these needs will determine their willingness to change, take on new tasks, and participate. The working environment should help to fulfill these needs. Work should be as interesting as possible; everyone should be given recognition in some way; everyone should be given some choice as to how and when to work; and a team spirit should be developed. Teams provide the opportunity to compete as well as belong, to contribute their unique skills to a group effort, to enjoy themselves, and to make choices on how to participate.

The security person is focused on survival, involving food, shelter, and safety. When psychological pain is experienced, the person may either move toward being a fulfilled person with a success identity or move toward a failure identity of weakness and irresponsibility. The fulfilled person meets needs and copes with psychological pain through flexibility and effective behaviors involving strength, responsibility, self-discipline, and confidence, which lead to an enlarged internal world and effective control of his/her life. The failure identity moves through three stages. The person first reduces psychological pain through giving up, not trying. When this is no longer sufficient, the person denies failure and takes on symptoms of acting out (anger), emotional and mental health problems (anxiety, compulsions, depression), psychosomatic disease (headaches, backaches, heart disease), or psychotic behavior. Eventually, the person may move into escaping pain and even finding pleasure in failure through becoming a negatively addicted person, for example, involved with drugs, alcohol, food, or gambling. Through this process, the person's internal world grows smaller. Although people are often not aware of it, they chose these behaviors as their best attempts to fulfil needs. Reality Therapy expects each person to make a judgment as to whether his/her behavior is responsible and, therefore, good for him/her and those with whom he/she is meaningfully involved. Reality Therapy involves an eight-step process developed to help people take responsibility for and change their own behavior. The process has been used in a variety of settings by professionals and nonprofessionals. The eight-step process consists of

(1) Make Friends — What Do You Want? What Do You Really Want?;
(2) Ask: What Are You Doing Now? or What Are You Choosing to Do Now?;
(3) Ask: Is It Helping? or Is It Against the Rules?;
(4) Make a Plan to Get What You Want or What You Really Want;
(5) Get a Commitment;
(6) Don't Accept Excuses;
(7) Don't Punish But Don't Interfere With Reasonable Consequences; Don't Criticize;
(8) Never Give Up. (Glasser, 1965).

Control Theory. In 1981 Glasser extended and advanced his concepts of Reality Therapy in *Stations of the Mind.* Expanding on the concepts in *Positive Addiction,* in which he set forth the idea that certain regular behaviors like running or meditation could become addictive in a positive, strengthening way (Glasser, 1976), and on the *Control System Psychology of William Powers* (1973), Glasser postulated that all of us are driven by powerful internal motivations that push us not only to survive but also toward belonging, worthwhileness, fun, and freedom. From our needs, we construct a complex, unique personal inner world. Our brain then acts as the control system that deals with the real world to try and control it so that it becomes as close as possible to our personal world. What happens in the outer world has little or no significance unless it relates to our inner world. There may arise a conflict between the old brain, which runs the body and controls physiology, and the new brain, the cerebral cortex, which controls doing, thinking, and feeling. In the new brain, we build up our perception of the world, like a picture album. When perceptions come in from the outer world through our senses, we compare those perceptions with our picture. If they do not match up, we have a perceptual error. We can handle that error three ways: by getting new information that corrects the error; redirection, using known behavior that may suppress our emotional pain or change something in the external environment to correct the error; or reorganization, a random search through potential behaviors to find one to reduce the error. Reorganization is a random system that may stumble onto negative or positive behavior. It is the only system capable of producing a new behavior, something we have never used before. Much of what we do all day is try to eliminate transient errors with new information. However, if that does not reduce the perceptual error, we use redirection, a behavior we know may get a desired result. Our two most effective error-reducing behaviors are thinking and doing. We usually redirect, but occasionally, we use reorganization.

Reorganization occurs when we have a large perceptual error and feelings of emotional pain have been generated because our inner world does not correlate with the outer world. If the new brain, in dealing with the outside world and perceptual errors, constantly calls on the old brain for physiological responses, the physiological responses may result in major body changes (psychosomatic disease). This theory requires that we remember that everyone lives in two worlds. People should make a thoughtful effort not to increase their own or other people's perceptual errors. This calls for using error-reducing behavior and working toward compromises between people's perceptions. We are not locked into any one behavior. We can reduce errors through any of the three components — doing, thinking, and feeling. We can change our actions (doing), change our thinking (the picture in our inner world), or change our feelings. Changing one will change the others. "You must accept that all of your life, any behavior you choose, good or bad, is your best choice at that particular time. If you start searching for fault, you necessarily criticize yourself, increase your error and become more sick or disabled. What you must learn to say is "I have an error, probably from a conflict, and I must figure out something better than what I am doing now" (Glasser, 1981). Sickness may be used to resolve the conflict (many a person gets out of a bad work situation after a heart attack or a back injury), but that is not a good solution (Glasser, 1981).

Peter Appel (1983) uses Reality Therapy and the control of perception concepts to provide a model for understanding social, biological, and psychological variables of adult development. He posits that

Each of us is an internally motivated being, whose perceptions of our needs and how to fill them, continually undergo change. These changes depend upon the physical, social, and psychological changes in our lives. The process of adult development involves the continuous comparison of the reference perceptions to our perceptions of reality to see if our needs are being met.

Both-Win Negotiation. Reality Therapy was adapted by Chester Karrass and William Glasser in *Both-Win Management* (1980). The essence of Reality Therapy is problem solving, for individuals, groups, or organizations (Glasser and Zunin, 1973). Chester Karrass and William Glasser applied the concepts of Reality Therapy and both-win negotiations to a way of working with employees that they called "Reality Performance Management" (RPM). Employees are viewed as having either a success or a failure identity. Feelings are what motivate people to do what they do. "How we feel, whether it's good or bad, is the psychological payoff (or price) that we receive or pay for how we behave" (Karrass and Glasser, 1980). The psychological payoff for success is pleasure. The cost of failure is psychological pain. Problem employees are moving toward a failure identity. They become lonely and less rational, with less and less to look forward to each day. Employees in the first stage of failure, the give-up persons, have a million excuses and put little effort into their jobs. They honestly believe that even if they make the effort, they won't succeed. People give up because they get a temporary burst of pleasure or relief from giving up. Signs a manager can look for that an employee is giving up include avoiding taking extra responsibility, lack of initiative, refusing to make decisions, procrastinating, excuses, shoddy work, and an overfocusing on procedures, not substance.

Because giving up works only temporarily, employees may move on to the second stage, symptom persons. They act out by fighting with others, disregarding rules and procedures, misplacing important papers, resisting authority, being absent at critical times, damaging equipment, waiting to be told what to do and following the directions explicitly with no thinking, griping maliciously and excessively, and hurting other people verbally or physically. They also may become emotionally upset and show symptoms of depression: uninvolvement; anxiousness; sadness; humorlessness; withdrawing; fatigue; slowing down work output; crying; or being sick, late, or absent excessively. A third set of symptoms involves psychosomatic illness: headaches, back problems, chronic fatigue, insomnia, shortness of breath, and some forms of heart trouble, ulcers, allergies, and arthritis. Occasionally, employees may even be psychotic, out of touch with reality, displaying thinking or behavior that makes sense only to them.

The third stage of failure is the negatively addicted person. Employees use an addiction to relieve the pain and find pleasure in failure. Alcohol is the most common addiction. Early signs may be subtle: reduced performance, absenteeism, increased sick leave, or sloppy work. There may be periods of normal work between inefficient performance and absenteeism. Over time, the periods of competence grow shorter.

Most managers when confronted with a problem employee apply what Karrass and Glasser call the "Upside-Down Theory." They do exactly the opposite of what they should do. They discuss, nag, resort to threats, and try to terminate. There is ever-worsening conflict, and the manager spends an inordinate amount of time on an ineffective battle of wills. The manager tends to bog down in criticisms and going over the history of failure and tries to tell the employee what to do instead of focusing on performance.

RPM puts the focus on the employee taking responsibility and on the current performance needed by using a modification of the eight Reality Therapy steps. First, the supervisor establishes and keeps a good relationship with each employee. This means giving recognition for things when they are going right, taking time to talk to employees when they are doing well, avoiding dealing with the employee at the height of a crisis, never criticizing in front of others, giving employees quality time, making work fun whenever possible, not overreacting, trying to avoid criticism, being honest, and when recognizing good work, being specific. Second, the supervisor uses the existing good relationship to get the employee to discuss frankly what the employee is not doing right while avoiding talking about past mistakes, not dwelling on feelings, and focusing on performance. Third, the supervisor asks the employee to evaluate his/her behavior in terms of its effect on the task or other workers. Fourth, the supervisor and employee negotiate a realistic, workable plan to handle the situation better, including performance targets. In negotiating the plan, the both-win negotiation process can be used, which involves making a plan that benefits both parties; full employee participation in making the plan; regular follow-up; and specific targets, standards, task descriptions, and milestones. Fifth, the supervisor gets the employee to agree to the plan and provides commitment to help where supervisor help is needed. Sixth, the supervisor does not ask for or accept excuses and the supervisor does not give excuses. The more the employee learns not to depend on excuses as crutches, the more the employee is helped to become stronger by focusing on performance. Excuses dilute ability, commitment, and initiative, and they relieve the person of responsibility. The goal is to build confidence. If necessary, the plan is renegotiated. Seventh, the supervisor lets natural consequences take over, not punishing, and limiting criticism, being sure that any criticism given is constructive not punitive. This means focusing on employee strengths, suggesting working together to find a better way, and focusing on the right ways, not wasting time talking about the wrong way. Eighth, the supervisor does not give up too easily (Karrass and Glasser, 1980).

Willa Bruce (1984) sees Reality Therapy as particularly amenable to use by managers because it is relatively quick and easy to learn and is action oriented. Bruce (1985) discusses how Reality Therapy and RPM can provide the manager with an effective way to deal with the problem employee. She also relates Chester Barnard's concepts of managerial responsibility in creating balance between organizational goals and employee aims and needs to Reality Therapy.

One study of managers trained with Reality Therapy using The Computer Consultant concluded that the likelihood of an employee becoming a problem was 0.66 (Dickey and Doughty, 1983). If a manager had been using Reality Therapy as a management technique, the likelihood was reduced to 0.40. If the employee became a problem and the manager did nothing, the likelihood of the problem being eliminated and the employee contributing to organizational effectiveness was 0.0095. If an EAP was used, the likelihood of the employee contributing to organizational goals was 0.48, if Reality Therapy was used it was 0.70, and if both were used it was 0.84 (Bruce, 1986).

Albert Ellis and Rational Emotive Therapy

Albert Ellis was born in Pittsburgh and grew up in New York City. He has a Ph.D. in clinical psychology and practices psychotherapy and marriage and family counseling in New York City. In the 1950s, he developed a theory of personality and a method of psychotherapy, Rational Emotive Therapy (RET), based on the assumption that an individual's irrational or faulty beliefs cause his/her dysfunctional behavior and destructive self-concept. It is primarily a person's beliefs, interpretations, and expectations, rather than the situation, that brings happiness or unhappiness. Ellis' work is heavily influenced by Stoic philosophy. He views the development of rationality along with a commitment to examine the deepest thought patterns as what is important for mental health. He also founded the Institution for Rational Living in New York. His extensive writings include *Executive Leadership: A Rational Approach* (1972), *Humanistic Psychotherapy: The Rational-Emotive Approach* (1973), *Handbook of Rational-Emotive Therapy* (1977) with Grieger, *Reason and Emotion in Psychotherapy* (1979), and *Theoretical and Empirical Foundations of Rational Emotive Therapy* (1979) with Whiteley.

As a theory of personality, Ellis' focus is on the person's belief system, rational and irrational, and the process by which irrational beliefs are maintained and lead to unhappiness and unproductive behavior. Ellis holds that society and parents teach irrational beliefs. He suggests irrational beliefs fall into three main categories: "I must be competent in everything and approved by everyone"; "others must treat me properly and when they don't they are worthless"; and "I must have everything I need easily and immediately" (Walrond-Skinner, 1986). People often fail to take advantage of opportunities to satisfy their needs because of their unconscious beliefs and assumptions. They are responsible for perpetuating their problems through cognitive habits that sabotage their efforts to change.

A fundamental principle of RET is that it is beliefs, rather than events, that cause psychological distress. RET focuses on identifying and changing irrational beliefs, changing "must," "should," and "have to" needs and demands, into want, wishing, and preferring. Ellis describes an ABC model: A = the activating event; B = the attitude or belief about the event; C = the consequences or emotional result. Ellis asserts that C is always the result of B, not A. The person's beliefs about the situation determine the feelings and dictate the actions. Irrational beliefs can be recognized by words or ideas such as "awful" and "should." The attitude behind "awful" is usually an unrealistic exaggeration, translating disappointments into disasters and making an unfortunate situation worse. The attitude behind "should" is an unrealistic demand, a demand to have things absolutely the way one wants with no inconvenience. RET focuses on using conscious effort and hard work to overcome upsetting ideas. It requires constantly challenging irrational ideas and replacing them with constructive ideas.

Cognitive restructuring is the process by which old beliefs are replaced by more rational and workable beliefs. This change takes self-support and practice and is most easily accomplished when there is also strong social support. Others can help to detect and dispute irrational beliefs, but it is the individual who must change them. Individuals should engage in critical thinking rather than passively accept society's propaganda and norms.

Ellis' treatment of many business and government executives lead to his applying RET to executives in organizations in *Executive Leadership: A Rational Approach* (1972). Ellis developed the concept of rational sensitivity as a way of becoming more sensitized to and perceptive of one's own and others' failings and becoming less condemning of failings. Rational sensitivity was focused on enhancing your own and others' authentic behaving. It promoted tolerance, open-mindedness, and flexibility. Ellis felt the prelude to controlling organizational processes was the ability to exert a large degree of self-regulation. Ellis used the ABC process to diagnose behavior; reduce irrationality; enhance decisiveness, efficient concentration, improved relations with others, self-discipline, and self-acceptance; and to deal with depression, hostility, and emotional upsets.

The workplace environment can be used to support more rational behavior by making information available to workers so they can rationally evaluate organizational change and make informed decisions; by providing workers with the opportunity to rationally discuss organizational policy and how it affects the employee's goals; and by providing a predictable structure within which employees can anticipate organizational behavior and plan accordingly. Organizations can also promote critical thinking by inviting employee participation in analysis and decision making. Critical thinking is learned through examining the evidence and experimentation. Organizations can also promote mental health by offering short-term counseling services to help workers examine in depth their self-sabotaging thoughts and identify their useless habitual ways of thinking (Corey, 1990).

Ellis, unlike Glasser, views man as not needing other people's love. Also, Ellis does not accept Glasser's need for self-worth but views valuing of oneself and existing as sufficient. Both focus on doing, thinking, and feeling, but Ellis focuses more on feeling and thinking and Glasser more on doing. Sewall (1982) suggests using a rational-reality approach for career counseling that combines aspects of the two.

RET has been used to reduce occupational stress. In one study of 53 working women, a training program of stress reduction that employed behavioral conditioning techniques of relaxation was compared with a training program using cognitive coping skills, including time management, RET, and assertiveness training (Higgins, 1986). Results indicated that both programs were effective and that participants of both programs reported less stress than the nonparticipants. The participants had lowered scores on two psychological indicators of stress, emotional exhaustion and personal strain. Neither program lowered absenteeism; however, absenteeism rates were already so low that it seemed unlikely that the programs would reduce them. Results were obtained with approximately six hours of instruction, indicating that even rela-tively brief programs can produce significant reductions and have potential to help workers cope with occupational stress.

Another study concluded that RET used in an EAP appears to be cost-effective and viewed by users as helpful (Klarreich, DiGiuseppe, and DiMattia, 1987). Of 431 employees using the EAP, 364 completed RET counseling. There was a 70 percent reduction in absenteeism, with a $2.74 cost-benefit ratio. A hidden savings was the small number of employees who had to be referred out (only 31 employees over a three-year period). The average number of one-half– to two-hour RET counseling sessions by a Ph.D.-level psychologist trained by Ellis was 4.1 sessions. Ellis (1985) has also written on the use of RET in EAPs. RET has also been used to address burnout (Richman and Nardi, 1985), for achieving peak performance in organizations (Spillane, 1985), and for leadership development (Ellis, 1975).

Existential, Gestalt, and Family Systems

Although existential and gestalt theories are not specifically focused toward work organizations, some of their concepts have been applied to that setting, and family systems theories in recent years have been increasingly applied to the workplace. As noted in Chapter 4, much of the adult behavior in the workplace may be related to early childhood experiences.

Existential

Existentialism focuses on concerns that are rooted in the individual's existence. Existentialists perceive identity as dynamic and always in the process of reconstruction and change. A person's changing perception about him/herself can cause radical shifts in mood and significantly affect mental health. Some choices may lead to feelings of anxiety and meaninglessness. Although that is normal, it can result in a temporary loss of will, which can affect the ability to complete routine work tasks. Mental health can be promoted and mental illness prevented by facing the anxiety caused by conflicts regarding four ultimate concerns: freedom, meaninglessness, isolation, and death. These four concerns spawn conscious and unconscious fears and reactions. Defense mechanisms such as denial, daydreaming, idealizing, and sublimation, which help a person to cope, must be broken through in order to develop a personal, meaningful response. Feelings of dissatisfaction or sadness may accompany defense mechanisms but usually are not severe enough to interfere with the ability to work or to produce mental illness. However, to lead a productive, committed, responsible, and creative life, one must break through the defenses (Yalom, 1970).

Organizations can enhance mental health in a number of ways, including creating a work environment that is pleasing, because beauty provides meaning and can enhance mental health; promoting discussions of issues; providing individual and small group counseling for times of stress or when a fellow worker is seriously ill or dies; providing recognition of the significance of individuals in organizations; recognizing that production will not always be high when an employee is having difficulties and not giving up on the employee; and training managers to understand psychological defense mechanisms and helping them to become more skillful in helping employees develop more creative solutions (Yalom, 1970).

Gestalt

Gestalt theory, developed by Fritz Perls, focuses on intrapersonal conflict that results from inner polarities. Each person is seen as a unique cluster of characteristics that are always in flux. The goal is to unify and integrate into a whole the constituent parts of self and of experiences. People seek coherence, but they may find it difficult to include parts of themselves that are in conflict and they may favor some characteristics while denying or suppressing others. The disconnected parts become unavailable as valuable inner resources. By repressing attributes that are seen as negative, some energy creativity is lost (Perls, 1969). By reframing the negative within the whole self-image, one enhances the ability to develop more adaptive spontaneous responses. This is seen as a useful self-motivational technique for the "Third Wave" (Holder, 1990).

Gestalt theory sees people as seeking out experiences that conform to their preconceived rules and expectations. People tend to ignore, discount, and isolate experiences that don't fit. People also dissociate or become alienated from parts of themselves and are left with a narrow or fragmented self-image. Mental illness may occur when persons become so disconnected within themselves and from their past and others that they have difficulty functioning. If the work role lacks congruence or is in conflict with the person's perceptions, the person may feel the need to change or quit and will suffer tension from not wanting to disengage. If the current self-image and life situation is significantly in conflict with the past, the person may lose the ability to move into the future with a strong identity and confidence. Mental health can be enhanced within an organization by providing opportunities for employees to be engaged in activities and discussions that give expression to diverse parts of themselves and that allow them to be creative and spontaneous. Individuals should be encouraged to be responsible for their work choices and to participate in finding solutions to problems. Challenging work and team projects can help employees remain engaged in their work. Workshops can be used to model how to integrate and give expression to diverse parts of the self at work and at home (Polster and Polster, 1973).

Family Systems

As discussed in Chapter 4, what has been learned about childhood learning and the family of origin can be applied in the workplace. Concepts of family therapy are increasingly being used in the workplace. Business therapy is an emerging field that is used to open communication among coworkers and is used to help executives discuss emotional issues that can lead to organizational trouble. One example is a manager at Connecticut Mutual Company who used a business therapist to help him overcome his autocratic management style and to conduct weekly group therapy. This led to a newly cooperative office. The organizational psychologist showed how the way people related in their childhood families was leading to their adult organizational behavior (Kaplan, 1986).

Parents profoundly affect the development of their children's personalities and how they relate to others. The home is where a sense of self and understanding of others is developed. Parents are the first authority figures, and siblings, relatives, and friends are leaders, followers, teammates, and competitors. Children learn how to trust or doubt, share or be selfish, persevere or quit, get angry or get even, and they learn about power and authority with their family and friends (Stark, 1992). The first attitudes about work are shaped by how children view their parents' attitudes toward work. In the workplace, when people feel insecure, they fall back on behaviors they learned in the past that made them feel more secure and in control. Many of these behaviors were learned in childhood, and they may or may not be functional for the adult in the workplace.

When people do not address and understand how family dynamics affect their attitudes and behavior at the office they are destined to unconsciously interpret events, actions, and communications on the basis of what they learned as children, instead of behaving as adults. Early experiences create for people an idea of how things "should be," so they gravitate naturally toward similar circumstances to create a sense of stability and familiarity for themselves. Instead of supervising and giving feedback, many supervisors "parent" their employees. They wield their power as parents once did, for example demanding respect and compliance "because we said so." On the other hand, employees may relate to their managers as they did to their parents, using the same strategies to gain attention, reacting the same way to criticism, carrying out their responsibilities with the same attention or lack thereof as they did as children, and they may relate to their coworkers as they did to their siblings. As familial influence extends to all aspects of work, people also carry with them into the work world their parents' ideas about how to gain and use power and how to establish a work persona (Stark, 1992).

Increasingly, adults coming into the work force are people who were affected by divorce during their childhoods. These are the children of the baby bust who were born in the period from the mid-1960s into the mid-1970s. Divorce will be an even greater influence for the workers of the future, because 50 percent of marriages now end in divorce. Some children of divorce learn coping behaviors that as adults may not be productive in the workplace. Among these behaviors are assuming the position of mediator and feeling overly responsible for resolving any problems that occur or expecting and accepting many different rules from many different sources without challenging discrepancies or problems or speaking up about differences (Stark, 1992).

Another set of problems may occur with persons who have come from homes in which there were problems with attachment. At the extremes, families may be either enmeshed or disengaged (Galvin and Brommel, 1982). In families where the parent or parents were overly attached to the children, the children may have had difficulty establishing independence and their own boundaries. As adults, they may have difficulty dealing with boundaries and knowing where boundaries are. They may be attracted to situations in which there are confused roles and boundaries. Some workplaces replicate an enmeshed family and will attract people who come from enmeshed families. On the other hand, children who come from homes where there is a lack of attachment may, as adults, seek negative reactions from people around them. This is because, as children, they learned negative attention was better than no attention. Provoking anger for them is a way to get undivided attention. They may also be overly controlling and overly critical of other people (Stark, 1992). They may make poor managers because they do not know how to allow others to be individuals. A manager who is overly controlling and critical will create more disengagement and withdrawal by employees. As the organization increasingly becomes an unfriendly environment, it may attract new employees who come from disengaged families.

Employees and managers sometimes wonder why an organization that is not functioning well seems to grow worse over time, with more and more of the personnel becoming dysfunctional. This is because if the problem is not identified and addressed early in a dysfunctional workplace, people tend to fall back on the more dysfunctional parts of their personalities and more dysfunctional persons are attracted as new employees to that workplace because, at an unconscious level, they recognize the dysfunctional environments in which they grew up. It is not just people's imagination that the workplace is growing more dysfunctional over time, it actually is, because the people in it are growing more dysfunctional. It is like a virus that is contagious and, if left untreated, spreads and becomes more difficult to stop.

It is important for managers to identify how their own families have affected how they respond to people in the workplace and how other people have been influenced by their families of origin. The manager can learn to use this knowledge to keep from personalizing conflict or discipline in the workplace. This knowledge can also help managers identify when a situation is serious enough for referral to an EAP or other professional help. Interpersonal communication training for employees can also include how families of origin influence the way they relate to people.

Early Trauma

Robert Isaacson (1982), a neuroscientist, has argued that traumatic memories tend to be well-entrenched because they are memories of lifesaving responses. These early learnings can lead to a compulsion to repeat. There may also be a neurological reason for severe, overreactive responses. Some researchers believe that enlarged neuronal imprints from stressful experience distort how adults react to stimuli. Ongoing painful experiences may have established circuits in the brain that are triggered when later events create feelings similar to the original events. When an adult who was traumatized as a child experiences a current situation similar to the original painful event, the original response may be triggered. Early emotional pain that was never addressed may remain buried and held in abeyance by the inhibiting mechanisms of ego defenses. When these feelings are buried and unaddressed the person tends to act them out. This may result in inappropriate behaviors with others when events trigger the early trauma or by turning the feelings inward, which may result in destructive illness and mental and physical disorders. Counseling may be required to address these issues, and persons may have to go through original pain work, validating their abuse and working through the original feelings and experiencing their buried anger, grief, and other emotions. Traumatized children may have been physically, sexually, or emotionally abused. They may also have been the victims of substance abuse.

MISUSE OF KNOWLEDGE

Managers can misuse the knowledge that they obtain about employees' psychological functioning and needs. Kanter and Mirvis (1989) claim that the human relationists discovered the right ideas but that greedy managers have used them for the wrong purpose. They believe many managers used the knowledge of the human resource movement just to get more out of their people. The human factor was treated as just another variable to manipulate and another investment, like physical plants. This resulted in disillusionment by employees. Any of these psychological and motivational approaches are open to abuse, and the manager needs to apply them in an ethical manner.

6

Creating a Mentally Healthy
Work Environment

The decade of the 1980s and the early 1990s have been a time of difficulty for many organizations, both public and private, as they have faced a changing world and tightening resources. This has resulted in organizations looking for ways to enhance their productivity and improve their workplaces.

CHANGING THE ORGANIZATIONAL CULTURE

Organizational culture is made up of many elements, including formal rules and procedures, informal rules of behavior, rituals, tasks, jargon, dress norms, and stories people tell about what goes on in the organization. Employers create and control many conditions that can create or alleviate stress and other problems that affect mental health in the workplace. Organizations need to create a culture that values people. Formal and informal systems need to be developed to support the culture and values, and an environment needs to be established to reinforce values and support the system. There is a need for future organizational change, not just individual change (Burrington, 1984).

William Bridges (1992) writes about organizational character. He believes there are as many characters as there are organizations, but for purposes of analysis and comparison, he refers to 16 basic categories, which are organized in the Organizational Character Index (OCI). His categories parallel the 16 basic personality types originally presented by Carl Jung (1953–71) and further developed by Katharine Cook Briggs and Isabel Briggs Myers (Myers, 1962) in their Myers-Briggs Type Indicator (MBTI) for identifying an individual's personality type. The OCI is not an adaptation of the MBTI, but it is based on the same four pairs of opposing tendencies adapted from Jung's work: extroversion or introversion; sensing or intuition; thinking or feeling; and judging or perceiving The OCI is an experimental tool for working with and in organizations. Character is seen as coming from the way the organization was set up by its founder; the type of business or profession; the employee group; its subsequent leaders; its history; and its organizational life cycle stage.

Extroverted organizations have open boundaries, allow access to decision making, collaborate on decisions, act quickly, experiment with different lines of action, trust oral communication, encourage interdepartmental cooperation, turn outside for guidance, seek assistance when in trouble, invite outsiders to celebrations, and have a motto such as "The answer is out there — we just have to find it"; introverted organizations have closed boundaries, prevent access to decision making, reach consensus after a decision is made, respond only after study, explore options in detail to find one line of action to try, trust written communication, experience interdepartmental mistrust, insist guidance must come from within, circle the wagons when in trouble, keep celebrations within the organization, and have a motto such as "The answer's within — we just have to figure it out" (Bridges, 1992, p. 15). Sensing organizations are at their best with detail, handle masses of data, prefer solid routines and incremental change, make improvements, see intuitive organizations as lost in the clouds and the future as an extension of the present, emphasize targets and plans, trust experience and authority, tend to organize functionally, and have as a motto something like "Change the structure"; intuitive organizations are at their best with the big picture, can spot emerging trends, are a little careless about routines, prefer transformational change, change their paradigms, see sensing organizations as stuck in the mud, believe the future can be created, emphasize purposes and vision, trust insight and creativity, often use cross-functional teams, and have a motto like "Change the belief systems" (Bridges, 1992, p. 20). Thinking organizations make decisions based on principles, think in terms of rules and exceptions, value what is logical, emphasize the objective, believe criticism leads to efficiency, encourage employees to live up to expectations, are a social machine, and have a motto such as "Do the right (or intelligent) thing"; feeling organizations make decisions based on values, think in terms of particular human situations, value what they care about, emphasize the people, believe support leads to effectiveness, encourage employees to do their best, are a social community, and have a motto such as "Work well together" (Bridges, 1992, p. 23). Judging organizations drive toward decisions, may be weak in information gathering, set clear and specific standards, define lots of things in detail, are often moralistic, and have a motto such as "Fish or cut bait"; perceiving organizations keep options open and seek more information, may be weak in decision making, set general standards, leave many things vague and undefined, are loose and fairly tolerant, and have a motto such as "Don't miss an opportunity" (Bridges, 1992, p. 26).

The 16 different types of organizational character are based on the possible mixes of extroverted (E), introverted (I), sensing (S), intuitive (N), thinking (T), feeling (F), judging (J), and perceiving (P). The OCI can be used to assess how organizations are likely to approach and deal with internal and external change. For example, extroverted organizations are readier to change in response to external forces but have more difficulty with internal pressures to change than do introverted organizations. Sensing organizations are likely to identify and handle effectively short-term changes with an incremental approach, while the intuitive organization is better at identifying and handling long-term changes through whole system transformations.

Organizational type also affects transition, the psychological process that is gone through when coming to terms with change. How each organizational type reacts to losses and endings is different:

> There aren't good characters and bad characters. There are simply the strengths and weaknesses of the particular character that an organization has. Neither extroversion nor introversion, thinking nor feeling, sensing nor intuition, judging nor perceiving is better than the other — except in particular circumstances. (Bridges, 1992)

Researchers have developed different perspectives about organizational culture. Meyerson and Marin (1987) have described three different theoretical viewpoints regarding organizational culture. The integration perspective focuses on all cultural manifestations being interpreted as consistently reinforcing the same themes, all members of the organization sharing in an organization-wide consensus, and the culture as being seen clearly with no ambiguity. The differentiation perspective sees cultural manifestations as sometimes inconsistent with ambiguity, with consensus occurring only within the boundaries of subcultures, with conflict often occurring between subcultures, and with ambiguity channeled so it does not intrude on the clarity that exists within the subcultures. The fragmentation viewpoint focuses on ambiguity as the essence of organizational culture, with consensus and disagreement being issue specific and constantly fluctuating, with no stable subculture or organization-wide consensus, and with clear consistencies and inconsistencies being rare.

Martin (1992) has gone on to explore those three perspectives in relationship to organizational change by using them with a case study of a Fortune 500 company with over 80,000 employees. The integration viewpoint is seen by employees as encouraging egalitarianism, fostering innovation, and expressing concern about the employees' physical and mental well-being. The integration perspective is the dominant view of organizational reseachers and practitioners in the United States. The core of the integration perspective is the desire for organization-wide consensus. Consensus can be in the form of action consistency, involving consistency between the espoused managerial values and formal and informal practices, or symbolic consistency, when changes such as dress norms or physical arrangements are made to serve as symbols of the organizational values. Culture is seen as existing to alleviate anxiety, provide control and predictability, and clarify ambiguity. Culture is defined in terms of that which is shared, but there is no standard agreement on what exactly is shared. Individual deviation is not readily recognized or accepted. Organizations with high integration may exclude from power those with values or identities that are different. Organizations with upper- and middle-class white men predominating in top management may tend to hire and promote similar individuals with shared values. Organizational change is seen as occurring when there are breaks in consistency in a deteriorating culture, followed by an organizational cultural transformation, in which there is establishment of a new culture.

The differentiation view challenges claims of egalitarianism and sees impediments to innovation and lack of concern for employee well-being in a setting of conflict and contradiction. Under supposed organizational unity, there is a hotbed of conflicting and overlapping subcultures. Inconsistency may occur in actions or ideology or may be symbolic. Consensus may occur within the subcultural boundaries, with ambiguity channeled outside those boundaries. Deviants may be viewed as heroic, although they also may be fired. Change is incremental, is localized within subcultures, and tends to be triggered by pressures in the segmented environment (Martin, 1992).

The fragmentation viewpoint focuses on ambiguity. There are neither clear consistencies nor clear inconsistencies as there are in integration and differentiation. There is no organization-wide or subcultural consensus. Issues generate temporary concern but do not coalesce into any kind of shared opinion. Confusion and unclarity surround egalitarianism, innovation, and concern for employee well-being. Employees are confused and uncertain about the organization's commitment. There are many interpretations of organizational actions. There is complexity without order and predictability. The organization, subcultures, and self are viewed as fragmented. Cultural change occurs through diffused power. Power is not concentrated at the organizational or subcultural level. Change is constant and can be driven by individuals. Change is not planned, and there may be a greater value on employee diversity (Martin, 1992).

Martin (1992) sees that in any organization at any point in time, all three perspectives (integration, differentiation, and fragmentation) can be operative. No single perspective can account for organizational complexity. Focusing on only one perspective ignores or distorts crucial aspects of an organization's culture. It would seem that if organizational culture is to be changed, attention must be paid to all three perspectives and how they operate, specifically in the organization seeking change.

Organizations in crisis may worsen. Devine (1984) suggests they may cope with crisis by exhibiting crisis syndrome characteristics, including becoming more centralized and authoritarian. This results in secondary crises as individuals cope with high anxiety by means of hostility, dependency, or work deterioration. To create a more mentally healthy workplace, many organizations need to make changes in their corporate cultures. For example, R. H. Macy & Company executives decided to change the entire Macy culture by eliminating the existing imperial atmosphere. They wished to personalize the organization and remove the pomposity. Macy's changes for the future had to be incorporated in a five-year plan required under bankruptcy reorganization. The approach of the executives, which was to be based on leading, not managing, was considered critical to the success of that plan. The focus was to be on empowering employees by giving employees information to make decisions and authority to carry them out (Rosenberg, 1992). This approach follows the decentralization focus of other organizations, such as Wal-Mart.

The approach of emphasizing leadership rather than management addresses the views of many employees who think that managers are in the way. Two management consultants, Rich Moran and George Bailey of Sibson & Company, San Francisco, who conducted focus groups involving more than 50,000 workers over three years all over the world, found that employees want to do their jobs and do them well. They want to contribute to a successful organization, but to do that, they need for managers to get out of their way and let them do it. Employees find that too often, management promises are not delivered. This leaves employees angry and cynical about the constant presentation of initiatives that come with the same promises of immediate improvement. They see this as a "program of the month" style, whether suggestion systems, customer service programs, quality improvement programs, or employee involvement programs. The research found that workers want to be customer/client driven but they often do not have a clear path to deliver the organization's resources. They are not satisfied with the status quo and believe their organizations can do better. They feel they are not consulted or listened to sufficiently. They want management to understand they know more than they are credited for, and they dislike being given insincere promises. Line employees view staff as siphoning off money better used elsewhere and see headquarters as useless (Cunniff, 1993).

This type of research supports the view that employees know what they want, and what they want is to be treated as adults. They want to be empowered. They want support from management to carry out their jobs, and they do not want to be overmanaged and treated as children within their organizations. Empowering people and treating them as adults is a healthy mental health approach. People who are empowered, are treated as adults, an have their self-esteem supported and encouraged are more mentally healthy individuals. When more employees function appropriately as healthy adults, the work environment becomes more and more functional and a better place in which to work, which again strengthens individual employees. This is a positive upward spiral of movement toward becoming and maintaining a mentally healthy work environment that will be a place where people will look forward to coming to work and will be productive.

More organizations are also striving to make the workplace a friendlier place. Various approaches to organizational outreach are being made because employers increasingly recognize that a happier work force means greater productivity, less absenteeism, better services or products, less labor strife, and less outlays on workers' compensation and medical benefits. A wide variety of approaches is being taken including approaches that recognize that the employee is not an entity unto his/herself but is part of a larger outside world that includes the family. IBM is building child day care centers to make their workplace more family friendly. Levi Strauss has an 18-member task force, which includes chief executives, managers, secretaries, and equipment operators, to explore ways the company can help solve family problems that affect the workplace. United Services Automobile Association encourages its 13,000 employees to use a wide array of health promotion programs, from a fish-stocked lake and sports fields to subsidized "dump your plump" cafeteria meals. They spend 2.7 percent of their budget on career training to promote from the ranks and provide college classes in 60 on-site classrooms for 1,800 employees. They pay graduate school tuition fees and provide self-improvement programs that can be used on their computer terminals. Tandem Corporation uses Friday night parties around a company pool to bring engineers and top executives together, while Wang Laboratories has an open-door policy that allows anyone to attend any company meeting (Mulligan, 1991).

The first step in creating a mentally healthy workplace is to take a serious look at the existing corporate culture. What values are held and reinforced; what is acceptable and unacceptable in the organization? Are these conducive to the mental health of the employees? Do these help employees to be empowered, act as adults, and strive to reach their full potential? Do they keep stress to a minimum? What are the healthy parts of the organization that should be kept and encouraged? What are the negative parts of the organization that should be changed, discouraged, and extinguished?

QUALITY OF WORKLIFE

Quality of worklife (QWL) is one way to look at the effectiveness of an organization and the quality of life at work for its employees. QWL has the goals of enhancing effectiveness of the organization and improving the quality of life at work for the employees. It is based on the assumptions that employees should be treated with dignity and respect; that they support what they help to create; that they want to understand how their organization functions and how their efforts contribute; and that they act more responsibly when treated as adults (American Society for Training and Development, 1983).

For many people, self-fulfillment through economic goals may be unattainable. This will probably be so for many people in the large birth cohort of the baby boom, where there have simply been too many people to be able to get up career ladders. This also may be true for many people caught in the economic shifts of the changing world economy, which will permanently dislocate some workers from their chosen career paths. With less economic fulfillment, QWL becomes more important for employees.

A midwest public utility, Minnesota Gas Company, which did QWL for many years has surveyed job applicants, employees, and managers for over 30 years. Their survey has also been administered by many other organizations. Minnesota Gas Company's data on over 57,000 people regarding preference for ten common job factors indicates employees' first two preferences are security and the type of work, with older and male workers preferring security and younger and female workers preferring the type of work. Other preferences in order of employee choice were advancement, a company/organization to be proud to work for, pay, pleasant and agreeable fellow workers, a considerate and fair supervisor, benefits, hours of work, and working conditions/physical environment. Older workers are more concerned with long-term factors such as advancement, benefits, and security, while younger workers are more interested in short-term concerns such as coworkers, hours, pay, and working conditions. Managers' order of preference was advancement, type of work, company, security, pay, supervisor, coworkers, benefits, working conditions, and hours, but managers' predictions of employees' preferences were not always correct (Sears, 1984).

Employee Assistance Programs (EAPs) may be successfully involved in QWL. They can help employees and employers take responsibility. Labor unions may also be successfully involved in QWL. EAPs and labor unions can be involved with management in strategic program planning, marketing, committee development, training, and program monitoring (Cohen-Rosenthal, 1985).

One way to examine the QWL is through employee attitude surveys. Employee attitudes and perceptions should be assessed periodically. The potential positive impact of regularly assessing the QWL in organizations has been noted (Lawler, 1982). Research indicates that there are relationships between organizational characteristics and employee morale, absenteeism, and performance. This has encouraged employers to undertake regular surveys of employees' attitudes and to monitor absenteeism and turnover rates. Early QWL focused on planning, availability of jobs, training, mobility, employment security, fringe benefits, and pay. Eventually, job safety, working conditions, and equitable distribution of job opportunities and wages were added. A good QWL environment has come to be defined as

> One that attracts employees, trains and develops them, advances them, provides them with enriching work experiences, invites their participation in job-related organization-wide decisions, and, at the same time, provides them with stable employment, an adequate income and benefits, fair treatment, due process and a safe and secure place to work. (Mirvis and Lawler, 1983)

QWL has been expanded from satisfaction with wages, hours, and working conditions to include worker satisfaction with all aspects of work and the work environment. Employees' job attitudes and behaviors are also reflected in their QWL.

Until recently, management sought to avoid responsibility for mental health in the workplace. Labor leader Leo Perlis, in his address "Labor's Plans for the 1980s," noted:

> When I worked as a twister in the silk mills in Patterson, New Jersey, there were loom fixers but no mind fixers. Nothing much has changed in the 40 years since then for most workers. There are still machine fixers in the workplace — but no mind fixers. There are still experts in production efficiency in mine, mill, and office — but no experts in emotional efficiency in the workplace. (Perlis, 1980)

In the 1980s and 1990s we are starting to develop experts in emotional efficiency, and more and more employers are coming to see that mental health is part of the QWL and that mental health problems are not just brought to the work site by the employees. The workplace itself is often a significant factor in the creation of conditions that cause mental health problems. Organizations recognizing this can bring about change to create healthy workplaces.

ORGANIZATIONAL POLICIES

Organizations can influence their corporate culture, respond to employee needs, and create more mentally healthy workplaces through their policies. There is also a societal view that employers have a responsibility to provide for their employees. A study of 2,207 people concerning their views as to whether employers should be responsible for providing counseling for employees for substance abuse and family problems and for providing child care concluded that a substantial majority of the general public believe that employers have some responsibility to provide social services to employees. Black and female respondents attributed more responsibility to employers, and higher education levels correlated to the belief employers should provide counseling programs. Those who were married and those with children were least likely to believe that employers had responsibilities for social services (Roff and Kelmmock, 1985).

Three of the major changes that are affecting the U.S. family are a decrease in the number of expanded families, a large increase in the number of single-parent families, and a majority of women working outside the home. Of single-parent homes, 90 percent are headed by women, and a growing number of women are choosing to have children alone. The baby boom generation has brought a new set of expectations to the workplace. Both women and men are more articulate about integrating work and family. Family-oriented benefits are increasingly being offered by employers or negotiated by unions. These include family leave, maternity and paternity leave, child and elder care, alternative work schedules, wellness and recreation programs, and EAPs. *Working Mother* magazine publishes a list of what they believe to be the best 100 companies for working mothers. The companies are chosen for setting a standard for the way every firm in the country should operate to improve the quality of life of U.S. families and increase productivity. Areas surveyed were pay and advancement for women, support for child care, and other "family-friendly" benefits such as job protected leave for childbirth, child care, and job flexibility. Benefits included million-dollar on-site child care centers offered by 56 of the 100 companies; after school and summer programs; sick child programs; job sharing; flextime; work at home; childbirth leaves; fitness centers; aquatic centers; and on-site classes for advanced degree work (Pabst, 1993).

Family Leave Policies

Parental and medical leave legislation was passed by Congress and signed by President Bill Clinton in February 1993. The family leave law covers employers of 50 or more employees. If allowing the leave would create a "substantial and grievous injury" to organizational operations, organizations may deny the benefit to salaried employees within the highest paid 10 percent of their work force. Employers may obtain up to three medical opinions and certifications on the need for the leave, and if employees do not return, employers can recapture the health care premiums they paid during the leave. Employees who have been employed for at least one year and for at least 25 hours per week are covered. Employees who are eligible can take up to 12 weeks of unpaid leave during any 12-month period for birth of a child; adoption of a child; need to care for a child, spouse, or parent with a serious health condition; and any serious health condition of their own that makes them unable to perform their job. Employees must receive their same job or an equivalent position upon their return, and employers must continue to pay any health care benefits they were providing. Workers on family leave are not eligible for unemployment or other government compensation during the leave. Some states have had their own family leave policy, which may have to be modified to fit the federal standard. State laws may be more extensive than federal law. The United States was the last industrialized nation to establish a national parental leave policy.

During the first half of the twentieth century, pregnant women were held to be unemployable. If they were employed and became pregnant, they were automatically terminated or forced to take lengthy unpaid leaves. They lost seniority and promotions and were not guaranteed their old jobs back after a maternity leave. The Pregnancy Discrimination Act of 1978 (PDA), an amendment to Title VII of the Civil Rights Act of 1964, now bars discrimination in employment based on pregnancy. Employers are free to provide any level of benefits they wish (or none at all) as long as they do not use pregnancy as a criterion for allocating those benefits. If an organization provides a broad base disability program, they cannot exclude pregnancy from coverage. In 1983 the Supreme Court ruled that PDA mandates equal maternity benefits for employees and wives covered under company medical insurance plans. This was to correct the problem of many dependents being given less coverage than employees.

Some states, including California and Montana, have laws going beyond PDA. The California law guarantees female workers up to four months of unpaid leave and guarantees the same or a similar job upon return to work when they become disabled because of childbirth or other pregnancy-related medical condition. Many women, however, continue to work throughout their pregnancies because they enjoy working or because they need the money or health insurance. Staying on the job longer was correlated in one study with a job involving less physical labor, more flexible working conditions, seniority, and higher levels of skill, training, and status (Chavkin, 1984). Although maternal employment is considered a risk factor for low birth weight, the manner in which employment might affect birth weight is poorly understood. A study has found that those who worked 40 or more hours per week were more likely than women who worked fewer hours to have a low birth weight delivery at 37 or more weeks (Peoples-Sheps et al., 1991).

Although most major organizations offer disability benefits to their pregnant employees, very few provide extended paid leaves. California, Hawaii, New Jersey, New York, Rhode Island, and Puerto Rico provide state temporary disability insurance (TDI) programs that provide some short-term disability for pregnant women. Some organizations in TDI states package TDI benefits and company benefits so that women receive their full salary while on maternity leave. Some employers allow employees to use vacation, sick, or personal leave as maternity leave. Some union contracts have provided for maternity leave. In Europe, five-month paid leaves are common, with Sweden offering nine months of parental leave, usable by the mother or father or shared by both, that replaces 90 percent of the salary of the person on leave. Most European countries also offer an additional year of unpaid, job protected leave.

The public sector and highly competitive industries have been most receptive to the provision of paternity leave, which is usually unpaid leave. However, organizations that provide paid maternity leave and not paid paternity leave could be subject to an equal rights discrimination claim, which they would be likely to lose.

Child Care Policies

With many employees having children who still require child care, being ensured of good child care is a primary concern of many workers. Having unstable child care can create considerable stress for parents while they are at work. The psychological strain can manifest itself in work-related attitudes and behaviors, including absenteeism (Brooke and Price, 1989). When child care arrangements fall through, parents may lose work days or be late to work, and this causes productivity problems. The "3-o'clock syndrome" refers to the stress parents feel when waiting for latchkey children to call after school to let their parents know they have reached home safely. Employers have an interest in child care issues because of these productivity issues. Also, good child care should be a concern of all employers and society because of the importance of raising a healthy generation of children. These are the citizens and workers of the future, and if they have good mental health as children, they will probably have good mental health as adults.

Since World War II, the need for child care for the children of working parents has increased dramatically. With 50 percent of all children under age six having mothers in the work force in 1987, up from 38 percent in 1977 (U.S. Department of Commerce, 1987), there is a need for employers to take an interest in helping their employees obtain good child care. Although the number of employers offering child care has increased markedly, the level of assistance still lags far short of the need. There is an unprecedented need for child care services, with many communities failing to meet that need. The number of latchkey children between ages 5 and 13 in 1987 was estimated by the Census Bureau to be 2,065,000 (7.2 percent) (U.S. Department of Commerce, 1987). Although on-site child care was a popular concept, it has given way to a variety of employer alternatives: child care resource and referral services; vacation, holiday, and summer camp programs; child care subsidies and accounts that may have tax benefits; purchase of slots for employees in existing community facilities; and consortium or community-shared child care facilities.

Employees' attitudes toward managing work and child care vary, depending on variables such as familial care, household employment configuration, dependent care profile, gender, and managerial status. Research suggests family support can help buffer employees from life stress (Cohen and Wills, 1985). A Department of Labor study found that female employees with one child under age six were absent nearly 13 days a year, compared with nearly 7 days for women with school-aged children (Klein, 1986). Studies tend to support the positive impacts of child care programs on productivity in terms of reducing absenteeism, tardiness, and turnover.

Eldercare Policies

Eldercare has increasingly become an issue because of longer life spans and what is referred to as the "sandwiched generation," people who still have children as dependents but also are having to care for elderly parents. Greater interest is also being taken because the more affluent live longer, and those in managerial and professional positions who have influence in organizations are likely to be impacted by this problem. Also, people are living longer, and with the end of mandatory retirement ages, more of them may stay in the workplace longer, and working spouses may have retired spouses who require eldercare.

Traditionally, women have been the caregivers for elderly parents, and this still continues to be true, but because so many women are now in the work force, this means caring for elderly parents also impacts the workplace. The day-to-day tasks of caring for an elderly parent may take a toll on an employee. With many services open only during working hours, an employee may use work time to confer with doctors, find home health care, and apply for Medicaid and other services. In a 1984 survey the New York Business Group on Health found excessive phone use by employees of aged relatives in nearly two-thirds of the 69 responding companies. Two-thirds to three-fourths of respondents mentioned absenteeism, lateness and the use of unscheduled days off as problems. Three-fifths of the companies reported excessive stress and physical complaints. Companies felt that responsibility for elderly parents negatively affected work, with nearly half reporting decreased productivity and work quality. The employee may be responsible for personal care, housekeeping, cooking, transportation, paperwork, and/or finances. Physical and emotional exhaustion may be the result, and stress may reduce the employee's productivity (Friedman, 1986).

Travelers Corporation found that one of every five of its employees over age 30 provided some care to an elderly parent. The average employee spent about 10 hours a week on parental care and had provided the care for an average of 5.5 years. Of the parents, 20 percent lived with the employee and 15 percent were in nursing homes; 35 percent lived far enough from the employee that travel was also a problem. Of employees, 40 percent managed their parents' finances and nearly 30 percent provided financial assistance (Friedman, 1986).

A University of Michigan School of Nursing study found that people caring for aged relatives were three times more likely to report symptoms of depression and four times more likely to report anger. A Duke University Center on Aging study found 33 percent of those caring for relatives with Alzheimer's disease used prescription drugs for depression, tension, and sleep disorders, compared with 10 percent of the general population. Exhaustion was common, and 22 percent of the caretakers used alcohol daily to relax or sleep. A Philadelphia study of 150 families found 26 percent of employed women had considered stopping work, and 28 percent of nonworking women had quit their jobs to care for their widowed mothers (Friedman, 1986).

Only a few organizations have eldercare policies for their employees, but this is expected to grow because of the demographics in the United States. Some organizations help employees who care for elderly parents through information programs, while others contract for services such as case management and counseling. Some provide seminars on the subject or their EAP conducts workshops. Other approaches are vouchers or subsidies for adult day care and the use of leaves and flexible work hours. Financial assistance remains a concern, because Medicare does not provide for glasses, dental care, or prescriptions and provides only limited long-term care services. Although 97 percent of the elderly are covered by Medicare, one-third have no private insurance to cover the gaps. Parents may have to spend themselves into near-poverty to receive Medicaid, although there are now some protections for the spouse. Indiana has a law that requires children to pay some parental costs. Although care of the elderly is a nontaxable benefit, that benefit is of little use to most employees, because in order to qualify, the elderly must be designated as a dependent of the employee for tax purposes. Unions are also interested in eldercare. A 1987 survey indicated that 30 percent of the responding unions were interested in negotiating eldercare in future contracts (Kemp, 1987).

Flexible Work Schedule Policies

More than one-fifth of the U.S. work force is engaged in part-time jobs, job sharing, or flexible work schedules. Flexible work scheduling has been a rapidly growing organizational policy. The scheduling of all employees to work at the same time may soon become a minority work situation. The interest in alternative work schedules has been reinforced by younger workers, who put a priority on activities other than work, the increasing number of working mothers, an increased interest by fathers in family activities, and the use of alternative schedules or shortened work weeks as a benefit or a cutback management approach when funding for increased wages is scarce.

The most popular of flexible work schedules, staggered work hours, allows employees to come and go at established times other than the traditional 8:00 to 5:00. Core times may be designated when employees must be present, and flex bands on either side of the core time allow for varying start and stop times. Lunch hours may also vary in length. A staggered work hour program might have one employee working 7:00 a.m. to 4:00 p.m. with a one-hour lunch while another employee works 10:00 a.m. to 6:30 p.m. with a 30-minute lunch.

A flexible work hour or flextime program allows employees to come and go on a varied schedule over the work week, perhaps working ten hours one day and four hours the next. Flextime started in West Germany around 1976 and then spread to Canada and then the United States. In Europe, a flex year is used by Beck-Felmeier KG department store in Germany. Employees contract for a certain number of hours per year. Small groups of employees within departments arrange work schedules. There is less absenteeism and tardiness and more concentration on work. The store also uses less backup personnel (Naisbitt and Aburdene, 1985). Another variation in scheduling that is becoming increasingly popular is the compressed work week. Work time is concentrated into fewer and longer days. Four 10-hour days or three 12-hour days are popular compressed work weeks.

Employees tend to choose hours with earlier reporting times and shortened lunch hours in order to have more time later in the day for errands and families. However, some people base their choices on their biological clock. For example, if they function best later in the day, they choose later work hours. A study of surveys taken in 25 federal agencies concluded that flextime results were positive, with employees and supervisors perceiving productivity improvements, absenteeism reduction, and near-elimination of tardiness (Ronen and Primps, 1980). Other studies have also confirmed positive behavior changes and productivity improvements (Golembiewski and Proehl, 1978; Maussen, 1980; Ronen, 1981). Research in a federal agency involving several hundred employees and using a pretest/posttest design indicates that alternative work schedules significantly increase employee satisfaction and reduce leave usage. The alternative work schedules included flextime and compressed work schedules. In the pretest, 11 percent of employees were very highly satisfied with their work schedule, while in the posttest, 29 percent were very highly satisfied. Sick leave decreased from 4.09 percent to 3.06 percent and annual leave decreased from 5.76 percent to 5.04 percent (Harrick, 1986). Other studies have also found increased employee satisfaction after implementation of alternative work schedules (Dunham and Pierce, 1983; Orpen, 1981).

Job sharing is another growing alternative, in which two people divide the time and responsibilities of a job. This has been a popular approach for younger and older workers and also may be a good solution for some people with disabilities and for some workers who work in hazardous working conditions, for example, when state law limits the amount of time spent on video display equipment or around certain substances.

Finally, telecommuting or home-based work/flexiplace is another alternative, which, although it has grown more slowly than originally projected, is beginning to be increasingly popular. Telecommuting involves work away from the central office, either at home or at a satellite location. The federal government, ten states, and many private organizations now have programs or pilots to develop this work approach (Kemp, in press). Telecommuting appears to have productivity benefits and mental health benefits for most workers, but the types of work and the types of employees who telecommute require careful assessment and selection, because not all jobs and personality types are well-suited to the approach. Some people do not do well working at home, because they find they need more social stimulation and find the isolation difficult.

Substance Abuse Policies

As noted earlier (Chapter 4), a drug-free workplace requires many employers to put into place substance abuse policies, including education, prevention, rehabilitation, and EAPs, and the Rehabilitation Act of 1973 and the Americans with Disabilities Act of 1990 provide partial protection for substance-abusing employees who come under the category of a qualified handicapped individual. Organizational policy may prohibit alcohol or drug use or possession at work; hold current alcohol and drug users to the same performance standards as other employees; require employees' behavior to conform to the organization's drug-free workplace policy; and discipline or fire an employee for poor performance or breach of work rules even if the cause is substance abuse impairment. Drug testing is not prohibited, but if used by the employer, the employer should have a clearly written policy regarding its use.

The federal government developed policies for federal employees and alcoholism under the Hughes Act (P.L. 91-616) as early as 1970. Substance abuse policy should focus on the organizational environment as well as the individual. As noted earlier, corporate cultures can encourage or discourage substance abuse. A "culture of drinking" that fosters and sanctions alcohol use can be replaced with a "culture of sobriety" (Fine, Akabas, and Bellinger, 1982). Where unions are present, organizational policy should be developed and implemented in association with the union. One study of whether supervisors' use of management-initiated policies on alcoholism is related to the presence of a union, the power of the union, and the supervisors' awareness of the union's policy positions found that the supervisors' awareness of union positions and some aspects of union power were positively related to the use of the policy. Union presence was also associated with greater use of alcoholism policy (Beyer, Harrison, and Hunt, 1980). EAPs should also be included in the process of developing a substance abuse policy. Hay (1986) provides a chart outlining development and implementation of drug abuse policy with EAP involvement.

Substance abuse policy should address disciplinary measures for violating attendance standards or other work rules, discharge for possession of drugs and alcohol on the work premises, being at work under the influence, and, if testing is to be used, standards for testing job applicants, standards for testing current employees (such as reasonable suspicion and fitness for duty), and courses of action to be taken if an employee refuses testing (Dees, 1986). The policy should also take into consideration substance abuse education, prevention, and rehabilitation. The substance abuse policy should include an EAP for assessment and referral to professional rehabilitation services. Because EAPs play a major role in secondary prevention of alcoholism (Kelsey, 1982), the EAP should have a clearly identifiable alcoholism component within its broad umbrella services (Jamieson, 1980). The policy should also address how many opportunities will be provided for rehabilitation at the company's expense (Denis, 1989).

As part of the EAP, a determination should be made as to whether to have a policy of constructive confrontation in substance abuse cases. The role of the supervisor in relation to occupational alcohol programs is identification of the problem employee, documentation of inadequate work performance, confrontation of the employee with the record, referral to the EAP or occupational alcohol program, and reintegration. Many job-based alcoholism policies and programs use constructive confrontation, and it is recommended by Trice and Roman (1978). They view the power inherent in work relationships as available to pressure the employee to return to an acceptable work level, and they see the critical factor as supervisory confrontation. However, not everyone agrees. Weiss (1985) sees constructive confrontation and job performance techniques used by EAPs as not very helpful in dealing with alcoholics but as warnings to employees not to be late or absent and to be "on their toes" for fear of being labeled "alcoholic" and subjected to confrontation. In research involving over 600 managers of a large corporation, the researcher concluded that oral discussions with both constructive and confrontational elements were positively associated with acceptance of help. The research found that a balance of constructive and confrontational was most effective and that alcoholism policies legitimated and encouraged action by supervisors (Trice and Beyer, 1984). Although supervisors may be no more likely than others to identify employees with alcohol problems, confrontation by the supervisor may have more impact (Foote and Erfurt, 1981). One study concluded that the success of problem drinkers in a workplace treatment setting was related to older age, longer length of service, and disciplinary referral (Beaumont and Allsop, 1984). A team evaluation as part of the management system may be helpful for confronting a substance-abusing employee. Team Evaluation and Management System (TEAMS) was developed to combine supervisor and associate evaluations. It provides a peer supplemental appraisal process in which the supervisor is one of four to eight raters on an employee self-selected evaluation team (Edwards and Sproul, 1986).

Smoking Policies

Nicotine is one of the most highly addictive substances. Studies have shown that smokers have higher rates of absenteeism and accidents, a greater number of health problems, and higher mortality rates. The Surgeon General of the United States has declared smoking to be hazardous to health because it has been linked to cancer, heart disease, emphysema, and other diseases. The Surgeon General has also declared passive, or secondhand, smoke from tobacco products to be a health hazard. "Passive smoking" refers to nonsmokers breathing the smoke from cigarettes, pipes, and cigars being smoked by other people. Employers have been success-fully sued by nonsmoking employees who have been exposed to secondhand smoke in the workplace. These lawsuits have been based on the employer's general duty under the Occupational Safety and Health Act to provide a reasonably safe work environment (*Kufahl* v. *Wisconsin Bell Co.* [Wisconsin Labor and Industrial Review Committee, No. 88-000676, 1990]). Employees have also claimed that their sensitivity to cigarette smoke qualifies as a handicap under the 1973 Rehabilitation Act and that the employer must accommodate them (*Vickers* v. *Veterans' Administration* [U.S Dist. Ct., Western Washington, 549 Fed. Supp., 1982]).

Many employers have smoking policies that limit smoking to designated areas or forbid any smoking in the work environment and allow smoking only outside the premises. Smoking policies may also include provision for education on the dangers of smoking, smoking cessation programs, and incentives for quitting smoking. The Administrative Management Society has estimated that 6,000 firms have some kind of policy that favors nonsmoking employees. A Bureau of National Affairs survey in 1991 found that 2 percent of companies hire nonsmokers exclusively, 8 percent have a stated preference for nonsmokers, and 7 percent allow individual supervisors to decide against hiring smokers (Clark, 1993).

There is still conflict in regard to policies that forbid employees to smoke, particularly off the job. Some employers, particularly those like fire departments, have been concerned about workers' compensation claims resulting from smoking rather than from smoke inhalation on the job. Other employers see hiring nonsmoking persons or prohibiting employees smoking on or off the job as a way to reduce health insurance costs. In 1987 an Oklahoma City firefighter was fired for smoking a cigarette during his lunch break under a policy that forbade smoking on or off the job. The dismissal was upheld. The judge ruled smoking was not comparable to the fundamental privacy rights based on intimacy issues and protected by the Constitution and the policy had a legitimate goal of protecting the health of employees who performed dangerous physical work. However, refusing to hire a smoker because of increased disability risk has been found unacceptable. In Minnesota in 1988, a job applicant who was refused a position because the employer claimed he was an increased disability risk won a discrimination case with the state Human Rights Commission. The Commission ruled that the employer's rejection, if it was based solely on concern about disability risk, was discrimination. In order to make such a refusal, the employer would have to prove that smoking would impair the person's job performance or injure other employees.

In response to increasing restrictions on employee smoking, 25 states and the District of Columbia have passed smokers' rights in the workplace laws that prohibit discrimination in hiring, firing, compensation, or other terms and conditions of employment based on whether or not the person smokes away from the job (Joel, 1993).

Diversity and Discrimination Policies

As mentioned earlier in this book, the work force is changing and becoming increasingly diverse in regard to gender, race, ethnicity, culture, disability, and medical condition. Organizational policies should reflect this fact and be in compliance with the laws involved (Title VII of the Civil Rights Act of 1964; Title 42 of the United States Code, Sections 1981 and 1983; Civil Rights Act of 1991; Americans with Disabilities Act of 1990; Age Discrimination in Employment Act; Equal Pay Act of 1963; First, Fifth, and Fourteenth Amendments to the U.S. Constitution; and state constitutions) and court decisions.

The employer should also strive to create an environment conducive to integrating a diverse work force. Focus should be placed both on creating a welcoming environment for increasing numbers of diverse employees entering the workplace and on reducing the fears and antagonism of existing workers. Policies should be in place to deal with sexual and other types of harassment. A number of federal decisions have held that Title VII of the Civil Rights Act of 1964 protects job applicants and employees from discrimination based on sexual orientation, and some states, such as California, have laws forbidding discrimination based on sexual orientation. It is essential to have good policies dealing with discrimination and harassment not only from the standpoint of meeting the law and preventing employer and managerial liability but also because of the damaging consequences to the mental health of employees who are discriminated against or harassed and the unhealthy environment that this creates, which can affect productivity and employee satisfaction and retention. To create a mentally healthy work environment requires confronting attitudes, norms, and the climate of acceptance for discriminatory and harassing behaviors in the workplace.

Surveillance and Monitoring

Computer monitoring, monitoring of telephone conversations, and other covert means of surveillance and monitoring are not uncommon in the workplace. Arguments for use of surveillance and monitoring are to decrease theft of organizational property, to improve productivity and customer service, and to prevent personal use by employees of organizational time and property. Employers need to seriously consider whether any surveillance and monitoring is necessary. If it is to be used, there should be a policy as to its use and the policy should be based on legitimate organizational purpose and be as narrowly defined as possible. Surveillance and monitoring raise legal and ethical concerns about privacy. Information gathered should be legal, and information regarding personnel should be restricted to personnel files, with access on a need-to-know basis. Failure to protect privacy can result in an invasion of privacy suit. Employers should also consider that productivity gains may be offset by losses as a result of reduced employee morale and stress.

The federal Employee Polygraph Protection Act of 1988 prohibits most private employers from requiring or even requesting job applicants or employees to submit to a lie detector test except for workplace theft or misconduct, as discussed below. The law does not cover federal, state, or local government employees or employees of contractors for the Federal Bureau of Investigation (FBI) or Department of Defense. Job applicants can also be screened by polygraph testing by security companies and pharmaceutical companies for specific positions in those companies. Discipline, discharge, or other negative actions cannot be taken for a refusal to take a polygraph test. An employee can be asked to take a lie detector test when workplace theft or other misconduct is resulting in loss to the employer, but there are specific restrictions: a specific incident or activity such as known theft, embezzlement, misappropriation, or sabotage must be under investigation; the employee tested must have had access; there must be reasonable suspicion that the employee was involved; and written notice of the incident being investigated and the reason for suspicion must be given at least 48 hours before the test and a copy of that notice must be kept in the files for at least three years. More than half the states also have polygraph protection laws that may be different or more restrictive than the federal. If polygraph testing is to be used in the organization, there should be a clearly written policy regarding its use in compliance with the law.

DESIGNING A HEALTHY ENVIRONMENT

Once the employer has determined the corporate culture that is desired and the policies necessary to establish that culture, attention can be paid to the physical and human changes required to create that culture and implement those policies.

Physical Environment

The physical environment affects the people who work in that environment. Taylor's studies (1911) and the establishment of scientific management, time, and motion studies, and other studies based on the effect of the physical environment have been premised on that idea. We now know that people react to their physical environment mentally and emotionally as well as physically. An employer should strive to create an optimum environment for the physical and mental health of the employees. An optimal environment will encourage brain and body efficiency, which will lead to reductions in illness, absenteeism, and stress and improve productivity. Poulton (1979) established an efficiency model based on the belief that environmental changes in atmospheric temperature and pressure affect efficiency. Noise, light, vibration, and glare also have an effect. Efficiency falls if the temperature, pressure, glare, noise, or vibration is too great or too little. The building, its physical condition and the numbers of people working in a work space may all have an effect. Different jobs are affected to a different degree by the extent of change in the physical environment. The work environment needs to be designed for optimum physical comfort and functioning by creation of an attractive and pleasant environment that people enjoy working in and a physically safe and secure and physiologically optimal environment. Workers are increasingly aware of the dangers of unsafe working environments, from "sick" buildings to the effects of smoking in the workplace to working with toxic and hazardous substances. As Sperry (1984) points out, it is not sufficient to focus programs on internal stressors; external stressors such as office design, lighting, air quality, and noise need to be considered for identification, reduction, and elimination of problems.

When the physical environment is changed to a more hospitable one, research has shown there are marked decreases in absenteeism and medical claims and increases in productivity. Absenteeism has been shown to decrease by as much as 15 percent and medical claims have decreased as much as 24 percent (Blanchard and Tager, 1985). The physical design of the workplace has been proven to affect the quality of workmanship as well as turnover (Becker, 1981).

Hazardous Work Environments

Many work environments are potentially hazardous to employees, ranging from workers who work in production processes with substances such as lead to secondary exposure to hazards such as radiation, asbestos, or high electrical currents when workers are exposed as a result of working with equipment or having work stations located near a hazardous source. For example, lead has long been recognized to cause health problems such as nephropathy among heavily exposed workers (Wedeen, 1984), and there may be a connection to hypertensive or cerebrovascular disease (Zenz, 1988). Mortality studies of lead workers have shown excesses of nonmalignant renal disease and cerebrovascular disease. An update on mortality rates in lead smelter workers found that among the workers studied who had high lead exposure, there was a diminishing excess of death from nonmalignant renal disease, a continued excess from kidney cancer, and an excess of cerebrovascular disease only in those with the longest exposure to lead (Steenland, Selevan, and Landrigan, 1992).

The Federal Occupational Safety and Health Administration (OSHA), a division of the Department of Labor, along with similar state agencies, regulates and monitors environmental hazards. The Occupational Safety and Health Act administered by OSHA applies to all private employers engaged in business affecting interstate commerce. The act requires employers to comply with two safety standards, a general standard applying to all workplaces and a specific standard applying to conditions in particular work environments. The general standard requires a workplace that is free from recognized hazards, including dangerous conditions or situations; conditions or situations that the employer knows about; or those that are generally considered hazardous in a particular industry. Those standards control temperature, noise, ventilation, maintenance, medical and first aid treatment, and personal protective equipment. The hazard communication rule, the right-to-know law, requires employers to inform workers of any and all hazardous chemicals or toxic substances used or produced in manufacturing or used in research, experimentation, or treatment. Training regarding handling is also required. The law originally applied only to chemical manufacturers but was extended to nonmanufacturers in 1988 and to the construction industry in 1989. In 1991 OSHA issued new regulations to protect workers from acquired immune deficiency syndrome (AIDS) and other communicable diseases. Those standards apply to approximately 4.9 million health care workers and another 700,000 workers who routinely come in contact with blood or body fluids as part of their jobs, including law enforcement, correctional facilities, the funeral industry, fire and rescue personnel, linen services, and research laboratories. OSHA estimated the regulations could prevent about 200 deaths and 9,200 blood borne infections per year at an approximate cost of $820 million a year (Ball, 1991). Employers must write exposure control plans and identify workers who may be at risk and train them on how to protect themselves. The regulations require employers to provide face masks, gloves, and gowns to workers who might be at risk. If employees might be exposed to hepatitis, employers must provide free hepatitis vaccinations and follow-up care. Employers in violation could be subject to OSHA penalties that apply to other federal safety laws, including fines up to $70,000 and jail terms. Public sector employees in 27 states with their own state OSHA plans do not come under federal OSHA laws, but the Department of Labor asked those states to adopt similar protections.

Workers who are exposed to hazardous work environments have several mental health concerns. Obviously, one concern is the stress of knowing that one may be working in an environment that may damage one's health or even result in one's death. This stress may be increased by insufficient data regarding the seriousness of the risk or a feeling of lack of control if the person believes he/she has no other choice than to work in a hazardous environment. Economics may play a role, in that the choice may be between working in the hazardous environment for higher pay and working for less pay in a less-hazardous environment. Although the Occupational Safety and Health Act provides protections from retaliation by the employer for an employee who refuses to work on a job the employee legitimately feels is unsafe, in order to support a family, workers may feel they must work in the more hazardous environment, and this may create feelings of conflict, anger, or alienation in the family as well as at the workplace. The family may also feel conflicted, angry, or alienated at the worker and the employer. If the worker's health is affected and the worker becomes ill and/or dies, these emotions may become intensified. If feelings of anger and hostility are turned toward the organization, it places the organization at risk for hostile acts taken against the organization, employer, or fellow employees. These feelings may also occur for workers and their families when the hazard is not an environmental hazard but is a human hazard, for example, police who face the danger of injury or death from other people. Unhealthy choices may be made for dealing with the stress of constantly working in the hazardous environment; the use of alcohol is a not-uncommon choice. In addition, as mentioned earlier, some hazardous work environments raise the potential of causing genetic damage, which not only may cause mental distress for employees and their families but also, if genetic damage occurs, may result in developmental disabilities and mental retardation in employees' children.

The first responsibility of the employer is to make the work environment as free of environmental and other hazards as possible. The organization should have policies and programs to help deal with any hazards that have not been eliminated, including monitoring programs of the work environment and of exposed employees. Employees should be kept up to date on all monitoring results. There should be staff responsible for workplace environment programs who oversee or coordinate all workplace environment programs that affect physical and mental health. This is essential to risk management and prevention. Training programs should be implemented to deal with all risk issues, and wellness and EAP programs should be coordinated to assist with prevention and with dealing with the physical and emotional effects.

Fetal Hazards

Under the Occupational Safety and Health Act, employers must inform employees and prospective employees about chemicals, toxic substances, and other substances in the workplace that there is reasonable cause to believe will cause mental or physical birth defects or be a hazard to the employee's reproductive system or a fetus if the employee is exposed to the substance on the job. However, in 1991 the U.S. Supreme Court in *United Auto Workers* v. *Johnson Control, Inc.* (No. 89-1215) banned fetal protection policies, policies in which employers do not allow women of childbearing age to work in certain hazardous (and also higher-paying) jobs. The court viewed these policies as excuses for denying women equal employment opportunity. The court also held that decisions about the welfare of future children was up to the parents. During the case, documentation was also provided of the fertility risk to males, and it was noted that reproductive males had not been banned from those jobs. In recent years, urology has spawned a new subspecialty, andrology, that focuses on male fertility. This is an outcome of increasingly worldwide male infertility. Substances that interfere with reproduction, genotoxins, can cause low sperm count, structural sperm abnormalities, testicular cancer, and birth defects. Increased levels of genotoxic substances in the environment have coincided with significant increases in the level of male infertility. "Sperm are so sensitive to genotoxins that some occupational health authorities have suggested that routine worker sperm counts be used to test the safety of industrial chemicals. If workers' sperm counts fell after the introduction of a new chemical, it could be presumed hazardous" (Castleman, 1985).

Management Development

Also very important to creating a mentally healthy work environment is having mentally healthy managers who know how to respect employees as adults and know how to work effectively with them. Bad managers can ruin a work environment by causing stress, bringing out unhealthy emotional and mental health responses in their subordinates, and causing a downward spiral in the effective operation of the organization. Selection of the right people for management is essential. Selection should be focused on looking for a candidate who relates well in an adult manner with other people. Being a good manager requires having good self-esteem and a healthy mental attitude toward self and others. Two different foundations of self-esteem, play/task-focused and self-focused, are probably determined early on by parents and other adults in their motivation of children. Children who learn to be play/task-focused develop into flexible, confident competitors because they enjoy figuring out what to do and see themselves doing it. Their self-esteem starts with an internal picture of themselves. They motivate and direct themselves by picturing themselves doing and then trying to act the way they first see themselves in the mental picture. Children who are self-focused look to others to define themselves. They motivate themselves by first looking outside at others. Happiness comes from peer approval or being better. These children develop a tentative confidence that is unreliable (Schwarzbeck, 1992). Managers need to have the good self-esteem that comes from the childhood foundation of being play/task focused. Thus, good managers are flexible and confident and operate from an internal picture of themselves accomplishing a task rather than being motivated by trying to superficially please others.

After selecting good candidates for management, the organization has a responsibility to see that they receive frequent training and reinforcement for developing their management skills, including their understanding of psychological theories of how people function and are motivated and how to have good verbal and nonverbal communication skills. Poor communication and feedback are listed among the organizational contributors to stress and burnout (Ivancevich and Matteson, 1987). The organization also needs to provide them with the resources to effectively carry out their job, including the support of an effective personnel office and EAP.

As Peters and Waterman (1982) have pointed out, the most successful U.S. companies share traits regarding the way they motivate employees. These shared traits are factors that make for a mentally healthy work environment. They include decentralization to give employees a role in decision making, building comradeship, and putting an emphasis on acknowledging good work. A premium is placed on keeping morale high and having fun. The result:

> Better performance, a higher level of contribution from the "average" (employee). . . . More significant, both for society and for the companies, these institutions create environments in which people can blossom, develop self-esteem and otherwise be excited participants in the business and society as a whole. (p. 86)

Participative management is aimed at increasing employee involvement in improving work practices, decision making, and organizational performance. Some of the techniques used are problem solving committees, quality circles, consultation meetings, ombudsmen, attitude surveys, and employee representation on policy making bodies. Research indicates that managers prefer more participation by their employees than currently exists and that managers who do use participatory techniques find they have a favorable impact on employee attitudes and performance. In a survey of over 200 managers in private and public organizations, it was found that the greatest participation gap between existing and preferred levels of participation was in employee representation on policy making bodies (Gilbert, 1988).

Organizational Development and Design

Existing organizations that do not have a good work environment have the ability to change. If the problems in the organization are longstanding, there will need to be a long-term commitment to change. The organization did not develop an unhealthy work environment overnight, and it is unrealistic to expect that it will heal itself overnight, either. In most cases in which the problems are serious, the organization will need to seek long-term help from professional consultants who specialize in organization development and have an understanding of how to create mentally healthy work environments. Consultants can serve as change agents, but they need long-term support from top management to really bring about change, and key individuals within the organization will have to become committed to bringing about change. As noted earlier, employees who have been in difficult work environments tend to regard change with suspicion or even hostility. They have probably seen other fad management techniques and approaches come and go. Resistance is likely to be high. That is why making a commitment to create a mentally healthy work environment cannot be a quick fix but must be a long-term commitment to years of hard work that involve identifying the kind of corporate culture the organization wants to have; changing policies and shifting resources to support that change; and implementing through training, incentives, and changed management styles that address employee participation, requirements, and expectations. Organizational development uses behavioral science concepts to improve organizational effectiveness and employee well-being.

Bridges (1992) believes that much of what passes for organizational development is "really little more than organizational repair." He thinks only two types of activity should be called "organizational development": finding out the inherent potentialities of the organization's basic character and compensating for its weaknesses so the potentialities can be realized and helping the organization to move through natural phases of growth to reach maturity. Team building, fostering creativity, visioning, and conflict resolution are not organizational development but are useful only if they are used to carry out one of the two developmental efforts. He sees it as important for the organization to accept its organizational character and dangerous to use self-denial. An organization must face its true organizational character in order to make decisions for changing it. Identifying and understanding the implications of organizational character also allow reinforcement of strengths or balancing of weaknesses with organizational development interventions or additions of personnel with a certain personality type. This approach can be used with career planning, team building, and leadership development.

Getting employees involved and committed is important to creating a positive work environment. Many approaches have been developed to do this, including job enrichment or enlargement, creating small semiautonomous groups with allocation of specific work to those groups, job rotation, training, job enrichment, teams, quality circles, total quality management (TQM), and integration of the positive policies and programs discussed elsewhere in this chapter.

Job enrichment and enlargement can be used to provide for the use of a variety of skills in a job, to encourage the completion of a whole task in order to see an outcome, and to increase satisfaction through more autonomy and responsibility. Work groups can be trained to do specific jobs, and members of those groups can be cross-trained so they can perform each other's work. Job rotation can be used within the group to add variety to the group. The group can be given more autonomy and responsibility over the jobs that they perform. Teams can be set up to perform specific work over a set period of time. The team is assigned members with the job skills required to perform the task of the team. The team is given autonomy and responsibility to carry out their task over a designated period of time. When the task is completed, team members are reassigned to new teams based on their skills in order to perform a new task. Quality circles involving the establishment of small groups, usually five to ten employees and their supervisor, who are trained in problem analysis, statistical techniques, and other skills necessary to identify work-related problems can be used to propose solutions; proposals are submitted to management for acceptance, modification, or rejection.

TQM can involve many of the organizational and management theories and approaches that have been developed, resulting in different organizations' programs looking quite different, but the main focus is on customer/client satisfaction through maintaining a goal of continual improvement, involvement of employees in decision making, team building, continuous training, and progress measurement. TQM has been practiced for years successfully in Japan and elsewhere. TQM is based on management principles advanced by Deming (1982, 1986), Juran (1964, 1979), and Ishikawa (1985). TQM is oriented to redistributing power away from hierarchically organized administrative elites and returning it to operatives along with input from the recipients of the services or goods. The benefits of TQM include improved access in response to consumer/customer input, improved quality from peer management, and reduced overall costs as the utilization of resources is streamlined (Hoefler, 1992).

President Bill Clinton in his "Putting People First Campaign" stressed his commitment to quality management and public sector application of TQM. As governor of Arkansas, Clinton worked with private companies and the Arkansas Industrial Development Commission to incorporate quality principles at the state level. Arkansas began six pilot programs in agencies in 1990 that have now become quality management initiatives in 34 agencies. President George Bush was involved with the establishment of TQM in the federal government, and a 1992 Government Accounting Office (GAO) survey found that almost 70 percent of the 2,800 civilian and Department of Defense (DOD) installations surveyed reported some kind of TQM initiative. The leading barriers to implementation reported were employee training factors, work force empowerment problems, and strategic planning issues. Of 20 listed obstacles the lowest-rated were process measurement problems and customer focused measurement issues. Employees did not believe they were empowered. The most difficult issue President Clinton will face in pursuing quality initiatives will be employee empowerment (Barkdoll and Leckey, 1993).

> For more than 100 years the ruling orthodoxy of public administration has limited the discretion of bureaucrats, preferring instead a system of laws enacted by elected officials. Recently though, elected officials have been besieged by interest groups, raising diverse, even contradictory, demands. This cacophony of interest precipitates political gridlock. . . . Now bringing quality to government means that civil servants will be empowered, individually and in teams, to put the interests of their customers, the taxpayers, foremost. Inescapably empowerment means greater powers of discretion for civil servants. The question is not how to "tame" the bureaucracy, but more how to empower it constructively. . . . Clinton will have to face the implications of federal executives exercising wide powers of discretion. (Barkdoll and Leckey, 1993)

For TQM to be successful, it must start with the members of the teams who use the processes, both managers and nonmanagers. "Measurement in TQM has one purpose — to support the team to accomplish its aims. Measurement has never improved quality; only people do that. To quote Deming: 'The most important losses or gains cannot be measured'" (Gilbert and Hyde, 1993).

WORKPLACE STRESS

Job stress involves having more work-related problems than one can cope with. Stress is present in all jobs and should be taken into consideration when hiring and orienting new employees. Stress is a key component in individual health, job satisfaction, organizational commitment, performance, and absenteeism (Hendrix, Steel, and Leap, 1991). Numerous factors can influence the ability of an employee to function on the job when subjected to stress, including age, health, psychological makeup, lifestyle changes, family problems, dual career problems, economic conditions, societal attitudes, type of job, organizational role, and management style (Dubinsky, 1985).

Women are now reporting stress-related illnesses at a rate that is nearly equal to that of men. Their incidence of heart disease and alcoholism is also rising. Hennessey (1983) believes that women face more stressors than their male counterparts because of confusion and conflict over perceptions regarding the appropriate roles for women in U.S. society. Double-bind expectations result for women from the demands on women to be successful employees while retaining most of the qualities of the traditional homemaker. Women have been raised with the expectation that they will be caretakers — passive, nurturing, submissive, and primarily concerned with meeting others' needs. In contrast, employees are expected to be assertive, risk taking, persevering, and able to allocate additional time beyond the standard work week to meet career and organizational goals. If a woman's behavior fits the successful employee, she may be faulted for being too aggressive and not meeting feminine standards, but if she is more traditionally feminine, she may receive little recognition and remuneration. "What the double bind amounts to is that the decision to either adopt or reject the style of behavior available to the woman in the workplace may place her in a position deleterious to her career interests" (Hennessey, 1983, p. 63). Women may adopt coping strategies, such as superwoman behavior, which uses perseverance and near-perfection of work to cope. Such perfectionism and unrealistic goals may lead to burnout and emotional and physical illness.

Some people are highly tolerant of stress. Individuals who do well under stress believe that life experiences are predictable and controllable, see change as normal in life and representing a challenge rather than a threat, and have commitment to their work, believing in its value and interest. Ryland and Greenfield (1991) believe that "sense of coherence" as a dispositional orientation or ability to select the right coping style in a given situation enhances the ability to cope with stress. Sense of coherence is an orientation based on a feeling of confidence that stress is structured, predictable, and explicable; resources are available to meet those demands; and the demands are challenges and worth investment and involvement (Antonovsky, 1987). Research has indicated that older workers appear to respond better to stress by seeing the stressors as opportunities rather than as threats (Mayes, Barton, and Ganster, 1991). Hardiness has also been associated with resistance to stress for men but as inconclusive for women (Wiebe, 1991).

Sources of stress include time pressure, repetitive tasks, machine-controlled jobs, sex discrimination, organizational politics, the lack of opportunity for job advancement, and incompatible managers or coworkers. Situational variables and personality variables may be involved. A study of racial differences found that black respondents were more likely than white respondents to identify a factor related to an individual, such as a supervisor, as a source of job stress. That finding suggested that blacks may encounter more work problems as a result of personal interactions (Stroman and Seltzer, 1991). Racial discrimination in the workplace may play a role in this.

Destructive coping techniques that may be used by employees include alcohol, smoking, excessive absences, and tensions at home (Foegen, 1981). One research study (Shinn et al., 1984) found that the most common coping response used by individuals was to focus attention on families, friends, and hobbies. Other research has shown that men tend to handle stress through problem-focused coping more than women (Folkman and Lazarus, 1980) and by distracting themselves by a nonwork activity, often exercise (McDonald and Korabik, 1991). Women are more likely to use selective ignoring (Fleishman, 1984) and to report talking to others to relieve stress (McDonald and Korabik, 1991).

Organizations that create hospitable work environments with low physical and mental stressors, low role conflict, enriched jobs, and good supervision tend to have employees who have less stress, are more committed to the organization, and have lower absenteeism. Organizational and job design, management development, and wellness programs, including screening for high cholesterol ratios, followed by interventions can be useful in improving individual health and creating a positive work environment (Hendrix, Steel, and Leap, 1991). Stress can be handled positively by individuals or by the organization through counseling, wellness programs, and other approaches. Some techniques that can be used to handle stress are physical exercise, fitness programs, hobbies, meditation, progressive relaxation, biofeedback, personal planning, assertiveness training, selection and placement procedures, employee training, flextime, career counseling, and quality circles (Dubinsky, 1985; Foegen, 1981). There are numerous stress tests available, but they are descriptive and tend to have vaguely defined norms. Such tests should be conducted only on a voluntary basis and in conjunction with employee counseling services (Ostell, 1986).

Workplace stress can lead to burnout. Burnout is "a psychological process, brought about by unrelieved work stresses that result in emotional exhaustion, depersonalization, and feelings of decreased accomplishment" (Ivancevich and Matteson, 1987). The term "burnout" was introduced into the professional literature in 1974 by a psychoanalyst who described the condition in alternative help-giving facilities (Ivancevich and Matteson, 1987).

Some of the symptoms of burnout are skipping rest and food breaks; increased overtime and no vacation; changed job performance, social withdrawal, emotional changes; self-medication with alcohol, tranquilizers, and other mood-altering drugs; increased physical complaints; and diminished sense of humor (Patrick, 1981). Other predictors of burnout are obsession with self, obsession with outside forces, a need for complete control, a fear of change, a need for constant excitement, and unrealistic expectations (Glicken, 1983).

Five stages in reaching burnout have been identified. Involvement is the first stage, when the person still feels committed and enthusiastic. If the job falls short of expectations, the psychological contract, the chance of burnout increase. The second stage, stagnation, is hardly detectable in the beginning as satisfaction diminishes and fatigue sets in. The employee begins to turn outside the workplace for satisfaction, to leisure, hobbies, social contacts, family, or increased substance use. The third stage, detachment, results in the employee becoming aware that something is missing from the work experience. The employee becomes chronically emotionally and physically tired, avoids challenges and opportunities, is increasingly negative about work, and begins just putting in time. The fourth stage, juncture, leads to growing self-doubts, lowered self-esteem, extreme cynicism toward customers or clients, increasingly troubled relationships, and increased absenteeism. At this point, the employee may fail to function adequately on the job and may even contemplate suicide. Some employees will quit their job at this time. The last stage, intervention, occurs when someone in the organization or outside it intervenes in some way that helps the employee recover morale, health, and productivity. Interventions may occur by referral to an EAP and entering counseling; entering a wellness program or individually beginning a health promotion and exercise program; or changes made in the workplace in regard to the work assignment, schedule, or environment. Some individuals themselves will, on their own, make the decision to change their attitude or perspective (Ivancevich and Matteson, 1987).

Organizations can create burnout through negative conditions such as excessive hours or paper work, insufficient training, no support for decisions, no power, lack of appreciation by supervisors or clients/customers, dehumanizing treatment, faulty rewards (including inadequate pay), lack of career advancement, lack of creativity, and repetitive work. Burnout may also be associated with employees who may come into the workplace with many distress symptoms. One study found that distress symptoms reported prior to beginning a job accounted for the greatest part of the variance in distress symptoms nine months later (Nelson and Sutton, 1990).

Some ways in which an organization can reduce the likelihood of burnout are seeking a fit between individual characteristics and the job and organizational structure, developing programs to help individuals deal with the stress that leads to burnout, and teaching and supporting self-diagnosis and individual adaptation strategies. Ellis' rational-emotive approach or Glaser's Reality Therapy can be used as appropriate treatments (Glicken, 1983). Workplace stress is one of the major reasons for the spread of wellness programs.

WELLNESS PROGRAMS

A growing body of research supports the link between lifestyle and health. This research and rising health care costs have led employers to take an interest in wellness or health promotion programs. Because very few group insurance plans cover wellness programs, most are paid for by employers. Employee wellness programs range from psychological workshops to physicals and conditioning. U.S. businesses competing with Japan have responded to wellness programs as a way to improve productivity and quality and cut health care costs (Feuer, 1985).

The predecessors of today's wellness programs are company-sponsored recreation and employee services programs, which began in the 1800s as a way to humanize the workplace. By the turn of the century, recreation programs were becoming a popular way to promote employee loyalty, fellowship, morale, and mental and physical development. The Recreation Association of American Industry, later the National Industrial Recreation Association (NIRA), was founded in 1940. During World War II, recreation programs were used to relieve stress and increase fitness. In the 1970s the focus became personal fitness as the President's Council on Physical Fitness and Sports, along with the business community, held the first national conference on physical fitness. In 1983 NIRA changed its name to the National Employee Services and Recreation Association (NESRA), in recognition of the wider range of services than just recreation.

There was a tremendous growth in recreation and fitness programs in the mid-1970s, and in 1984, NESRA reported there were over 50,000 companies with recreation and fitness programs (Finney, 1984). A survey of 309 business managers conducted by the American Management Association found that 47 percent of the respondents offered wellness programs (McKendrick, 1987). A Department of

Health and Human Services survey found that at least 50 percent of employers with more than 100 employees have some kind of health promotion program (Vokel, 1987). A survey of the frequency of work site health promotion activities in private sector work sites with 50 or more employees (reported in 1989) found 65.5 percent of the 1,358 respondents had one or more areas of health promotion activity. The most prevalent types of activity were smoking cessation (35.6 percent), health risk assessment (29.5 percent), back problem prevention and care (28.5 percent), stress management (26.6 percent), exercise/fitness (22.1 percent), off-the-job accident prevention (19.8 percent), nutrition education (16.8 percent), blood pressure control and treatment (16.5 percent), and weight control (14.7 percent). The average number of activities for all work sites was two and for work sites with activities, three. The larger the work site, the more likely were the programs to be offered. The most activity was in the Western region and the least in the Northeast. Programs varied by type of industry, with utilities/transportation/communication and financial/real estate/insurance firms being the most likely to offer activities. The majority of employers paid the entire program cost (Fielding and Piserchia, 1989). Wellness programs are relatively new in union contracts; however, some unions such as the National Association of Government Employees, International Brotherhood of Police Officers, and the United Food and Commercial Workers International Union have negotiated wellness programs (Kemp, 1987).

Wellness programs range from elaborate programs to simple incentives. Pepsico has a large facility at their New York headquarters with programs for smoking cessation, karate, prenatal aerobics, tai-chi, and video golf, while Xerox has two gyms, racquetball courts, and an exercise trail. Vermeer Manufacturing Company has a program that donates money to employees' favorite charities based on exercise, and Flex Company has a program that gives gift certificates to employees who quit smoking. Programs may be at the work site, subsidized in off-site locations, or contracted for.

One way to classify wellness programs is in four general categories: early intervention, behavior risks, healthy behavior through corporate culture, and reducing exposure to hazardous or toxic substances or stress (Rosow and Zager, 1985). Early intervention programs involve identification and treatment of biological or disease risks that lead to illness. Early detection programs for screening for diabetes, glaucoma, and hypertension fall in this category, as do EAPs for mental health issues. Some programs have mandatory elements, for example, mandatory joint union-employer alcohol rehabilitation programs. Behavior risk programs focus on detecting and controlling high-risk behavior such as smoking, stress, eating problems, and inadequate physical activity. Healthy Behavior through Corporate Culture programs focus on making healthy behaviors part of the corporate culture, involving corporate image and esprit de corps; this approach may include attractive work environments and nutritional foods in cafeterias and vending machines. Reducing exposure to hazardous or toxic substances or stress involves programs such as noise reduction, safety and accident prevention, defensive driving, and organizational seat belt policies. Sperry (1984) sees wellness programs as involving education, risk appraisal, intervention, and fitness. Stress management and other programs that focus only on internal stressors are viewed by Sperry as insufficient, because external stressors also need to be identified and eliminated or reduced. Initially, most wellness programs were begun to save money by reducing medical care expenditures, but by 1986, the focus had broadened. Additional goals now include employee relations, improved morale, recruitment, benefits, increased productivity, lower absentee rates, less turnover, improved relations with unions, and enhanced company spirit (Fink, 1986).

A study of Kennecott Copper Corportion's Insight Program found a 52 percent improvement in attendance, a 75 percent decrease in nonindustrial health and accident insurance, and a 55 percent reduction in medical, surgical, and hospital costs. A study at the New York State Department of Education showed a decline in sick leave use after establishment of a wellness program. Prior to the program, 66.5 hours of sick leave per employee were used, while after the program was initiated, 42.5 hours were used. Canada Life Insurance experienced a 22 percent decrease in absenteeism and a 13.5 percent reduction in turnover after instituting a fitness program. Studies show that regular participation in recreation and fitness activities increase task performance while decreasing stress and anxiety. In contrast to average office workers whose efficiency decreases 50 percent during the final two hours of the work day, program participants have been found to work at full efficiency all day (Finney, 1984).

Psychosocial factors contribute significantly to dissatisfaction and intent to change in regard to handling stress, weight, nutrition, exercise, alcohol use, and cigarette smoking. Personal efficacy is significantly related to dissatisfaction and intent to change. Job stress and anxiety are more likely to predict dissatisfaction and intent to change, while health knowledge has little effect on either (Davis et al., 1984). Research indicates that when corporate fitness programs have low participation rates, it is because they fail to make a strong connection between health and success. Inner-directed employees who set their own goals are most likely to participate. Outer-directed people, who in the research study make up a greater share of the employees, are more likely to participate in health activities if they perceive it to bring higher social status and contribute to success (Edmondson, 1987).

EMOTIONAL HEALTH PROGRAMS

Sonnenstuhl (1986) coined the term "emotional health program" to cover all programs concerned with preventing, identifying, and treating personal problems that adversely affect job performance, including counseling, EAP, mental wellness, special health services, and alcoholism. Basically, three types of employee problems appear in the workplace: short-lived preoccupations; problems due to an underlying personality disorder; and deeply embedded problems, such as emotional disorders (1 in 6 employees), alcoholics (1 in 10 employees), and drug abuse (1 in 20 employees) (Miles, 1985). A study of 73 companies conducted in the mid-1980s to determine the number of emotionally disturbed employees and services for them found that a full range of mental disorders was reported but that 40 percent of the respondents had no procedure to deal with emotional problems at work (Madonia, 1985). An EAP may include many emotional health programs, or an organization may use an EAP and other separate emotional health programs such as specialized counseling and mental wellness programs.

Employee Assistance Programs

EAPs provided by employers are designed to help employees deal with personal problems that seriously affect job performance. The philosophy behind EAPs is that it is more desirable both economically and socially to rehabilitate previously proven and trained employees than to terminate them.

R. M. Macy and Company and Northern State Power Company in Minneapolis have provided employee assistance since 1917, and Metropolitan Life Insurance began employee counseling in 1919, but most EAPs began in the 1940s with employer concerns about alcoholism among white-collar workers. Gradually these programs evolved and began treating the emotional, mental, and financial problems caused by substance use. Caterpillar Tractor Company established the first broadbrush EAP in 1945.

Purposes

EAPs serve multiple purposes. They are a way to deal with troubled employees who cost employers billions of dollars annually and to enhance productivity. EAPs are seen by some employers as part of the employee benefits package, including a benefit for employees' families. Some employers see them as a way to reduce health costs over time (Dellovo, 1986). EAPs can also play a role in risk management. The Risk and Insurance Management Society sees troubled employees as a risk management problem because the human factor is the main problem in workplace accidents and a healthy employee costs less for health care benefits and workers' compensation (Rosati, 1986). Risk management techniques can be applied to problem employees by identifying the source of loss, evaluating loss size, designing a program to minimize risk, estimating program costs, and comparing costs with lost savings. Loss control, claim management, funding for exposure, safety, and accident prevention and elimination are all risk management functions that relate to EAP programs (Hurley, 1986). EAPs can recoup losses from employee absenteeism, inadequate job performance, and other problems by applying risk management concepts (Weaver, 1979). Some EAPs take on a preventive role as well as a rehabilitative role. For example, alcoholism and other drug abuse require prevention as well as rehabilitation that requires an organizational and environmental approach as well as an individual focus. However, this is a major weakness of many EAPs, because many of them are primarily focused on working with the individual employee, rather than dealing with the organizational environment as a whole. In some cases, dealing with individual employees and their families is not sufficient; the organization as a whole has problems that should be addressed, and EAPs should have the capability to deal with organizational problems as well as individual problems.

Types of EAPs

A 1987 survey of the first 50 of the Canadian Business Top 500 companies found that nearly two-thirds of them had EAPs (Conlon, 1987). Some EAPs, however, are only paper programs (Bureau of National Affairs [BNA], 1987). There are various types of EAPs. Some organizations have internal organization-run programs (such as Metropolitan), while other programs are sponsored and provided by unions or are joint labor-management sponsored progams, some organizations contract for services through contractors such as Human Affairs, and some smaller organizations group together to receive services through a consortium. Internal EAPs are involved with a higher percentage of alcohol cases than external EAPs (BNA, 1987). Minter (1986) provides a model for analysis in the form of an evaluation format that can be used as part of a self-assessment to decide whether to develop an in-house or contracted EAP. If an employer decides to contract for EAP services, several issues should be considered, including the agency's track record, fee structure, philosophy, and image. Hellan and Campbell (1981) provide a guide for selecting an EAP contractor, with a set of questions to ask potential contractors.

A 1982 nationwide survey of 500 EAP administrators with a 73 percent response rate found 72 percent of respondents worked in business, 12 percent in general government, and 16 percent in school districts, colleges, labor unions, and private nonprofit organizations.

Four-fifths of the in-house programs did their own assessment and referral, but only 10 percent provided in-house counseling. Eighty-six percent of the programs were broadbrush, and 37 percent of the programs were cosponsored by the organization and unions (Intveldt-Work, 1983). A survey of 66 EAPs by *Personnel* found 33 percent of the programs were in-house (Levine, 1985b).

Most EAPs allow for both supervisor referral and self-referral. A few programs allow for mandatory supervisor referral, which requires the employee to go to the EAP, but most EAPs provide for only voluntary supervisor referral. The supervisor makes the referral, and it is then up to the employee whether or not to visit the EAP. EAPs are a benefit to supervisors because they allow the supervisor to focus on work performance, demonstrate concern, and make an early identification of employees with job-endangering personal problems, while giving those supervisors a professional source to which to refer employees with those problems.

Many EAPs now receive more self-referrals than supervisor referrals. Sonnenstuhl (1986), in research within a company with 6,000 employees, found that the referral process, as described through employee interviews, is a distinctly social process in which employees are aware of their own discreditable attributes. The decision to refer oneself evolves from a complex set of formal and informal social controls. It is not a change in the attribute but how the person perceives it that leads to referral.

Utilization

Generally, 10–20 percent of employees will use an EAP each year. A survey of state government EAPs found the programs provided the following services: referral (97 percent), training of managers (97 percent), employee education (88 percent), individual counseling (76 percent), hot line (45 percent), and group counseling (30 percent) (Kemp, 1985). A survey of 309 business managers conducted by the American Management Association showed that 48 percent of the respondents offered some type of EAP, with substance abuse counseling the most prevalent form of counseling (McKendrick, 1987). An American Society for Personnel Administration survey also reported alcoholism treatment as the most-used service and the one most frequently perceived as effective (Ford and McLauglin, 1981). A survey of EAPs for state employees found the most frequent services used, in order of frequency, were alcohol rehabilitation, individual psychological counseling, drug abuse counseling, stress management, interpersonal relations, marital and family counseling, financial counseling, legal counseling, career counseling, physical ill health, and life-style (Kemp, 1985). A survey of 68 companies reported the frequency of services as alcoholism (100 percent), drug abuse (85 percent), family emotional crisis (74 percent), psychiatric

(72 percent), financial (48 percent), and legal (45 percent) (Kiefhaber and Goldbeck, 1980). Personal Performance Consultants, Inc., a national EAP provider based in St. Louis, reported their EAP use as 27 percent emotional, 23 percent marital, 22 percent family/child, 15 percent alcohol/drug, 5 percent office/job, 4 percent legal, 3 percent financial, and 1 percent medical (Lydecker, 1985). An Administrative Management Society survey showing types of services prevalent in companies with EAPs found the following services: alcohol/drug abuse counseling (82 percent), preretirement counseling (69 percent), termination counseling (52 percent), career counseling (50 percent), marital counseling (43 percent), financial counseling (40 percent), and legal counseling (28 percent) (Bailey, 1986).

A study by the Human Resources Group in New York found that psychological disorders and substance addiction accounted for 67 percent of EAP referrals (39 percent psychological trauma and 28 percent addictions). The study was based on 399 cases from 13 major companies that were referred to EAPs in 1983. Stress was the most common psychological trauma (29 percent), followed by depression (20 percent) and anxiety (18 percent). Of addictions, 73 percent involved alcohol and 10 percent, cocaine. Of those referred, 66 percent were salaried employees, 48 percent were male, the average age was 36.9, and the average length of employment was 7.5 years (Levy, 1986). Another study found that absenteeism was the most common work performance problem causing formal supervisory referral, while awareness of slipping was the reason most noted for informal supervisory referrals. Interpersonal relations predominated for self-referrals, and more people with substance abuse problems were self-referred rather that referred by supervisors (Martin et al., 1985). A survey of 66 EAPs by *Personnel* found that the most frequent problems were alcoholism, drug dependency, marital problems, financial problems, personality problems with supervisors or coworkers, and legal problems (Levine, 1985b). Thus, utilization varies widely over EAPs.

Demographics influence the nature of the work-related and personal problems experienced by EAP users. A study of 14,000 cases in a large organization indicated that older employees over 50 had more health-related problems, chemical dependency problems that had impacts off the job, issues requiring legal referral, and problems requiring benefits clarification, while younger employees who were under 26 had more problems in relationship to policies/procedures, intimate relations and work relationships. Whites had more intimate relations problems, such as identity, relationship, and sexual, while American Indians came more than other groups for alcohol problems on and off the job. Although there were few gender differences, females had more problems involving intimate relations and work relations, and males had more problems involving chemical dependency impacting on the job. Managers also had more problems involving chemical dependency impacting on the job (Gomez-Mejia and Balkin, 1980).

A study to determine if there are key characteristics that separate employees who do not utilize EAP services from those who do found that nonutilizers tended to be middle and upper management and professional, older (50+), male, and with high stress jobs (Braun and Novak, 1986). EAPs often find executives and professionals hard to reach (BNA, 1987; Ford and McLauglin, 1981). Perceptions of nonutilizers included denial of the problem or need for services; self-reliance; use of an EAP was seen as devaluing them; the EAP was seen as for others; and the EAP was perceived as not confidential. Utilizers' views were trust in the EAP service; being open to change; having received peer referral; seeing the service as free and convenient; having supervisors that supported the utilization; seeing it as an alternative to job loss; and perceiving there was a need for help (Braun and Novak, 1986).

EAPs can develop specific programs to address specific groups, such as older workers (Kemp, 1984a), public employees (Little, 1981), women (Martorano and Morgan, 1987; Milstead-O'Keefe, 1981), executives (McGurrin, 1987), and persons with disabilities (Orzolek, 1987). They can also develop programs to address specific problems, such as aging parents (Nasatir, 1985) and dual careers (Stringer-Moore, 1981).

Training can increase the number of individuals seeking EAP services. For example, the Impact of Drug Abuse on the Family, a training model designed to overcome problems of defensiveness that highlights the negative effects of drug abuse on families when tied into a large corporation through a safety focus and a work/family theme resulted in a 50 percent increase in drug referrals to the EAP, with 75 percent of those being self-referrals. Drug referrals rose from the third highest presenting problem to number one (Mattox, 1985). The type of professionals providing services through the EAP may also influence the type of referrals.

Effectiveness

EAPs are perceived to be cost-effective, although documentation has been scarce (BNA, 1987). There is a slowly growing body of evaluation research (Mann, 1989). A 1984 survey of 50 companies found the use of EAPs resulted in a 33 percent decline in sick benefit use, a 65 percent decline in work-related accidents, a 30 percent decline in workers' compensation claims, and a 74 percent decline in time spent on supervisor reprimands (Lydecker, 1985). An Administrative Management Society survey found that a 30 percent reduction in absenteeism and a 23 percent decline in turnover occurred at the surveyed companies (Bailey, 1986). Several companies have attributed savings to EAPs: Illinois Bell Telephone reported 46 percent fewer cases of sickness disability among 402 employees, International Harvester found a 39 percent decrease in disability payments for 342 employees, and General Motors, Fisher Body Division experienced a 52 percent reduction in grievance and disciplinary actions (Ray, 1982). The U.S. Post Office reported an EAP benefit-cost ratio of 5:1 (Norris, 1983). One state study of 24 employees using an EAP found 20 employees reduced sick time (Kemp, 1985). An evaluation of a corporate EAP based on a review of 95 case files and a survey of 60 employee participants found that 65 percent of therapists reported a successful outcome while 90 percent of the participants viewed their own treatment as successful (Gam et al., 1983). Dale Massi, a professor of social work and specialist in EAP who conducted a major evaluation for the U.S. Department of Health and Human Service's EAP, believes a company usually spends 60 percent less to rehabilitate an employee who is performing poorly because of personal problems than to replace that worker (Topolnicki, 1983).

Change

EAPs grew rapidly and changed radically in the 1980s. Most large employers in the public and private sectors now offer some type of EAP, and many smaller employers are finding ways to receive EAP services, for example, through consortia. Movements to license and credential EAP practitioners are underway. The Association of Labor-Management Administrators and Consultants on Alcoholism (ALMACA), now the Employee Assistance Professionals Association (EAPA), the National Council on Alcoholism, and the Occupational Program Consultants Association developed standards for employee alcohol assistance programs in 1981. A certification process for employee assistance professionals has been developed by EAPA. In addition to EAPA, there is another professional association, the Employee Assistance Society of North America. Some states have considered EAP regulation. California placed regulation of EAPs under Knox-Keene legislation, which regulates Health Maintenance Organizations (HMOs) (Cagney, 1987). There has been a tremendously rapid growth in the establishment of EAPs, especially entrepreneurial, private, profit-making ones. Some EAPs have been integrated into HMOs (Fallon and Lenney, 1987), and more EAPs also are becoming involved in health promotion and wellness.

Critical Incident Stress Debriefing

As discussed earlier employees can be placed under critical incident stress as a result of the types of jobs they do, such as police, fire, and ambulance services, or through exposure to violence or disaster in the workplace. If left unaddressed, this stress can lead to posttraumatic stress disorder, workers' compensation claims, resignations, and even suicides. Critical incident stress can be acute or cumulative. Some psychological signs are apathy, anger, denial, impaired judgment, loss of objectivity, and underutilization of skills. Some physical signs are headaches, back aches, chronic fatigue, insomnia, lethargy, loss of appetite, and nervousness.

Organizations that have frequent critical incident exposure have found critical incident stress debriefing teams to be effective. Such teams are made up of individuals specially trained to deal with the impact of a critical incident and accelerate the return of personnel to their normal functioning. Team members may include professional psychologists or counselors, clergy persons, and specially trained organizational staff members. The team conducts debriefing of all personnel who have been exposed to the original critical incident. Such debriefings usually take two to four hours. Employees may be required to attend but are not required to actively participate. The debriefing can deal with factual and emotional elements. Resources then are made available for anyone needing additional counseling or support.

Organizations that rarely have critical incidents can use the services of their EAP. The EAP can do individual or group debriefings as required by the incident. If they do not have an EAP, they may be able to hire a counselor in the community with experience in critical incidents. In some cases where the incident has community-wide implications, such as a shooting at a school, large numbers of mental health professionals may be required and will volunteer their services. Management should be sure that a mental health professional with critical incident and posttraumatic stress experience is put in charge of seeing that all helping professionals and volunteers are properly trained and briefed to assist the employees and customers/clients/students. Debriefing should occur as soon as possible, preferably within 24 hours, but can be done even as late as six months after the incident.

Not all stressful situations are critical incidents and require debriefing. In deciding whether a debriefing session is necessary, several factors should be considered: the uniqueness of the event in terms of how far outside the normal limits of expectations was its impact; whether there were fatalities or serious injuries; the danger it posed to the workplace; the number of people affected; the emotional impact of the event on those people; and the difficulty in returning the workplace to normal (Van Fleet, 1992).

CONFLICT RESOLUTION AND REDUCTION

As noted earlier, with violence becoming more prevalent and murder becoming the third most common cause of death in the workplace, it is increasingly important for organizations to develop conflict resolution and reduction programs. Earlier, programs were described for addressing the stresses involved in terminations and layoffs. Another program that is valuable is to use mediation to resolve disputes. Mediation is a common process of dispute resolution between management and unions under collective bargaining agreements, but it can also be used in other settings. Increasingly, mediation centers are available in communities. They became popular to resolve divorce and child custody cases and were sometimes required by the courts. However, many such centers now handle more business sector cases than domestic cases.

Mediation is aimed at finding solutions in a time-efficient and cost-effective way and is oriented to the both-win concept, so that both parties will walk away feeling satisfied and without resentment. Mediation clients pay on a flat scale per hour for uncomplicated cases and panel mediations. Mediation is a good way to resolve differences with dissatisfied customers/clients and avoid conflict or litigation. Mediation techniques can also be used to resolve differences between employees. Mediation is effective because it brings disputing parties face to face, sometimes for the first time. A mediator allows short and relatively controlled expressions of emotion, which may have to be gotten out of the way before a resolution is possible. The mediator lays down ground rules and helps the disputants listen to each other without interruptions and with respect. The mediator asks each party to state their situation, asks questions, and helps the parties start talking to each other. The mediator provides a feeling of safety and helps bring disputants to agreement through questioning and by filling in information gaps. Mediators can use approaches such as the Harvard Negotiation Project's principled negotiation to reach successful resolutions satisfactory to both parties. The principled negotiation process avoids bargaining over positions that endanger ongoing relationships and avoids soft negotiation or being nice, which results in unwise agreements. Instead, it focuses on separating the people from the problem, focuses on interests and not positions, invents options for mutual gain, and finds and uses objective criteria for decision making (Fisher, Ury, and Patton, 1991). In addition, mediation and conflict resolution skills can be taught to employees to reduce conflict and workplace violence in organizations.

7

Financing Employee Mental Health Care

Creating a mentally healthy workplace is based on both a managerial philosophy of valuing employees as adults and as people and on the knowledge that mentally healthy workplaces will lead to the outcomes employers seek: employee satisfaction, attendance at the job, retention for a reasonable period of time, performance in producing the goods/services of the organization, and productivity. Obviously, there are costs in creating a mentally healthy workplace, but an employer must weigh those costs against the costs of having an unhealthy workplace. It will be less expensive for employers in the long run to have a mentally healthy workplace than to have the high costs of an unhealthy workplace that eventually comes from employee dissatisfaction and unhealthy behaviors, including substance abuse and mental and physical health problems; poor attendance at the job; high rates of turnover; increased labor relations, discipline, and grievance problems; and poor performance in the quantity and/or quality of the goods/services produced, leading to overall poor productivity.

All organizations can do many things in relationship to creating policies and using managerial approaches to establish a mentally healthy work environment with little cost. The extent/elaborateness of other approaches and programs developed to create a mentally healthy workplace will vary by the size and the resources of the organization. However, even small organizations with few resources can use many low cost options to create a mentally healthy workplace. The previous chapters have discussed many ways to create mentally healthy workplaces through a variety of approaches with various cost levels. This chapter will focus on financial issues related to providing mental health care to employees, including insurance coverage for mental health and substance abuse, the use of managed care, workers' compensation, and public sector coverage for people with disabilities.

INSURANCE

Group health insurance is not a required benefit. Some 35 million Americans have no health insurance, and perhaps twice that number are underinsured. Many of these employees work for small employers who provide no health insurance benefits. Yet, by 1986, employers paid for about half of the $465 billion spent on health care. About 10 percent of all payroll costs went to employee health care expenditures (Howard, 1987). With rising health care costs, employers have been increasingly concerned about the cost of providing health insurance coverage to their employees. A survey of 45 organizations in 1985 showed that 78 percent of them had already taken steps within the previous two years to cut costs of health care benefits. Four of those organizations planned to add an EAP as part of their cost cutting approach to reduce medical expenditures (Levine, 1985a).

If employers provide group health insurance, there are some rules they must follow, based on federal and state laws. Employers have a wide variety of benefit plans to choose from for their employees. Many of these plans require a contribution from covered employees, including deductibles and co-payments. The employers select the plan or plans they wish to offer. If several plans are offered, the cost to the employee may vary by which plan is chosen. Many state laws require employers who offer health insurance to provide certain mandated minimum coverages. Some states mandate treatment for mental illness and/or treatment of alcoholism and drug abuse. As of 1989, 28 states mandated some degree of mental health coverage and 29 states mandated alcohol treatment (Blue Cross and Blue Shield, 1989). Maryland, for example, mandates employers with health insurance benefits to offer at least 30 days of inpatient care each calendar year of benefit coverage for mental health (Bailey, 1989). Massachusetts mandates $500 of outpatient mental health insurance coverage and 60 days of inpatient care (Frank, 1990). By 1990, at least 40 states required coverage for alcohol and drug rehabilitation in company health insurance plans (Miller, 1990). In the early 1990s, the California legislature proposed requiring mental health coverage to be the same as physical health coverage; no insurance plan could provide less coverage for mental health than for physical health. However, as of 1993, that legislation had not passed. Mandated insurance coverages raise concerns about their effect on small businesses (McGuire, 1992), and they meet resistance from small businesses. The laws are complex and vary greatly from state to state, so employers should check with their state health insurance commissioner to determine mandatory insurance requirements.

An employer who does not offer required coverage can be held liable for medical expenses incurred by employees as a result of that failure to provide coverage. Federal law requires employers after 1986 to offer workers over age 65 the same health insurance coverage offered younger workers and their spouses. If participation in the plan is mandatory, employers cannot make their older workers pay any more than younger workers to belong. If participation is voluntary, premiums charged to older workers cannot be any higher than the actuarial tables show costs for older workers in relation to costs for younger workers. Under the Pregnancy Discrimination Act, employers must provide the same health insurance coverage that they provide to all employees with other disabilities to women who cannot work because of childbirth or disabilities related to pregnancy.

Consolidated Omnibus Budget Reconciliation Act of 1986

The Consolidated Omnibus Budget Reconciliation Act of 1986 (COBRA) requires employers of 20 or more employees to offer their employees the opportunity to continue their heath insurance for themselves, their spouses, and their dependents if they are terminated for any reason except gross misconduct. The law covers the maximum premium the employee can be charged and the minimum period for extension of coverage. The law also allows for the employee and their covered dependents to convert to an individual policy at the end of the continuation period, but at that point, individual rates may be charged. An employer and the insurance company can be held liable for any additional expense incurred by an employee as a result of not being offered continuation of group health insurance coverage. Also, many states have similar laws, and some cover employers with smaller numbers of employees or even all employers with group health insurance plans.

Mental Health Coverage

One of the major problems with insurance coverage for mental health is that it generally is treated differently than physical health. Mental health coverage is usually less and more restricted than parts of the health insurance package that deal with physical health problems. Mental health insurance coverage has been a controversial issue, and much opposition remains. Opponents argue that psychotherapy should not be included in insurance programs because emotional distress is universal and everyone may suffer from such distress at some time. If treatment is begun, it may continue indefinitely (McGuire, 1981).

Prior to the 1950s, mental health care was largely available only in state-run mental institutions and a few private-pay psychiatric hospitals. Coverage for mental illness first became available through major medical contracts of commercial insurers in the 1950s

(Goldman, Sharfstein, and Frank, 1983). Federal employees began to have access to limited mental health care in the 1950s, and by 1960, their mental health benefits were similar to their physical health benefits. Coverage for outpatient treatment under major medical policies early on was the same for mental illness as for any other illness. As utilization rose, the cost of outpatient treatment became a concern. Contributing to the problem was a lack of guidelines to control utilization. Because of the confidential nature of psychotherapy, therapists were reluctant to release information and preferred to retain control of the therapy and how long it would last (Upton, 1983). As insurance companies raised premiums, employers complained of rising costs and insurance companies reduced mental health benefits.

By the 1970s, the majority of insurance companies had maximum limits per year and per lifetime for mental health coverage. Most companies also paid no more than 50 percent of treatment costs. By using higher premiums in conjunction with higher co-payments, insurance companies tried to decrease the demand for mental health services (McGuire, 1981). There were five major providers of health insurance plans that covered mental health services: stock and mutual health insurance company plans; nonprofit open-panel hospital service or medical service corporation plans (Blue Cross and Blue Shield); closed panel health maintenance organization (HMO) group practice plans like Kaiser Permanente; foundations of fee-for-service practitioners; and employee indemnity plans through self-insurance by the company or union (Dorken et al., 1976).

During the 1970s and early 1980s, employers again were not very concerned about the cost of mental health care because the cost of mental health care, psychiatric treatment and substance abuse treatment was a relatively small part of the total health care expense (Wagman and Schiff, 1990). A survey of the 145 members of the Business Group on Health in the late 1970s found that of 79 companies replying, they all provided mental health benefits and many provided benefits for dependents as well. The most commonly covered mental health problems were depression, substance abuse, and schizophrenia. Family, marital, and sexual problems were beginning to be included more often. Half of the employers paid all of the premium, while the other half required some employee cost sharing. Most companies had no data indicating the cost of the mental health benefit versus the rest of the insurance coverage. The companies at that point saw mental illness as just another disease. Benefits of providing mental health coverage were believed to be lowered employee absenteeism (53 percent), improved employee productivity (53 percent), improved employee morale (52 percent), fewer instances of severe mental illness (51 percent), reduced hospital utilization (46 percent), and lower total insurance premiums

(16 percent). Problems identified were identifying employees in need of assistance (66 percent), removing the stigma associated with treatment (53 percent), motivating employees to obtain treatment (50 percent), training supervisors to detect mental illness and make necessary referrals (41 percent), developing company policy on confidentiality (34 percent), and assuring no negative consequences to employment status for those who did obtain treatment (25 percent) (Goldbeck, 1977).

By the end of the 1980s, that picture was changing. In 1985, employers spent only 6 percent of their health costs for mental health and substance abuse treatment, but by 1990, employers were spending 15–30 percent of their health costs for mental health and substance abuse, and costs were increasing at a rate of 25 percent annually (Bartlett, 1990). A survey of 90 large employers found that more than 95 percent of them were reporting extensive increases in utilization and costs for mental, nervous, and chemical dependency problems and individual claims were running as high as $10,000 (Bailey, 1989).

There is a growing demand for increased utilization of inpatient and outpatient mental health services. Outpatient services are increasing faster than inpatient services, but the number of hospital admissions and inpatient days is also increasing, although the stays for individual patients are shorter (Miller, 1990). However, evidence was also appearing in the late 1970s and during the 1980s of the mind and body connection and that spending money for psychotherapy or other mental health treatment could save money elsewhere. The ability of mental health services to decrease productivity losses from illness and absenteeism and to lower medical and social costs encouraged employers to provide access to mental health services; however, at the same time, rising costs began to discourage that provision.

By 1984, most states mandated mental health coverage for their employees. However, the 1980s also saw employers decreasing mental insurance benefits in an effort to control costs, and in the 1980s, more large employers were offering their employees a choice of health care plans with various high and low options. Some of these options tended to have less coverage for mental health services and/or more restrictions on their use. Providing benefits through a variety of policy providers and seeking competition was sometimes done to control cost. However, restructuring health benefits and using carrier competition may not curtail costs but may actually increase them (Chenoweth, 1989).

By the 1990s, limits on inpatient and outpatient coverage were common. The most common day limits were 30 to 60 days per inpatient episode or per year. Outpatient care typically had limits on total expenses of $1,000–$2,000 and carried a 50 percent coinsurance rate (American Psychiatric Association, 1989). The discriminatory coverage for mental disorders is seen in the statistics, which show that in the late 1980s, 12 percent of the payment for treatment of mental illness came from private insurance, compared with 25 percent for general medical conditions (Ridgely and Goldman, 1989).

Substance Abuse Coverage

There is particular concern about coverage for substance abuse. By the late 1980s, General Motors was experiencing substance abuse treatment costs absorbing some 20 percent of health care expenditure, with inpatient costs accounting for 90 percent of that expenditure (Bailey, 1989). From 1980 to 1983, inpatient costs associated with chemical dependency increased 42 percent. Costs rose with the increase in the length of treatment. By 1976, many 14-day inpatient programs were extended to 21 days, and then, many 21-day programs were extended to 28 days. By 1990 some programs charged as much as $25,000 for 28 days (Miller, 1990).

Inpatient hospitalization treatment may not be the best option for all treatment of substance abuse; outpatient treatment may be as effective (Bensinger and Pilkington, 1985; Miller, 1990). Maresfield Enterprises expanded its employee medical benefits to cover inpatient treatment of substance abuse but found that productivity and absenteeism did not improve with the increased hospital admissions and insurance premiums. Outpatient programs may be more effective and cost-efficient for some types of patients, including those who turn to substance abuse during a sudden trauma and possibly those with a history of intermittent substance abuse who suffer a sudden trauma or whose substance abuse increases. Some chronic substance abusers may use inpatient facilities as a respite from unhappy lives rather than to get well (Weiss, 1987). Limiting the number of times that inpatient treatment will be provided is one way to address that problem.

A combination of inpatient and outpatient may be effective. General Motors has a program contracted through Connecticut General Insurance Company that designs programs to maximize the effectiveness of utilization. Employees can be placed in halfway houses where they receive treatment but are expected to continue to work during treatment. An employee who drops out of their recovery plan and does not resume it is liable for part of the cost of treatment. Repeaters are also charged as a way of discouraging the revolving door syndrome (Ham, 1989).

It should not be automatically accepted that the now-common 28-day inpatient program for substance abuse treatment is necessary for everyone treated. There is no clinical evidence that the 28-day program is the best way to treat substance abuse. Many substance abuse counselors are recovering abusers, and they may use the 28-day program because they are familiar with it (Bartlett, 1990). In 1991, a 28-day inpatient program could cost $15,000–$20,000 while a comparable outpatient program cost $3,000–$5,000 (Woolsey, 1991). Substance abuse can often be effectively treated much less expensively on an outpatient basis, and it makes little sense to have insurance programs that provide for only inpatient treatment of substance abuse or encourage its use by providing better reimbursement for inpatient than for outpatient treatment.

Cost

Most mental health and substance abuse insurance coverages favor inpatient treatment, in that they provide more or better coverage for inpatient than for outpatient. Some policies will cover inpatient treatment 100 percent but outpatient treatment 50 percent or less. In fact, some policies will cover inpatient only, not outpatient treatment. This results in unnecessary hospitalization that uses up to 70 percent of mental health care dollars (Bartlett, 1990). Problems with rising costs for mental health and substance abuse care have been fueled by this willingness to pay for or pay more for inpatient treatment, which is the most expensive type of treatment. Costs have also been fueled by employees feeling they should use their maximum benefit, for example, if there is a 60-day maximum, employees believing that they should use their full benefit. This has been made worse by there being little focus on treating individuals rather than focusing on an overall standard and also by the fact that there is no agreement on the amount of time required in treatment for mental health and substance abuse problems (Woolsey, 1991). A study of patients with serious mental illness who were treated in a public mental health system showed that annual treatment costs could be substantially reduced with the use of day hospital treatment. Two cohorts of psychiatric patients were followed for 12 months after admission. The substitution of the day hospital provided a cost savings of 31 percent per hospital episode, and readmission rates did not rise (Dickey et al., 1989).

By the mid-1980s, inpatient care accounted for 70 percent of national mental health care expenditures. In 1984,mental health costs had reached $237.6 billion, and 7–10 percent of claims dollars were going to mental health (Lee, 1987). In 1985, mental health and substance abuse treatment accounted for 5 percent of employer-paid health care costs, but by 1990, mental health and substance abuse costs were 30 percent (Bartlett, 1990). By the late 1980s, the cost of providing mental health and substance abuse care was rising faster than medical costs (Duva, 1989). The employer cost of providing mental health and substance abuse benefits to employees in January 1991 was $282 per employee. The six months from May 1990 to

January 1991 saw an increase of 36 percent in the cost of mental health and substance abuse benefits to employees (Kenkel, 1991).

Limiting Mental Health Coverage and Cost Sharing

There is resistance to providing mental health coverage equal to physical health coverage. There is a fear that such expanded insurance will increase demand and costs (Frank, 1990). Capped benefits and increased co-payments are used to restrict utilization and control costs. Cost sharing focuses on getting employees to pay a greater share of the cost through deductions, co-payments, and caps and may result in lack of treatment of lower income employees or use of inappropriate and more expensive treatment.

In 1983, New York state began providing their workers with complete coverage for outpatient psychotherapy. One year later, the state's medical insurance bill tripled to more than $31 million, although utilization rose only 8 percent. The state then put a ceiling on the amount of reimbursement that would be made per psychotherapy visit (Chenoweth, 1989). A study released in 1990 reported that mental and nervous care benefits accounted for more than $43 million in 1986. Another study showed that Virginia's mandated services rose in cost from $28.3 million in 1986 to $41.6 million in 1988 (Frank, 1990). A survey of 1,943 companies in 1991 revealed that 87 percent of employers were restricting inpatient treatment of mental disorders and substance abuse, up from 75 percent in 1990. Eighty-five percent of employers were using a maximum dollar amount payable per lifetime for inpatient care, up from 35 percent in 1990 (Kenkel, 1991).

These costs have to be weighed against their benefits. Capping benefits or increasing co-payments may result only in keeping needy individuals out of treatment programs (Bartlett, 1990). Although these methods may produce immediate savings, they do not solve the basic problem of service provision and probably will not save money in the long run. Studies indicate that mental health interventions produce an average reduction of 19–34 percent in general health care use. Cutting back on mental health services could be counterproductive in the long run (Chenoweth, 1989). "If you don't offer these benefits, those problems will end up manifesting themselves somewhere else in your benefit plan, somewhere on the medical side" (Harty, 1991).

There is already a problem in the treatment of the U.S. patient. At least 50 percent (and probably much more) of all inpatient treatment costs are related to mental health and substance abuse problems (Woolsey 1991). Even though only a small percentage of illnesses and disorders are only biophysical, the psychosocial model of illness is little used by doctors in the United States. In a survey of 1,000 general medical clinic patients, only 16 percent of their complaints were explained by a biophysical view of disease (Kroenke and Mangelsdorff, 1989). This means that most complaints are associated with psychological and social causes. Yet, physicians are trained to see the presentation of complaints in a biophysical way, which can lead to inappropriate treatment and a lack of focus on prevention. A survey of general practitioners and family medicine faculty revealed that the problems in medical practice that generated the most difficulties were depression, chronic back pain, geriatric problems and sexually transmitted disease (Leclere et al., 1990). Physicians did not like to deal with these major complaints that had significant components of psychological and social causation. Research has shown that as medical students move through their training there is a shift by many students toward the biophysical model and away from the psychosocial model and away from treating patients with psychological problems. A negative orientation toward psychological problems and alcoholic, geriatric, and acquired immune deficiency syndrome (AIDS) patients appears to increase with medical school training (Merrill et al., 1991).

Medical school has been likened to a four-year tug-of-war between competing "climates of value" (technology versus humanism, a scientific versus a literary approach, a disease versus a person, competence versus caring) (Good and Good, 1989). The increase in NPO (Negative Orientation) scores between freshmen and seniors and the similarity in senior' NPO scores found in three medical schools would support the view that the psychosocial model of illness loses out in this tug of war. (Merrill et al., 1991)

During times of high health care costs and tight budgets, employers need to be careful about reductions in mental health care coverage. Employees may not be as aware of the significance of mental health care coverage as they are of physical health care coverage, and they may be more willing to accept a reduction in mental health care benefits. However, employers and managers need to be long-term focused and recognize that mental health problems will appear in the physical health system and will be treated inappropriately and at higher cost if mental health care coverage is not provided. Corporation managers focused on short-term financial accounting and public administrators focused on short-term political gains need to change their short-term focus for long-range planning. This is the only way the United States will be competitive with other countries. This long-range focus needs to be taken in regard to mental health provision, cost, and productivity.

Bartlett (1990) feels that insurers need to change their philosophy regarding mental health benefits by putting the emphasis on quality care and treatment of each individual in the most independent setting possible. Also, employers need to take an interest in the content of therapy. Different forms of psychotherapy have different results. With more employees using psychotherapy, employers need to be aware of the different types of psychotherapy and the appropriateness of different therapies to different situations. They should not consider all psychotherapy the same, the "uniformity myth." Short-term psychotherapy may result in no insurance premium increases, but it also may not improve the worker's situation and productivity. Long-term psychotherapy may raise insurance premium costs above the increases in worker productivity (Klarreich, DiGiuseppe, and DiMattia, 1987). Managed care may help the employer find the most appropriate care for each situation.

COST CONTROL AND MANAGED CARE

Suzanne Gelber, a consultant with the benefits division of Towers, Perin, Forster, and Crosby Inc. of New York, encourages employers to review the design of their mental health and substance abuse benefits to ensure that the plans do not encourage employees to seek the most costly care (Woolsey, 1991). There is a substantial variation in cost and level of service of care for treating mental health problems by different providers. Providing full coverage of inpatient treatment encourages long and inappropriate hospital stays. This is demonstrated by the increase in adolescent psychiatric hospitalization, which has increased 350 percent from 1982 to 1987 (Bartlett, 1990). Utilization studies show that adolescent care is the leading cause of increasing employers' costs (Woolsey, 1991). This results from the treatment of employee's children who are covered under dependent coverage. Thus, one way to address costs is to provide coverages that encourage outpatient treatment or treat it equally with inpatient treatment and encourage the ability to use various treatments. This will encourage the correct level of care being used, not a level of care more intensive and expensive than necessary. Various approaches have been used to contain costs, including managed care.

Managed Care

Managed mental health care focuses on the development and implementation of mental health benefit plans that control costs while assuring appropriateness of care and quality. Managed care involves a prepaid health plan or insurance program where beneficiaries receive medical services in a coordinated manner in order to eliminate unnecessary medical services. Typically, managed care involves strict utilization review and controlled access. Managed care requires the employee to receive permission from a gatekeeper, such as a primary care physician, utilization review nurse, or employer designated professional such as an employee assistance program (EAP) professional, before receiving specialist and/or inpatient care.

Managed health care plans can incorporate cost-effective alternatives into existing indemnity programs. One of these approaches is the addition of case management. Managed care focuses on assessing the individual who needs treatment and determining the appropriate level of care. Under a case management approach, the objectives can be adjusted as the client's need for care changes. Managed care can be implemented by indemnity insurers, self-insured employers, HMOs, or preferred provider organizations. Managed care is more recent to the mental health field, because it began with general medical care.

Managed care may involve a multidisciplinary approach by using physicians, clinical nurses, health counselors, psychologists, and social workers to match patients' needs with an appropriate specialist. Case managers may take extensive clinical histories and, after considering the diagnosis, devise a goal-oriented treatment plan and monitor patients' and caregivers' performance. All inpatient care is approved ahead of time and then monitored. Outpatient care is also monitored. There is a tendency to emphasize outpatient care whenever possible. Case managers focus on outliers, cases that have unusually long lengths of stay or unusually high costs compared with other cases in the same category. This is the same approach taken in Medicare's prospective payment system based on Diagnostic Related Groups (DRGs). Case management programs can identify catastrophic cases through diagnosis, age, and treatment setting. Catastrophic admissions are associated with freestanding psychiatric hospitals rather than general hospitals or substance abuse facilities. Catastrophic length of stay in substance abuse facilities is associated with dual diagnoses, a psychiatric and a substance abuse disorder. Long-stay admissions are concentrated in the Northeast, while high-cost admissions are more likely to occur in the West, South, and Northeast (Goldstein et al., 1988).

The clinical, ethical, and financial aspects of managed care have been reviewed from the perspectives of insurers, providers, and payers (Broskowski, 1991; Newman and Brickline, 1991), and managed health care is not always looked upon favorably by providers. They tend to view managed care as withholding treatment in order to make money. Administrators at pyschiatric hospitals in the mid-1980s in a *Modern Healthcare* survey felt psychiatric case managers have made it very difficult to deliver adequate patient care (64 percent), case managers have demanded discharge of patients too early (62 percent), case management or gatekeeping systems have led to inappropriate placements (24 percent), case management firms rarely explained their review criteria (42 percent), and review criteria were applied inconsistently (52 percent). Thus, a good managed care program should have a good quality assurance (QA) system to make sure quality is maintained while costs are controlled (Newman and Brickline, 1991).

There is considerable tension between psychiatric providers and managed care (Kim, 1988), and some believe that the most serious problem with managed care is that their profits depend on denial of care (Pinheiro, 1992). The incentive for managed care is to reduce service utilization, while the incentive for the providers is to utilize all care available. Most managed care companies are publicly held companies that focus on maximizing the shareholders' income. However, they also have an incentive to not withhold services, because if the patient gets sicker, the patient could cost the company more money. Providers want to use all their available knowledge and services and to reduce the likelihood for a malpractice suit.

Utilization Review

Utilization review is a part of managed care. Utilization review seeks to curtail medically unnecessary treatment and unnecessarily long-term treatment. Although utilization review reduces lengths of stay, overall, it is not able to make a major impact on the total cost of health care (Wagman and Schiff, 1990). Utilization review typically reduces costs 10–15 percent (Bartlett, 1990).

Health Maintenance Organizations

HMOs usually include mental health care. In 1987, of the 648 HMOs in the country, 99 percent included mental health benefits (Ernest and Witney, 1986). HMOs are exclusive providers. The employee must use providers who are either based in a specific clinic or on a closed panel of contracted providers. If employees choose to receive services outside the HMO providers, unless it is an emergency, they are responsible for the full costs. HMOs are regionally based and provide services within a specified geographic region. They provide services based on contracts that are based on a per capita fee. HMOs use utilization review extensively, and the primary care physician is usually the gatekeeper for specialist care. Permission from the HMO's utilization review professional is usually required for inpatient treatment. Some clinic-based HMOs have their own staff of counselors to address mental health problems. There are also mental health HMOs made up of a closed panel of mental health providers who contract to provide mental health services just through their provider list.

Kaiser Permanente has shown that mental health services and psychotherapy can be economically included in prepaid health plans and that failure to include them actually jeopardizes the effective functioning of medical services by visits from patients who have emotional, rather than organic, reasons for their physical symptoms. Patients who received psychotherapy at a Kaiser Permanente HMO in San Francisco had reduced emotional distress and reduced medical utilization. Of the medical visits at the HMO, 60 percent were for psychosomatic disorders, and the emotionally distressed patients had higher medical utilization. Brief psychotherapy was more effective than continuous, long-term psychotherapy, and the costs of psychotherapy were more than offset by the savings from the reduced medical utilization (Cummings and VandenBos, 1981). An analysis of 58 studies of psychotherapy and medical utilization showed decreased medical utilization following psychotherapy in 85 percent of the studies, with medical utilization declining 10–33 percent and hospital length of stay declining 1.5 days (Mumford et al., 1984).

It is not the provision of mental health services but the way that they are provided that can cause financial problems (Cummings, 1979). A study of the multiyear patterns of ambulatory mental health care in a population continuously eligible to receive fee-for-service care found that among 14,000 people who were eligible for all of a three-year period, 14 percent used outpatient mental health services at least once in a three-year period. When compared with three-year HMO data, it was found the probability that a nonuser becomes a user is roughly the same for fee-for-service and HMO clients, but the probability of continuing use in the next year is much less in the HMO. The HMO effect on mental health care was primarily on the visits per user rather than on the number of users (McGuire and Fairbanks, 1988).

Some HMOs limit the number of mental health care visits. Limitations on visits puts the focus on brief psychotherapy approaches. This will work well for some clients but may not for others. However, it may have the benefit of decreasing the dropout rate. One study indicated that dropout rates from psychotherapy were lower when treatment duration was specified at outset rather than being open ended (Sledge et al., 1990). Some HMOs provide as much access as other types of coverage. In some treatment settings, for example, the Milwaukee Clinical Campus of the University of Wisconsin Medical School, there is no difference in the number of visits for HMO patients compared with other patients (Blackwell, Gutmann, and Gutmann, 1988).

There are providers who support managed care and see HMOs as able to provide well-designed, targeted, clinical behavioral medicine that can improve health outcomes and save money. In addition, they can be used to increase self-care competence and empower patients to participate in health care, because 70–90 percent of all symptoms are self-diagnosed and self-treated without professional help. Also, nearly a third of patients' visits to doctors are for bodily symptoms as an expression of psychological distress; another third are behavioral choices, such as substance abuse, smoking, or poor nutrition; and even in the remaining patients with medical disease, the course of the illness may be strongly influenced by mood, coping skills, and social support. Psychological and behavioral interventions can help patients more directly address their problems and become less dependent upon medical care (Sobel, 1992). For example, in one study of 452 elderly patients admitted for surgical repair of fractured hips, patients receiving screening for psychiatric consultations received more psychiatric consultations but had a reduced hospital length of stay of 1.7–2.2 days and a savings of $270,000, for a program cost of $40,000 (Strain et al., 1991). In another study involving providing continuous emotional support for women during labor, the supported group versus the controls had 56 percent less Cesarean sections, 85 percent less epidural anesthesia, 70 percent fewer forceps deliveries, 61 percent less oxytocin, a 25 percent decline in the duration of labor, and 58 percent less neonate hospitalization. The program cost was only $200 per intervention (Kennell et al., 1991).

Preferred Provider Organizations

Preferred Provider Organizations (PPOs) contract with health care providers to provide services at a reduced or discounted cost. The PPO plan then requires a lower deductible or co-payment by employees who use the list of contracted providers, usually from no co-payment to 10 or 20 percent. If employees choose to use a provider not on the list they pay a higher deductible and co-payment, usually a 30–40 percent co-payment. Mental health providers may be contracted with, to provide savings of usually 20–30 percent (Bartlett, 1990). PPOs, like HMOs, use utilization review extensively.

Exclusive Provider Organizations

Exclusive Provider Organizations (EPOs) are similar to PPOs and HMOs. They are contracted with to provide services at a reduced or discounted fee like a PPO, but like an HMO, they are the only provider that the employee can attend and receive coverage of payment. If another provider is seen, the employee must pay for the service. Employers or employers' EAPs may contract for certain mental health or substance abuse services with an exclusive provider for mental health or substance abuse treatment. For example, an EAP in Bakersfield has an EPO contract for inpatient substance abuse treatment. Exclusive provider organizations can provide services for mental health and/or substance abuse treatment at a 40–50 percent savings (Bartlett, 1990).

Employee Assistance Programs as Managed Care

EAPs can assess, make referrals, and, in some cases, provide treatment. EAPs can serve as gatekeepers to mental health and substance abuse programs. EAPs can operate as a form of managed care by making a correct assessment and sending the person to the correct treatment. Some EAPs may also coordinate managed mental health care by contracting for substance abuse services through a specific hospital or clinic. This can be done to control costs through a reduced cost contract while controlling for quality.

Some EAPs have the professional staff available to actually provide treatment. Employer-provided EAPs may provide an indefinite amount of outpatient treatment without using the employee's insurance, but most contracted EAPs provide a set number of visits (usually three to ten) under the costs of the contract with the employer, and the employee's insurance is used after those visits are used up. EAPs may also provide preventive services. The cost of an EAP compared with other benefits is low, because only a minority of employees use it. Coverage for the intensive treatment needed by a few can be handled through a two-tiered insurance arrangement by encouraging the use of the EAP as a gatekeeper for referral to appropriate and cost-effective services. Employees seeking counseling on their own can be required to pay a greater percentage of the cost of the services, for example, 50 percent, while those referred through the EAP pay only 20 percent of the cost of the services (Lydecker, 1985).

It is crucial that the EAP works well with the benefit structure and guides employees to treatment programs that are appropriate. This will reduce health care costs in the long run by guiding employees to appropriate treatment early (Bartlett, 1990). Research involving 223 companies in Houston, Texas, found that companies with EAPs experienced a higher number of claims for nervous and mental disorders but that there was no significant difference in overall insurance costs. EAP companies also experience a much lower rate of increase in insurance costs (14 percent versus 22 percent). Those findings supported the "off-set effect principle" that treating psychological disorders reduces medical care. The EAP companies also had more control over inpatient utilization and lower deductibles and lower lifetime dollar limitations (Madonia, 1987). Lockheed estimated $1 million in annual savings on life insurance premiums over five years from their wellness program (Naisbitt and Aburdene, 1985). There may also be reduced premiums for offering an EAP or wellness program (Williams, 1986).

National Health Insurance

Debate about national health insurance has been ongoing in the United States for many years. The United States and South Africa remain the only industrialized nations without some form of national health care. Various health plans have been proposed over the years; some have included mental health services, and others have not. Opponents to mental health coverage in national health insurance programs argue that the poor would be subsidizing the rich because people with higher incomes use psychotheapy more. Although people with higher incomes do tend to use specialized mental health services more, lower income people tend to use general medical personnel for their mental health problems. This use of medical services is much more expensive than the appropriate use of mental health services (Cummings, 1979). Including mental health service coverage on an equal footing with physical health service coverage in any national health service plan would mean more-appropriate and less-expensive service.

The American Public Health Association (APHA) has a resolution supporting universal access to mental health care. The resolution recommends

> That any national or state plan for universal access to health care provide for the treatment of psychiatric disorders on an equal basis with other disorders; and Recommends that any national or state plan for universal access to health care provide access to a range of community-based treatment, support and rehabilitation services for persons with long-term, disabling mental illness. (APHA, 1993)

In September 1993 the Clinton administration introduced national health care legislation. Mental health care was included, but with lesser coverage than physical health care.

Even without a national health system, health care in the United States is increasingly concentrated in fewer hands. National networks of services controlled by megacompanies are growing in the health care industry. Ten to 12 major corporations, predominately insurance corporations, are becoming major providers. There is also a growth in national networks in the provision of private mental health care and in contracted EAPs. This raises questions about the ability of smaller and more diverse service providers to survive in the marketplace (Brous, 1986). Although service provision is growing in the private sector, the public sector remains involved in providing benefits to employees for mental health problems, including workers' compensation.

WORKERS' COMPENSATION

The modern concept of safety laws and workers' compensation originated in Europe at the end of the nineteenth century as a result of industrialization. Approximately a decade after their origination in Europe, they reached the United States. Until that time, an injured worker had to bring suit for damages against the employer and had the burden of proof to show that the injury was caused by the employer's negligence. If the employer could prove that the worker's negligence (contributory negligence) had contributed to the injury, the worker would recover nothing. Also, employers could use as a defense the fellow-servant rule, which prevented the injured worker from collecting damages if another employee caused the injury, or the assumption of risk doctrine, which stated that an employee assumed certain risks as an employee. These defenses meant that most industrial injuries were not compensated. Workers' compensation laws were developed to protect employers against lawsuits that could expose the employer to huge damage awards and to protect employees from the costs of medical care and loss of income while unable to work. In 1911, workers' compensation was begun, and it is the oldest widespread social program in the United States.

State Programs

Workers' compensation laws are state laws, with requirements varying from state to state. California has the largest system in the United States, covering more than 12 million workers and in 1989 paying more than $10 billion in claims' costs (Koll, 1991). California employers in 1989 paid 50 percent above the U.S. average (Ferguson, 1991), and in 1992 most employers paid between 3 percent and 4 percent of their payroll for workers' compensation (Green, 1992). The state programs are administered by state workers' compensation boards or commissions. They establish the specific rules defining how the system works and may also have lists of approved health care professionals who may treat injured or ill employees. Most states make workers' compensation mandatory for employers, regardless of the number of their employees. In some systems, if the employer can prove he has sufficient financial resources, the employer may self-insure and pay claims out of the organization's own funds instead of buying insurance. The system is no-fault and requires no proof of who is responsible. This approach reduces court cases and provides benefits to employees without the delay of court proceedings. In Nevada, North Dakota, Ohio, Washington, West Virginia, and Wyoming, employers must insure employees through a state workers' compensation insurance fund rather than through private insurance companies. In most cases, employees cannot sue the employer or a fellow worker for work-related damages. About a dozen states exclude employers of only a few employees (3–5) in nonhazardous businesses. New Jersey, South Carolina, and Texas have elective programs. If an employer is not covered, the employee may sue that organization for damages and the employer may not use contributory negligence as a defense. A small number of employees are excluded, for example, some maritime, railroad, and federal employees who are covered by federal law and some agricultural laborers and part-time housekeepers in private homes (Joel, 1993). In 1986 there were 86 million workers covered by workers' compensation programs.

Workers' compensation insurance has been rising faster than the rate of inflation. Some of these costs are related to the fact that medical costs have been rising faster than the rate of inflation. Broadening the definition of what constitutes a workers' compensation claim, increased litigation and legal fees, and court actions that slow the compensation process are also increasing system costs (Lavan, 1990). Increasing costs and widening parameters have created calls for system reform. Some analysts believe that if costs are not controlled, the system will have to be completely restructured. In that eventuality, there have been proposals to treat workers' compensation as an employee benefit rather than a statutory right (Kiell, 1989).

Employers cannot discipline or fire an employee who files a workers' compensation claim (Joel, 1993). An employer may have to continue the benefits even if there is a subsequent firing for cause. *Cousins* v. *Georgia-Pacific Corporation* (Maine Supreme Judicial Court, No. 5988, 1991) ruled that an employee's right to benefits does not end because he/she is fired, even for cause, as long as the original injury made him/her eligible for the benefits in the first place. Employees file a workers' compensation claim when they believe they have been injured or are ill because of a work-related cause. The injury or illness must be either specific as a result of a single event or exposure or cumulative as the result of repetitive mental or physical trauma or exposure. If the employee's doctor says that an injury or symptom is related to job stress but the employer or insurance carrier disagrees the parties may choose an Agreed Medical Expert (AME) to resolve the difference. If the employer still disagrees with the claim, the workers' compensation board holds a hearing to arbitrate the dispute. Basically, eligibility is based on injury/illness being related to occurring during work time, being in a location where the employee was supposed to be or could have reasonably been expected to be, in the line of duty while doing a task associated with the job, and when there is a cause and effect relationship between the job and the injury. Work-related accidents caused by intoxication or addiction to alcohol or drugs normally do not qualify for benefits. However, if employers serve alcohol at a party or picnic, they may be liable. Employees accidentally injured while asleep on the job generally are ruled to qualify for benefits (Joel, 1993). Thus, employees who are suffering from mental health problems that could cause them to be fatigued would put the employer at risk of a compensable claim. Occupational diseases to be compensable must result from continued exposure to a recognized hazard of a particular job. Different states have different standards of proof in regard to how much they will require the hazard to be related to the work versus how much the hazard is caused by outside factors. Workers also are not generally compensated for self-inflicted injuries (Joel, 1993).

The employer may have to pay benefits during the dispute process, but if the employee loses, the employee may have to reimburse the employer. Appeals may be made, including to the courts. The employer's insurance pays all medical bills and pays benefits based on a percentage of the employee's average weekly income, 66.66 percent of gross up to a maximum cap in most states. In California in 1992, the maximum payable benefit was $336 per week. The payment is less than full income because the employee does not have to pay income taxes on workers' compensation benefits. Some states require the employer to continue group health insurance while the employee is unable to work.

Workers' compensation laws require employers to carry insurance that will pay all medical expenses and protect the worker from loss of income for work-related injuries and illnesses. Workers are also entitled to receive rehabilitation services. Vocational rehabilitation may be more expensive than all other claim costs and may run over $20,000. Vocational rehabilitation is available to workers who cannot return to their usual occupation or the occupation they were performing at the time of their injury. Employees may receive vocational rehabilitation benefits if they are medically able to benefit from vocational rehabilitation and if they want to participate in vocational rehabilitation. This in the long run is the best approach, because vocationally rehabilitated employees will be able to return to work and will not remain unproductive and a cost to society. It is in the interests of the employer to provide psychological support to the employee by keeping in touch, offering emotional support, encouraging use of the EAP, aiding in rehabilitation, and trying to get the worker back into the workplace as soon as possible. Such support helps workers return to work as soon as possible and return to being productive. It also reduces costs, provides an environment that other employees will recognize as supportive of workers, and will enhance morale.

When the condition allows, the employee can return to light duty before returning to full duty. The employer is obligated to provide that work only if the employer has it available. One way for employers to control costs is to see that they make light duty available. If the employee cannot return to full earning capacity, workers' compensation pays the difference between what the employee would have been able to earn before the accident/illness and what the employee is able to earn with the disability. If the worker is permanently disabled, most states use a schedule listing a specific number of weeks of benefits to be paid, depending on how much each injury is perceived to be worth. The payments are often paid out as a lump sum. California uses percentages that range from 0 for an injured worker with no residual effect from an injury to 100 percent for a worker who can no longer work at all. In the case of death, the spouse is usually paid a modest burial allowance and the worker's full weekly benefits for life or until remarriage. Dependents may receive benefits, usually until age 18. In California, these benefits are on a schedule that varies with the age and number of dependents. A claim involving young children and a dependent spouse may run over $200,000.

Currently there is an effort to abandon the free market system for a managed care approach. Twenty-nine states have "free choice" systems that allow employees to choose their own doctor. Many states do not allow employers to negotiate and contract with health care providers for workers' compensation, but employers are increasingly interested in moving toward HMOs or other managed care, while labor unions oppose this approach. California is a free choice state, but the law allows employers to contract with PPOs for workers' compensation cases. Under this approach, if an employee does not specify a doctor at the time of hire, the employer has the option to choose a doctor for the employee. Of the companies that belong to the California Workers Compensation Institute, 77 percent have signed contracts with PPOs. This type of managed care is estimated to save approximately 22 percent (Doherty, 1989).

Mental Health Coverage

Mental disorders are among the most recent types of injuries/illnesses added to workers' compensation coverage. These types of claims in some states have increased dramatically in the past ten years. In the 1970s there were very few mental stress claims, but now the numbers are growing rapidly, and employees are winning awards for claims related to depression, anxiety, nervous disorders, and migraines. In 1989, stress claims made up 15 percent of all occupational disease claims, an increase from 5 percent in 1980 (De Carlo, 1989). The costs of mental stress related claims vary widely. In 1984 a study by the National Council on Compensation Insurance indicated that the average cost for all workplace injuries in a 13-state sample was $7,500, but mental stress claims were more expensive, with an average cost of $10,000–$15,000 (Lavan, 1990).

Some on-the-job accidents/diseases will be covered by the Americans with Disabilities Act (ADA). To come under ADA, the injury/disease must cause substantial limitation to major life activities or result in the person having a record of such an impairment or being regarded as having such an impairment. The employer may not check into an applicant's workers' compensation history prior to selection but may make such a check after offering a job. The employer may refuse to hire or can fire only if the person with the disability is unable to perform the job without posing a significant risk to him/herself or others and only if the risk cannot be eliminated or reduced through a reasonable accommodation. ADA does not require the employer to provide a light duty job if there is none available or to create a job the employee could do (ADA, 1992).

Mental disorders can be categorized into three groups: physical/mental claims, mental/physical claims, and mental/mental claims. The first type of claim involves a physical injury leading to a mental disability, such as a worker who develops a depression after suffering a fall. Compensation would be rated based on the mental disturbance being created by the physical injury. This type of claim is recognized in almost every jurisdiction in the United States. The physical injuries are normally serious and lead to depression or other psychological conditions. The mental/physical claims occur when a mental stress condition causes a physical injury, for example, when an employee develops an ulcer after a stressful negotiation process. That type of claim is also compensable in nearly all jurisdictions. The mental/mental claim is the result of a mental stress condition. This type of claim is subject to claims by employees that they suffered a stress disorder after receiving a poor performance review (Borba and Camilleri, 1987) or even termination. The first two types of claims have a physical component, and there is tangible evidence to support the claim. Mental/mental claims are more difficult to deal with because of their subjective nature in terms of evaluation of mental stress conditions or loss of mental capabilities. It is also difficult to prove how much of the disability is related to the work situation and how much to other factors, such as personal relationships, financial problems, or personality disorders. It may be necessary to determine if the person was mentally ill before the claim and/or whether the work-related stress merely aggravated an existing condition (Lavan, 1990). These claims are covered by only a few state laws and are relatively new to the field, and the laws regulating them tend to be vague (Joel, 1993).

The National Council on Compensation Insurance in 1985 identified five categories of how states rule on mental/mental claims: did not compensate for those claims (9 states); permitted compensation if the source of the mental stress is a sudden, frightening, or shocking event (8); permitted compensation if the source of the mental stress is unusual or in excess of everyday life and employ-ment stress (11); allowed compensation even if the mental stress event was not sudden (7); and did not yet have a defined policy on such claims (15) (Borba and Camilleri, 1987).

In one case that involved psychiatric disability based on a condition resulting from an abnormal working condition, *Marico* v. *Workmens' Compensation Appeal Board* (Pennsylvania Common-wealth Court, No. 1 1092 C.D., 1989, 1991), it was ruled that the presence of a mouse in the workplace was not sufficient to support a claim of psychiatric trauma being work-related, because mice are a common workplace pest.

Stress Claims

Stress can be defined as any demand that creates a tension or threat that requires an individual to make an adaptation in life-style and that is widespread in the workplace (Gadzella et al., 1990). Both physical and social factors can influence behavioral health changes. Job pressure, harassment, excessive work load, ineffective manage-ment, and job insecurity can all cause stress and adversely impact the psychological well-being of the employee (Stellman, 1987). Eco-nomic and demographic changes have had a profound impact on the increase in stress claims. The decline in industrial jobs and the rise in a service and knowledge based economy have led to an increase of new jobs in the stressful service sector and jobs that are mentally, rather than physically, oriented. Corporate mergers, plant closings, relocations, and layoffs are increasingly the norm and lead to stress and stress claims. The demise of the traditional family and the increase of dual-income families has led to greater pressures on families. There are also more and more women in the work force, and many of them have multiple roles and responsibilities in relationship to family and work, which create stress (Lavan, 1990). Many states have expanded the types of cases that are compensable under workers' compensation laws, and the legal system has been changing, with courts recognizing stress disorders as legitimate claims. The rise in the number of attorneys also makes available many attorneys to pursue cases. There are a rising number of employees who settle their stress claims in court instead of through the workers' compensation system. This shows a failure of the system to meet the needs of all the claimants and opens employers to uncertainties regarding liability. This problem was addressed by the California Supreme Court in *Cole* v. *Fair Oaks Fire Department* (233 Cal. Rptr. 308). The court held that employees' claims for injuries that arise during the course of employment must be brought under the employer's workers' compensation insurance, not in a private lawsuit, whether or not the employer was at fault for the injury. The California Supreme Court in *Foley* v. *Interactive Data Corporation*

(233 Cal. Rptr. 308). found that an employee may not recover, in a private lawsuit, damages for emotional suffering that he/she experiences when an employer breaks the employment agreement.

In a survey of human resource managers and company medical directors, 72 percent of them felt that mental health problems resulting from stress at work were very pervasive. They also reported that each year, 20 percent of their work force suffered from anxiety disorders or stress-related illness (Lavan, 1990). It is estimated that each employee who suffers from a stress-related illness loses an average of 16 days of work per year (Allen, 1990). Many of these stress-related illnesses may be compensable under workers' compensation. Certain traumatic events, such as narrowly escaping a traffic accident when driving, are a part of the job, and even being reprimanded by a supervisor may be compensable. If an employee was suspected of forging a check and was distraught over the investigation, the employee might not be compensated, because forgery is not within the scope of the job, but if the employee were found innocent he/she could be compensated for the stress arising from the investigation (Allen, 1990). Employers have become increasingly hesitant to terminate employees for fear of emotional distress and a stress disorder case (Lavan, 1990).

Some occupations are more prone to stress than others. The National Institute for Occupational Safety and Health in the 1980s compared stress disorders among all occupational groups in regard to the highest incidence of stress-related diseases, such as heart disease, hypertension, ulcers, and nervous disorders. They found occupations of laborer, secretary, inspector, clinical lab technician, and office manager to be the most stressful. Jobs with large numbers of assignments to complete or repetitive tasks can be very stressful (Stellman, 1987). Another study reported innercity school teacher, police officer, air traffic controller, medical intern, firefighter, waiter, assembly-line worker, customer service representative, securities trader, and newspaper editor as the ten most stressful jobs (*Men's Health*, 1992). Also, people occupying lower-level jobs at the staff and mid-management levels report higher levels of stress than do executives, which may be due to the executive's ability to delegate responsibilities to the staff and mid-level managers, who are then accountable for carrying them out (Gadzella et al., 1990). People between the ages of 19 and 40 scored higher on stress tests than individuals between the ages of 41 and 63; this may be the result of older employees learning how to better deal with stress and perform their jobs more efficiently (Gadzella et al., 1990). Women score higher than men on tests of overall stress, probably because they hold jobs involving routine, boring tasks, requiring long hours at low pay, and their job responsibilities are often combined with the primary responsibility for the family (Stellman, 1987). Thus stress-related disorders are a legitimate health concern in the workplace and will be likely to impact certain employees more than others. A stress or psychological disability claim by a police officer can cost from $260,000 to $350,000, not including administrative costs, claims handling costs, overtime, replacement, or turnover costs (Mathis, 1983).

California is one of only six states that allow claims based on gradual stresses of daily work. States that allow stress claims that are not sudden but result gradually may have difficulty distinguishing how much of the stress was caused outside the workplace. In California, only 10 percent of the stress must be connected to work. Thus, marital problems, substance abuse, commuting, or many other factors may cause the greater share of the stress, but the claim remains completely compensable, with no reduction in the claim for outside causes of the emotional distress. In California, cumulative injuries can include psychic and mental disturbances that are the result of mental stress. In California, stress-related claims rose 430 percent from 1980 to 1986, to account for 1.7 percent of all claims (DeCarlo, 1989). Between 30,000 and 40,000 stress-related mental disability claims are filed each year, and 98 percent of them are litigated. In 1987, it cost around $6,000 to litigate the claims, and nearly 80 percent were settled out of court (Jacobs, 1989). The California system is one of the most liberal workers' compensation systems in the country (Jacobs, 1989; Weaver, Vellings, and Green, 1992).

Employers are liable even for preexisting conditions if they are exacerbated by the employment. Employment does not have to be the only cause of the injury; it merely has to be a contributing factor. A 1982 case involving an Albertson's cake decorator found the "industry takes the employee as it finds him." What is significant is the amount of stress perceived by the worker in the workplace, not how much stress a normal person might tolerate. "His perception of the circumstances is what ultimately determines the amount of stress he feels. . . . All that is required is that the employment be one of the contributing causes without which the injury would not have occurred" (*Albertson's Inc.* v. *Workers' Compensation Appeal Board* [1982, California Compensation Cases 47:460–67]). The Albertson case is a mental/mental case, and after it, the mental/mental stress claims in California increased dramatically. California Workers' Compensation Institute (CWCI), a research organization composed of workers' compensation insurers in California, has found mental/mental psychiatric claims to be the fastest-growing category of all workers' compensation claims in California. The majority of cases are caused by a cumulative exposure to stresses occurring over a period of time. In approximately 70 percent of cases, job pressures are cited as the cause of disability. The greater share of these job pressures comes from alleged harassment by supervisors and co-workers. Other causes claimed are job termination, discrimination, and demotion (CWCI, 1990). Only 10 percent of mental/mental stress claims occur because of a single traumatic event. Also, the average claimant for mental/mental stress claims is an older woman working in a white-collar job, and 20 percent of the claims are filed in the first four months of employment (CWCI, 1988).

The costs of workers' compensation have soared in California. The cost rose from around $4 billion in 1984 to about $11 billion in 1991. CWCI found that in 1985, for claims that had been settled and closed in California, the average cost of the stress claims was $11,389, including $8,649 for permanent disability, $784 for temporary disability, $172 for vocational rehabilitation, and $1,784 for medical treatments. The distribution of benefits is very different from other workers' compensation claims, because the costs for medical treatment, vocational rehabilitation, and temporary disability are much lower, and permanent disability accounts for 76 percent of the benefit dollar (CWCI, 1990). Mental stress claims are particularly expensive in California, because 98 percent of them are litigated (CWCI, 1990). California employers have to pay the medical and legal costs for a worker's claim, even if the claim proves baseless. The employer bears all of the expense, including for the defense attorney, the insurer's attorney, all medical evaluations by both sides, transportation for the employee to medical evaluations, the cost of obtaining medical records for both attorneys, any diagnostic tests ordered by the two sets of evaluating physicians, and compensation for time the employee loses from work attending legal depositions or medical evaluations. The claim costs the employee nothing. If the employee wins a settlement, his/her attorney's fees come out of the settlement, usually 10–12 percent. Insurers tend to settle mental health stress claims because it is cheaper to buy them out through settlement for an average $8,649 for permanent disability while other costs are low than to risk providing for lifetime medical care, a vocational rehabilitation plan, and lost wages over the two or three years it would take to settle the case in cout (CWCI, 1990).

Attempts to Reduce Claims

The employer should have policies and programs that eliminate or reduce stress in the workplace. Many organizations use their EAPs to help address mental health and stress problems. Wellness programs are also used by some organizations to attempt to reduce stress and prevent claims. Organizations are becoming more aware of the importance of reducing stress factors in the work environment by doing away with impossible deadlines, unclear job rules, and managers who are too hard driving and controlling. Managers should be receptive to employee complaints about stress, and whenever possible, solutions should be found to those complaints. A stress management plan should prevent problems.

As the CWCI (1988, 1990) research points out, alleged harassment by supervisors and coworkers is a major cause of claims, and older women in white-collar jobs are often claimants. This may be a result of sexual discrimination and sexual harassment in the workplace, and creating a work environment free of those problems could have a positive effect on claims. Also, a substance abuse policy should be enforced, because substance abuse may contribute to mental health and stress claims.

Organizations are also more aware of the importance of matching the right person to the right job. Some individuals respond better to stress than others. The Workmen's Compensation Research Institute found that 20 percent of stress-related claims come from workers who have been in a new job for less than four months and 43 percent of stress claims come from persons who have been in their job for less than one year (CWCI, 1988). This points out the importance of seeing that the individual with the right skills to meet the job requirement is hired, promoted, or assigned to the job. This requires careful evaluation of the tasks and duties of the job, the skills and knowledge needed, and the abilities of the job candidates. Correct selection and placement should reduce the number of stress-related claims. The interview can be used to help make the right selection. The interview itself is a stressful situation and observing the interviewee's actions during the interview will give important clues as to how the person deals with stressful situations. For jobs involving stress, questions can be asked in the interview such as how the interviewee performs under strict deadlines, as a way to determine how the person reacts to stress and the resume/application can be reviewed to identify factors in past work history that might indicate problems with stress (Allen, 1990). In addition, personnel files should be well-documented. Favorable performance evaluations should not be given when an employee is not performing well, and critical incidents should be recorded. Performance problems such as frequent absenteeism, poor quality work, or insubordination may be linked to an inability to cope with stress (Allen, 1990). Prompt action should be taken. Appropriate actions would include transfer to a less-stressful job, referral to the EAP, documentation of disciplinary procedures, and termination. These actions should be taken to remove employees from jobs that have too much stress for them to handle. This will prevent damage to the employee and the workplace and will prevent workers' compensation claims.

Unfortunately, some mental health disabilities are subject to fraudulent claims or malingering. Stress is a claim particularly subject to this problem. According to the CWCI, mental stress claims increased nearly 700 percent in California from 1979 to 1988, and nine of ten claimants filing such claims were successful. It may be difficult to separate the claims that are legitimate from the minority who are abusing the system.

Unfortunately, some states such as California, Colorado, and New Jersey, suffer from a considerable amount of fraud in their systems. In Oregon, officials believed that one in four workers' compensation claims were fraudulent, until a fraud crackdown. In Los Angeles, hustlers around the unemployment office downtown try to talk workers who come for unemployment into filing workers' compensation claims instead. They ask people if when they were working their back or hands ever hurt, or if they had eye trouble, sleeplessness, or stress. Although it is illegal under California law for "cappers" to recruit clients and patients, the law is treated as largely unenforceable. The Spanish-speaking community has been targeted by television, radio, and newspaper advertising by workers' compensation doctors and lawyers. At one wood furnishing factory, half the workers said they personally knew of phony claims with typical settlements of $5,000–$7,000 for the worker (Scott, 1992). In addition, clinics would generate many times that amount in billings per patient. A 1991 California law makes it a felony punishable by fines of up to $50,000 or jail sentences of up to five years to intentionally commit a fraud seeking workers' compensation. Lawyers and doctors who commit fraud can face professional discipline, including loss of their state license. The Bureau of Fraudulent Claims was established to investigate and prosecute claims suspected of falling within the bill's definition, and insurers are mandated to report suspected fraud to the Bureau or their local district attorney.

PUBLIC SECTOR COVERAGE FOR PEOPLE WITH DISABILITIES

Many people with serious mental illness or mental retardation receive their medical coverage through the public sector through Medicare or Medicaid.

Medicaid

Medicaid is a government medical program designed for low income people. Medicaid patients make up about one-fourth of all patients treated for psychiatric disorders in general hospitals (Mechanic and Rochefort, 1992). Approximately half of Medicaid costs are paid for by the federal government and half by the state government. Eligibility, benefit levels, and restrictions vary from state to state. There are usually limits on the length of reimbursable stay per admission and limits on daily allowable charges. Usually 12–15 days are allowed in general hospitals (Sharfstein, Frank, and Kessler, 1984). If patients require a longer inpatient stay, they are usually sent to a state mental hospital. Another difficulty with care under Medicaid is that community care is highly fragmented, and there is poor coordination between hospital care and community care (Mechanic, 1991). It is difficult to substitute outpatient care for inpatient care. Many psychiatric patients may be admitted repeatedly as inpatients for short periods of stay during major episodes of their illness but may not receive treatment between such episodes (Mechanic, 1993).

There is growing interest in developing managed care systems for persons on Medicaid. Existing HMOs or special HMOs just for persons with serious and long-term mental illness can be used. A study in Hennepin County, Minnesota, in which persons with mental illness on Medicaid were randomly assigned to already existing prepaid plans, included 35 percent of the Medicaid beneficiaries in the county. Those assigned to the HMOs were found to use community mental health services in a manner very much like that of fee-for-service Medicaid patients. The mainstreaming programs did maintain specialty community-based services, but community services were less likely to be reimbursed for the prepaid patients. The program did allow patients to continue to visit their prior service providers without obtaining a physician referral, and that did weaken the HMOs' financial control (Christianson et al., 1992).

Medicare

Medicare is a federal program designed to provide medical coverage for the aged but it also provides medical coverage for permanently and totally disabled individuals. Some people with disabling mental disorders qualify for Medicare coverage. At the end of 1988, about 620,000 people were receiving Social Security Disability Insurance (SSDI) benefits because of a psychiatric mental disorder. That is the largest single diagnostic group, approximately 22 percent of all disabled workers, who collect the benefits. Approximately 36 percent of disabled workers under age 30 have a mental disorder and 38.9 percent of those aged 30 to 39 (U.S. Social Security Administration, 1989). Employment and functional impairment criteria must be met to qualify. Upon qualification, a cash benefit is provided (approximately $527 average monthly benefit in 1987), and after 24 months of eligibility for benefits, the individual is automatically enrolled under Medicare. In 1987 there were approximately 3 million people qualified for Medicare because of SSDI or kidney disease, and approximately 70 percent of those with disabilities received some medical service, at a cost of around $8.5 billion (11.2 percent of

Medicare expenditures). In 1988 there were 51,200 admissions to psychiatric hospitals, and the rate of psychiatric admissions fell from 21.1 per 100,000 in 1987 to 16.6 in 1988. This was a continuation of a trend (U.S. Social Security Administration, 1989).

Medicare enrollees may also purchase additional insurance from the private sector, called Medigap insurance, to cover some of the costs not covered under Medicare. Research indicates that disabled Medicare enrollees with emotional disorders or mental illness are as likely as other disabled Medicare enrollees to have private health insurance. However, persons with mental disabilities and Medicare coverage are more likely to receive care as an inpatient. This may result from Medicare limits on outpatient coverage for psychiatric care and close to full coverage for care in psychiatric units in general hospitals (Rubin, Wilcox-Cox, and Deb, 1992). Restrictions may be placed on payment for inpatient care under the prospective payment system, which pays under the appropriate DRG. Outpatient services are limited by a dollar cap and co-payments. Medicare does not cover inpatient care for anyone aged 22–64 in a specialty mental hospital or institution for mental disease. This affects care in state mental hospitals and in nursing homes.

CONCLUSION

Thus, one of the difficulties in providing for a mentally healthy work environment is the fact that when persons are identified as having a mental health problem and are referred by an EAP, they may have difficulty paying for treatment. Even if the employer's insurance covers mental health, that coverage may be limited and biased toward inpatient care. Employers should review their cultures, policies, programs, and financing mechanisms to ensure the establishment and retention of a mentally healthy work environment.

Appendix: Mental Health in the Workplace Resources

The following resources are available for additional information.

AIDS Referral Service
P. O. Box 6003
Rockville, MD 20849-6003
800-458-5231

Alcohol, Drug Abuse, and Mental Health Administration
Department of Health and Human Services
5600 Fishers Lane
Rockville, MD 20857
301-433-3673

Alzheimer's Association
P. O. Box 5675-AL
Chicago, IL 60680-5675
800-272-3900
312-335-8882 (TDD)

Alzheimer's Disease Education and Referral (ADEAR) Center
National Institute on Aging
U.S. Department of Health and Human Services
9000 Rockville Pike
Building 31, Room 5C-27
Bethesda, MD 20205
800-438-4380
(Publishes an annual progress report on Alzheimer's disease and provides other information and resources to professionals and others seeking information on Alzheimer's disease)

American Association for Marriage and Family Therapy
1100 Seventeenth Street, N.W., 10th Floor
Washington, DC 20036
800-374-2638
(Offers local referrals and general information)

American Association of Retired Persons
601 E Street, N.W.
Washington, DC 20049
202-434-2260
(Social Outreach and Support Section offers information and referrals)

American Geriatrics Society
770 Lexington Avenue, Suite 300
New York, NY 10021
212-308-1414
(Offers information and referral to local chapters)

American Psychiatric Association
1400 K Street, N.W.
Washington, DC 20005
(Information on mental health)

American Psychological Association
750 First Street, N.E.
Washington, DC 20002-4242
202-336-5700
(Information on depression and mental health)

Equal Employment Opportunity Commission
1801 L Street, N.W.
Washington, DC 20507
202-366-9305, 202-663-4001
202-755-7687 (TDD)

Immigration and Naturalization Service
425 I Street, N.W.
Washington, DC 20536
202-514-1900

Institute for Rehabilitation and Disability Management
Washington Business Group on Health
777 North Capitol Street, N.E., Suite 800
Washington, DC 20002
202-408-9333 (Voice/TDD)
202-408-9332 (FAX)

IRS Tax Credit/Deduction Americans with Disabilities Act
Office of Chief Council
CC:PSI:6
1111 Constitution Avenue, N.W., Room 5111
Washington, DC 20224
202-566-3292

Job Accommodation Network
West Virginia University 809, Allen Hall
P. O. Box 6112
Morgantown, WV 26506-6122
800-526-7234 (Voice/TDD)
800-526-4698 (within WV)

National Institute on Aging
9000 Rockville Pike
Building 31, Room 5C-27
Bethesda, MD 20205
800-222-2225
(Information on a range of mental health issues)

National Institute on Alcohol Abuse
5600 Fishers Lane
Rockville, MD 20857
301-433-3885

National Institute on Drug Abuse
5600 Fishers Lane
Rockville, MD 20857
301-662-HELP (Mon.–Fri. 9 A.M.–3 P.M. EDT; Sat.–Sun. Noon–3 P.M.)
800-662-9832 (Spanish language)
301-433-6480; 800-843-4971

National Institute on Mental Health
5600 Fishers Lane
Rockville, MD 20857
301-433-3673

Occupational Safety and Health Administration
200 Constitution Avenue, N.W.
Washington, DC 20210
202-523-8151

Office on the Americans with Disabilities Act
Civil Rights Division
U.S. Department of Justice
P. O. Box 66118
Washington, DC 20035-6118
202-514-0301
202-514-0381 (TDD)

U.S. Department of Labor
200 Constitution Avenue, N.W.
Washington, DC 20010
202-523-8271
202-523-8305 (Wage and Hour Division)

References

Aberth, John. (1987). "Personnel World: Pre-Employment Testing Is Losing Favor." *Personnel Journal* (September):96–104.

Abramowitz, M. and M. Hamilton. (1986). "Drug Testing on the Rise." *Washington Post* (September 7):D1.

Abrams, L. (1987). "An Employer's Role in Relapse Prevention." *The ALMACAN* (July):20–22.

Ackoff, R. (1967). "Management Misinformation-Systems." *Management Science* 14:147–56.

Adler, Nancy J. (1981). "Re-entry: Managing Cross-Cultural Transitions." *Group and Organizational Studies* 6, 3:341–56.

Alcohol, Drug Abuse, and Mental Health Administration (ADAMHA). (1991). *What You Can Do About Drug Use in America*. Washington, DC: ADAMHA.

Alcohol, Drug Abuse, and Mental Health Administration (ADAMHA) (1983). *Statistical Abstract*. Washington, DC: ADAMHA.

Alderfer, Clayton P. (1989). "Theories Reflecting My Personal Experience and Life Development." *The Journal of Applied Behavioral Science* 25, 4:351–65.

Alderfer, Clayton P. (1972). *Existence, Relatedness, and Growth: Human Needs in Organizational Settings*. New York: Free Press.

Alderfer, Clayton P., R. E. Kaplan, and K. K. Smith. (1974). "The Effect of Variables in Relatedness Need Satisfaction on Relatedness Desires." *Administrative Science Quarterly* 19:507–32.

Allen, David S. (1990). "Less Stress, Less Litigation." *Personnel* (Summer):32–34.

Amchin, Jess. (1991). *Psychiatric Diagnosis: A Biopsychosocial Approach Using DMS III-R*. Washington, DC: American Psychiatric Press, Inc.

American Psychiatric Association. (1989). *Coverage Catalog* (2nd ed.). Washington, DC: American Psychiatric Association.

American Psychiatric Association. (1987). *Diagnostic and Statistical Manual of Mental Disorders* (3rd edition, revised). Washington, DC: American Psychiatric Association.

American Public Health Association. (1993). "Resolution: Universal Access to Mental Health Care." Washington, DC: American Public Health Association.

American Society for Training and Development (1983). *Quality of Work Life: Perspectives for Business and the Public Sector*. New York: Addison-Wesley.

"Americans with Disabilities Act [ADA] Could Restrict Use of Psychological Tests." (1992). *Mental Health Law Reporter* (October):94.

Amundson, N. E. and W. A. Borgen (1982). "The Dynamics of Unemployment: Job Loss and Search." *Personnel and Guidance Journal* 60, 9:562–64.

Anderson, Charlene and Carolyn Stark. (1986). "Emerging Issues from Job Relocation in the High Tech Field: Implications for Employee Assistance Programs." *Employee Assistance Quarterly* 1, 2:37–54.

Anderson, Jeffrey and Susan Berger. (1991). "Physical Illness and Psychological Functioning: An Interview with Jeffrey Anderson, M.D." *The California Therapist* (January/February):54–59.

Andrews, F. M. and S. B. Withey (1976). *Social Indicators of Well-Being.* New York: Plenum.

Anglin, M. D. and Y. Hser (1990). "Treatment of Drug Abuse." In J. Q. Wilson and M. Tony (Eds.), *Drugs and Crime.* Chicago: University of Chicago Press.

Angrist, Burt. (1990). "Cocaine in the Context of Prior Central Nervous System Stimulant Epidemics." In Nora D. Volkow and Alan C. Swann (Eds.), *Cocaine in the Brain.* New Brunswick, NJ: Rutgers University Press.

Annas, George J. (1989). "Who's Afraid of the Human Genome?" *The Hastings Center Report* 9:19–21.

Anthony, W. A. (1980). *The Principles of Psychiatric Rehabilitation.* Baltimore: University Park Press.

Anthony, W. A. and R. P. Liberman. (1986). "The Practice of Psychiatric Rehabilitation: Historical, Conceptual, and Research Based." *Schizophrenia Bulletin* 12:542–59.

Antonovksy, S. (1987). *Stress and Coping.* San Francisco: Jossey-Bass.

Appel, Peter. (1983). "Adult Development from the Perspective of Reality Therapy." *Journal of Reality Therapy* 3:5–9.

Argyris, Chris. (1957). *Personality and Organization.* New York: Harper & Row.

Ashbaugh, J., P. Leaf, R. Manderscheid, and W. Eaton. (1983). "Estimates of the Size and Selected Characteristics of the Adult Chronically Mentally Ill Population Living in U.S. Households." *Community Mental Health Journal* 3:3–24.

Atwood, Joan D. and Robert Chester. (1987). *Treatment Techniques for Common Mental Disorders.* Northvale, NJ: Jason Aronson.

"Autism Seems to Cluster in Families." (1990). *Idaho Press Tribune* (August 20):8A.

Bailey, Nancy C. (1989). "Does Managed Mental Health Care Have a Future?" *Business and Health* 7:26–28.

Bailey, William E. (1986). "Putting Together the Pieces." *Management World* (March):32–33, 37.

Ball, Karen. (1991). "OSHA Regulations on AIDS, Hepatitis Overdue, Say Unions." *Chico Enterprise-Record* (December 14):9B.

Ban, Carolyn and Norma M. Riccucci. (1991). *Public Personnel Management: Current Concerns-Future Challenges.* White Plains, N. Y.: Longman Publishing Group.

Barkdoll, Gerald L. and Thomas J. Leckey (1993). "President-Elect Clinton as Quality Manager." *PA Times* 16, 1:8.

Barker, Peggy R., Ronald W. Manderscheid, Gerry E. Hendershot, Susan S. Jack, Charlotte Schoenborn, and Ingrid Goldstrom. (1992). "Serious Mental Illness and Disability in the Adult Household Population: United States, 1989." *Advance Data* 218 (September 16). Washington, DC: National Center for Health Statistics, Centers for Disease Control.

Barnard, Chester. (1948). *The Functions of the Executive.* Cambridge, MA: Harvard University Press.

Barr, J. K., K. W. Johnson, and L. J. Warshaw. (1992). "Supporting the Elderly." *Milbank Quarterly* 70, 3:509–33.

Barris, R., V. Dickie, and K. B. Baron. (1988). "A Comparison of Psychiatric Patients and Normal Subjects Based on the Model of Human Occupation." *Occupational Therapy Journal of Research* 8:3–23.

Barry, A. (1989). "A Phased Approach to Retirement Training." *Personnel Management* 21:52–57.

Bartlett, John. (1990). "Mental Health Benefits: The New Frontier." *Best's Review: Life-Health Insurance Edition* (October):52–54, 152.

Beaumont, P. B. and S. J. Allsop. (1984). "An Industrial Alcohol Policy: The Characteristics of Worker Success." *British Journal of Addiction* 79, 3:315–18.

Becker, F. D. (1981). *Workspace: Creating Environments in Organizations.* New York: Praeger.

Bellamy, G. T., L. E. Rhodes, D. M. Mank, and J. M. Albin. (1989). *Supported Employment a Community Implementation Guide.* Baltimore: Paul H. Brookes.

Bennett, Dudley. (1980). *Successful Team Building Through TA.* New York: AMACOM, American Management Association.

Bennett, Dudley. (1976). *TA and the Manager.* New York: AMACOM, American Management Association.

Bensinger, Ann and Charles F. Pilkington. (1985). "Treating Chemically Dependent Employees in a Non-Hospital Setting." *Personnel Administrator* (August):42–52.

Benson, Bruce Paul. (1990). *Serving the Dislocated Worker.* New York: Proma.

Bergin, A. E. (1985). "Proposed Values for Guiding and Evaluating Counseling and Psychotherapy." *Counseling and Values* 29:99–116.

Berne, Eric. (1976). *Beyond Games and Scripts.* New York: Grove Press.

Berne, Eric. (1972). *What Do You Say After You Say Hello?* New York: Grove Press.

Berne, Eric. (1966). *Principles of Group Treatment.* New York: Grove Press.

Berne, Eric. (1964). *Games People Play.* New York: Grove Press.

Berne, Eric. (1963). *The Structure and Dynamics of Organizations and Groups.* New York: Grove Press.

Berne, Eric. (1961). *Transactional Analysis in Psychotherapy.* New York: Grove Press.

Beyer, Janice M., M. Trice Harrison, and Richard E. Hunt. (1980). "The Impact of Federal Sector Unions on Supervisors' Use of Personnel Policies." *Industrial and Labor Relations Review* 33, 2:212–31.

Bibby, Candace. (1992). "The EAP's Role in Downsizing." *EAP Digest* 12, 5:14.

Black, C. (1981). *It Will Never Happen to Me.* Denver: M.A.C.

Blackwell, Barry, M. Gutmann, and L. Gutmann. (1988). "Case Review and Quantity of Outpatient Care." *American Journal of Psychiatry* 145:1003–6.

Blackwell, Barry and Gregory L. Schmidt. (1992). "The Educational Implications of Managed Mental Health Care." *Hospital and Community Psychiatry* 43, 10:962–64.

Blair, Brenda R. (1987). *Supervisors and Managers as Enablers.* Troy, MI: Performance Resource Press, Inc./Johnson Institute.

Blakeney, Roger N. (1986). "A Transactional View of the Role of Trust in Organizational Communication." *Transactional Analysis Journal* 16:95–98.

Blakeney, Roger N. (1983). "The Organizational, Group, and Individual Levels of Analysis in Organizational Behavior." *Transactional Analysis Journal* 13:58–64.

Blanchard, M. and M. Tager. (1985). *Working Well: Managing for Health and High Performance.* New York: Simon and Schuster.

Blue Cross and Blue Shield. (1989). *Mandated Coverage Laws Enacted Through 1988* Washington, DC: Blue Cross/Blue Shield.

Borba, Phillip S. and Michael Camilleri. (1987). "Compensating Workers for Mental Disorders." *Business and Health* (October):10–11.

Bouricius, J. K. (1989). "Negative Symptoms and Emotions in Schizophrenia." *Schizophrenia Bulletin* 15, 2:201–08.

Bradford, L. P. and M. I. Bradford. (1979). *Retirement: Coping with Emotional Upheavals.* Chicago: Nelson-Hall.

Bradshaw, John. (1990). *Homecoming: Reclaiming and Championing Your Inner Child.* New York: Bantam Books.

Braun, Abby L. and Donald E. Novak, Jr. (1986). "Non-Utilization." *EAP Digest* (November/December):52–55.

Bray, R. M., M. E. Marsden, and M. R. Peterson. (1991). "Standardized Comparisons of the Use of Alcohol, Drugs, and Cigarettes Among Military Personnel and Civilians." *American Journal of Public Health* 8, 7:865–69.

Bremer, Kamala and Deborah A. Howe. (1988). "Strategies Used to Advance Women's Careers in the Public Services: Examples from Oregon." *Public Administration Review* 48, 6:975–81.

Bridges, William. (1992). *The Character of Organizations: Using Jungian Type in Organizational Development.* Palo Alto, CA: Consulting Psychologists Press.

Brocher, T. (1976). "Diagnosis of Organizations, Communities, and Political Units." *Bulletin of the Menninger Clinic* 40:513–30.

Brodsky, Melvin. (1990). "Foreign Labor Development." *Monthly Labor Review* 11, 12:50–52.

Brooke, P. P., Jr., and J. L. Price. (1989). "The Determinants of Employee Absenteeism: Test of a Causal Model." *Journal of Occupational Psychology* 62:1–19.

Broskowski, A. (1991). "Current Mental Health Care Environments: Why Managed Care is Necessary." *Professional Psychology: Research Practice* 22:6–14.

Brous, James T. (1986). "EAPs and the Super-Med Trend." *EAP Digest* (July/August):31–37.

Bruce, Willa. (1986). "Reality Therapy Proven to Be an Effective Management Strategy: A Report of a Computer Model." *Journal of Reality Therapy* 5:15–24.

Bruce, Willa. (1985). *Reality Therapy as a Means of Dealing with the Problem Employee.* Blacksburg: Virginia Polytechnique Institute.

Bruce, Willa. (1984). "Reality Therapy as a Management Strategy: An Idea Whose Time Has Come." *Journal of Reality Therapy* 4, 1:16–20.

Buckingham, S. L. and W. G. VanGorp. (1988). "Essential Knowledge about AIDS Dementia." *Social Work* (March–April):112–15.

Bureau of National Affairs (BNA). (1990). *Employee Relations Weekly* (April 16):510.

Bureau of National Affairs (BNA). (1987). *Employee Assistance Programs: Benefits, Problems, and Prospects: A BNA Special Report.* Washington, DC: Bureau of National Affairs.

Burger, Frank P. (1992). "You Be the Arbitrator." *EAP Digest* 12, 3:10.

Burrington, Debra D. (1984). "An Organization's Culture Can Forecast Employee Health." *EAP Digest* 5:32–41.

Butynski, W., D. Canova, and J. Rada. (1990). *State Resources and Services Related to Alcohol and Other Drug Abuse Problems: Fiscal Year 1989.*

Washington, DC: National Association of State, Alcohol and Drug Abuse Directors.

Cagney, Tamara. (1987). "Knox Keene: Regulation and Implications for the Future of EAP." *The ALMACAN* (October):14–18.

Caldwell, Michael F. (1992). "Incidence of PTSD Among Staff Victims of Patient Violence." *Hospital and Community Psychiatry* 43, 8:838–39.

California Workers' Compensation Institute (CWCI). (1990). "Mental Stress Claims in California Workers' Compensation: Incidence, Costs and Trends." In *CWCI Research Notes*. San Francisco: CWCI.

California Workers' Compensation Institute (CWCI). (1988). "Mental Stress Claims." In *CWCI Research Notes*. San Francisco: CWCI.

"Californians Flunk Drug Tests." (1990). *Chico Enterprise Record* (May 24):1A.

Carmel, H. and M. Hunter. (1989). "Staff Injuries from Inpatient Violence." *Hospital and Community Psychiatry* 40:41–46.

Castleman, Michael. (1985). "Toxics and Male Infertility." *Sierra* (March/April):49–52.

Cawood, James S. (1991). "On the Edge: Assessing the Violent Employee." *Security Management* (September):131–36.

Centers for Disease Control (CDC). (1990). "Occupational Homicides Among Women: United States, 1980–1985." *MMWR* 39:544–53,551–52.

Centers for Disease Control (CDC). (1987). "Traumatic Occupational Fatalities: U.S., 1980–1984." *MMWR* 36:461–64, 469–70.

Chambers, Carl D. and Leon Brill (Eds.). (1973). *Methodone Experiences and Issues*. New York: Behavior Publications.

Champney, Timothy F. and Laura Cox Dzurec. (1992). "Involvement in Productive Activities and Satisfaction with Living Situation Among Severely Mentally Disabled Adults." *Hospital and Community Psychiatry* 43, 9:899–903.

Chaplin, J. P. (1968). *Dictionary of Psychology*. New York: Laurel.

Chavkin, Wendy. (1984). "Parental Leave: What There Is and What There Should Be." *Ms* 13:115.

Chenoweth, David. (1989). "Employers Must Reassess Worker Mental Health Coverage." *Occupational Health and Safety* 58:52–53.

Cherskov, Myk. (1987). "Substance Abuse in the Workplace." *Hospitals* 6:68–73.

Chess, S. (1969). *An Introduction to Child Psychiatry* (2nd ed.). New York: Grune & Stratton.

Chorover, Stephen L. (1974). "Psychosurgery: A Neuropsychological Perspective." *Boston University Law Review* 54:231–48.

Christ, H. C., L. S. Weiner, and R. T. Moynihan. (1986). "Psychosocial Issues in AIDS." *Psychiatric Annals* 16:173–79.

Christen, J. C. and N. Nykodym. (1986). "TA: A Training and Development Tool: The Consultant's Perspective." *Organizational and Development Journal* 4:85–86.

Christianson, J., N. Lurie, M. Finch, I. S. Moscovice, and D. Hartley. (1992). "Use of Community-Based Mental Health Programs by HMOs: Evidence from a Medicaid Demonstration." *American Journal of Public Health* 83:790–96.

Clark, Charles S. (1993). "Can an Employer Ban Off-the-Job Smoking by Employees? Many Do." *Chico Enterprise-Record* (January 30):5B.

Clayman, Charles B. (Ed.). (1988). *The American Medical Association Guide to Prescription and Over-the-Counter Drugs*. New York: Random House.

Clifton, Laurie. (1989). "Senior News: Medicating the Elderly." *Chico Enterprise-Record* (March 3):1B.

Cohen, S. and T. A. Wills. (1985). "Stress, Social Support and the Buffering Hypothesis." *Psychological Bulletin* 98:310–57.

Cohen-Rosenthal, Edward. (1985) "QWL and EAPs: Making the Connection." *EAP Digest* (May/June):42–52.

Cole, M. (1984). "How to Make a Person Passive-Aggressive or the Power Struggle Game." *Transactional Analysis Journal* 14:191–94.

Collar, Martha. (1992). "Double Trouble for Some 'Type A' Personalities." *Air North* (June):28.

Conlon, Patrick. (1987). "Show You Care." *Canadian Business* 60, 4:108–11.

Cook, R. F. (1989). "Drug Use Among Working Adults: Prevalence Rates and Estimation Methods." In S. W. Gust and J. M. Walsh (Eds.), *Drugs in the Work Place*. Washington, DC: Government Printing Office.

Corey, Gerald. (1990). *Theory and Practice of Group Counseling*. Pacific Grove, CA: Brooks/Cole Publishing.

Cosgrove, Susan and Thomas A. McLellan. (1992). "Rebels in the Workplace: Referral and the Resistant Client." *EAP Digest* 12, 5:38–40.

Council of State Governments. (1983). *State Administrative Officials: Classified by Function*. Lexington, KY: Council of State Governments.

Council on Ethical and Judicial Affairs, American Medical Association. (1991). "Use of Genetic Testing by Employers." *Journal of the American Medical Association* 13, 266:1827–30.

Cournos, F. (1987). "The Impact of Environmental Factors on Outcome in Residential Programs." *Hospital and Community Psychiatry* 38:848–52.

"Court Rules Patient Workers Must Get Paid." (1974). *Psychology Today* (April):29.

Craig, Delores E. and William E. Boyd. (1990). "Characteristics of Employers of Handicapped Individuals." *American Journal on Mental Retardation* 95, 1:405–18.

Crant, J. Michael and Thomas S. Bateman. (1990). "An Experimental Test of the Impact of Drug-Testing Programs on Potential Job Applicants' Attitudes and Intentions." *Journal of Applied Psychology* 75, 2:127–31.

Crowne, Sidney. (1987). "Assessment of Psychotherapy: What Happens to Untreated Patients?" In Richard L. Gregory (Ed.), *The Oxford Companion to THE MIND*. New York: Oxford University Press, pp. 661–63.

Cummings, Nicholas. (1979). "The Anatomy of Psychotherapy Under National Health Insurance." In *Psychology and National Health Insurance: A Sourcebook*. Washington, DC: American Psychological Association.

Cummings, Nicholas and G.R. VandenBos. (1981). "The Twenty Year Kaiser-Permaente Experience with Psychotherapy and Medical Utilization: Implications for National Health Policy and National Health Insurance. " *Health Policy Quarterly* 1, 2:159–75.

Cunniff, John. (1993). "Employees Want Less Interference at Work." *Chico Enterprise-Record* (January 16):7B.

Cushna, Bruce, Ludwik S. Szymanski, and Peter E. Tanguay. (1980). "Professional Roles and Unmet Manpower Needs." In Ludwik S. Szymanski and Peter E. Tanguay (Eds.), *Emotional Disorders of Mentally Retarded Persons*. Baltimore: University Park Press, pp. 3–18.

Cutting, J. and D. Murphy. (1990). "Preference for Denotative as Opposed to Connotative Meanings in Schizophrenics." *Brain and Language* 38, 3:459–68.

Dackis, Charles A. and Mark S. Gold. (1990). "Medical, Endocrinological, and Pharmacological Aspects of Cocaine Addiction." In Nora D. Volkow and Alan C. Swann (Eds.), *Cocaine in the Brain*. New Brunswick, NJ: Rutgers University Press.

Davey, Bruce W. (1984). "Personnel Testing and the Search for Alternatives." *Public Personnel Management Journal* (Winter):361–73.

Davidson, Dan. (1988). "Employee Testing: An Ethical Perspective." *Journal of Business Ethics* 7:214–16.

Davis, H. D., P. A. Honchar, and L. Suarez. (1987). "Fatal Occupational Injuries of Women, Texas 1975–1984." *American Journal of Public Health* 77:1524–27.

Davis, Keith E., L. Kirby Jackson, Jennie Kronenfeld, and Steven Blair. (1984). "Intent to Participate in Worksite Health Promotion Activities: A Model of Risk Factors and Psychosocial Variables." *Health Education Quarterly* 11, 4:361–67.

Deb, S. (1982). "Psychoanalysis as an Applied Science." *Samiksa* 36:57–70.

DeCarlo, Donald. (1989). "Don't Stress Claims Broadside You." *Business and Health* (January):44–45.

Dees, Rusch O. (1986). "Testing for Drugs and Alcohol: Proceed with Caution." *Personnel* 63, 9:53–55.

Dellovo, Robert J. (1986). "Employee Assistance Programs Benefit the Troubled Employee." *Pension World* 22, 4:46–48.

DeLuca, M. (1991). "Independence Day." *Restaurant Hospitality* 75:135.

Dembronski, T. M. and P. T. Costa. (1988). "Assessment of Coronary-Prone Behavior: A Current Overview." *Annotated Behavioral Medicine* 10:60–63.

Deming, W. E. (1986). *Out of the Crisis.* Cambridge, MA: Massachusetts Institute of Technology, Center for Advanced Engineering Study.

Deming, W. E. (1982). *Quality, Productivity, and Competitive Position.* Cambridge, MA: Massachusetts Institute of Technology, Center for Advanced Engineering Study.

Denis, A. (1989). "Alcoholics and Drug Abusers: How Many Second Chances Are They Owed?" *Employment Relations Today* 16:211–18.

Devine, Irene. (1984). "Organizational Crisis and Individual Response: New Trends for Human Service Professionals." *Canadian Journal of Community Mental Health* 3, 2:63–72.

Dickey, Barbara, Paul R. Binner, Stephen Leff, Mary K. Uyeda, Mark J. Schlesinger, and Jon E. Gudeman. (1989). "Containing Mental Health Treatment Costs through Program Design: A Massachusetts Study." *American Public Health Association* 79, 7:863–67.

Dickey, J. and D. Doughty. (1983). Unpublished Manuscript. Cited In Willa Bruce (1985). *Reality Therapy as a Means of Dealing with the Problem Employee.* Blacksburg: Virginia Polytechnic Institute.

Dilley, J. W. and A. B. Boccellari. (1988). "AIDS Dementia Complex: Diagnosis and Management." *Focus* 3:1–3.

Disabatino, M. (1976). "Psychological Factors Inhibiting Women's Occupational Aspirations and Vocational Choices: Implications for Counseling." *Vocational Guidance Quarterly* 25:43–49.

Doherty, Kathleen. (1989). "It's High Noon for Worker's Comp." *Business and Health* (December):36.

Dominguez, C. M. (1991). "The Glass Ceiling and Workforce 2000." *Labor Law Journal* 42:715–17.

Dorken, Herbert et al. (1976). *The Professional Psychologist Today.* San Francisco: Jossey-Bass.

"Drug Abuse Falls in U.S., but Climbs Worldwide." (1993). *Chico Enterprise-Record* (February 16):5C.

Dubin, R. (Ed.). (1976). *Handbook of Work, Organization and Society.* Chicago: Rand McNally.

Dubinsky, A. J. (1985). "Managing Work Stress." *Business* 35, 3:30–35.

Dunham, Randall B. and J. Pierce (1983). "The Design and Evaluation of Alternative Work Schedules." *Personnel Administration* 28, 4:66–67.

Dunham, Randall B. and Frank J. Smith. (1979). *Organizational Surveys: An Internal Assessment of Organizational Health*. Glenview, IL: Scott, Foresman.

Dunner, David L. (1988). "Mania." In Joe P. Tupin, Richard I. Shader, and David S. Harnett (Eds.), *Handbook of Clinical Psycho-Pharmacology*. Northvale, NJ: Jason Aronson.

Duva, Joseph. (1989). "Costs Force Change in Mental Health Plans." *Business Insurance* (September 11):40.

Eaton, L. and F. Menolascino. (1982). "Psychiatric Disorders in the Mentally Retarded: Types, Problems and Challenges." *American Journal of Psychiatry* 139:1297–1303.

Edmondson, Brad. (1987). "The Inner-Directed Work Out." *American Demographics* 9:24–25.

Edwards, Mark R. and J. Ruth Sproul. (1986). "Confronting Alcoholism Through Team Evaluation." *Business Horizons* 29, 3:78–83.

Elkiss, H. (1991). "Reasonable Accommodation and Unreasonable Fears: An AIDS Policy Guide for Human Resource Personnel." *Human Resource Planning* 14:183–89.

Ellis, Albert. (1985). "A Rational-Emotive Approach to Acceptance and Its Relationship to EAPs." In S. H. Klarreich, J. L. Francek, and E. C. Moore (Eds.), *The Human Resources Management Handbook*. New York: Praeger, pp. 325–30.

Ellis, Albert. (1979). *Reason and Emotion in Psychotherapy*. Secaucus, NJ: Citadel Press.

Ellis, Albert. (1975). "A Rational Approach to Leadership." In R. N. Cassel (Ed.), *Leadership Development: Theory and Practice*. Boston: Christopher, pp. 23–54.

Ellis, Albert. (1973). *Humanistic Psychotherapy: The Rational-Emotive Approach*. New York: Julian Press.

Ellis, Albert. (1972). *Executive Leadership: A Rational Approach*. Secaucus, NJ: Citadel Press.

Ellis, Albert and J. M. Whiteley. (1979). *Theoretical and Empirical Foundations of Rational Emotive Therapy*. Los Angeles, CA: Wilshire.

Ellis, Albert and R. Grieger. (1977). *Handbook of Rational-Emotive Therapy*. New York: Springer.

Equal Employment Opportunity Commission (EEOC). (1991). *Technical Assistance Manual for the Americans with Disabilities Act*. Washington, DC: EEOC.

Ernst and Whitney, Inc. (1986). *Health Care Risk Contracting*, No. J58654. New York: Ernst and Whitney.

Esajian, Jeanie. (1991). "Evolving Treatment of Adolescents Coordinates Psychological and Biological Strategies." *Psychosource* (Summer):1, 8.

Evans, Daryl Paul. (1983). *The Lives of Mentally Retarded Persons*. Boulder, CO: Westview Press.

Fallon, Anthony and Jill Lenney. (1987). "EAPs and HMOs: The Genesis of a New Partnership." *EAP Digest* 7, 4:29–32.

Faulstich, M. E. (1987). "Psychiatric Aspects of AIDS." *American Journal of Psychiatry* 144:551–55.

Feldman, Ronald A., Arlene Rubin Stiffman, and Kenneth G. Jung. (1987). *Children at Risk: In the Web of Parental Mental Illness*. New Brunswick, NJ: Rutgers University Press.

Ferber, M. A. and B. G. Birnbaum. (1981). "Labor Force Participation Patterns and Earnings of Women Clerical Workers." *Journal of Human Resources* 13:129–34.

Ferguson, Tim W. (1991). "Pain and Suffering of Workers Comp Spreads to Statehouses." *The Wall Street Journal* (July 23):A15.

Ferman, L. A. and J. G. Gardner. (1979). "Economic Deprivation, Social Mobility, and Mental Health." *Mental Health and the Economy.* Kalamazoo, MI: Upjohn Institute for Employment Research.

Festinger, Leon. (1973). *A Theory of Cognitive Dissonance.* Evanston, IL: Row, Peterson.

Feuer, Dale. (1985). "Wellness Programs: How Do They Shape Up?" *Training* 22:24–32.

Fielding, Jonathan and Philip V. Piserchia. (1989). "Frequency of Worksite Health Promotion Activities." *American Journal of Public Health* 79, 1:16–20.

Finch, Ellen S. (1985). "Deinstitutionalization: Mental Health and Mental Retardation Services." *Psychosocial Rehabilitation Journal* 8, 3:36–48.

Fine, Michelle, Sheila Akabas, and Susan Bellinger. (1982). "Cultures of Drinking: A Workplace Perspective." *Social Work* 27, 5:436–40.

Finegan, Jay. (1990). "Coping With Drugs." *Inc.* (November):122.

Fink, Wendy. (1986). "Employers Use Wellness to Hike Worker Morale." *National Underwriter: Life & Health Insurance Edition* 15:23.

Finney, Craig. (1984). "Corporate Benefits of Employee Recreation Programs." *Parks and Recreation* 18, 9:12, 16.

Firth, Jenny and David A. Shapiro. (1986). "An Evaluation of Psychotherapy for Job Related Distress." *Journal of Occupational Psychology* 59:109–11.

Fisher, Roger, William Ury, and Bruce Patton. (1991). *Getting to Yes: Negotiating an Agreement Without Giving In.* Boston: Houghton Mifflin.

Fisher, Seymour and Roger Greenberg. (1985). *The Scientific Credibility of Freud's Theories and Therapy.* New York: Basic Books.

Fleischman, J. A. (1984). "Personality Characteristics and Coping Patterns." *Journal of Health and Social Behavior* 25:229–44.

Fletcher, Olive. (1986). "Should the Test Score Be Kept a Secret?" *Personnel Management* (April):44–46.

Foegen, J. H. (1981). "Work-Generated Pressure: Mental Health Time Bomb." *Management World* 10, 7:39–40.

Folkman, M. and R. S. Lazarus. (1980). "An Analysis of Coping in a Middle-Aged Community Sample." *Journal of Health and Social Behavior* 21:219–39.

Fontaine, C. M. (1983). "International Relocation: A Comprehensive Psychosocial Approach." *EAP Digest* 3, 3:27–31.

Foote, Andrea and John C. Erfurt. (1981). "Effectiveness of Comprehensive Employee Assistance Programs at Reaching Alcoholics." *Journal of Drug Issues* 11, 2:217–32.

Ford, Robert and Frank S. McLauglin. (1981). "Employee Assistance Programs: A Descriptive Survey of ASPA Members." *Personnel Administration* 26:29–35.

Fosler, R. Scott, William Alonso, Jack A. Meyer, and Rosemary Kern. (1990). *Demographic Change and the American Future.* Pittsburgh: University of Pittsburgh Press.

Fowler, Allen. (1991). "An Even-Handed Approach to Graphology." *Personnel Management* (March):40–43.

Frank, J. D. (1973). *Persuasion and Healing: A Comparative Study of Psychotherapy.* Baltimore: Johns Hopkins Press.

Frank, Richard D. (1990). "Employer Mental Health Coverage." *Health Affairs* 8, 2:31–42.

Franklin, Deborah. (1991). "The Puzzle of Addiction: Who's Vulnerable and Why?" *The Washington Post* (March 26): *Health,* pp. 12–15.

Franzem, Joseph. (1987). "Easing the Pain." *Personnel Administrator* (February):48–55.

Friedman, Dana E. (1986). "Eldercare: The Employee Benefit of the 1990s?" *Across the Board* (June):45–46.

Friedman, M. and D. Ulmer. (1984). *Treating Type A Behavior and Your Heart* . New York: Knopf.

Friedman, M. and R. H. Roseman. (1974). *Type A Behavior and Your Heart*. New York: Knopf.

Friedman, Paul R. (1974). "The Mentally Handicapped Citizen and Institutional Labor." *Harvard Law Review* 87:567.

Fritz, Gregory K., Judith Williams, and Michael Amylon. (1989). "After Treatment Ends: Psychological Sequllae in Pediatric Cancer Survivors." *American Journal of Orthopsychiatry* 58, 4:552–61.

Gadzella, Bernadette, Dean W. Ginther, Maryjane Tomcala, and George W. Bryant. (1990). "Stress as Perceived by Professionals." *Psychological Reports* (December):981–85.

Galvin, K. M. and B. J. Brommel (1982). *Family Communication: Cohesion and Change*. Glenview, IL: Scott-Foresman.

Gam, John, William I. Sauser, Kenneth V. Evans, and Charles V. Lair. (1983). "The Evaluation of an Employee Assistance Program." *Journal of Employment Counseling* 20, 3:99–106.

Gardner, Jr., Lytt I. (1991). "Substance Abuse in Military Personnel: Better or Worse?" *American Journal of Public Health* 81, 7:837–38.

Garrison, Carol Z., Robert E. McKeown, Robert F. Valois, and Murray L. Vincent. (1993). "Aggression, Substance Use, and Suicidal Behaviors in High School Students." *American Journal of Public Health* 83, 2:179–84.

Garrity, Thomas F., J. Morley Kotchen, Harlley E. McKean, Diana Gurley, and Molly McFadden. (1990). "The Association Between Type A Behavior and Change in Coronary Risk Factors Among Young Adults." *American Journal of Public Health* 80, 11:1354–57.

Gawin, F. H. and E. Ellinwood. (1988). "Cocaine and Other Stimulants." *New England Journal of Medicine* 318:1173–82.

Geller, Jeffrey L. (1992). "Communicative Arson." *Hospital and Community Psychiatry* 43, 1:76–77.

Gibbs, J. T. (1982). "Psychosocial Factors Related to Substance Abuse Among Delinquent Females: Implications for Prevention and Treatment." *American Journal of Orthopsychiatry* 52:261–70.

Giffin, K. (1967). "The Contribution of Studies of Source Credibility to a Theory of Interpersonal Trust in the Communication Process." *Psychological Bulletin* 68:104–20.

Gilbert, G. Ronald and A. C. Hyde. (1993). "Implementing Quality Management: Point/Counter Point." *PA Times* 16, 1:8.

Gilbert, J. (1988). "Managerial Attitudes Toward Participative Management Programs: Myths and Reality." *Public Personnel Management* 17, 2:109–23.

Glasser, William. (1981). *Stations of the Mind*. New York: Harper and Row.

Glasser, William. (1976). *Positive Addiction*. New York: Harper and Row.

Glasser, William. (1972). *The Identity Society*. New York: Harper and Row.

Glasser, William. (1969). *Schools Without Failure*. New York: Harper and Row.

Glasser, William. (1965). *Reality Therapy: A New Approach to Psychiatry*. New York: Harper and Row.

Glasser, William and L. M. Zunin. (1973). "Reality Therapy." In R. Corsini Itasca (Ed.), *Current Psychotherapies*. Itasca, IL: F. E. Peacock.

Glicken, Morley D. (1983). "A Counseling Approach to Employee Burnout." *Personnel Journal* 62, 3:222–28.

Goldbeck, Willis B. (1977). "Corporate Mental Health Benefits." In *Background Papers on Industry's Changing Role in Health Care Delivery*. New York: Springer-Verlag.

Goldman, H., S. Sharfstein, and R. Frank. (1983). "Equity and Parity in Psychiatric Care." *Psychiatric Annals* 13:488–91.

Goldstein, Jill M., Ellen L. Bassuk, Stephen K. Holland, and Danya Zimmer. (1988). "Identifying Catastrophic Psychiatric Cases." *Medical Care* 26, 8:785–97.

Goldstrom, I. and R. Manderscheid. (1972). "The Chronically Mentally Ill: A Descriptive Analysis from the Uniform Client Data Instrument." *Community Support Services Journal* 2:4–9.

Golembiewski, R. T. and C. W. Proehl, Jr. (1978). "A Summary of the Empirical Literature on Flexible Working Hours: Character and Consequences of a Major Innovation." *Academy of Management Service Review* (October):37–42.

Gomez-Mejia, Luis R. and David B. Balkin. (1980). "Classifying Work-Related and Personal Problems of Troubled Employees." *Personnel Administrator* 25:27–32.

Good, M. J. and B. J. Good. (1989). "Disabling Practitioners: Hazards of Learning to Be a Doctor in American Medical Education." *American Journal of Orthopsychiatry* 59:303–09.

Goodwin, D. W., F. Schuslsinger, J. Knop, S. Mednick, and S. B. Guze. (1977). "Psychopathology in Adopted and Nonadopted Daughters of Alcoholics." *Archives of General Psychiatry* 34:1005–09.

Gostin, L. (1991). "Genetic Discrimination: The Use of Genetically Based Diagnostic and Prognostic Tests by Employers and Insurers." *American Journal of Law and Medicine* 17:109–44.

Graedon, Joe and Theresa Graedon. (1988). *50+: The Graedons' People's Pharmacy for Older Adults*. New York: Bantam Books.

Green, Sephen. (1992). "Reform Attempts Run into Entrenched Opposition." *The Sacramento Bee* (February 9):A15.

Greenberger, R. A. (1983). "Firms Are Confronting Alcoholic Executives with Threat of Firing." *Wall Street Journal* (January 13):1.

Grossman, H. J. (1983). *Classification in Mental Retardation*. Washington, DC: American Association on Mental Deficiency.

Gustafson, Mickie. (1992). *Losing Your Dog: Coping with Grief When a Pet Dies*. New York: Bergh Publishing.

Hafner, H. (1986). "The Risk of Violence in Psychotics." *Integrative Psychiatry* 4:138–42.

Hahn, D. L. (1974). "The Importance of Pay." In R. P. Quinn and L. J. Shephard (Eds.), *The 1972-1973 Quality of Employment Survey: Continuing Chronicles of an Unfinished Enterprise*. Ann Arbor, MI: Survey Research Center.

Hale, Robert E. (1992). "Psychiatric Lessons from the Persian Gulf War." *Hospital and Community Psychiatry* 43, 8:769.

Hales, T., P. J. Seligman, S. C. Newman, and C. L. Timbrook. (1988). "Occupational Injuries Due to Violence." *Journal of Occupational Medicine* 30, 6:483–87.

Hall, D. T. and K. E. Nougain. (1968). "An Examination of Maslow's Need Hierarchy in an Organizational Setting." *Organizational Behavior and Human Performance* 3:12–35.

Hall, R.C.W. and J. R. Joffe. (1972). "Aberrant Response to Diazepam: A New Syndrome." *American Journal of Psychiatry* 129:738–42.

Ham, Faith Lyman. (1989). "A Cooperative Effort That's Paying Off." *Business and Health* 7:40–42.

Hamilton, Jean A., Sheryle W. Alagna, Linda S. King, and Camille Lloyd. (1987). "The Emotional Consequences of Gender Based Abuse in the Workplace: New Counseling Programs for Sex Discrimination." *Women and Therapy* 6, 1:155–82.

Haney, Daniel Q. (1992). "Alzheimer's Drug Maker Optimistic, Despite Disappointing Results." *Chico Enterprise-Record* (November 6):15C.

Harding, C. M., G. W. Brooks, T. Ashikaga, and J. S. Strauss. (1987). "The Vermont Longitudinal Study of Persons with Severe Mental Illness." *American Journal of Psychiatry* 144:718–26.

Hargrave, George and D. Hiatt. (1987). "Law Enforcement Selection with the Interview, MMPI and CPI: A Study of Reliability and Validity." *Journal of Police Science and Administration* (January):110–17.

Harper, M. S. (1986). "Introduction." In M. S. Harper and B. D. Lebowitz (Eds.), *Mental Illness in Nursing Homes: Agenda for Research*. Rockville, MD: National Institute of Mental Health.

Harrick, E. (1986). "Alternative Work Schedules, Productivity, Leave Usage, and Employee Attitudes: A Field Study." *Public Personnel Management* 15:159–69.

Harty, Sara J. (1991). "Companies Employ Managed Care in Mental Health Plans." *Business Insurance* (August 26):26.

Hay, David J. (1986). "The EAP Role in Formulating a Company Drug Policy." *The ALMACAN* (July):16–18.

Health and Welfare Canada. (1988). *Mental Health for Canadians*. Ottawa: Minister of Supply and Services.

"Health: Upjohn Defends Its Besieged Sleeping Pill." (1991). *Chico Enterprise-Record* (December 22):8E.

Heffron, Florence. (1989). *Organization Theory and Public Organizations*. Englewood Cliffs, NJ: Prentice-Hall.

Hellan, Richard T. (1986). "An EAP Update: A Perspective for the 80s." *Personnel Journal* 65, 6:51.

Hellan, Richard T. and William J. Campbell. (1981). "Contracting for EAP Services." *Personnel Administrator* (September):49–51.

Hendrix, William H., Robert P. Steel, and Terry L. Leap. (1991). "Development of a Stress-Related Health Promotion Model." *Journal of Social Behavior and Personality* 6, 7:141–62.

Hennessey, Marenn T. (1983). "Stress, Women and the Workplace: An EAP Responds." *EAP Digest Annual*, pp. 62–65.

"Heroin Use." (1990). *The Economist* (September 8):33.

Hersey, P. K., H. Blanchard, and W. Natemeyer. (1979). *The Social Psychology of Organizations*. Englewood Cliffs, N.J.: Prentice-Hall.

Herzberg, Frederick. (1966). *Work and the Nature of Man*. New York: Thomas Y. Crowell.

Herzberg, Frederick, B. Mausner, and B. Snyderman. (1959). *The Motivation to Work*. New York: Wiley.

Heylighen, Francis. (1992). "A Cognitive-Systemic Reconstruction of Maslow's Theory of Self-Actualization." *Behavioral Science* 37, 1:39–58.

Higgins, N. E. (1986). "Occupational Stress and Working Women: The Effectiveness of Two Stress-Reduction Programs." *Journal of Vocational Behavior* 29:66–78.

Hirschhorn, L. and T. Gilmore. (1980). "The Application of Family Therapy Concepts to Influencing Organizational Behaviors." *Administrative Science Quarterly* 25:18–37.

Hoefler, James M. (1992). "Total Quality Management (TQM) in Hospital Administration: An Old Set of Ideas Whose Time Has Come?" *Journal of*

Human Services 11, 1:20–29.

Holder, Robert J. (1990). "Human Energy: A Self-Motivational Technique for the Third Wave." *Organizational Development Journal* (Fall):26–31.

Hollingsworth, David K. and Carol J. Mastroberti. (1983). "Women, Work, and Disability." *Personnel and Guidance* 61, 10:587–91.

Hollister, Leo. (1978). "Psychopharmacology." In John C. Shershow (Ed.), *Schizophrenia: Science and Practice*. Cambridge, MA: Harvard University Press.

Holoviak, Stephen J. and Sharon Brookens Holoviak. (1984). "The Benefits of In-House Counseling." *Personnel* 61,4:58.

"Hostages Recall Angry Gunman Threatened to Start Shooting Babies." (1991). *Chico Enterprise-Record* (September 23):8C.

House, R. J. and L. A. Wigdor. (1967). "Herzberg's Dual Factor Theory of Job Satisfaction and Motivation: A Review of the Evidence and a Criticism." *Personnel Psychology* 20:369–89.

Howard, James S. (1987). "Employee Wellness: It's Good Business." *D&B Reports* 35:34–37.

Hubbard, R. L., M. E. Marsden, J. V. Rachal, H. J. Harwood, E. R. Cavanaugh, and H. M. Ginzburg. (1989). *Drug Abuse Treatment: A National Study of Effectiveness*. Chapel Hill: University of North Carolina Press.

Hudson, Christopher G. (1993). "The United States." In Donna R. Kemp (Ed.), *International Handbook of Mental Health Policy*. Westport, CT: Greenwood Press.

Hurley, Susan. (1986). "Measuring the Value of Employee Assistance Programs." *Risk Management* 33, 6:56.

Institute of Science and Technology. (1986). "Coping with Involuntary Job Loss and Building a New Career: Worker's Problems and Career Professionals' Challenges." *Journal of Career Development* 12, 4:48–53.

Intveldt-Work, Susan. (1983). "Staffing Patterns, Relationships Profiled in Nationwide EAP Survey." *The ALMACAN* 13, 6:6–7, 15.

Inwald, Robin E. (1988). "Five Year Follow-Up Study of Department Terminations as Predicted by 16 Preemployment Psychological Indicators." *Journal of Applied Psychology* 73:703–10.

Inwald, Robin E. (1984). "Assessment: How to Evaluate Psychological/Honesty Tests." *Personnel Journal* (May):40–46.

Isaac, Rael Jean and Virginia C. Armant. (1990). *Madness in the Streets*. New York: Free Press.

Isaacson, Robert L. (1982). *The Limbic System*. New York: Plenum Press.

Ishikawa, I. (1985). *What is Total Quality Control? The Japanese Way*. Englewood Cliffs, NJ: Prentice Hall.

Ivancevich, J. M. and M. T. Matteson. (1987). *Stress and Work: A Managerial Perspective*. Glenview, IL: Scott-Foresman.

Jacobs, Harvey E. (1988). "Vocational Rehabilitation." In R. P. Liberman (Ed.), *Psychiatric Rehabilitation of the Chronic Mental Patient*. Washington, DC: American Psychiatric Press.

Jacobs, Harvey E., S. Kardashian, and R. K. Kreinbring. (1984). "A Skills-Oriented Model for Facilitating Employment Among Psychiatrically Disabled Persons." *Rehabilitation Counseling Bulletin* 31:273–77.

Jacobs, Harvey E., Donald Wissusik, Rosemary Collier, Debra Stackman, and Derek Burkeman. (1992). "Correlations Between Psychiatric Disabilities and Vocational Outcome." *Hospital and Community Psychiatry*. 43, 4:365–69.

Jacobs, Rahul. (1989). "Stress on the Job? Go to California." *Fortune* (July 31):32.

Jamieson, J. K. (1980). "Jamieson Urges Alcoholism Emphasis in Employee Program Efforts." *Labor-Management Alcoholism Journal* 11:207–10.

Janus, Irving L. (1982). *Group Think*. (2nd Ed.). Boston: Houghton Mifflin.

Jemelka, R., E. Trupin, and J. A. Chiles. (1989). "The Mentally Ill in Prisons: A Review." *Hospital and Community Psychiatry* 40:481–90.

Jeppesen, J. (1974). "Transactional Analysis in Management." Middle-Management Leadership Seminar-X390.

Joel III, Lewin G. (1993). *Every Employee's Guide to the Law*. New York: Pantheon Books.

Johnston, William B. and Arnold E. Packer. (1987). *Workforce 2000*. Indianapolis, IN: Hudson Institute.

Jones, J. S., B. Stanley, J. J. Mann, A. J. Frances, J. R. Guido, L. Traskman-Bendz, R. Winchel, R. P. Brown, and M. Stanley. (1990). "CSF 5-HIAA and HVA Concentrations in Elderly Depressed Patients Who Attempted Suicide." *The American Journal of Psychiatry* 147:1225–27.

Jones, Rochelle. (1980). *The Big Switch, New Careers, New Lives After 35*. New York: McGraw-Hill.

Jones, W. H. (1979). "Grief and Involuntary Career Change: Its Implications for Counseling." *Vocational Guidance Quarterly* 27, 3:196–201.

Jung, Carl G. (1953–71). *Collected Works*. London: Blackwell.

Juran, J. M. (1964). *Managerial Breakthrough*. New York: McGraw-Hill.

Juran, J. M., F. M. Gryna, Jr., and R. S. Bingham (Eds.). (1979). *Quality Control Handbook*. New York: McGraw-Hill.

Kanter, Donald L. and Philip H. Mirvis. (1989). *The Cynical Americans*. New York: Jossey-Bass.

Kaplan, David and Charlie A. Ziegler. (1985). "Class, Hierarchies, and Social Control: An Anthropologist's Comment on Theory Z." *Human Organization* 44:83–88.

Kaplan, Gary. (1986). "Business on the Couch." *Nation's Business* 74, 5:49–52.

Kaplan, S. G. and E. G. Wheeler. (1983). "Survival Skills for Working with Potentially Violent Clients." *Social Casework* 64:339–46.

Karrass, Chester L. and William Glasser. (1980). *Both-Win Management*. New York: Lippincott and Crowell Publishers.

Karp, D. A. (1989). "The Social Construction of Retirement Among Professionals 50–60 Years Old." *The Gerontologist* 29:750–60.

Kelsey, James E. (1982). "A Practical Approach to Prevention." *Labor-Management Alcoholism Journal* 11:142–43.

Kemp, Donna R. (In press). "Telecommuting in the Public Sector." *Public Productivity and Management Review*.

Kemp, Donna R. (1987). *Supplemental Compensation and Collective Bargaining*. Alexandria, VA: International Personnel Management Association.

Kemp, Donna R. (1985). "State Employee Assistance Programs: Organization and Services." *Public Administration Review* 45, 3:378–82.

Kemp, Donna R. (1984a). "Employee Assistance Programs: A Resource for Older Workers." *International Employee Benefits Foundation Digest* 21, 10:8–9.

Kemp, Donna R. (1984b). "Resident Advocates: A Mechanism for Protecting the Rights of Institutionalized Mentally Retarded Persons." *Journal of Mental Health Administration* 11, 2:48–51.

Kemp, Donna R. (1983). "Assessing Human Rights Committees: A Mechanism for Protecting the Rights of Institutionalized Mentally Retarded Persons." *Mental Retardation* 21, 1:13–16.

Kemp, Donna R. (1981). *Implementation of Rights in Institutions for Mentally Retarded*. Occasional Paper. Waukegan, IL: National Association for Superintendents of Public Residential Facilities for the Mentally Retarded.

Kenkel, Paul J. (1991). "More Firms Limit Mental Health Plans." *Modern Healthcare* (January 7):7–17.

Kennel, J., M. Klause, S. McGrath, S. Robertson, and C. Hinkley. (1991). "Continuous Emotional Support During Labor in a US Hospital: A Randomized Controlled Trial." *Journal of the American Medical Association* 265:2197–2201.

Kiefhaber, Anne and Willis B. Goldbeck. (1980). "Industry's Response: A Survey of Employee Assistance Programs." In Richard H. Edgal, Diana C. Walsh, and Willis B. Godbeck (Eds.), *Mental Wellness Programs for Employees.* New York: Springer-Verlag, pp. 19–26.

Kiell, Matthew. (1989). "Recutting the Worker's Comp Pie." *Safety and Health* (April):44–45.

Kiesler, C. A. and A. E. Sibulkin. (1987). *Mental Hospitalization: Myths and Facts about a National Crisis.* Beverly Hills: Sage.

Kiloh, L. G. (1982). "Electroconvulsive Therapy." In E. S. Paykel (Ed.), *Handbook of Affective Disorders.* New York: Guildford Press, pp. 262–75.

Kim, Howard. (1988). "Tension Typifies Relationship between Psychiatric Providers, Managed Care." *Modern Healthcare* (October):84–88.

Kirman, B. H. (1973). "Clinical Aspects." In J. Wortis (Ed.), *Mental Retardation and Developmental Disabilities: An Annual Review.* New York: Brunner/Mazel.

Klarreich, Samuel H., Raymond DiGiuseppe, and Dominic J. DiMattia. (1987). "Cost Effectiveness of an Employee Assistance Program with Rational-Emotive Therapy." *Professional Psychology* 18:140–44.

Klein, B. (1986). "Missed Work and Lost Hours." *Monthly Labor Review* 109:26–30.

Klingner, Donald, Nancy G. O'Neil, and Gamal Sabet. (1987). "Drug Testing in the Public Workplace." SPALR Occasional Paper in Public Personnel Administration #1. Washington, DC: American Society for Public Administration Section on Personnel Administration and Labor Relations.

Koll, Juri. (1991). "The State of Cal Workers' Comp." *The Comp Examiner* (November):1–2, 4, 6.

Konovsky, Mary A. and Russell Cropenzano. (1991). "Perceived Fairness in Employee Drug Testing." *Journal of Applied Psychology* 76:698–99, 705.

Koskinene, Lennart. (1992). "Expression 1." In Mickie Gustafson, *Losing Your Dog.* New York: Bergh Publishing.

Kovach, Jeffery L. (1986). "Psychological Testing Is Fair: True or False?" *Industry Week* 8:44–47.

Krausz, Rosa R. (1986). "Power and Leadership in Organizations." *Transactional Analysis Journal* 16:85–94.

Kriegel, Robert and Marilyn Kriegel. (1990). *The C Zone: Peak Performance Under Pressure.* New York: Anchor Press/Doubleday.

Kroenke, K. and A. D. Mangelsdorff. (1989). "Common Symptoms in Ambulatory Care: Evaluation, Therapy, and Outcome." *American Journal of Medicine* 86:262–66.

Kubler-Ross, Elizabeth. (1969). *On Death and Dying.* New York: McMillan.

Kupfer, Andrew. (1988). "Is Drug Testing Good or Bad?" *Fortune* (December 19):133–40.

Kurpius, D. J. (1985). "Consultation Interventions: Successes, Failures, and Proposals." *The Counseling Psychologist* 13:368–89.

Kurtz, L. David, C. Patrick Fleenor, Louis E. Boone, and M.Virginia Rider. (1989). "CEOs: Handwriting Analysis." *Business Horizons* (January–February):41–43.

Labbate, Lawrence A. and Michael P. Snow. (1992). "Posttraumatic Stress Symptoms Among Soldiers Exposed to Combat in the Persian Gulf." *Hospital and Community Psychiatry* 43, 8:831–33.

Lappe, Marc. (1987). "The Limits of Genetic Inquiry." *The Hastings Center Report.* 17:5–10.

Lavan, Helen. (1990). "Employee Stress Swamps Worker's Comp." *Personnel* (May 1990):61–64.

Lawler, Edward E. (1982). "Strategies for Improving the Quality of Work Life." *American Psychologist* 37:486–93.

Learnard, Linda T. and Elizabeth Devereaux. (1992). "A Model for Community Practice." *Hospital and Community Psychiatry* 43:869–71.

Leclere, H., M. D. Beaulieu, G. Bordage, A. Sindon, and M. Couillard. (1990). "Why Are Clinical Problems Difficult? General Practioners' Opinions Concerning 24 Clinical Problems." *Canadian Medical Association Journal* 143:1305–15.

Lee, Frederick C. (1987). "Purchasers Address Escalating Psychiatric and Substance Abuse Utilization." *Employees Benefits Journal* 12:9–13.

Lehmann, Timothy. (1978). "Developmental Stages and Chronological Ages for Males and Females." In Vivian Rogers, Colleen Ryan, Robin Sutton, and Nancy Winn (Eds.), (1985), *A Life Transitions Reader.* Lawrence: University of Kansas Press.

Levin, Pamela Fox, Jeanne Beauchamp Hewitt, and Susan J. Misner. (1992). "Female Workplace Homicides." *American Association of Occupational Health Nurses Journal* 40, 5:229–36.

Levin-Landheer, Pam. (1982). "The Cycle of Development." *Transactional Analysis Journal* 12:129–39.

Levine, Hermine Z. (1985a). "Benefit Cost Cutting." *Personnel* 62, 7:56–63.

Levine, Hermine Z. (1985b). "Employee Assistance Programs: Consensus On." *Personnel* 62, 4:14–19.

Levinson, Daniel J. (1978). "Tasks and Periods in the Evolution of the Life Structure." In Vivian Rogers, Colleen Ryan, Robin Sutton, and Nancy Winn (Eds.), (1985), *A Life Transitions Reader.* Lawrence: University of Kansas Press.

Levy, Robert. (1986). "Demographics of EAP Referrals." In *EAP Digest Annual 1983–1984.* Troy, MI: Performance Resource Press, pp.223–26.

Little, Charles D. (1981). "Counseling the Public Employee." *Supervisory Management* 26, 6:16–18.

London, M., R. Crandall, and G. W. Seals. (1977). "The Contribution of Job and Leisure Satisfaction to Quality of Life." *Journal of Applied Psychology* 62:328–34.

Lord, D. B. (1983). "Parental Alcoholism and the Mental Health of Children: A Bibliography and Brief Observations." *Journal of Alcohol and Drug Education* 29:1–11.

Louis, M. (1980). "Surprise and Sense Making: What Newcomers Experience in Entering Unfamiliar Organizational Settings." *Administrative Science Quarterly* 25:226–51.

Lousig, Gregory. (1990). "Alternatives to Drug Testing." *Security Management* (May):51.

Luborsky, Lester, L. Singer, and L. Luborsky. (1975). "Comparative Studies of Psychotherapies." *Archives of General Psychiatry* 32:995–1008.

"Lukewarm Turkey." (1989). *Scientific American* (March):32.

Lusk, Sally L. (1992a). "Violence Experienced by Nurses' Aides in Nursing Homes." *American Association of Occupational Health Nurses Journal* 40, 5:237–41.

Lusk, Sally L. (1992b). "Violence in the Workplace." *American Association of Occupational Health Nurses Journal* 40, 5:212–13.

Lydecker, Toni H. (1985). "Reshaping Employee Assistance Programs." *Association Management* 37, 11:80–84.

Lydiard, R. B., E. F. Howell, M. T. Laraia, and M. D. Fossey. (1989). "Depression in Patients Receiving Lorazepam for Panic." *American Journal of Psychiatry* 146:629–31.

Madonia, Joseph. (1987). "The Impact of EAPs on Health Insurance." *EAP Digest* 7, 4:47–50.

Madonia, Joseph F. (1985). "Handling Emotional Problems in Business and Industry." *Social Casework* 66, 10:587–93.

Maidani, Ebrahim A. (1991). "Comparative Study of Herzberg's Two-Factor Theory of Job Satisfaction Among Public and Private Sectors." *Public Personnel Management* 20, 4:28–48.

Makin, Peter J., Cary L. Cooper, and Charles J. Cox. (1989). *Managing People at Work*. Westport, CT: Quorum Books.

Malan, D. (1973). "The Outcome Problem in Psychotherapy Research." *Archives of General Psychiatry* 29:719–29.

Mann, Everett. (1989). "Evaluation of Employee Assistance Programs." In Donna R. Kemp, *Employee Assistance Programs: An Annotated Bibliography*. New York: Garland Publishing.

Marmor, J. (1974). *Psychiatry in Transition: Selected Papers of Judd Marmor*. New York: Brunner/Mazel.

Marriner, A., (Ed.). (1992). *Contemporary Nursing Management*. St. Louis, MO: Mosby.

Martin, David W., Virginia M. Heckel, G. Kenneth Goodrick, Janet M. Schreiber, and Virginia L. Young. (1985). "The Relationship Between Referral Types, Work Performance, and Employee Problems." *Employee Assistance Quarterly* 1, 2:25–36.

Martin, Joanne. (1992). *Cultures in Organizations: Three Perspectives*. New York: Oxford University Press.

Martorano, Joseph T. and Maureen Morgan. (1987). "How EAP Counselors Can Help PMS Sufferers." *EAP Digest* 10:69–72.

Maslow, Abraham H. (1970). *Future Reaches of Human Nature*. New York: Viking Press.

Maslow, Abraham H. (1965). *Eupsychian Management*. Homewood, IL: Dorsey-Irwin.

Maslow, Abraham H. (1962). *Toward a Psychology of Being*. New York: Van Nosbrand.

Maslow, Abraham H. (1954). *Motivation and Personality*. New York: Harper.

Maslow, Abraham H. (1943). "A Theory of Human Motivation." *Psychological Review* 50:370–96.

Mathis, R. William. (1983). "How Workers' Compensation Injury Affects Police Officers." *The Police Chief* (November):72–74.

Matteson, Michael T. and John M. Ivanevich. (1987). *Controlling Work Stress*. San Francisco: Jossey-Bass.

Mattox, Joe A. (1985). "Helping Drug Addicted Employees." *Training and Development Journal* 39, 12:60–61.

Maussen, D. (1980). *The Impact of Flextime on Organizational Functioning*. Washington, DC: Office of Personnel Management.

Mayes, Bronston T., Mary E. Barton, and Daniel C. Ganster. (1991). "An Exploration of the Moderating Effect of Age on Job Stressor-Employee Strain Relationships." *Journal of Social Behavior and Personality* 6, 7:289–308.

Mayo, Elton. (1933). *The Human Problems of an Industrial Civilization*. New York: Macmillan.

McDonald, Lisa M. and Karen Korabik. (1991). "Sources of Stress and Ways of

Coping Among Male and Female Managers." *Journal of Social Behavior and Personality* 6, 7:185–98.

McDuff, David R. (1992). "Social Issues in the Management of Released Hostages." *Hospital and Community Psychiatry* 43, 8:825–28.

McGregor, Douglas. (1960). *The Human Side of Enterprise.* New York: McGraw-Hill.

McGuire, Thomas G. (1992). "Estimating the Costs of a Mental Health Benefit: A Small-Employer Mandate." In Richard G. Frank and Willard G. Manning, Jr. (Eds.), *Economics and Mental Health.* Baltimore: Johns Hopkins University Press, pp. 240–62.

McGuire, Thomas G. (1981). *Financing Psychotherapy: Costs, Effects, and Public Policy.* Cambridge, MA: Ballinger.

McGuire, Thomas G. and Alan Fairbanks. (1988). "Patterns of Mental Health Utilization Over Time in a Fee-for-Service Population." *American Journal of Public Health* 78, 2:134–56.

McGurrin, Lisa. (1987). "The Executive Alcoholic and the Conspiracy of Silence." *New England Business* 9:31–35.

McKendrick, Joseph E. (1987). "Cafeteria Plans: What's on the Menu?" *Management World* 16:16–17.

Mechanic, David. (1993). "Editorial: Managed Care for the Seriously Mentally Ill." *American Journal of Public Health* 82, 6:788–89.

Mechanic, David. (1991). "Strategies for Integrating Public Mental Health Services." *Hospital and Community Psychiatry* 42:797–801.

Mechanic, David and David Rochefort. (1992). "A Policy of Inclusion for the Mentally Ill." *Health Affairs* 11:128–50.

Meier, Robert, R. Farmer, and D. Maxwell. (1987). "Psychological Screening of Police Candidates: Current Perspectives." *Journal of Police Science and Administration* (September):210–15.

Men's Health. (1992). "Survey." Cited in "Health Watch," *Chico Enterprise-Record* (December 27):7C.

Menolascino, Frank J. (1989). "Overview: Promising Practices in Caring for the Mentally Retarded-Mentally Ill." In Robert J. Fletcher and Frank J. Menolascino (Eds.), *Mental Retardation and Mental Illness.* Lexington, MA: Lexington Books, pp. 3–14.

Menolascino, Frank J. (1983). "Overview: Bridging the Gap Between Mental Retardation and Mental Illness." Frank J. Menolascino and Brian M. McCann (Eds.), *Mental Health and Mental Retardation: Bridging the Gap.* Baltimore: University Park Press, pp. 3–64.

Merrill, Joseph M., Zenaido Camacho, Lila F. Laux, John I. Thornby, and Carlos Vallbona. (1991). "How Medical School Shapes Students' Orientations to Patients' Psychological Problems." *Academic Medicine* 66, 9:54–56.

Meyerson, Debra and Joanne Martin. (1987). "Cultural Change: An Integration of Three Different Views." *Journal of Management Studies* 18:1–26.

Miles, J. B. (1985). "How to Help Troubled Workers." *Commuter Decisions* 17, 3:66–76.

Miller, Angela Browne. (1990). "Employee Utilization of Addiction Treatment." *Employee Assistance Quarterly* 5, 4:13–31.

Milstead-O'Keefe, Robin J. (1981). *Empowering Women Alcoholics to Help Themselves and Their Sisters in the Workplace.* Dubuque, IA: Kendall/Hunt.

Milwid, Beth. (1987). *What You Get When You Go For It.* New York: Dodd, Mead.

Minter, Jack. (1986). "A Contracted or In-House EAP?" In *EAP Digest Annual 1983–1984.* Troy, MI: Performance Resource Press, pp. 41–43.

Mirvis, Philip H. and Edward E. Lawler II. (1983). "Accounting for the Quality of Work Life." *Journal of Occupational Behavior* 5:200.

Mitchell, J., H. E. Jacobs, and F. Yen. (1987). "Costs and Response Rates in a Community Follow-up for a Psychiatric Vocational Rehabilitation Program." *Rehabilitation Counseling Bulletin* 31:273–77.

Moccia, John A. (1983). "The Desperate Alternative." *Federal Probation* (June):70–72.

Modjeska, Lee. (1988). *Employment Discrimination Law*. Rochester, NY: Lawyers' Co-Operative.

"Moms Reap Benefits from Work." (1990). *Idaho Free Press* (December 24):A11.

Mook, D. G. (1987). *Motivation: The Organization of Action*. New York: Norton.

Moss, Kathryn. (1992). *Employment Complaints Filed by People with Mental Disabilities*. Washington, DC: Mental Health Policy Resource Center.

Muchowski, P., T. Gorski, and M. Miller. (1982). *Counseling for Relapse Prevention*. Independence, MO: Herald House/Independence Press.

Mufson, Dianne. (1986). "Selecting Child Care Workers for Adolescents: The California Psychological Inventory." *Child Welfare* (January/February):83–87.

Mulligan, Hugh A. (1991). "Putting 'Umph' into the Workplace." *Chico Enterprise-Record* (July 13):8A.

Mumford E., H. J. Schlesinger, and D. Anderson. (1984). "A New Look at Evidence about Reduced Cost of Medical Utilization Following Mental Health Treatment." *American Journal of Psychiatry* 141:1145–58.

Murphy, Kevin R., George C. Thorton, and Kristin Prue. (1991). "Influences of Drug Testing on Job Characteristics." *Journal of Applied Psychology* 76:447–49, 452.

Murray, Thomas. (1983). "Warning: Screening Workers for Genetic Risk." *The Hastings Center Report* 13:5–8.

Myers, Isabel Briggs. (1962). *The Myers-Briggs Type Indicator Manual*. Princeton, NJ: Educational Testing Service.

Naisbitt, John and Patricia Aburdene. (1985). *Reinventing the Corporation*. New York: Warner Brothers.

Nasatir, Marilyn. (1985). "Aging Parents: A Support Group at Work." *Activities, Adaptation and Inquiries* 6, 4:81–87.

National Advisory Mental Health Council (NAMHC). (1990). *National Plan for Research on Child and Adolescent Mental Disorders*. Washington, DC: National Institute of Mental Health.

National Center for Health Statistics. (1990). *Vital Statistics of the United States, Volume II, Mortality, Part A, 1988*. Hyaattsville, MD: National Center for Health Statistics (DHHS publication PHS 90-1102).

National Institute of Mental Health (NIMH). (1992). Unpublished estimate. Washington, DC: Statistical Research Branch. In Peggy R. Barker, Ronald W. Manderscheid, Gerry E. Hendershot, Susan S. Jack, Charlotte A. Schoenborn, and Ingrid Goldstrom. (1992). "Serious Mental Illness and Disability in the Adult Household Population: United States, 1989." *Advance Data*. 218 (September 16). Washington, DC: National Center for Health Statistics, Centers for Disease Control.

National Institute of Mental Health (NIMH). (1990). *Mental Health, United States, 1990*. In R. W. Manderscheid and M. A. Sonnenschein (Eds.), DHHS Pub. No. (ADM) 90-1708. Washington, DC: U.S. Government Printing Office.

National Institute of Mental Health (NIMH). (1986). *Mental Health, United States, 1985*. In C. A. Taube and S. A. Barrett (Eds.), DHHS Pub. No. (ADM) 86-1378. Washington, DC: U.S. Government Printing Office.

National Institute on Aging. (1992). *1992 Progress Report on Alzheimer's Disease.* Washington, DC: Department of Health and Human Services.

National Institute on Alcohol and Alcohol Abuse. (1981) Statistics. Washington, DC: National Institute on Alcohol and Alcohol Abuse.

National Institute on Drug Abuse. (1991). *National Household Survey.* Washington, DC: National Institute on Drug Abuse.

National Institute on Drug Abuse. (1981). *Demographic Trends and Drug Abuse (1980–1985).* Washington, DC: National Institute on Drug Abuse.

Neece, Benson, Widing and Associates, Inc. (1991). *The Question and Answer Forum.* New York: Neece, Benson, Widing and Associates, Inc.

Nelson, Debra L. and Charlotte Sutton. (1990). "Chronic Work Stress and Coping." *Academy of Management Journal* 33, 4:859–69.

Neugebauer, Richard. (1980). "Formulation of Hypotheses about the True Prevalence of Functional and Organic Psychiatric Disorders among the Elderly in the United States." In B. P. Dohrenwend, B. S. Dohrenwend, M. S. Gould, B. Link, R. Neugebauer, and R. Wunsch-Hitzig (Eds.), *Mental Illness in the United States: Epidemiological Estimates.* New York: Praeger.

Newman, R. and P. M. Bricklin. (1991). "Parameters of Managed Mental Health Care: Legal, Ethical and Professional Guidelines." *Professional Psychology: Research and Practice* 22:26–35.

Newman, Robert G. (1977). *Methadone Treatment in Narcotic Addiction.* New York: Academic Press.

"New Technologies May Compromise Confidentiality — News Update." *EAP Digest* 12, 5:19.

Norris, Willatt. (1983). "Industry's Hangover Cure." *Management Today* (July):75.

Nykodym, N., W. Ruud, and P. Liverpool. (1986). "Quality Circles: Will Transactional Analysis Improve Their Effectiveness." *Transactional Analysis Journal* 16:182–87.

Nykodym, N. W., W. R. Nielsen, and J. C. Christen. (1985). "Can Organizational Development Use Transactional Analysis?" *Transactional Analysis Journal* 15:278–84.

O'Brien, P. C., A. R. Childness, and I. O. Arndt. (1988). "Pharmacological and Behavioral Treatments of Cocaine Dependence." *Journal of Clinical Psychiatry* 49:17–22.

Office of Technology Assessment (OTA). (1990). *The Effectiveness of Drug Abuse Treatment: Implications for Controlling AIDS/HIV Infection.* Washington, DC: OTA.

O'Reilly, C.A., III. (1978). "The Intentional Distortion of Information in Organizational Communications." *Human Relations* 31:173–93.

Orpen, C. (1981). "Effect of Flexible Working Hours on Employee Satisfaction and Performance: A Field Experiment." *Journal of Applied Psychology* 6:113–15.

Orzolek, Cathy. (1987). "Making EAP Accessible to the Multi-Disabled." *The ALMACAN* (June):14–18.

Ostell, Alistair. (1986). "Where Stress Screening Falls Short." *Personnel Management* 18:34–37.

Oster, Gerry, Daniel Huse, Shelley A. Adams, Joseph Imbimbo, and Mason W. Russell. (1990). "Benzodiazephine Tranquilizers and the Risk of Accidental Injury." *American Journal of Public Health* 80, 12:1467–70.

O'Sullivan, Christine M. (1992). "The Impaired Manager's Impact on the Work Group." *EAP Digest* 12, 3:20–23, 44–46, 50.

O'Sullivan, Christine M. (1988). "Alcohol and Abuse: The Twin Family Secrets."

In G. Lawson and J. Cooperride (Eds.), *Alcoholism and Special Populations*. Rockville, MD: Aspen Systems.

Ouchi, William G. (1981). *Theory Z: How American Business Can Meet the Japanese Challenge*. Reading, MA: Addison-Wesley.

"Outpatient Treatment for Chemical Dependency on Increase." (1992). *Psychsource* (Summer):1–2.

Pabst, Georgia. (1993). "Magazine Cites 100 Companies as the Best for Working Mothers." *Chico Enterprise-Record* (February 4):5C.

Padus, Emrika. (1986). *The Complete Guide to Your Emotions and Your Health*. Enmaus, PA: Rodale Press.

Pape, Patricia A. (1992). "Relapse Prevention with the Female Client." *EAP Digest* 12, 3:34–39.

Parkes, Colin Murray. (1972). *Bereavement*. New York: International Universities Press.

Parsons, Julie A., Jack G. May, Jr., and Frank J. Menolascino. (1984). "The Nature and Incidence of Mental Illness in Mentally Retarded Individuals." In Frank J. Menolascino and Jack A. Stark (Eds.), *Handbook of Mental Illness in the Mentally Retarded*. New York: Plenum Press.

Pati, G. C. and G. Stubblefield. (1990). "The Disabled Are Able to Work." *Personnel Journal* 69:30–34.

Patrick, P. K. (1981). *Health Case Worker Burnout*. Chicago: Blue Cross.

"Peak Ages for Developing Mental Illness Are Childhood, Adolescence." (1990). *The Nation's Health* (November):7.

Peck, M. B. (1970). "A Small-Group Approach to Individual and Institutional Change." *International Journal of Group Psychotherapy* 20:435–49.

Peoples-Sheps, Mary D., Earl Siegel, Chirayath M. Suchindran, Hideki Origasa, Andrea Ware, and Ali Barakat. (1991). "Characteristics of Maternal Employment during Pregnancy: Effects on Low Birth Weight." *American Journal of Public Health* 81, 8:1007–12.

Perlis, Leo. (1980). "Labor's Plans for the 1980s." In N. Sherman, Stanley Yolles, A. Pasquale, and Leonard W. Krinsky (Eds.), *Mental Health and Industry* New York: Human Sciences Press, pp. 40–42.

Perls, Fritz. (1969). *In and Out the Garbage Pail*. Lafayette, CA: Real People Press.

Perry, S. W. and J. Markowitz. (1986). "Psychiatric Interventions for AIDS-Spectrum Disorders." *Hospital and Community Psychiatry* 17:1001–06.

Peters, Thomas J. and Robert H. Waterman, Jr. (1982). *The Search for Excellence: Lessons from America's Best-Run Companies*. New York: Harper and Row.

Philips, D. A. and D. J. Milliken. (1980). *So the Boss Has a Problem*. Center City, MN: Hazelden Foundation.

Philips, I. (1971). "Psychopathology and Mental Retardation." In F. Menolascino (Ed.), *Psychiatric Aspects of the Diagnosis and Treatment of Mental Retardation*. Seattle: Special Child Publications.

Pinheiro, Marcio. (1992). "The Selling of Clinical Psychiatry in America." *Hospital and Community Psychiatry* 43, 2:102–04.

Plog, Stanley C. and Miles B. Santamous. (1980). *The Year 2000 and Mental Retardation*. New York: Plenum Press.

"Poetic Man Hacks Ex-Wife's Hard Disk; Infects Computer with Virus." *Chico Enterprise-Record* (December 9, 1992):3E.

Pollock, H. M. (1944). "Mental Disease Among Mental Defectives." *American Journal of Psychiatry* 101:361–63.

Polster, Erving and Miriam Polster. (1973). *Gestalt Therapy Integrated*. New York: Random House.

Poulton, E. C. (1979). *The Environment of Work*. New York: Thomas.

Powers, William T. (1973). *Behavior: The Control of Perception*. Chicago: Aldine.

Preferred Health Care. (1987). *Mental Health Claims Costs.* Katonah, NY: Preferred Health Care.

Price, R. W. and B. J. Brew. (1988). "The AIDS Dementia Complex." *The Journal of Infectious Disease* 158:1079–83.

Ray, J. S. (1982). "Having Problems with Worker Performance? Try an EAP." *Administrative Management* (May):48.

Regier, D. A., J. K. Myers, M. Kramer, L. N. Robins, D. G. Blazer, R. L. Hough, W. W. Eaton, and B. Z. Locke. (1984). "The NIMH Epidemiologic Catchment Area Program: Historical Context, Major Objectives, and Study Population Characteristics." *Archives of General Psychiatry* 41:934–41.

Rendely, Judith, Robert M. Holmstrom, and Stephen A. Karp. (1984). "The Relationship of Sex-Role Identity, Life Style, and Mental Health in Suburban American Homemakers: Sex-Role, Employment, and Adjustment." *Sex Roles* 11:23–28.

Repetti, Rena L., Karen A. Mathews, and Ingrid Waldron. (1989). "Employment and Women's Health: Effects of Paid Employment on Women's Mental and Physical Health." *American Psychologist* 44, 11:1394–01.

Reskin, B. F. and H. I. Hartman. (1986). *Women's Work, Men's Work.* Washington, DC: National Academy Press.

Restak, Richard. (1988). *The Mind.* New York: Bantam Books.

Reuter, Peter. (1988). "Testing and Deterrence." *Journal of Policy Analysis and Management* 7:554–56.

Rice, Marc. (1992). "Disabilities Act Takes Effect, But Compliance Will Be Slow." *Chico Enterprise-Record* (January 26):5A.

Rich, C. L., D. Young, and R. C. Fowler. (1986). "San Diego Suicide Study." *Archives of General Psychiatry* 43:577–86.

Richman, D. R. and T. J. Nardi. (1985). "A Rational-Emotive Approach to Understanding and Treating Burnout." *Journal of Relational Emotive Therapy* 3:55–64.

Ridgely, M. Susan and Howard H. Goldman. (1989). "Mental Health Insurance. " In David A. Rochefort (Ed.), *Handbook on Mental Health Policy in the U.S.* New York: Greenwood Press, pp. 341–61.

Riley, Mary. (1990). *Corporate Healing: Solutions to the Impact of the Addictive Personality in the Workplace.* Troy, MI: Performance Resource Press.

Risley, T. R. and J. Sheldon-Wildgen. (1980a). "Invited Peer Review: The AABT Experience." *Behavior Therapist* 3:5–9.

Risley, T. R. and J. Sheldon-Wildgen. (1980b). "Suggested Procedures for Human Rights Committees of Potentially Controversial Treatment Programs." *Behavior Therapist* 3:9–10.

Robins, E. S. Glassner, J. Kayes, R. Wilkinson, and G. Murphy. (1959). "The Communication of Suicide Intent: A Study of 134 Consecutive Cases of Successful (Completed) Suicide." *American Journal of Psychiatry* 115:724–33.

Robins, L. N., J. E. Helzer, M. Weissman, H. Orvaschel, E. Gruenberg, J. D. Burke, and D. A. Regier. (1984). "Lifetime Prevalence of Specific Psychiatric Disorders on Three Sites." *Archives of General Psychiatry* 41:949–58.

Roff, Lucinda L. and David L. Kelmmock. (1985). "Employers' Responsibility for Social Services." *Social Work* 30, 5:445–47.

Ronen, S. (1981). *Flexible Working Hours: An Innovation in the Quality of Work Life.* New York: McGraw-Hill.

Ronen, S. and S. Primps. (1980). "The Impact of Flextime on Performance and Attitudes in 15 Public Agencies." *Public Personnel Management* 9, 3:210–17.

Room, Robin. (1991). "The U.S. General Population's Experience with Responses to

Alcohol Problems." In Walter B. Clark and Michael E. Hilton (Eds.), *Alcohol in America*. Albany: State University of New York.

Rosati, Mark. (1986). "Risk and Insurance Management Society Conference: Employee Assistance Programs." *Business Insurance* 20:11.

Rosenberg, Joyce M. (1992). "New Executives Creating New Culture at Macy." *Chico Enterprise-Record* (November 28):9A.

Rosenfeld, Albert. (1992). "The Medical Story of the Century." *Longevity* (May):42–53.

Rosentahl, N. D., C. J. Carpenter, S. P. James, B. L. Parry, S.L.B. Rogers, and T. A. Wehr. (1986). "Seasonal Affective Disorder in Children and Adolescents." *American Journal of Psychiatry* 143:356–58.

Rosow, Jerome and Robert Zager. (1985). *Improving Health-Care Management in the Workplace*. New York: Pergamon Press.

Rotman, Richard E. (1983). "Psychological Testing: Can It Help You Hire the Right Person?" *Public Relations Journal* (June):22–24.

Rotter, Julian. (1990). "Internal Versus External Control of Reinforcement." *American Psychologist* 45, 4:489–93.

Rubin, Jeffrey, Virginia Wilcox-Cox, and Partha Deb. (1992). "Private Health Insurance and the Use of Medical Care by Disabled Mentally Ill Medicare Enrollees." In Richard G. Frank and Willard G. Manning (Eds.), *Economics and Mental Health*. Baltimore: Johns Hopkins University Press, pp. 218–39.

Rusch, Frank R., Carolyn Hughes, John R. Johnson, and Kathleen E. Minch. (1991). "Descriptive Analysis of Interactions between Co-Workers and Supported Employees." *Mental Retardation* 29, 4:207–12.

Rusch, Frank R. and C. Hughes. (1989). "Overview of Supported Employment." *Journal of Applied Behavior Analysis* 22:351–63.

Russell, M., C. Henderson, and S. B. Blume. (1985). *Children of Alcoholics: A Review of the Literature*. New York: Children of Alcoholics Foundation Inc.

Ryland, Elisabeth and Sue Greenfield. (1991). "Work Stress and Well Being." *Journal of Social Behavior and Personality* 6, 7:39–54.

Sadusk, J. R. (1966). "Non-Narcotic Addiction: Size and Extent of the Problem." *Journal of the American Medical Association* 196:707–09.

Sagan, Leonard A. (1987). *The Health of Nations*. New York: Basic Books.

Salancik, G. and J. Pfeffer. (1977). "An Examination of Need-Satisfaction Models of Job Attitudes." *Administrative Science Quarterly* 22:427–55.

Sanzotta, Donald. (1977). *Motivational Theories and Applications for Managers*. New York: AMACOM.

Sax, S. and S. Hollander. (1972). *Reality Games*. New York: Popular Books.

Schachner, Michael. (1990). "Supervisors Should Look for Drug Abuse." *Business Insurance* (May):7.

Schaef, A. W. and D. Fassel. (1988). *The Addictive Organization*. San Francisco: Harper and Row.

Schneid, Thomas D. (1992). *The Americans with Disabilities Act: A Practical Guide for Managers*. New York: Van Nostrand Reinhold.

Schwartz, Harold I. (1992). "An Empirical Review of the Impact of Triplicate Prescription of Benzodiazepines." *Hospital and Community Psychiatry* 43, 4:382–85.

Schwartz, Howard S. (1983). "Maslow and the Hierarchical Enactment of Organizational Reality." *Human Relations* 36, 10:933–56.

Schwartz, Jackie. (1982). *Letting Go of Stress*. New York: Pinnacle Books.

Schwarzbeck, Charles. (1992). "Building Confidence in Later Childhood." *Chico Enterprise-Record* (November 28):2B.

"Scientists Home in on Test to Detect Alzheimer's Disease." (1992). *Chico Enterprise-Record* (November 1):7.

Scott, Richard E. (1992). "Surge in Workers Comp Fueling Effort Against Insurance Fraud." *Chico Enterprise-Record* (January 27):1A.

Sears, David L. (1984). "What Do Employees Want?" *Management World* (October):14–16.

Segal, Steven P. and Pamela Kotler. (1989). "Community Residential Care." In David A. Rochefort (Ed.), *Handbook on Mental Health Policy in the United States*. Westport, CT: Greenwood Press, pp. 237–66.

Sewall, K. S. (1982). "A Comparing and Contrasting of Reality Therapy and Rational Emotive Therapy." *Journal of Reality Therapy* 1:18–21.

Shafer, Michael S., P. David Banks, and John Kregel. (1991)."Employment Retention and Career Movement Among Individuals with Mental Retardation Working in Supported Employment." *Mental Retardation* 29, 2:103–10.

Shaffer, David. (1993). "Suicide: Risk Factors and the Public Health." *American Journal of Public Health* 83, 2:171–72.

Shaffer, David, M. S. Gould, and P. Fisher. (1992). *Study of Completed and Attempted Suicides in Adolescents*. Rockville, MD: National Institute of Mental Health.

Sharfstein, S., R. Frank, and L. Kessler. (1984). "State Medicaid Limitations for Mental Health Services." *Hospital and Community Psychiatry* 35:213–15.

Sheehy, Gail. (1974). *Passages*. New York: Dutton.

Sherman, P. (1985). "Helping the Impaired Executive." *The ALMACAN* (November):20–22.

Shinn, M., M. Rosario, H. Morach, and D. E. Chestnut. (1984). "Coping with Job Stress and Burnout in the Human Services." *Journal of Personality and Social Psychology* 46:864–76.

Shore, Harvey. (1984). "Employee Assistance Programs: Reaping the Benefits." *Sloan Management Review* 2513:69.

Shostrom, E. (1965). "An Inventory for the Measurement of Self-Actualization." *Educational and Psychological Measurement* 24:207–18.

Siegel, Bernie. (1986). *Love, Medicine and Miracles*. New York: Harper & Row.

Simonton, Carl, Stepanie Matthews-Simonton, and James Creighton. (1978). *Getting Well Again*. New York: Tarcher.

Simpson, H. M. (1986). "Epidemiology of Road Accidents Involving Marijuana." *Alcohol, Drugs and Driving Abstracts and Reviews* 2, 3–4:15–30.

Singer, Benjamin D. (1980). "Crazy Systems and Kafka Circuits." *Social Policy* 11:46–54.

Sirrocco, A. and H. Koch. (1977). *Nursing Homes in the U.S. 1972–1974: National Nursing Home Survey*. Vital and Health Statistics, Series 14, No. 17, DHEW Publication No. (HRA) 78-1812. Washington, DC: U.S. Government Printing Office.

Skinner, B. F. (1961). *Contingencies of Reinforcement*. New York: Appleton-Century-Crofts.

Sledge, W. H., K. Moras, D. Hartley, and M. Levine. (1990). "Effect of Time-Limited Psychotherapy on Patient Dropout Rates." *American Journal of Psychiatry* 147:1341–47.

Smith, Blake D. and Carl Salzman. (1991). "Do Benzodiazepines Cause Depression?" *Hospital and Community Psychiatry* 42, 11:1101–02.

Smits, J. Stanley and A. Larry Pace. (1988). "Employee Assistance: Workplace Substance Abuse: Established Policies." *Personnel Journal* (May):88–93.

Sobel, David S. (1992). "Mind Matters and Money Matters: Is Clinical Behavioral Medicine Cost Effective?" Oakland, CA: Kaiser Permanente Medical Care Program.

Soderstrom, Carl A., J. M. Birschbach and P. C. Dischinger. (1990). "Injured Drivers and Alcohol Use: Culpability, Convictions, and Pre- and Post-Crash Driving History." *Journal of Trauma* 30, 10:1208–13.

Solomon, J. and M. Hanson. (1982). "Alcoholism and Sociopathy." In J. Solomon (Ed.), *Alcoholism and Clinical Psychiatry*. New York: Plenum Medical, pp. 111–27.

Sonnenstuhl, William J. (1986). *Inside an Emotional Health Program*. Ithaca, NY: ILR Press.

Sovner, R. (1987). "Behavioral Psychopharmacology." In J. Stark, F. J. Menolascino, M. Albarielli, and V. Gray (Eds.), *Mental Retardation and Mental Health*. New York: Springer-Verlag.

Sovner, R. (1986). "Limiting Factors in the Use of DSM-II for Mentally Ill/Mentally Retarded Persons." *Psychopharmacology Bulletin* 22:1055–59.

Sperling, Dan. (1988). "Treating Pre-Menstrual Syndrome: PMS Isn't Just in a Woman's Mind." *USA Today* (September 1):4D.

Sperry, Len. (1984). "Health Promotion and Wellness Medicine in the Workplace: Programs, Promises, and Problems." *Individual Psychology Journal of Adlerian Theory, Research and Practice* 40, 4:401–11.

Spillane, R. (1985). *Achieving Peak Performance: A Psychology of Success in the Organization*. Sydney: Harper and Row.

Stahl, S. (1990). "Novel Pharmacological Approaches for the Treatment of Schizophrenia." Unpublished paper presented at International Conference of Schizophrenia, July 1990, Vancouver, B.C.

Stark, Amy. (1992). *Because I Said So*. New York: Pharos Books.

Stedman, Donald J. (1971). *Mental Retardation Programs*. Washington, DC: Department of Health, Education, and Welfare.

Steenland, Kyle, Sherry Selevan, and Philip Landrigan. (1992). "The Mortality of Lead Smelter Workers: An Update." *American Journal of Public Health* 82, 12:1641–44.

Steinglass, P. (1987). *Family Therapy with Alcoholics: A Review*. New York: Basic Books.

Stellman, Jeanne Mager. (1987). "Environmental Factors Affecting Job Stress." *Business and Health* (October):16–17.

Strahm, G. (1990). "Prevalence of Selected Mental Disorders in Nursing and Related Care Homes." In National Institute of Mental Health, *Mental Health*. 90(1708):Ch. 6. Washington DC: National Institute of Mental Health.

Strain, J. J., J. S. Lyons, and J. S. Hammer. (1991). "Cost Offset from a Psychiatric Consultation-Liason Intervention with Elderly Hip Fracture Patients." *American Journal of Psychiatry* 148:1044–49.

Stringer-Moore, Donna. (1981). "Impact of Dual Career Couples on Employers: Problems and Solutions." *Public Personnel Management Journal* 10, 4:393–400.

Stroman, Carolyn A. and Richard Seltzer. (1991). "Racial Differences in Coping with Job Stress." *Journal of Social Behavior and Personality* 6, 7:309–18.

Strupp, H. H. (1978). "Psychotherapy Research and Practice; An Overview." In A. E. Bargin and S. Garfield (Eds.), *Handbook of Psychotherapy and Behavior Change*. New York: Wiley.

"Study Addresses Employee Resistance to a Company Move — News Update." (1992). *EAP Digest* 12, 5:20.

Summers, J. A. (1981). "The Definition of Developmental Disabilities: A Concept in Transition." *Mental Retardation* 19, 6:259–65.

Super, D. E. (1963). *"Career Development: Self-Concept Theory."* Research Monograph No. 4 Princeton, NJ: College Board.

Taylor, Frederick. (1911). *The Principles of Scientific Management.* New York: Harper and Row.

Taylor, P. J. (1986). "The Risk of Violence in Psychotics." *Integrative Psychiatry* 4:12–24.

Taylor, Stephen and Thomas W. Zimmerer. (1988). "Viewpoint: Personality Tests for Potential Employees: More Harm Than Good." *Personnel Journal* (January):60–64.

Thornburg, L. (1992). "Practical Ways to Cope with Suicide." *HR Magazine* (May):63.

Thorton, John F., Mary V. Seeman, Elizabeth D. Plummer, and J. Joel Jeffries. (1985). "Schizophrenia: The Medications." Toronto, Canada: Merrill Pharmaceuticals Professional Services Department (12-85-571).

Tines, Jeffrey, Frank R. Rusch, Wendy McCaughrin, and Ronald W. Conley. (1990). "Benefit-Cost Analysis of Supported Employment in Illinois: A Statewide Evaluation." *American Journal on Mental Retardation* 95, 1:44–54.

Topolnicki, Denise M. (1983). "Love and Money: 'Marital Aid Inc.'" *Money* 12, 7:124.

Traiforos, A. (1990). "The Role of Organized Labor in Rehabilitation." *Rehabi USA* (Fall):12–14.

Trice, Harrison M. and Janice M. Beyer. (1984). "Work-Related Outcomes of the Constructive-Confrontation Strategy in a Job-Based Alcoholism Program." *Journal of Studies on Alcohol* 45, 5:393–404.

Trice, Harrison M. and Paul M. Roman. (1978). *Spirits and Demons at Work.* Ithaca, NY: Cornell University Press.

U.S. Census Bureau, Department of Commerce. (1993). Cited in "Asian-Americans Fastest Growing Minority Group." *Chico Enterprise-Record* (February 21):9A.

U.S. Census Bureau, Department of Commerce. (1989). Cited in "U.S. Population Boom Predicted to Go Bust in 2038." *Chico Enterprise-Record* (February 1):7D.

U.S. Census Bureau, Department of Commerce. (1984). *Projection of the Population of the United States by Age, Sex, and Race 1983–2080.* Washington, DC: Government Printing Office.

U.S. Congress, Office of Technology Assessment (OTA). (1990). *Genetic Monitoring and Screening in the Workplace.* Washington, DC: U.S. Government Printing Office.

U.S. Congress, Office of Technology Assessment (OTA). (1988). *Biology, Medicine, and the Bill of Rights.* Washington, DC: U.S. Government Printing Office.

U.S. Congress, Office of Technology Assessment (OTA). (1982). *The Role of Genetic Testing in the Prevention of Occupational Disease: Summary.* Washington, DC: U.S. Government Printing Office.

U.S. Department of Commerce. (1992). *Statistical Abstract of the United States 1992.* Washington, DC: U.S. Department of Commerce.

U.S. Department of Commerce. (1990). *Statistical Abstract of the United States 1990.* Washington, DC: U.S. Department of Commerce.

U.S. Department of Commerce. (1989). *Human Resources Planning.* Washington, DC: Commerce Clearing House.

U.S. Department of Commerce. (1988). *Statistical Abstract of the United States 1988.* Washington, DC: U.S. Department of Commerce.

U.S. Department of Commerce. (1987). *Statistical Abstract of the United States 1987.* Washington DC: U.S. Department of Commerce.

U.S. Department of Health and Human Services. (1987). *Prevention and Control of Stress Among Emergency Workers.* Rockville, MD: National Institute of Mental Health.

U.S. Department of Health, Education, and Welfare. (1975). *Mental Retardation and the Law.* Washington, DC: U.S. Department of Health, Education, and Welfare, p. 44.

U.S. Department of Labor. (1989) "New Survey Measures Extent of Drug-Testing Programs in the Workplace." In *News.* Washington, DC: U.S. Department of Labor.

U.S. Department of Labor. (n.d.). "What Works: Workplaces Without Drugs." Washington, DC: U.S. Department of Labor.

U.S. General Accounting Office (GAO). (1992). *Employee Drug Testing: Estimated Cost to Test All Executive Branch Employees and New Hires.* Washington, DC: GAO.

U.S. General Accounting Office (GAO). (1988). *The Fair Labor Standards Act: Extending the Act to State and Local Government Employees.* Washington, DC: GAO.

U.S. Senate. (November 9, 1989). *Human Genome Initiative Hearings Before the Subcommittee on Science, Technology, and Space of the Committee on Commerce, Science, and Transportation, U.S. Senate.* Washington, DC: U.S. Government Printing Office.

U.S. Social Security Administration. (1989). *Annual Statistical Supplement, 1989.* Washington, DC: U.S. Social Security Administration.

Underhill, R. (1982). "TA Training for Management Development." *Transactional Analysis Journal* 12:199–202.

Upton, David. (1983). *Mental Health Care and National Health Insurance.* New York: Plenum Press.

Valenstein, Elliot S. (1986). *Great and Desperate Cures: The Rise and Decline of Psychosurgery and Other Radical Treatments for Mental Illness.* New York: Basic Books.

Van Fleet, Frederick M. (1992). "Debriefing and the Critical Incident." *EAP Digest* 12, 3:28–33.

Vokel, Marta. (1987). "Kicking the Smoking Habit." *United* (February):40.

Vroom, V. H. (1964). *Work and Motivation.* New York: Wiley.

Wacker, D. P., L. Fromm-Steege, W. K. Berg, and T. H. Flynn. (1989). "Supported Employment as an Intervention Package: A Preliminary Analysis of Functional Variables." *Journal of Applied Behavior Analysis* 22:429–39.

Wagman, Jacqueline Bloom and Jeannette Schiff. (1990). "Managed Mental Health Care for Employees: Roles for Social Workers." *Occupational Social Work Today* 6:53–65.

Wahba, M. A. and L. G. Bridwell. (1976). "Maslow Reconsidered: A Review of Research on the Need Hierarchy Theory." *Organizational Behavior and Human Performance* 15, 2:212–40.

Waldrop, J. (1991). "The Cost of Hiring the Disabled." *American Demographics* 13:12.

Wallgren, K. (1975). "Managerial Corral." *Transactional Analysis Journal* 5:373–75.

Wallner, Teut. (1975). "Hypotheses of Handwriting Psychology and Their Verification." *Professional Psychology* (February):8–16.

Walrond-Skinner, S. (1986). *Dictionary of Psychotherapy*. New York: Routedge and Kegan.

Weaver, Charles A. (1984). "Employee Assistance Programs." In Jerry S. Rosenbloom (Ed.), *The Handbook of Employee Benefits*. Homewood, IL: Dow-Jones-Irwin, p. 317.

Weaver, Charles A. (1979). "EAPs: How They Improve the Bottom Line." *Risk Management* 26:22–26.

Weaver, Nancy, Mary Lynne Vellings, and Stephen Green. (1992). "Workers' Comp Critically Injured. " *The Sacramento Bee* (February 9):A1, A4.

Wedeen, R. (1984). "Occupational Renal Disease." *American Journal of Kidney Disease* 4:241–57.

Wegscheider, S. (1981). *Another Chance: Hope and Help for the Alcoholic Family*. New York: Science and Behavior Books.

Weiss, Lisa K. (1987). "Cutting the Cost of Substance Abuse Treatment." *Compensation and Benefits Review* 19, 3:37–44.

Weiss, Richard M. (1985). "Determining the Effects of Alcohol Abuse on Employee Productivity." *American Psychologist* 40, 5:578–81.

Weissman, M. M., E. S. Gershon, K. K. Kidd, B. A. Prusoff, J. F. Leckman, E. Dibble, J. Hamovit, W. D. Thompson, D. L. Pauls, and J. J. Guroff. (1985). "Psychiatric Disorders in the Relatives of Probands with Affective Disorders." *Archives of General Psychiatry* 41:13–21.

White House. (1989). *National Drug Control Strategy*. Washington, DC: U.S. Government Printing Office.

"Who's Been Peeking at Our Genes." (1991). *California Republic* (February 26):16.

Wiebe, Debrah. (1991). "Hardiness and Stress Moderation." *Journal of Personality and Social Psychology* 60, 1:89–99.

Williams, C. (1987). "Peacetime Combat: Treating and Preventing Delayed Stress Reactions in Police Officers." In T. Williams (Ed.), *Post-Traumatic Stress Disorders: A Handbook for Clinicians*. Cincinnati, OH: Disabled American Veterans.

Williams, Kenneth R. (1986). "Linking Risk Avoidance and Insurance Coverage." *Personnel Administrator* 31:68–75.

Wilson, Phillip G., Mark F. O'Reilly, and Frank R. Rusch. (1991). "Analysis of Minority-Status Supported Employees in Relation to Placement Approach and Selected Outcomes." *Mental Retardation* 29, 6:329–33.

Wisdom Simulators, Inc. (1992). *Hold Your Fire*. Cited in "Conflict Resolution, PC Style." *EAP Digest* 12, 5:18.

Woititiz, J. G. (1983). *Adult Children of Alcoholics*. Hollywood, FL: Health Communications.

Woolsey, Christine. (1991). "Containing Mental Health Benefit Costs." *Business Insurance* (November 11):52–53.

World Health Organization (WHO). 1977). *Manual of the International Statistical Classification of Diseases, Injuries, and Cause of Death*. Geneva: WHO.

World Health Organization (WHO). (1946). "Preamble." *Constitution*. Geneva: WHO.

Wright, Jim. (1984). "EAP: An Important Supervisory Tool." *Supervisory Management* 29, 12:16–17.

Yalom, Irvin D. (1970). *Existential Psychotherapy*. New York: Basic Books.

Zare, Nancy. (1990). "The EAP and Organizational Development." *EAP Digest* (May/June):27–56.

Zenz, C. (Ed.). (1988). *Occupational Medicine*. Chicago: Year.

Zunker, Vernon G. (1990). *Career Counseling: Applied Concepts of Life Planning*. Brooks/Cole: Pacific Grove.

Index

ABOUT THE AUTHOR

DONNA R. KEMP is Professor and Graduate Coordinator in Public Administration and Political Science at California State University, Chico. She previously was a planner and program manager for the State of Idaho and held academic positions in Idaho, South Carolina, and Bakersfield, California. Her research is focused on public personnel management and health and mental health policy. She is the author/editor of three books including *International Handbook on Mental Health Policy* (Greenwood Press, 1993), and many journal articles and other publications.